Fundamentals of Psychoanalytic Technique

A Norton Professional Book

Fundamentals of Psychoanalytic Technique

A Lacanian Approach for Practitioners

BRUCE FINK

W. W. Norton & Company
New York • London

For information about permission to reproduce
selections from this book, write to
Permissions, W. W. Norton & Company, Inc.,
500 Fifth Avenue, New York, NY 10110

Production Manager: Leeann Graham
Manufacturing by Quebecor World Fairfield Graphics

Library of Congress Cataloging-in-Publication Data

Fink, Bruce, 1956-
    Fundamentals of psychoanalytic technique : a Lacanian approach for
practitioners / Bruce Fink. — 1st ed.
        p.; cm.
    Includes bibliographical references and index.
    ISBN-13: 978-0-393-70508-9 (hardcover)
    ISBN-10: 0-393-70508-0 (hardcover)
    1.   Psychoanalysis. 2.   Lacan, Jacques, 1901-1981.   I. Title.
    [DNLM: 1.   Lacan, Jacques, 1901-1981. 2.   Psychoanalytic
Therapy—methods. WM 460.6 F499f 2007]
RC506.F4245 2007
616.89′17—dc22   2006102242

W. W. Norton & Company, Inc., 500 Fifth Avenue, New York, N.Y. 10110
www.wwnorton.com

W. W. Norton & Company Ltd., Castle House, 75/76 Wells St., London W1T 3QT

1   3   5   7   9   0   8   6   4   2

To my analysands and supervisees,
past and present.

Contents

Preface

It is from my analysands that I learn everything, that I learn what psychoanalysis is.
— Lacan (1976, p. 34)

It always seemed to me that analysis was not so much a matter of technique but of the kind of work the analyst inspires the analysand to do in the course of analysis. My presumption was that different analysts could potentially use rather different techniques to encourage more or less the same kind of work. But the more I have spoken with different psychoanalytic groups around the United States, the more I have become convinced that the kind of technique being taught in societies and institutes today does not merely fail to foster what I understand to be analytic work, it precludes it. Contemporary approaches to psychoanalytic treatment seem to me to have lost sight of many of the fundamental insights achieved by Freud, Lacan, and other analytic pioneers and to have adopted views stemming from psychology, particularly developmental psychology, that contradict basic tenets of psychoanalysis—tenets as fundamental as the unconscious, repression, repetition compulsion, and so on.

I have thus taken the somewhat brazen step of preparing a primer of technique that seeks to keep those basic tenets solidly in its sights. My focus here is on what strikes me as elementary technique (though it seems not to be nearly as elementary to many clinicians as I would have thought it to be), not on long theoretical explanations of the basic tenets. With this in mind, I have written for readers with no previous knowledge of Lacan and little prior knowledge of psychoanalysis in general. This primer will, I hope, be of use to beginners and to more seasoned clinicians as well, albeit for different reasons.

It should be clear from the outset that the techniques presented here work for me—I find that I am able to achieve a great deal of what I believe psychoanalysis seeks to achieve by employing them—and that they are not likely to work for everyone else or to work as well for everyone else. One must also bear in mind that, generally speaking, *nothing works with everyone*. Nevertheless, based on my experience with the considerable number of clinicians (graduate students in clinical psychology, social workers, psychiatrists, psychologists, and psychoanalysts) whom I have supervised over the past dozen or so years, I have reason to believe that these techniques can be helpful to many practitioners, often transforming their practices fairly radically in a few short months. This is why I have decided to present them in this form.

The majority of the techniques proposed here are designed for work with neurotics, not psychotics. I do not discuss the distinction between neurosis and psychosis at any length here, as I have done so extensively elsewhere (Fink, 1995, 1997, 2005b), but in my view a rather different approach to technique is required in work with psychotics, and I give a brief sketch of that different technique in Chapter 10. If, as I propose, repression should be the analyst's guiding light in directing treatment with neurotics, the absence of repression in psychosis implies that we need to direct treatment with psychotics differently. Whereas many contemporary analysts seem to believe that the majority of the patients seen in our times are not suffering from "neurotic-level problems," I would argue that the majority of analysts can no longer recognize "neurotic-level problems" precisely because repression and the unconscious are no longer their guiding lights (Lacan, on the other hand, argues that analysts must be "dupes" of the unconscious, in the sense that they must follow the unconscious wherever it may lead, even if that means allowing themselves to be led around by the nose, so to speak; see Lacan, 1973–1974, November 13, 1973). This leads analysts to confuse neurosis with psychosis and to formulate an approach to psychoanalytic work that supposedly applies to one and all. (Indeed, the main "diagnostic" distinction made in our times seems to be that between "high functioning" and not-so-high-functioning individuals.) I believe that the approach to neurosis that I present here is applicable to the vast majority of patients seen by most clinicians today (there are, of course, exceptions) and practitioners may come to share this belief with me after reading about the approach to the treatment of psychosis I offer in Chapter 10.

The experience of conducting psychoanalyses is so complex that no one could ever cover all facets of it, even in a lifetime of writing. My selection of topics here has been informed in particular by what seems to me to be left out in the basic training of analysts and psychotherapists today. I do not, for example, devote much space here to discussions of affect or countertransference (except in Chapter 7) because they are so heavily emphasized in other texts—so much so that they need, in my view, to be counterbalanced. Nor do I devote much space to articulating the later and final stages of an analysis, as this is designed to be a somewhat introductory text. In this sense, this book is anything but a standalone training manual; it should be supplemented by many other readings, a short list of which can be found in the bibliography.

I have tried in the course of this book to compare and contrast my approach with other approaches, when possible, but I am aware that experts on these other approaches may find my knowledge of them lacking. As Mitchell & Black (1995, p. 207) put it, "at present it is very difficult to find any psychoanalyst who is really deeply conversant with more than one approach (e.g., Kleinian, Lacanian, ego psychology, self psychology). The literature of each school is extensive and each clinical sensibility finely honed, presenting a challenging prospect to any single analyst attempting to digest it all." I have spent the better part of 25 years grappling with Lacan's at times torturous French and striving to find ways to put his insights into practice. Only now am I beginning to get a better feel for the broader psychoanalytic landscape, and some of my attempts to compare and contrast my approach with other approaches are bound to come off as somewhat caricatural.

The non-Lacanian analysts I discuss here are those whose work I have found most accessible and cogent, even when I do not in the slightest agree with their points of view (regarding, for example, "normality," "projective identification," and so on). Since my goal is not to present other approaches in an exhaustive manner, I obviously do not do justice to these analysts' ideas: I take certain of their statements out of context and simplify their views, which leads to an inevitable loss of subtlety. I have, nevertheless, tried to avoid the use of secondary sources—that is, commentaries on these analysts' ideas—finding that, as in virtually every other field, original thinkers' ideas are often more comprehensible and convincing. When I have relied upon secondary sources as an initial guide, I have always gone back to the original sources to verify their accuracy, and I have been surprised at how little care analysts take in reading and interpreting each other's work, even when that work is written in a relatively straightforward manner; virtually every conclusion I preliminarily drew about an analyst's theoretical views based on commentaries had to be seriously revised, if not jettisoned altogether! I had been aware, prior to beginning this project, that most English-language commentaries on Lacan's work are seriously flawed, and I had blithely chalked that up to the difficulty of his writing and to the fact that so few English speakers are genuinely fluent in French. Now it appears to me that other factors must be at work as well.

As I indicate in my subtitle, I am not purporting to provide some sort of definitive Lacanian approach here, but merely *a* Lacanian approach; Lacan's work is so voluminous and complex that it can be used to justify a number of different (though no doubt related) approaches, and there may well be as many varied Lacanian approaches as there are Lacanians—if not more! After all, like everyone else, Lacanian analysts have a tendency to change their views over the course of a lifetime. Given my intention here to provide an introductory text on technique, I have simplified many of Lacan's formulations; I have in no way attempted to supply historical perspective on the development of concepts like interpretation and transference from his early work to his later work, and I only hint at or refer to more subtle and complex articulations, especially those from the 1970s, in footnotes. (Similarly, in my attempt to keep the main text as accessible as possible, I have generally relegated more detailed commentary on and critique of other analysts' viewpoints to the rather copious footnotes.) I have not sought here to hew to any particular orthodoxy, especially as that would require somehow reconciling the instances in which Lacan contradicts his earlier views in his later writings. Instead I have presented his ideas on technique that make the most sense to me and that work best for me; and I have attempted to present them more or less in the order in which they are employed in an actual analysis, at least up until Chapter 6.

People in the English-speaking world are likely to believe that Lacanians are something of a fringe group, since their numbers are so small in the United States, Canada, Australia, and the United Kingdom. However, the tide probably has now turned: Given the phenomenal growth in the number of Lacanians in Europe and South America over the past few decades and the equally phenomenal decline in the number of new psychoanalytic trainees in the English-speaking world, above all in the classical training institutes associated with the International Psychoanalytic Association (see Kirsner, 2000), there actually may be more analysts practicing in a Lacanian fashion in the world today than there are analysts of any other tendency. This is certainly not to say that they all agree with each other—there are over a dozen different Lacanian schools—or that even a small fraction of them would agree with the majority of what I say here.

To simplify my use of pronouns in this book I have adopted the following convention: In odd-numbered chapters, the analyst is always a she and the analysand is always a he; in even-numbered chapters, the roles are reversed. All translations of French works, where no extant English edition is referenced, are my own; when English editions are cited, I have nevertheless modified the translations in many cases, often quite radically (for comments on translation, see Fink, 2005a). All references to Lacan's *Écrits* are to the French pagination included in the margins of the English edition (2006).

I would like to add a special word of thanks here to Héloïse Fink and Luz Manríquez for their inspiration and guidance regarding the choice of the Fugue in A flat major from *The Well-Tempered Clavier* by Johann Sebastian Bach for the front cover; to Deborah Malmud, Michael McGandy, and Kristen Holt-Browning at Norton for being such a pleasure to work with; and to Yael Baldwin for her helpful comments on an early version of the manuscript, which led to many additions and improvements.

Pittsburgh, 2006

Fundamentals of Psychoanalytic Technique

1

Listening and Hearing

Freud remarked that there is perhaps a kind of speaking that is worthwhile precisely because up until now it was merely interdicted—which means spoken between, between the lines. That is what he called the repressed.

— Lacan (1974–1975, April 8, 1975)

THE PSYCHOANALYST'S first task is to listen and to listen carefully. Although this has been emphasized by many authors, there are surprisingly few good listeners in the psychotherapeutic world. Why is that? There are several reasons, some of which are primarily personal and others of which are more structural, but one of the most important reasons is that we tend to hear everything in relation to ourselves. When someone tells us a story, we think of similar stories (or more extreme stories) we ourselves could tell in turn. We start thinking about things that have happened to us that allow us to "relate to" the other person's experience, to "know" what it must have been like, or at least to imagine how we ourselves would have felt had we been in the other person's shoes.

In other words, *our usual way of listening is centered to a great degree on ourselves*—our own similar life experiences, our own similar feelings, our own perspectives. When we can locate experiences, feelings, and perspectives of our own that resemble the other person's, we believe that we "relate to" that person: We say things like "I know what you mean," "Yeah," "I hear you," "I feel for you," or "I feel your pain" (perhaps less often "I feel your joy"). At such moments, we feel sympathy, empathy, or pity for this other who seems like us; "That must have been painful (or wonderful) for you," we say, imagining the pain (or joy) we ourselves would have experienced in such a situation.

When we are unable to locate experiences, feelings, or perspectives that resemble the other person's, we have the sense that we do *not* understand that person—indeed, we may find the person strange, if not obtuse or irrational.

1

When someone does not operate in the same way that we do or does not react to situations as we do, we are often baffled, incredulous, or even dumbfounded. We are inclined, in the latter situation, to try to correct the other's perspectives, to persuade him to see things the way we see them and to feel what we ourselves would feel were we in such a predicament. In more extreme cases, we simply become judgmental: How could anyone, we ask ourselves, believe such a thing or act or feel that way?

Most simply stated, *our usual way of listening overlooks or rejects the otherness of the other.* We rarely listen to what makes a story as told by another person unique, specific to that person alone; we quickly assimilate it to other stories that we have heard others tell about themselves or that we could tell about ourselves, overlooking the differences between the story being told and the ones with which we are already familiar. We rush to gloss over the differences and make the stories similar if not identical. In our haste to identify with the other, to have something in common with him, we forcibly equate stories that are often incommensurate, reducing what we are hearing to what we already know.[1] What we find most difficult to hear is what is utterly new and different: thoughts, experiences, and emotions that are quite foreign to our own and even to any we have thus far learned about.

It is often believed that we human beings share many of the same feelings and reactions to the world, which is what allows us to more or less understand each other and constitutes the foundation of our shared humanity. In an attempt to combat a certain stereotype of the psychoanalyst as a detached, unfeeling scientist rather than as a living, breathing human being, certain practitioners have suggested that the analyst should regularly empathize with the analysand, highlighting what they have in common, in order to establish a solid thera-peutic alliance. Although these practitioners have a number of good intentions (for example, to debunk the belief in the analyst's objectivity), expressions of empathy can emphasize the analyst's and analysand's shared humanity in a way that whitewashes or rides roughshod over aspects of their humanity that are unshared.[2]

---

[1] This is true of most forms of identification: Certain facets of things or experiences must almost always be effaced or ignored in order for an identity to be established between any two of them. As Casement (1991, p. 9) put it, "the unknown is treated as if it were already known."

[2] Freud (1913/1958, pp. 139–140) recommended that the analyst show the analysand some "sympa-thetic understanding." However, he did not mean by this that we should profess to be like the analysand or that we should agree with him or believe his story, but that we should show that we are very atten-tive, listening carefully, and trying to follow what he is saying (the German term he uses, *Einfühlung*, is often translated as *understanding, empathy,* or *sensitivity*). Margaret Little (1951, p. 35) astutely asserted that "The basis of empathy . . . is identification." My viewpoint here is diametrically opposed to that

I would propose that the more closely we consider any two people's thoughts and feelings in a particular situation, the more we are forced to realize that there are greater differences than similarities between them—we are far more different than we tend to think![3] In any case, the alliance-building supposedly accomplished by an empathic response on the analyst's part (like "that must have been painful for you," in response to what the analyst believes must have been a trying life event, say the break-up of a long-term relationship) can be accomplished just as easily by asking the analysand to describe his experience ("what was that like for you?"), which has the advantage of not putting words in the analysand's mouth (see Chapter 2). In the work I do supervising psychotherapists of many ilks, I find that the comments that are most often intended by the therapist to be empathic and to foster in the patient a sense of being "understood" generally miss the mark, the patient responding, "No, it wasn't painful. Actually, it was a lot easier than I thought—I never felt better!" The analyst who succumbs to the temptation to respond empathically

---

of those who believe, like McWilliams (2004, p. 36), that "the main 'instrument' we have in our efforts to understand the people who come to us for help is our empathy" and who are convinced, like Heinz Kohut (1984, p. 82), of the analyst's ability to employ "vicarious introspection," "the capacity to think and feel oneself into the inner life of another person." Lacan (2006, p. 339) suggested that analysts' invocations of empathy often involve "connivance." The fact is that for an analyst to think or feel herself "into the inner life" of an analysand, she must ignore all the ways in which they are different, all their obviously nonoverlapping particularities—in other words, she must fool herself into believing they are fundamentally alike, lopping off any and all difference. But A can be said to be equal to A only in mathematics.

I myself have heard a wide variety of conflicting accounts of what empathy is (the philosophical and psychoanalytic traditions provide many vastly different definitions of it). I have even once heard it said that the empathic thing to do on certain occasions is to show no empathy—when, for example, a patient would take it as a sign of paternalism or condescension, something which, let it be noted, usually cannot be known in advance (such was the case of Marie Cardinal in The Words to Say It, 1983; see especially pp 27–28). It seems to me that proponents of empathy in therapy are forced to engage in serious conceptual acrobatics to justify its applicability in all cases.

[3] This is one of the many places where I differ radically in viewpoint from someone like McWilliams (2004, p. 148), who proffered, "we are all much more similar than we are different as human beings," although she tempered this point of view later on in her book (p. 254). Malan (1995/2001) made the same assumption when he argued that:

> One of the most important qualities that psychotherapists should possess . . . is a *knowledge of people*, much of which may come not from any formal training or reading but simply from personal experience. Which of us has not experienced, in ourselves or those close to us, the potential dangers of apparently innocent triangular situations; or the use of tears not merely as emotional release but an appeal for help? (p. 3)

The fact is that *many people* have not experienced the things he mentions. In my view, identifying with or trying to see ourselves as similar to people who are different from us (racially, culturally, linguistically, denominationally, socioeconomically, sexually, or diagnostically) does not help us understand or assist them.

often finds that she is actually not on the same page as the analysand at that precise moment.[4]

In effect, we can understand precious little of someone's experience by relating it or assimilating it to our own experience. We may be inclined to think that we can overcome this problem by acquiring much more extensive experience of life. After all, our analysands often believe that we cannot understand them unless we look old and wise, unless we seem right from the outset to have had a good long experience of life. We ourselves may fall into the trap of thinking that we simply need to broaden our horizons, travel far and wide, and learn about other peoples, languages, religions, classes, and cultures in order to better understand a wider variety of analysands. However, if acquiring a fuller knowledge of the world is in fact helpful, it is probably not so much because we have come to understand "how the other half lives" or how other people truly operate, but because we have stopped comparing everyone with ourselves to the same degree: Our frame of reference has shifted and we no longer immediately size everyone else up in terms of our own way of seeing and doing things.

In the early days of my psychoanalytic practice, a woman in her fifties came to see me and tearfully told me a story about how she had gotten married, divorced, and later remarried to the same man. I was quite incredulous, thinking at the time that this sort of thing only happened in Hollywood, and must have had a surprised or bewildered look on my face. Needless to say, the woman felt I was being judgmental and never came back. She was right, of course: I was trying to imagine myself in her shoes and found it quite impossible or at least unpalatable.

Our usual way of listening is highly narcissistic and self-centered, for in it we relate everything other people tell us to ourselves. We compare ourselves to them, we assess whether we have had better or worse experiences than they have, and we evaluate how their stories reflect upon us and their relationship with us, whether good or bad, loving or hateful. This, in a word, is what Lacan refers to as the *imaginary* dimension of experience: The analyst as listener is constantly comparing and contrasting the other with herself and constantly sizing up the other's discourse in terms of the kind of *image* it reflects back to her—whether that be the image of someone who is good or bad, quick or

---

[4] Consider the first definition of empathy given by *Webster's Third New International Dictionary* (unabridged): "the imaginative projection of a subjective state, whether affective, conative, or cognitive, into an object so that the object appears to be infused with it: the reading of one's own state of mind or conation into an object." If one is to express some empathy regarding what the analysand himself has described as a very tough situation, it is often enough to give the analysand a compassionate look or register that one has heard what he is saying with a warmer than usual "hmm" that is not inflected as a question.

slow, insightful or useless. The imaginary dimension concerns images—our own self-image, for example—not illusion per se (Lacan, 2006, pp. 349–350).[5]

When operating in the imaginary dimension of experience, the analyst is focused on her own self-image as reflected back to her by the analysand and hears what the analysand says only insofar as it reflects upon her. Her concern here is with what the analysand's discourse means to her and what it means about her.[6] Is he angry at her? infatuated with her? Is he depicting her as intelligent, trustworthy, and helpful or as dense, untrustworthy, and unhelpful? When he is ostensibly complaining about his mother, the analyst wonders whether he is not in fact leveling his criticism at her, she wanting to be seen as the good mother, not the bad mother. When he is discussing his grades, his GRE scores, or his income, the analyst is mentally comparing her own grades, scores, and income with his.

Listening for all this makes the analyst constitutionally incapable of hearing a great many things that the analysand says—first and foremost slips of the tongue, which, as they are often nonsensical, do not immediately reflect upon the analyst and thus are generally ignored by her. When the analyst is operating primarily within the imaginary dimension or register, everything that cannot

---

[5] Even Winnicott (1949, p. 70), whose perspectives are generally so different from Lacan's and my own, says of patients that they "can only appreciate in the analyst what [they themselves are] capable of feeling. In the matter of motives, the obsessional will tend to be thinking of the analyst as doing his work in a futile obsessional way." He goes on to say similar things of patients in other diagnostic categories. The same is obviously true of analysts-in-training and of many more experienced analysts as well when they listen to their patients.

Curiously enough, even some psychodynamic therapists recommend making use of this narcissistic way of listening rather than encouraging us to listen in some other way. Malan (1995/2001, p. 26), for example, recommended that the therapist "use his knowledge of his own feelings in a process of identification with the [patient]; to know not only theoretically but intuitively what [is] needed." He further claimed that "the psychiatrist needs to identify himself with the patient and try to see what he himself would feel in the same situation" (p. 28). This approach bears a curious affinity to something described in Edgar Allan Poe's The Purloined Letter (1847/1938), in which a boy is able to beat all of his classmates in the game of "even or odd" (perhaps better known as "odds or evens" or "one strikes three shoot") by trying to identify with the level of intelligence of his opponent, trying to make his own face take on the same look of relative intelligence or stupidity as his opponent's face, and thereby guessing whether the other person will simply switch from even to odd or whether he will do something more complicated. This strategy involves nothing more than what Lacan (2006, p. 20) called the purely imaginary dimension of experience.

[6] Many people at first read psychoanalytic literature in much the same way, looking primarily to understand themselves as they read about theory and about others' analyses. As noted in Chapter 7, analysts who privilege the interpretation of transference try to make a virtue of this vice. Gill (1982) approvingly mentioned Lichtenberg & Slap (1977) who:

> . . . argue that within the analytic situation the analyst is always "listening" to how the analysand is experiencing him (the analyst). In other words, no matter what the apparent focus of the patient's remarks or even silences is, "one or (usually) more aspects of the patient's sense of himself interacting with his environment invariably has relevance to his relation with the analyst." (p. 72)

easily be compared with her own experiences (her own sense of self—in short, her own "ego," as I shall use the term) goes unattended to and, indeed, often remains simply unheard.[7] Since only things that are more or less immediately meaningful can be so compared, whatever is not immediately meaningful or comprehensible—slurs, stumblings, mumbling, garbled speech, spoonerisms, pauses, slips, ambiguous phrasing, malapropisms, double and triple entendres, and so on—is set aside or ignored. Whatever does not fall within her ken, within her own universe of experience, is overlooked or disregarded.

This essentially means that *the more the analyst operates in this imaginary mode, the less she can hear.* Our usual way of listening—both as "ordinary citizens" and as analysts—primarily involves the imaginary register and makes us rather hard of hearing. How, then, can we become less deaf?

Deferring Understanding

Within himself as well as in the external world, [the analyst] must always expect to find something new.

— *Freud (1912b/1958, p. 117)*

The unconscious shuts down insofar as the analyst no longer "supports speech," because he already knows or thinks he knows what speech has to say.

— *Lacan (2006, p. 359)*

If our attempts to "understand" ineluctably lead us to reduce what another person is saying to what we think we already know (indeed, that could serve as a pretty fair definition of understanding in general),[8] one of the first steps we must take is to *stop trying to understand so quickly.* It is not by showing the

---

[7] Lacan (2006, p. 595) referred to this as the "dyadic relation," by which he meant that the analytic relationship is construed in such cases as nothing more than a relationship between two egos.

A supervisee of mine once let a patient break off his therapy after a slight lifting of his deep depression. When I asked her why she had not tried to keep him in therapy to see if his depression could be further dissipated, she explained that it seemed to her that there were good reasons to think life depressing— isn't some depression, she retorted, a sensible response to life in our times? I pointed out to her that, regardless of her theoretical perspective on the matter, she seemed to be assuming that her patient's reasons for being depressed were the same as hers (or what she believed to be hers), when his might well have been entirely different from hers. In comparing his reasons to her own, she was excluding or failing to hear the ways in which they potentially differed. See Lacan's (1990) highly original take on sadness and depression as a moral failing or moral weakness, at times going as far as a "rejection of the unconscious" (p. 22), which is equivalent in this context to foreclosure (see Chapter 10).

[8] "To explain a thing means to trace it back to something already known" (Freud, 1900/1958, p. 549; see also Freud, 1916–1917/1963, p. 280). Patrick Casement (1991, pp. 3, 8–9) said much the same

analysand that we understand what he is saying that we build an alliance with him—especially given the fact that our attempts to show him that we understand often fall flat and demonstrate the exact opposite—but, rather, by listening to him in a way that he has never been listened to before. Since "the very foundation of interhuman discourse is misunderstanding" (Lacan, 1993, p. 184), we cannot rely upon understanding to establish a solid relationship with the analysand. Instead, we must "exhibit a serious interest in him" (Freud, 1913/1958, p. 139) by listening in a way that demonstrates that we are paying attention to what he says in a fashion hitherto unknown to him.

Whereas most of those who have listened to him in the past have allowed him to speak only briefly and then responded with their own stories, perspectives, and advice,[9] the analyst allows him to speak at great length, interrupting him only to ask for clarification about something he said, for further details about something, and for other similar examples. Unlike most of those who have listened to the analysand before, the analyst takes note of the fact that the analysand used the exact same words or expressions to characterize his wife early in the session and his grandmother half an hour—or even several sessions—later. If she focuses on what the analysand's discourse means about her, she cannot so easily remember many of the particulars of what the analysand says, whether they concern the analysand's early life events, brothers' and sisters' names, or current relationships.

The less the analyst considers herself to be targeted by the analysand's discourse, and the less she concerns herself with how that discourse reflects upon her, the more of it she will be able to remember quite effortlessly.[10] (I generally take it as a bad sign when an analyst can only summarize in her own words what the analysand said and cannot remember any of it verbatim.) The less she uses herself as the measure of all things in the analysand's discourse, the more easily she can approach the latter on its own terms, from its own frame of reference. It is only in this way that she can hope to explore the

---

thing and emphasized the importance of deferring understanding and "learning from the patient" how different he is from all those the analyst has encountered before, whether in the clinic or the literature.

[9] Regarding advice-giving, Lacan (1993, p. 152) said, "It's not simply because we know too little of a subject's life that we are unable to tell him whether he would do better to marry or not in such and such circumstances and will, if we're honest, tend to be reticent—it's because the very meaning of marriage is, for each of us, a question that remains open."

[10] As Lacan (1968a, p. 22) put it, "If you allow yourself to become obsessed with what in the analysand's discourse concerns you, you are not yet in his discourse." This is one of the reasons why it is virtually impossible for an analyst to do psychoanalysis with a relative or close friend: It is not simply that the transference may sour relations between the analyst and the relative or friend (Freud mentioned that the analyst who takes a family member or friend into analysis must be prepared to permanently lose all friendly contact with that person), but that the analyst is likely to have difficulty listening in any mode other than the imaginary mode.

world as the analysand sees and experiences it, not from the "outside"—that is, by imposing her own way of functioning in the world, her own modus vivendi, on to the analysand—but to a greater or lesser degree from the "inside" (I am obviously employing such terms in a very approximate way here).[11]

This does not mean that the analyst must ultimately come to see the analysand's world the way he himself sees it, for the analysand generally only sees a part of it, not wanting to see other parts of it, in particular those parts that he considers unsavory or finds unpleasant or repulsive.[12] Although she listens intently to the story as told by the analysand, she must not believe everything she hears, even if she is often best advised not to express a great deal of disbelief at the outset. In most cases, skepticism as to whether we are hearing the whole story—whether of a particular event or of the analysand's life in general—or just a carefully orchestrated rendition of certain parts of it should be introduced only gradually; otherwise, the analysand may get the impression that we do not believe anything he says and follow the all-too-common inclination to find someone who will. This may be especially important when the analysand is experiencing marital problems and has come primarily at the insistence of his wife; if he does not find at least a temporary ally in his analyst—someone who seems to believe at least much of his side of the story—he will likely flee in search of a practitioner who is willing to side with him.

On the other hand, an adolescent who is used to successfully duping adults is often better met with skepticism on the analyst's part right from the outset; should the analyst seem to be buying the story—that the adolescent has not, in fact, done anything wrong and is simply the victim of circumstances, for example—the analysis is likely to crash before it ever gets off the ground, so to speak. Early expressions of skepticism also make sense with people who have been in therapy before or who are already quite familiar with psychoanalytic theory.

In everyday discourse, we generally show other people that we are listening to what they are saying by nodding or saying "yes" or "yeah," all of which imply assent—that we agree, that we are buying the story we are being told. Analytic discourse, on the other hand, requires something different of us: It requires

---

[11] Lacan (1976, p. 47) remarked, "I don't believe at all that there is an inner world that reflects the outer world, nor the contrary. I have tried to formulate something that indisputably assumes a more complicated organization."

[12] Indeed, were the story the analysand tells about his world the whole story, there would be nothing more to be said and nothing to be done about it, except perhaps taking some very practical action like leaving home or getting divorced. If the analysand is loath to take such action, it is probably related to something that he has left out of his rendition of the story.

us to show that we are listening intently without suggesting that we either believe or disbelieve what we are hearing.

The analyst also should eschew conventional ways of expressing attentiveness to what someone is recounting, such as saying "interesting" or "fascinating," as these comments are hackneyed and often suggest a condescending and distant perspective. They also suggest that the analyst thinks she understands what the analysand has said. Instead, she should cultivate a wide range of "hmms" and "huhs" (not "uh-huhs," which have come to signify agreement, at least in American English) of various lengths, tones, and intensities, which can be used to encourage the analysand to go on with what he is saying, to further explain something, or simply to let the analysand know that she is following or at least awake and inviting him to continue. One of the advantages of such sounds is that their meaning is not easily identifiable and the analysand can thus project many different meanings onto any one particular sound.

For example, a "hmm" sound I occasionally make to indicate simply that I have heard something an analysand has just said is sometimes interpreted as a skeptical sound by an analysand who is not too comfortable with the perspective he has been propounding—that is, he believes I am calling his perspective into question. I often have had no such intent when making that particular sound, but the "hmm" is sufficiently ambiguous that an analysand who is suspicious of his own motives or perspectives can "hear" it as a request for him to explore the latter. He projects his own suspicions onto me, and his own suspicions can only come to the fore and be discussed when they are attributed to me first.

Given that the implicit rules of everyday conversation require that each party be allowed to speak in turn (however much these rules are violated by many of the people we encounter in everyday life!), the analyst must encourage the analysand to keep talking even when the usual conventions would require that the analysand give it a rest and let the analyst chime in. This means that the analyst's listening is not passive—indeed, it must be quite active. The analyst who gives the analysand little or no eye contact and/or who writes down virtually everything the analysand says is likely to provide scant encouragement of the analysand's speech. If the analyst is to engage the analysand in the analytic process, she herself must be anything but a detached, objective observer—she must manifest her own active engagement in the process. The more she is engaged, the more engaged the analysand is likely to feel—assuming, that is, that the analyst's engagement is of a certain open, interested, and encouraging type and not of a defensive, smothering, or self-disclosing type. One of my analysands occasionally says that during our sessions he has the sense that he is "surfing on the waves of [my] 'hmms' and 'huhs'"; he tends to comment on that particularly at moments when he feels that those waves are less abundant than usual—that is, when he feels that I am not listening as actively as usual.

This points to one way in which the "analyst's neutrality" is a myth—the analyst is anything but a neutral, indifferent, inactive figure on the analytic stage. Chapter 4 addresses this issue in more depth.

"Free-floating Attention"

As soon as anyone deliberately concentrates his attention to a certain degree, he begins to select from the material before him; one point will be fixed in his mind with particular clearness and some other will be correspondingly disregarded, and in making this selection he will be following his expectations or inclinations. This, however, is precisely what must not be done. In making the selection, if he follows his expectations he is in danger of never finding anything but what he already knows.

— *Freud (1912b/1958, p. 112)*

What does the analyst listen for? This question presumes that there is something *in particular* that the analyst should be listening for, whereas experienced analysts generally agree that no matter what they might expect to come out in any given analysis, they are always surprised by what they find. Freud (1912b/1958, p. 111) rightly recommended that we approach each new case as though it were our first, in the sense that we should presume nothing about what will transpire, employing "evenly-suspended attention," also known as "evenly hovering attention" or "free-floating attention," so that we will be able to hear whatever appears in the analysand's "free associations." "Free-floating attention" is what allows us to hear what is new and different in what the analysand says—as opposed to simply hearing what we want to hear or expect in advance to hear. We cultivate the practice of such attention (which is not at all easy to sustain) as part of our attempt to recognize the otherness of the other, the other's differences from ourselves.[13]

---

[13] Free-floating (or evenly hovering) attention is, as Freud (1912b/1958, p. 112) said and Lacan (2006, p. 471) reiterated, supposed to be the analyst's counterpart to the analysand's "free association." Yet one of the first things one notices as a practitioner is that the analysand's associations seem to be anything but free. The analysand finds himself obliged to dance circles around certain topics rather than go directly toward them, or to veer away from them altogether when the memories and thoughts associated with them are overly charged.

But what exactly is "free-floating attention"? It is not a kind of attentiveness that latches on to one particular statement the analysand makes and—in the attempt to etch it in one's mind, think it through, or connect it to other things— misses the analysand's next statement. It is rather an attentiveness that floats from point to point, from statement to statement, without necessarily trying to draw any conclusions from them, interpret them, put them all together, or sum them all up. *It is an attentiveness that grasps at least one level of meaning and yet hears all the words and the way they are pronounced as well*, including speed, volume, tone, affect, stumbling, hesitation, and so on.

Lacan (2006) ironized about certain analysts' search for a third ear (above all, Theodor Reik), with which to presumably hear an occult meaning, a meaning beyond the meanings that can already be found in the analysand's speech:

> But what need can an analyst have for an extra ear, when it sometimes seems that two are already too many, since he runs headlong into the fundamental misunderstanding brought on by the relationship of understanding? I repeatedly tell my students: "Don't try to understand!" . . . May one of your ears become as deaf as the other one must be acute. And that is the one that you should lend to listen for sounds and phonemes, words, locutions, and sentences, not forgetting pauses, scansions, cuts, periods, and parallelisms. (p. 471)

Lacan's point here is that when the analyst becomes obsessed with understanding the meaning that the analysand is consciously trying to convey, with following all the intricacies of the story he is telling, she often fails to listen to the way in which the analysand conveys what he says—to the words and expressions he uses and to his slips and slurs. Better to plug up the ear that listens only for meaning, he suggests, than to render the ear that listens to speech itself superfluous by adding a third one. When, for example, the analysand begins a sentence with "on the one hand," we can be pretty sure he has another "hand" in mind; yet by the time the first "hand" is laid out, he may well have forgotten the second "hand," in which case he is likely to say, "Well anyway," and blithely turn to something else. The analyst must not, however, take it so lightly: What, indeed, was that other hand? Its importance derives from the very fact that it has been (at least momentarily) forgotten.

Getting caught up in the story being told is one of the biggest traps for new analysts and, not surprisingly, they get most easily caught up in the story the closer it seems to their own interests or the more closely it seems to concern or reflect upon them as individuals or clinicians. What is most important to the analysand, especially at the beginning of the analysis, is that the analyst—like anyone else he talks to in other walks of life—grasp his point, the conceptual point he is trying to make. He rarely begins analysis with the explicit hope that the analyst will hear something in what he is saying that is different than the point he is consciously trying to get across. The analyst, on the other hand, must wean herself from listening in the conventional way and realize that it is often of far less importance to understand the story or point than it is to hear the way in which it is delivered.

Free-floating attention is a practice—indeed, a discipline—designed to teach us to *hear without understanding*. Apart from the fact that understanding generally tends to bring the analyst herself front and center, introducing a plethora of imaginary phenomena (for example, comparing herself to the analysand and worrying about her self-image as reflected back by the analysand's speech, as I indicated earlier), there is often precious little that could be understood anyway in the analysand's discourse. Why is that?

The Story Makes No Sense (or Too Much Sense)

The unconscious is not about losing one's memory; it is about not recalling what one knows.
— *Lacan (1968b, p. 35)*

The analysand tells a story about himself that is highly partial, in both senses of the term: He leaves out a great deal of the story—feeling that it is not important, germane, or flattering to himself, or having simply "forgotten" it— and he presents the story as though he played a crystal-clear role in it as the hero, the victim, "the good guy," or (less commonly) the jerk or criminal. The story he tells is always piecemeal, fragmentary, riddled with gaps and holes, and essentially comprehensible to no one but him, for only he is privy to what has been left out (although sometimes he, too, is in the dark) and only he fully embraces his own perspective on his predicament. Even then, he himself may be of two minds (or even more) about his own participation in the story: In session, he may try to convince the analyst, and thereby convince himself, that he was nothing but a victim in the situation, but he may not fully endorse that view in his heart of hearts. Part of the analyst's job is to ensure that the part of him that does not endorse this view has a chance to speak its piece and gets a fair hearing, so to speak.

Often the story as told simply makes no sense to a listener, no matter how creative or intuitive, because too much is being left out; the analyst's task, in such cases, is to draw the analysand out in an attempt to fill in the gaps (which recalls Freud's notion that the main purpose of an analysis is to fill in the gaps in the analysand's history).[14] In other cases, however, the story is wrapped up very nicely and neatly, with a pretty bow on top, and yet it seems incommensurate with the affect attached to it, does not make any sense in the context of the analysand's life as it has thus far been portrayed, or seems too cut and dried. Indeed, the analysand may seem extremely content with his explanation of the event in question and yet the analyst may wonder why, if he is so at peace with the explanation, it is being mentioned at all. Something about it does not fit, does not make any sense—it is not a problem with the story itself, but with the fact that it is being told in an analytic session at this particular point in the therapy.

If we could say that there is, indeed, something in particular that the analyst listens for, it is for what does not fit, does not make sense, or seems to make too much sense and therefore seems problematic. These are all related to *repression*. When the analysand truncates his story by suppressing certain elements, he may be doing so consciously, knowing that he is trying to present himself in a certain way (whether flattering or unflattering) to the analyst, but he may also be doing so unconsciously, for reasons of which he is not aware. He may not be aware (and may resist becoming aware) of the way in which he situates the analyst in his psychical economy—of the type or quality of transference he has to her—or of what he is trying to achieve in relation to her. Similarly, he may have truly forgotten certain elements of the story and may recall them only after a considerable quantity of analytic work.

Important details may be left out of the analysand's account of a specific story that takes only minutes to recount, but they may also be left out of the broader portrait that he paints of his life. An analysand told me early on in his therapy that he was a "scoundrel" and that he felt he had always had a "diabolical core." Yet nothing in the story of his life that he told me during the first several weeks of consultations suggested anything particularly unsavory or dishonorable. The worst behavior he seemed to be able to point to was trampling on a neighbor's newly planted seedling as a child, and the working assumption I initially formed was that he had a highly critical superego (perhaps encouraged by his father's accusation early in life that he had stolen money that he had in fact found on the ground). It took several months of sessions before he recalled, through his associations to a couple of dreams, the circumstances surrounding a family

---

[14] See Freud (1916–1917/1963, p. 282). Consider how many times Freud had to get the Rat Man to tell the story of the pince-nez (the crisis that brought him into analysis) before he could piece it together. Note too that Freud suggests that "we can express the aim of our efforts in a variety of formulas: making conscious what is unconscious, lifting repressions, filling gaps in the memory—all these amount to the same thing" (p. 435).

member's hospitalization and a former partner's pregnancy, his guilt feelings about which he had never spoken of before. The reasons for his harsh view of himself—which he himself did not really understand, since he thought of himself as essentially a good person—came into focus when he recalled these incidents and it was his recollection and discussion of them that allowed some of this harshness to finally dissipate.

Analysis as a Logic of Suspicion

An "act of speaking" [Un "dire"] is akin to an event. It is not a quick glimpse or a moment of knowing. . . . Not all speech [parole] is an act of speaking, otherwise all speech would be an event, which is not the case, and we would not speak of "worthless words."
— Lacan (1973–1974, December 18, 1973)

It is equivocation, the plurality of meanings, that favors the passage of the unconscious into discourse.
— Lacan (1976, p. 36)

Repression is our guiding light in psychoanalysis (if you will excuse the paradoxical nature of the metaphor, repression usually being associated with darkness). Virtually everything we do as analysts should be designed to get at the repressed in a more or less direct manner. This is why our constant focus is on what is being left out of the equation, out of the story, out of the picture the analysand paints of himself and of his life. This is why we give special attention to the details of a story that were "accidentally" left out the first time the story was told. This is why our ears perk up when the analysand is suddenly unable to recall the name of his best friend. This is why we are intrigued when a sentence is interrupted and started anew somewhere else (our concern being with the break in the narrative, not its continuity). This is why, like Freud (1900/1958, p. 518), we give extra weight to elements of a dream that were forgotten during the first telling and only remembered later when the analysand is associating to his dream. This is why we may find the stray or offhanded comment he makes on the way out the door after the session to be the most important.

To the analyst, every story the analysand tells is suspect. Not only is it likely to be incomplete or too pat, but it is also probably being told here and now for certain strategic or tactical purposes—to please or displease the analyst, to get a rise out of her, to win or lose her hypothetical love, to prop up or destroy a certain image—purposes that may not be out in the open and yet play an important role in the ultimate shape and form the story takes.

The notion that we must approach each new analysand on his own terms, as though he were our first, does not imply that we must act as if we know nothing at all about psychoanalysis— as if we do not know that the presence of symptoms in the analysand's life is indicative of repression (since symptoms represent the return of the repressed), that slips of the tongue and bungled actions are mini-symptoms that also represent the return of the repressed, that the subject's rhetoric can help us pinpoint repression (the most important element in a list often being reserved for last—"my friends and siblings, not to mention my mother," an example of paralipsis or preterition—and the most likely answer to a question often being mentioned under the guise of negation—"The person who punished me the most? I don't think I could say it was my father").[15]

Psychoanalysts have been led to examine the analysand's myriad rhetorical ploys in terms of the kinds of defensive moves they involve. Just as dreams form in accordance with condensation and displacement—associated by Lacan (2006, pp. 511–515) with metaphor and metonymy—which disguise unconscious wishes, the analysand's discourse functions in accordance with a plethora of other mechanisms designed to keep the unconscious down. The analysand spontaneously employs rhetorical figures (that are well-known to grammarians and linguists) to keep from saying certain things and to keep certain ideas from surfacing. He eventually fails in this endeavor: Things do slip out, and the analyst, trained to detect these rhetorical ploys—"the psychoanalyst is a rhetorician," said Lacan (1977–1978, November 15, 1977)—learns where to intervene in order to foil them.

When someone uses a *mixed metaphor*, for example, it is often because one of the words in the metaphor that first came to mind is disturbing to that person. One of my analysands once said "stop beating around the issue" when the term "bush" seemed too sexually charged, too likely to bring up sexual thoughts he did not want to discuss (it is sometimes astonishing how quickly such substitutions can be made). We might equally imagine someone saying

---

[15] It should be clear from my examples that when I say that we must not act as if we know nothing at all about psychoanalysis, I do not mean that it is important for us to "know" that bulimia is due to x, y, or z, or that stuttering is due to p, q, or r. This kind of "knowledge accumulated in the course of an analyst's experience concerns the imaginary" and "is of no value in [the process of] training analysts" (Lacan 2006, p. 357); the causes of symptoms in different subjects are often so different anyway as to render such global claims useless. What I mean is that it is important for us to keep in mind the most basic theoretical principles of psychoanalytic theory: that a fear often covers over a wish, that expressions of disgust are often signs of repression, that people get a kick out of many things that they say they find repulsive or profess to be afraid of, that "bungled actions are the only actions that are always successful" (Lacan, 2007, p. 65), and so on. In such cases, psychoanalytic theory allows us to see far more than we would see otherwise. As Bowlby (1982) said, "Because of his large store of relevant information about the appearance and habits of birds and plants, the experienced naturalist sees far more than does the tyro" (p. 111).

"stop circling around the bush" when there is a certain sadistic or masochistic thought about beating that the person wants to keep out of sight and out of mind.

Mixed metaphors are very common in analysis and in everyday life as well. Of course, at times they can simply imply that the person does not really know the metaphors he is half-using, but most native speakers know at least a lot of the idiomatic expressions they use by heart, and they can be immediately made to wonder why they changed the wording by the analyst simply repeating the changed wording back to them. The mixed metaphor "beating around the issue" can be understood as a compromise formation between "beating around the bush" and "skirting the issue." In rhetorical terms it might be called *catachresis*, which designates a misuse of words. In either case, it suggests to the attentive clinician that *something is being avoided* or that another train of thought is interfering with the completion of the initial train of thought.

Let us consider another rhetorical device or trope: *Litotes*, also known as understatements, are used constantly in sessions, and they are often preceded by a slight pause. One analysand of mine was about to say (as he indicated later), "I really lust after my best friend's wife," but toned it down by saying, "I don't find her unattractive." The slight pause he introduced, combined with the highly constructed double negative, suggested to me that something was likely going unsaid; as it turned out, a certain thought was being circumvented because the analysand had judged it unacceptable, thinking "How can I be so low as to lust after my best friend's wife?"

Another analysand neglected to provide the last two intended words—"to stop"—of a sentence that she began as follows: "It [her parents holding her down and tickling her until she could barely breathe] would be fun up to a point and then I'd want it . . ." The *ellipsis* of the words "to stop," which she perhaps felt were obvious given the context, suggested to me a rather different train of thought to which she was perhaps loath to give direct expression: that she would want it to go on forever, get more intense, or even lead to something sexual. I could have said to myself, "I know what she means even if that is not what she said," but when I repeated back her incomplete phrase, "you'd want it . . ." she mentioned that she had been distracted while saying it by indistinct thoughts of an embarrassing kind. Such an ellipsis or elision might have gone unnoticed by her friends in everyday conversation but in the analysis served as a kind of index or telltale sign of concealment.

As I have indicated elsewhere (Fink, 2004, pp. 72–75), many other rhetorical devices, such as pleonasm, digression, periphrasis, retraction, and irony, can take on a defensive quality, especially in the analytic context. I hope that these three examples suffice to make it clear to what extent such figures of speech are not "mere manners of speaking," as the analysand is inclined to think of them, and that the attentive listener can learn to read them as mile markers along the road toward the repressed. The unconscious at work in dreams employs condensation and displacement, and the analysand in talking about his dreams employs virtually all of rhetoric's figures and tropes. *To the analyst, nothing is ever "just a figure of speech."* The analyst's mode of listening attends to both what is presented and what is not presented, to both what is enunciated and what is avoided. In essence, it reads all speech as a compromise formation, as produced by competing forces.

When the analyst focuses exclusively on the story or conceptual point being made, she usually cannot hear the figures of speech being employed and thus hears only one level—the level of the meaning the analysand is consciously trying to convey. She fails then to read the several different staffs upon which the music of the analysand's discourse is actually written.

Hearing Only What We Expect To Hear

The essence of language has never been to serve the function of communication.
— Lacan (2005a, p. 106)

The perceptum *[what is perceived] is already structured [by language].*
— Soler (2002, p. 33)

There are, of course, still other reasons why it is so difficult for the analyst to hear exactly what the analysand says, at least some of which are related to the interaction between language and perception. Neurobiologists and psychiatrists have shown how important "sensory gating" is for the ability to tune out distracting perceptual stimuli that seem unimportant to the task or goal one has at hand (Green, 2001, pp. 77–79). A great deal of work on the brain and perceptual systems has been done that suggests that many people who end up being classified as autists, schizophrenics, and psychotics more generally (although I am not suggesting that there are not important differences among them) often "feel 'bombarded' by sensory input and cannot filter out . . . irrelevant stimuli" (p. 78), "irrelevant stimuli" being those perceptions that they do not necessarily wish to pay attention to at any particular moment but that distract them nevertheless. In other words, they are not able to tune out many stimuli the way the majority of people can, the latter having a "gate," as it were, that lets in certain stimuli and keeps out others based on a supposed assessment of what is important and what is not that takes place outside of consciousness, prior to consciousness. Only those stimuli that make it through the gate—only those that are deemed relevant to the task at hand—are actually allowed into consciousness.

This research seems to be borne out at the clinical level by the many cases of "sensory overload" reported by psychotic patients, in which noises that had previously gone unheard or that had blended into the background begin to become overwhelming (loud, insistent, and unignorable), smells that had previously either been enjoyed or unnoticed suddenly become unbearably strong and repulsive, and colors, shapes, or motion that had previously not stood out suddenly monopolize consciousness and overpower it. The moment at which these perceptions begin to impinge on such subjects is often a very stressful one, signaling that the subject is in danger of experiencing a psychotic break or episode (prolonged sleep deprivation can bring on a similar inability to "gate" stimuli in those who are not psychotic). In certain autistic and schizophrenic subjects, on the other hand, difficulty filtering stimuli can be permanent, not necessarily indicating an imminent danger of any kind; the difficulty does not come and go as it does in cases of paranoia, where breaks may be followed by apparent remission and then further trouble at a later date.

Although the most biologically-minded researchers consider the difficulty filtering out stimuli to be a strictly physiological problem, resulting from some malformation of a specific brain structure or some chemical imbalance, it strikes me as equally (if not more) likely that language plays a significant role in the ability to filter stimuli, for those who are unable to filter perceptions in the usual manner generally do not speak or think in quite the same way as those who can filter such perceptions. Perhaps it is not gating difficulties that cause problems with language acquisition but problems with language acquisition that cause gating difficulties.

Language is not assimilated in the same manner by such subjects, nor does it function in the same manner for them as it does in what I will call "ordinary neurotics." As I have argued elsewhere (Fink, 1997, 2005b), there are at least two major different ways of coming into being in language, what we might call the "ordinary neurotic way" and the "psychotic way." The ordinary neurotic way leads to the usual predominance of language-based thinking (as opposed to visual or other ways of thinking), a split between conscious and unconscious (and the widespread conflict of feelings referred to in psychoanalysis as "ambivalence," certain feelings being conscious and others unconscious, loosely speaking),[16] and the ability to hear both literal and figurative meanings of an

---

[16] See Chapter 7 for a discussion of the relationship between affect and repression. Miller (2002, p. 25) characterized the difference between the neurotic and psychotic ways of coming into being

expression at the same time. The psychotic way leads to language learning by imitation alone, no split between conscious and unconscious (and thus no ambivalence per se), and an inability to hear both literal and figurative meanings of an expression at the same time.

Rather than try to explain this in detail here, I will illustrate it with some comments that Temple Grandin (Grandin & Johnson, 2005), a researcher who studies animal behavior, autism, and the relationship between them and who considers herself to be autistic (rightly so, no doubt), makes about her own relationship to language:

> I got in fights [in high school] because kids teased me. They'd call me names like "retard," or "tape recorder." They called me tape recorder because I'd store up a lot of phrases in my memory and use them over and over again in every conversation. (p. 1)
>
> I almost never remember specific words and sentences from conversations. That's because autistic people think in pictures; we have almost no words running through our heads at all. (p. 10.)
>
> When I talk to other people I translate my pictures into stock phrases or sentences I have "on tape" inside my head. . . . I *am* a tape recorder. That's how I am able to talk. The reason I don't sound like a tape recorder anymore is that I have so many stock phrases and sentences I can move around into new combinations. (p. 18)
>
> Animals and autistic people don't seem to have repression. . . . I don't think I have any of Freud's defense mechanisms, and I'm always amazed when normal people do. One of the things that blows my mind about normal human beings is denial. . . . People [in a] bad situation can't see it because their defense mechanisms protect them from seeing it until they're ready. That's denial, and I can't understand it at all. I can't even imagine what it's like.
>
> That's because I don't have an unconscious. . . . While I don't know why I don't seem to have an unconscious, I think my problems with language have a lot to do with it. (p. 92)[17]

Grandin makes it clear that she cannot classify stimuli into dangerous and not dangerous the way verbal people can—which for many years made her

---

in language as follows: "Without the Name-of-the-Father [that is, in psychosis], there is no language but only llanguage," a Lacanian term that is briefly discussed in a later footnote. He goes on to say, "Without the Name-of-the-Father, there is no body, strictly speaking, there is what is corporal, the flesh, the organism, matter, and images. There are bodily events, events that destroy the body."

[17] Grandin (1995, pp. 49, 85) indicates elsewhere that she believes that autism and schizophrenia are "neurological disorders," but her comments allow us to think otherwise.

constantly fearful of innocuous noises (like the beeping sound trucks make when they back up)—and thus cannot ignore stimuli the way most people have been shown to in study after study, in which they simply do not see things they do not expect to see in a specific context, whether it is a "lady wearing a gorilla suit" in the middle of a basketball game, or a large aircraft parked on a runway when the subjects are pilots preparing to land a plane on that same runway (Grandin & Johnson, 2005, pp. 24–25). In what is referred to as "inattentional blindness" (Mack & Rock, 1998), most of us—but not Grandin or many psychotics—screen things out before they reach consciousness and ultimately see and hear largely what we are expecting to see and hear.

For those of us who come into language in the "usual neurotic way," our immersion in language is so extensive and colors our world so thoroughly that we selectively see and hear what the social/linguistic context has led us to expect to see and hear. What falls outside of our expectations is often simply neither seen nor heard.[18]

This can be a serious liability for the clinician: Even the most well-intentioned clinician almost automatically hears what, to her mind, it would make sense for the analysand to be saying in a particular context, as opposed to hearing what the analysand is actually saying, which may be quite out of the ordinary and even nonsensical. Even the most attentive analyst often hears only what the analysand likely meant to say, filtering out the analysand's slight slip of the tongue or slur. Throughout our lives we learn to find meaning in what others are saying to us, even if it is sometimes rather incoherent, and this often involves seeing a whole image (or gestalt) where only a partial one was presented, or hearing a whole coherent thought when only a partial or incoherent thought was enunciated. We learn to fill in the gaps, supply missing words, rectify the grammar, and correct malapropisms—and we do all of this in our heads without even becoming conscious of it, for the most part.

Our own ignorance of certain vocabulary and expressions can make us hear one thing in the place of another (as those who have struggled to learn a foreign language are often well aware: When people speak to us in that foreign language

---

[18] Grandin's work can also help us realize why a neurotic and a psychotic often have a very difficult time understanding each other: They operate on fundamentally different principles. Often, like Grandin, we "can't even imagine what it's like" to be in the other's shoes. Grandin makes this point eloquently in her many discussions of most humans' inability to see things from the point of view of the animals they work with or live with. See also her *Thinking in Pictures* (Grandin, 1995).

Lacan (2007, pp. 52–53) indicated that sensation and perception are never pure, but are instead strained through our symbolic/linguistic filters.

we are inclined to hear terms and expressions that we have already learned in the place of ones that are unfamiliar but perhaps sound somewhat similar). If, for example, the analysand says that he "was sedulously attempting to persuade the Exchequer" to do something, and the analyst does not know the words "sedulously" or "Exchequer," she may hear something else altogether, such as "was assiduously (or credulously) attempting to persuade the spell checker." Even though that may not make a whole lot of sense in the context, it may be the best the analyst can do to find meaning in it given the subset of the English language she understands (no one can possibly understand all of it). What we hear when someone speaks is referred to in linguistics as "the ribbon of sound" (Saussure, 1916/1959); spoken words tend to run together, forming a sort of uninterrupted ribbon, and it is not always entirely clear where one word ends and the next begins (a problem some may be quite familiar with once again from learning foreign languages).

We are used to almost automatically cutting the ribbon up into discrete units on the basis of the language as we think we know it, as well as on the basis of what we are expecting to hear in general and what we have come to expect from a particular interlocutor. This constant activity aiming at making sense of what we hear is such that hearing itself fades behind meaning making; perception itself is suppressed in favor of interpretation. The result is that we become constitutionally deaf, in a certain sense.

To practice psychoanalysis, however, we have to break ourselves of this ingrained habit, and this often takes quite a bit of work. Practitioners occasionally tell me that their patients make no slips or slurs, but in my experience most people make a slip every five or ten minutes (some more, some less, of course) and the problem is rather that practitioners are not attuned to them. How can they become attuned to them? One useful exercise is to listen to news announcers, whether on the radio or television, and practice listening for slips and stumblings as opposed to listening for content. It is perhaps best to listen first to programs that one is not especially interested in, so that the content does not monopolize one's attention. It is perhaps also best at first not to look at the television, because seeing the speaker is likely to interfere with one's hearing (many analysts have remarked that they hear patients on the couch better than those sitting across from them, not because they are physically closer but because the analysts are not distracted by their patients' looks, facial expressions, and so on). Once one is able to regularly hear the slips and slurs in speech about matters that are of not much interest, one can then turn to programs that are closer to one's own heart, practicing focusing on the ribbon of sound as much as possible while still taking in the meaning, but without dwelling upon it or trying to do anything in particular with it (for

example, comparing it with things heard before or fathoming its implications).

Once a clinician becomes attuned to slips and verbal stumblings, she will
begin to notice them in herself and in friends and colleagues; yet it may still take
some time before she can hear them in sessions with analysands because she
is even more focused on meaning in the analytic situation than elsewhere. To
perfect our ability to pay free-floating attention to what analysands actually
say, we must often, in the words of the music teacher, "practice, practice,
practice."

Pitfalls of Training

*I could label what I am saying in my seminar this year as providing you with your
edupation, provided we emphasize the fact that it is those who [do not allow themselves to
be] dupes of the unconscious who go astray.*

— *Lacan* (1973–1974, *January 8, 1974*)

Many other things contribute to making the analyst constitutionally incapable
of hearing a great deal of what the analysand says (for example, a high degree
of obsessionality), not the least of which is our training itself. In many training
programs, whether in social work, psychology, psychoanalysis, or psychiatry,
students are encouraged to believe that there are such things as "expert knowledge systems"—systems of "knowledge" like that found in the *DSM*—and that
it is our task as clinicians to simply apply them to the best of our ability as
quickly as possible. I have heard individual teachers in all of the above fields tell
students that they should dispense the expert knowledge they have acquired
to their clients or patients, and if they do not do so they are deliberately flout-
ing all of the (so-called) empirically validated treatment (EVT) protocols and
evidence-based therapies (EBTs). Psychology and psychiatry have, after all,
they argue, now been placed on a scientific footing, taking the guesswork out
of clinical practice. Practitioners need but listen in a somewhat cursory manner
to figure out where a particular patient figures in the diagnostic manuals that
have received the seal of approval, so to speak, from the relevant APA, for those
manuals (and their supplements) will tell them which techniques to employ. If
we begin to listen only for the patterns or sets of patterns that we have been
taught to identify and treat, we are likely to turn a deaf ear to anything that
does not appear on our *DSM* radar screen.

Fortunately, not every program or every teacher truly believes in the scientific foundations of clinical practice or fosters checklist approaches to diagnosis

and treatment! Indeed, the medical establishment itself—which is often taken by psychologists and psychoanalysts as the establishment to emulate in as many ways as possible (including respectability, social prestige, income, and supposed scientificity)—has been repeatedly taken to task in recent decades for having little if any evidence for the vast majority of the procedures and treatments it prescribes, many of which have been halted or taken off the market, and is recognized even by numerous doctors to function far more as an art than a science.[19] But the very structure of higher education and its place in our culture often encourages clinicians to believe that, with their upper-level diploma, they have received in trust expertise in their field and have little to learn from further study or from their patients. Continuing education credits are viewed by many as puerile exercises at best and generally just another hoop to be jumped through. Regardless of whether continuing education courses are the best means of reminding clinicians that clinical practice entails a lifelong learning process, practitioners should be reminded that their education has generally managed to show them but the tip of the iceberg and that they would do well to remain avid readers in their fields and open to even the seemingly least profound comments made by their least "insightful" patients.

---

[19]David Eddy, M.D., Ph.D. (the chairman of the Center for Health Policy Research & Education at Duke University, who spearheaded the movement toward "evidence-based medicine") estimates that only 15% of what physicians do is backed by "hard evidence" (that is, clinical trials), and many other doctors and healthcare quality researchers place their estimate in the 20% to 25% range (Carey, 2006). The so-called standard of care in medicine—that is, the treatment that physicians are expected to provide in a specific instance (so as not to be accused of malpractice, for example)—is thus rarely on firm ground; and even when it is thought to be on a firm scientific footing, it should be kept in mind that the conclusions of up to a third of clinical trials in medicine are later overturned (Carey, 2006, p. 77). Those who believe that psychotherapy research has already managed to replicate medicine's "scientific basis" do not seem to be reading the literature in either field!

I will not enter here into the complex debates about the history and philosophy of science that are so germane to claims about the scientificity of medicine, psychoanalysis, and psychology. For a brief discussion, see Fink (1995, Chapter 10).

2

Asking Questions

It is often more important to sustain the problem raised than it is to solve it.
— Lacan (1998b, p. 425)

GIVEN THE DEGREE to which repression and transference lead the analysand to truncate and tailor the stories she tells the analyst, a good deal of the analyst's work consists of asking her questions so that she will fill in missing details, finish sentences that have trailed off, and explain what she means by certain things she says. This is an area in which the analyst's own resistance to the analytic process is likely to manifest itself; it is also an area in which the analyst is likely to say far more than he needs to.

During the preliminary meetings—that is, during the longer or shorter period of face-to-face sessions (lasting up to a year or more) that precede the use of the couch—the analyst can place a question mark after something the analysand has said simply by raising an eyebrow or giving the analysand a quizzical look. Such a question mark is not, however, terribly precise, for the question raised could concern the whole of what the analysand has just said, just the last part, the way it was said, or the fact that the analysand got angry or laughed while saying it—in short, it does not point to anything in particular. In this case, the analysand is free to interpret the raised eyebrow or quizzical look however she likes, whether as a sign of disapproval or criticism, as suggesting that she does not know what she is talking about, or as a request for further elaboration. Hence the importance, especially with analysands prone to thinking that the analyst is critical of everything they say, of more precise questioning. Given, however, the degree to which all speech is potentially ambiguous, the less the analyst says, the more precise his question is likely to be (except, as we shall see further on, when he employs a deliberately open-ended formulation like "What about that?"). Long, involved questions often lose

24

or confuse the analysand, and they almost always make what the analysand has just said recede into the background, if not be completely forgotten.

If the analysand says, "I had a great many difficulties in elementary school due to all the moving around my family did," and the analyst wants to know what kind of difficulties, it usually suffices to simply ask "Difficulties?" Should the analyst instead ask, "Can you give me some examples of that?" he may be met with examples of the different moves her family made from city to city instead of examples of her difficulties. Less is often more when asking questions, and should the analysand respond to the query "Difficulties?" simply by saying "Yes, difficulties," the analyst can easily add, "What kind of difficulties?"

Precision is not, of course, always what is most productive; sometimes the analysand hears something in the analyst's question that the analyst had not intended, and her response to the question she heard is often far more interesting than the response (given later) to the question he had intended to raise. This is because she is likely to project (as we all do) things she herself has already been thinking onto what the analyst says.[1]

Nevertheless, it is often of the utmost importance that the analyst bring the analysand to discuss particular events—and such unconscious formations as dreams, daydreams, and fantasies—in great detail, and in particular ensure that the details that the analysand is the most inclined to omit get articulated at some point. Once the analyst is attuned to the kinds of rhetorical strategies analysands employ to skirt topics and avoid what they consider to be unsavory or reprehensible details, he must often work quite hard to ensure that those topics do not remain forever skirted and that those details are not indefinitely avoided. Although the analyst must not force the analysand to reveal things she is not yet ready to face, he must not shy away from encouraging her to talk about painful or difficult subjects.

This is where the analyst's own resistance may well come in, for it is much easier for the analyst to sit back and allow the analysand to talk about whatever she feels like talking about than it is to work with her to articulate the trying and traumatic experiences in her past. The analysand may be reluctant to delve into painful matters, but if the analyst responds by backing off and does not show the analysand that he wants her to talk about these things—if not today, then tomorrow (and he must not forget to bring them up tomorrow if she does not do so spontaneously)—he allows the treatment to be directed by his own

---

[1] It should not be thought that the analyst's speech (whether in the form of questions or statements) is any less prone to ambiguity than the analysand's, for *all speech* is potentially polyvalent and can be heard in more than one way. In any event, the meaning of what one says is always determined by other people: Meaning is determined in the place of the Other (see Fink, 2005b, pp. 574–575).

resistance rather than by his desire as an analyst to always pursue the analysis ever further.

Analysands often know at some level that they need to talk about (and often even *want* to talk about) their trying experiences and disturbing fantasies, yet they find it difficult to discuss them with the analyst (for a wide variety of reasons, including fear of rejection, fear of making real something that heretofore they have only considered to be a will-o'-the-wisp in their minds, and fear of exciting the analyst with their revelations).[2] Even after three years of analysis, one of my analysands was ashamed to tell me that, when he was a teenager, he had found a dildo in his mother's closet; he felt it did not fit in with what we were talking about (his anxiety about writing) when it came to his mind in session, and he only reluctantly discussed it when I prompted him to tell me what had occurred to him. His reluctance to discuss the subject was due to the fact that he did not like what it implied about his parents' relationship and how it resonated with some of his own sexual fantasies and practices.

If the analyst fails to encourage his analysands to discuss these things, they are likely to come to one or more of several conclusions: that the analyst is not particularly interested in them or committed to their having a successful analysis, that the analyst finds their life and fantasies reprehensible and does not want to hear about them, that the analyst cannot bear to hear about them, or that perhaps they are not so important to talk about after all. Any of these conclusions will defeat the analysis in short order.

In formulating questions to draw analysands out about their trying experiences and painful memories, the analyst does well to use the exact same words and expressions as the analysand, as opposed to formulating things in his own terms. Translation (into one's own terms) is betrayal—betrayal of the letter, and often of the spirit, of the analysand's discourse. When I occasionally, cannot recall the exact term an analysand used to characterize something or someone and put another term in its place, the analysand often lets me know right away that that was not what she said. Once, when I wanted to repeat

---

[2] As Freud (1914a/1958) reminded us, analysands are often surprisingly ignorant of their own thoughts and fantasies at the beginning of treatment and have to be encouraged to pay attention to them:

> The initiation of the treatment in itself brings about a change in the patient's conscious attitude to his illness. He has usually been content with lamenting it, despising it as nonsensical and under-estimating its importance; for the rest, he has extended to its manifestations the ostrich-like policy of repression which he adopted towards its origins. Thus it can happen that he does not properly know under what conditions his phobia breaks out or does not listen to the precise wording of his obsessional ideas.... He must find the courage to direct his attention to the phenomena of his illness. (p. 152)

It is obviously up to the analyst to inspire in him the courage to do so.

something an analysand had said as part of a question and could not remember the exact phrase, I said, "So you made love after your argument?" and the analysand sharply corrected me: "We had sex." (Clearly, there was no love involved in her view, and she had not used the phrase "made love.") Words are not indifferent or interchangeable: better to stick with the verbatim text. This is true regardless of how extreme the analysand's language is, and even if her language is potentially offensive to the analyst's sensibilities (hopefully his own analysis will have tempered most of the latter). Shying away from repeating the four-letter words the analysand employs (often with considerable affective charge) suggests that the analyst disapproves of such language—or worse, of the body parts or activities associated with them—or cannot abide the crude reality of the analysand's life or fantasy life. This too will defeat the analysis in short order.[3]

In certain circumstances, the analyst must help the analysand articulate experiences by asking a plethora of exploratory questions, without which the analysand feels lost or at sea, overwhelmed by the memories of what may have been a rather inchoate experience. These questions should avoid vague terms like *abuse*, which can mean different things to different people, and should take the smallest steps possible, allowing the analysand to correct and fill in details. "He touched you with his fingers?" is far preferable to "He molested you?"

In talking with one of my analysands about his horror at his seemingly sexual reaction to the sight of dead bodies, I needed to ask dozens of questions to circumvent his reluctance to even think about it. He was incapable of freely associating to it because of his sense that it was terribly immoral for him to have sensations in his penis upon seeing a dead body (he had seen dead bodies in films on the Nazis)—to his mind, it proved he was a monster. The guilt he felt seemed somewhat alleviated after it became clear that it was the fact that a dead body did not move in a harmonious, unified fashion but rather like a disconnected collection of fragmented body parts, that led to a kind of shrinking feeling in his penis (in an effort to avoid having it become disconnected like those other body parts, one might surmise). He could deal

---

[3] This is not to suggest that the analyst need introduce crude terminology on his own. He should simply follow the analysand's lead and avoid circumlocutions: He should not be afraid to call a spade a spade. This is not to suggest, either, that the analyst must stress every last bit of sexual terminology the analysand uses or obsessively follow every last sexual association possible. Nevertheless, sexuality is an important part of life and certain contemporary analysts seem to have forgotten that; they would do well to pay more attention to the way sexual terminology and innuendo permeate our language and the way sex goes to the core of the subject's sense of self and colors so many of her relationships.

The analyst should also avoid any temptation to employ vocabulary that goes over the analysand's head (e.g., introduce psychoanalytic jargon with which the analysand may not be familiar).

with castration anxiety far more easily than with the sense that his sexual tastes were so perverted as to exclude him from the realm of all human feeling. Nevertheless, his initial self-recriminations—based on his presentiment that such a sensation in his penis must surely consign him to the ranks of an Adolf Hitler or a Gilles de Rais—were so strong that I had to ask question after question to get him to overcome his resistance to talking about it. It seems that no relief from such self-reproaches would have been possible without that.

When working with analysands in a tongue other than their mother tongue, the analyst must keep in mind that the analysand may at times be translating from her native language into the language the analyst understands, and that translation is very often treason: It betrays or, indeed, fails to betray (in the sense of giving away) a certain meaning. The analyst must ask the analysand at times how certain central words or phrases in her discourse, and in her dreams and fantasies in particular, would be expressed in her mother tongue, and get her to pronounce them aloud even though the analyst does not know that language; for it is often only once the analysand hears the words pronounced aloud that she can associate to them on the basis of their sound (words with different meanings are often pronounced more or less identically) or their double or triple meanings.

An analysand whose mother tongue was not English once told me an "unpleasant dream" in which he was a salesman selling "stocks," and although he called upon many people, no one seemed to want them and he had to beg them to buy his "stocks." The only associations he had before coming to the session were to a conference he was organizing and to the fact that he felt he had to beg certain big-name speakers to speak at it. It struck me right from the outset that the word *stocks* as employed by the analysand was ambiguous and a bit odd, given the context, and when I asked him what he meant by it he confirmed my suspicion that he meant something more like what we would typically refer to as "goods" or "merchandise" in American English. I then asked him if there was some word in his mother tongue that he had had in mind. He replied that there was, and I asked him to pronounce it out loud—much to his astonishment, as it was obvious to him that I did not speak his mother tongue. I admit that I was hard-pressed to repeat it back to him very accurately, so that he could hear it pronounced by some other person (we tend to hear "the same thing" differently when it is enunciated by another person; we hear the ambiguities and double entendres in another's speech more easily than in our own because our attention is often focused primarily on our intended meaning when we ourselves speak), but I did my best to reproduce the sound and asked him if it evoked anything for him. When it did not, I asked him if it had any other meanings in his mother tongue. He reflected for a moment and then laughed, saying that it also meant gift and penis.[4] This allowed us to begin to talk about another possible meaning of the dream, related to the fact that he felt that neither his wife nor any other woman was sufficiently excited by him and that he had recently resorted to begging them to sleep with him—a topic he had not known how to bring up, since he found it too humiliating to broach. One might say that his dream, in selecting a word that meant goods, gift, and penis, had furnished a way to broach it, a way that would have remained untapped had we not explored the meaning of the word in his mother tongue.

A number of complications can arise when an analysand does analysis in a tongue other than her mother tongue (not to mention when the analyst conducts an analysis in a tongue other than his mother tongue), but one the analyst should be particularly attentive to is interlinguistic phenomena, such as when a word or name as pronounced in one of the languages the analysand speaks means something different or refers to someone else in another of the languages she speaks. Such "crossover" words or names are, in my experience conducting analyses with French speakers living in the United States, often key to deciphering dreams (they constitute particularly felicitous disguises employed by the dreamwork in bilingual and partially bilingual people), and when the analyst works with an analysand whose mother tongue he does not speak he must do his best to keep an eye out for them and encourage his analysand to do so as well.[5]

---

[4] Regarding the kinds of plays on words that are possible in one language and not another, Lacan (1973, p. 47) said the following: "A specific language is nothing but the sum total of the equivocations that its history has allowed to persist in it."

Laughter can play many different roles and mean many different things in analysis, as we shall see in the course of this book; here I would simply like to emphasize the importance of noticing and asking about laughter that follows a comment made by the analysand, as it often indicates that something came to mind that is equally if not more important than the comment the analysand has just made. A male analysand of mine was talking about what he would miss were his mother to die, and the second thing he mentioned was his enjoyment of her smell on the bed sheets when he took naps in her bed after she had gotten up. He laughed after he said this, and I initially thought that he had laughed because he felt silly saying it when he had not napped in her bed in some 20 years. However, when he paused after laughing I decided to ask what had made him laugh. He indicated that he had suddenly remembered that once, after reading some psychoanalytic literature and finding out from his mother that she had never breastfed him, he had openly accused her of being the cause of all his "oral fixations." This was particularly striking in light of the fact that in the previous session he had associated his father with his "oral fixations" and had accused his mother of being against everything associated with his father. It is likely that he would not have put the fleeting memory that led him to laugh into words had I not prompted him to do so. Laughter is something we must pay very close attention to in psychoanalysis!

[5] Interpreters of certain literary texts must keep an eye out for them as well. Consider the following somewhat nonsensical example from James Joyce's *Finnegans Wake*: "Who ails tongue coddeau aspace of dumbillsilly?" When pronounced aloud it sounds like the French "Où es ton cadeau, espèce d'imbécile?" ("Where is your gift, you idiot?"). This example is discussed in Lacan (2005b, p. 166).

Such words need not be complete homonyms or spelled in exactly the same manner. In one case, an analysand told me about a dream in which he was sucking a woman's toe. Rather than immediately assuming that the big toe was a phallic symbol (although, of course, I did not rule out that eventuality),[6] I asked him how one would say "big toe" in his mother tongue and he pronounced a word that evoked "umbrella" in English. His immediate association was that as a child, he had once been bored and started playing with an umbrella that had a very sharp point; he repeatedly thrust the sharp point into the soft mud near his feet, but then missed and hit his big toe, wounding it so severely that he had to go to the hospital. In describing how badly he had injured his toe, he slipped and instead of saying that the toe was very swollen, he said, making an exaggerated gesture with his hands above his lap to show how big it was, "the umbrella was swollen." The connection between this self-inflicted injury and a kind of self-castration (the big toe as an umbrella-like object that can be extended or retracted, sucked, and so on) hinged on a relationship between parts of words in two different languages. The dream was far more complicated than this one simple connection—relating to his sense that he should have been punished by his father for his overly intimate relationship with his mother—but this simple connection might not have been made so easily had I failed to inquire about his mother tongue. The analyst cannot possibly know all languages, cultures, or customs and thus must continually inquire if he is to ever know what different things, terms, and activities mean to an analysand.[7]

God Is in the Details

Psychoanalysis involves allowing the analysand to elaborate the unconscious knowledge that is in him not in the form of a depth, but in the form of a cancer.
                                    —Lacan (1973–1974, June 11, 1974)

I am often surprised, when talking with the clinicians I supervise, that they are unable to answer some of the simplest questions I raise about their analysands, such as the names of members of the analysand's family and how old the analysand was when certain events occurred. It would seem that over the past 100 years, analysts have come to think that names and dates are of little

---

[6] See Freud's (1905a/1953, p. 155, footnote 2) comments on feet.
[7] See, on this point, Lacan's (1988a, pp. 196–198) account of his work with a patient from northern Africa and my comments on it (Fink, 2004, pp. 9–10).

importance! Yet time and again, important connections can be found between names of family members and names of boyfriends and husbands; time and again, an event an analysand reports as having taken place at one moment in time actually took place somewhat earlier or later than she originally remembered, making it coincide with another event whose importance the analysand has repeatedly downplayed. If the analyst has not bothered to ask about the analysand's age or grade in school when each event occurred, no connection between the events can be made.

One of my analysands told me that he made a "conscious decision" in junior high school not to pursue what he really wanted, having concluded that no man gets the woman he really wants (he said he saw guys all around him who were pining for their "ideal woman" but who ended up alone and disappointed). Yet he had no recollection, he said in response to a question I asked, of what was going on at the time that he made this conscious decision. I recalled that he had told me, in response to another question of mine a couple of weeks before, that a particular event had occurred when he was 14 (coinciding for most people with junior high), an event that had "changed everything" for him. He and his younger sister had, for many years prior, engaged in sexual play, and at age 14 he for the first time ejaculated during this play. He did not know what was happening to him when it occurred, and both he and his sister seemed quite shaken by it; his sister was never willing to engage in such sexual play again despite his efforts to "win her back." It seems that his conscious decision not to pursue what he really wanted (his sister, in this case, and his mother as well, as it turned out) might well have been a way of making the best of a bad situation.

Although this analysand at times emphasized how upset he felt about this change in his relationship with his sister, at other times he downplayed its importance; when I asked if the conscious decision was not in fact made around the time of this change, he assured me that the change had occurred a couple of years before that. "At least I certainly hope so," he continued, "otherwise I wouldn't have been just a kid [when I was playing around with my sister]." It would seem that in the later session he felt a need to change the date of the turning point in his relationship with his sister from 14 to 12 so that he would not feel so responsible, not feel that he was almost an adult at that point who "should have known better." If I had not kept track of the date, I would have allowed the analysand's defense (against the idea of being an almost-adult "corrupter of youth") to prevail rather than establish a connection between his loss of this close contact with his sister and his giving up on his own desire. Note that the analysand had not forgotten either the event that "changed everything" in his relationship with his sister or the "conscious decision" he made; what was unconscious—that is, what had been repressed—was the link between them. And indeed, repression often works by making a link between two different events or thoughts disappear.[8]

At the very next session he wondered if it was not precisely because he thought of his sister as the ideal woman for him that he was led to introduce another man into his sexual fantasies: To directly imagine being with his sister would be too taboo and would put a stop to the fantasy (a certain amount of disguise being necessary in most fantasies). Instead, he eroticized the relationship between her and another man in his fantasies, just as he did in his later teens when he introduced his sister to his best friends. He had been perplexed by the role of the male go-between in his sexual fantasies for a long time; the age-14 connection allowed him to find a first interpretation of it and eventually allowed his fantasies to find other avenues and permutations.

Getting What We Ask For

Swear to tell the truth, nothing but the truth, the whole truth, and that is precisely what will not be said. If the subject has the slightest idea of it, that is precisely what he will not say.
                                                                              — Lacan (1976, p. 35)

It is well known that the answers we receive depend in large part on the questions we ask. If we ask voters to rate a preestablished list of issues in terms of their importance to them, we may not be any the wiser regarding what issues are of the most importance to them, for we may not have included the right issues on the list. If we do not leave a few blanks on the page that the voters can fill in themselves with their own issues, we are likely to remain in the dark as to what is of most concern to them.

Similarly, our best bet in analytic work is to ask very open-ended questions rather than asking, "Did that make you laugh or cry?" (a common response

---

[8] Important links can also exist, of course, between thoughts, fantasies, and events that were not contemporaneous or even close together in time or space due to what Freud referred to as "deferred action" (*Nachträglichkeit*); see Fink (1995, pp. 26, 64).

An analysand told me one day that his sister once performed oral sex on him when he was around eight; a few weeks later he told me that the first time a girl ever performed fellatio on him was when he was around 16 and that he could not stand it. When I said, "But it happened before," he replied, "Oh, you're right—you know me better than I do!" He had obviously never made the connection between the two events; in this sense, we might say that the connection or link between them had been broken through the action of repression. Nevertheless, his reaction to the second event was no doubt colored by his experience of the first and by what the first had come to mean in the intervening years as he learned about sexuality.

being "Neither, it made me sick to my stomach!"). Rather than propose an A or B, or even an A, B, or C, to choose from, we generally do best to avoid putting words in the analysand's mouth. Rather than trying to guess at the analysand's likely reaction to a situation, it often makes far more sense to simply say, "And?" or "What was that like?" or "How did you react?" (I mentioned exceptions to this rule of thumb earlier, in which far more precise questions are called for.) This makes it easier for the analysand to respond however she likes.

The way we formulate questions determines in part the response that we get: If we say, "Was that painful for you?" we are likely to get a response that includes the term "painful," whereas the analysand may have emphasized something completely different had we simply asked, "What about that?" I find open-ended questions particularly useful in working with dreams and fantasies. One day an analysand of mine told me that he was only able to remember a tiny snippet of a dream, something about his father and a raincoat. He expressed his conviction that there was too little there to work with, but, in my typical fashion, I asked, "What about a raincoat?" "Nothing," he replied. "Nothing?" I queried after a pause of ten or more seconds. In the interim an image of a particular raincoat had come to him, and he soon recognized it as the one his father had been wearing one day in a store when the analysand, as a young boy, had accidentally latched onto the wrong raincoat and in short order found himself out in the store's parking lot standing with a stranger. Prior to this moment he had never remembered how the story ended, but suddenly he recalled seeing his father not too far away in the parking lot and running over to him. His father picked him up in his arms and hugged him, "kind of like he wanted me. . . . Maybe he did want kids after all." The analysand's mother had devoted considerable effort to convincing him that his father had never wanted children and this had affected his relationship with his father quite negatively.

The more open-ended the question, the more unexpected, unpredictable, and often more productive the answer.

"I Don't Know Why"

I don't discover the truth—I invent it.
—Lacan (1973–1974, February 19, 1974)

If, in the early stages of an analysis, the analyst asks many questions, it is at least in part to get the analysand to start asking herself questions. For it is only once the analysand has begun to raise her own questions and begun to wonder about the why and wherefore of her own experiences that she has truly entered analysis. Prior to that time she may well be there because her spouse demanded that she go or because her boss strongly recommended that she seek help; as cooperative as she may be in diligently striving to answer the questions the analyst poses to her, she is still not really there for herself, for her own reasons, for her own motives, to figure something out for herself.

As Lacan (2006, p. 251) put it, the subject is a question, and we can only be sure that the analysand has a subjective stake in the analysis when she formulates a question (or more than one question) of her own. It is her investment in this question—whether it be why she is so angry all the time, why she developed the sexual orientation she developed, why she has been unable to pursue the field that interests her the most or pursue anything she wants at all—that will motivate her search for some answer via dreams, daydreams, fantasies, and the whole range of her life events. It is this question that makes her continue the analysis even when it becomes difficult or painful.

This question is thus an important motor force of the analysis, yet there is no clear-cut or surefire way for the analyst to bring about the formulation by the analysand of such a question.[9] Each analysand is different: Some have formulated a question long before they ever arrive at the analyst's office, some seem to never formulate a question at all (apart from questions like "What's the matter with my spouse?" or "What are we doing here anyway?"), and some can be incited to formulate a question after a longer or shorter series of preliminary meetings.[10] The latter such analysands, after the analyst has explicitly or implicitly raised the question "Why?" (Why do you think you view a man 20 years your junior as a father figure? Why do you think you keep getting into competitive arguments with him? Why did you feel you *had* to tell your mother about your alcoholism the day you first went into detoxification?) repeatedly, take that questioning approach as their own. Specific questions the analyst raises during sessions are increasingly pondered in the interval between sessions and eventually the analysand seems to adopt a questioning stance of her own.[11] When she recalls an incident from her past in association with a

---

[9] Freud postulated that the motor force of the analysis was the patient's will to get better, but we very often find that the patient above all simply wishes to have things go back to the way they were before, not truly to get better (see Fink, 1997, Chapter 1).

[10] This wide variability among analysands means that the opening moves by which the analyst attempts to intrigue the analysand and get her "hooked" on the adventure that is psychoanalysis are infinitely varied, unlike chess in which the opening moves are quite limited in number.

[11] Analysts from other psychoanalytic perspectives would be likely to characterize this in other ways—for example, as identification with or introjection of the analyst by the analysand or as the fostering in the analysand of an "observing ego." For reasons that will become obvious in Chapters 5 and 7, I am

dream, she thinks "I don't know why I acted that way at that time" and asks herself *why* she did.

It would seem that the analyst by repeatedly asking "why?" becomes associated, in certain cases, with a desire to know why. Lacan (1998a, p. 1) suggested that our general attitude in life is a will not to know: not to know what ails us, not to know why we do what we do, not to know what we secretly seem to enjoy, not to know why we enjoy what we enjoy, and so on. A strong motive, a considerable investment, is required for us to overcome that will not to know, and one of the trickiest tasks for the analyst is to find a way to inspire in his analysands such an investment. Perhaps it is at least in part the analyst's will to know, as demonstrated in his continual questions, that inspires a desire to know in his analysands; it is his persistent asking of questions that allows him to become the cause of the analysand's wondering, the cause of the analysand's desire to know why.[12]

more inclined here to refer to Lacan's (2006, p. 628) well-known statement, "Man's desire is the Other's desire."

[12] As I have indicated elsewhere (Fink, 1997, pp. 11–14), it is the point at which the analysand formulates broad questions of her own about the why and wherefore of her direction in life that marks the end of the preliminary face-to-face meetings; in other words, this is the point at which the analyst should consider moving the analysand to the couch.

The analyst must, of course, be careful not to ask so many questions as to begin to direct what can and cannot be talked about in sessions. The general topics addressed and direction of sessions should be left up to the analysand, except when she is obviously avoiding important work.

3

Punctuating

It is a fact, which can be plainly seen in the study of manuscripts of symbolic writings, whether the Bible or the Chinese canonical texts, that the absence of punctuation in them is a source of ambiguity. Punctuation, once inserted, establishes the meaning; changing the punctuation renews or upsets it; and incorrect punctuation distorts it.

—Lacan (2006, pp. 313–314)

A SPEAKER CAN BE THOUGHT of as providing a certain punctuation of his own discourse, akin to the punctuation found in written texts, by pausing at certain points, stressing certain words, rushing through or mumbling others, repeating specific phrases, and so on. This is the preexisting punctuation, in a sense—the punctuation that corresponds to the reading of his discourse suggested by the speaker himself, the punctuation that corresponds to the meaning the speaker himself attributes to his own speech. This preexisting punctuation sometimes allows for only one reading, a reading that may be superficial and uninteresting, even to the speaker (it is all too easy to read, in that sense), but sometimes it makes the text difficult to read in any way whatsoever. The listener is at times faced with mumbling (which can make a particularly important or sensitive point hard to follow), with selective stress on one part of a statement when it is another part of the statement that seems more important, or with well-paced speech about mundane subjects followed by a torrent of words about more sensitive topics (the very rush of the words seeming to belie a wish to conceal). Here the preexisting punctuation seems to obscure the speaker's meaning or present his words in such a way that only the meaning he wants to convey is discernible in them.

The analyst—in attempting to slow the analysand down, get him to repeat more clearly words that he has muttered under his breath, and explain himself a bit more fully—tries to bring about a shift in that preexisting punctuation. An analysand of mine once placed a period after the comment "My brother was of no importance." In an effort to turn that period into a comma and encourage the analysand to elaborate upon the comment, I responded with a quizzical "Hmm?" which led him to pause a moment and then say that something a friend once told him had just occurred to him: "I hate my brother; why shouldn't I kill him?" Adding a question mark (as we saw in Chapter 2) can lead to the addition of a further statement that completely reverses the meaning of the preceding statement (someone whom one might want to kill hardly seems to be "of no importance"!).

Part of the analyst's task is to provide a slightly different punctuation, a punctuation that brings out meanings in the "text" of the analysand's speech that had not been visible before. Texts like the Bible or Aristotle's works—which often had no punctuation whatsoever in their earliest forms—can be understood quite differently if we punctuate them in one way instead of another, and debates have raged for centuries over their correct interpretation. We need not begin with the assumption in the analytic situation that there is any one correct punctuation or interpretation of the analysand's speech, to conclude nevertheless that some ways of punctuating are more productive than others. We begin with a text that has a certain ready-made punctuation provided by the analysand and attempt to read it in a way that destabilizes or upsets the analysand's take on its meaning and is thus transformative for the analysand.

Aiming at the Repressed

With our free-floating attention we hear what the analysand said, sometimes simply due to a kind of equivocation, in other words, a material equivalence [two words or expressions that sound exactly alike]. We realize that what he said can be understood completely differently. And it is precisely in hearing it completely differently that we allow him to perceive from whence his thoughts emerge: They emerge from nothing other than the ex-sistence of llanguage. Llanguage ex-sists elsewhere than in what he believes his world to be.[1]
— Lacan (1973–1974, June 11, 1974)

How does one know what to punctuate? After all, the analysand makes a very wide variety of statements; which ones should be punctuated?

Since part of the psychoanalyst's overall strategy with neurotics (once a certain amount of trust has been put by the analysand in the analyst due

---

[1] Llanguage (*lalangue*) is a complex concept in Lacan's work, and I will not go into it here except to say that it is what allows two words (such as *sects* and *sex*) to sound exactly alike when spoken.

to her attentive listening to the analysand) is to aim at the repressed, one answer is easy: One can punctuate—that is, reiterate, repeat with emphasis, or emphatically say "hmm" after—any (and potentially every) manifestation of the unconscious.[2] There are far more of these than the usual slips of the tongue or sudden forgetting of what the analysand was about to say, but it is astonishing the degree to which people who have been practicing for a long time do not hear or follow up on even these blatant manifestations.

Here are some other examples of obvious or not-so-obvious manifestations of the unconscious:

- Words are often begun, then stopped, and then begun anew, sometimes allowing for another reading. For example, one of my analysands stumbled as she ostensibly tried to say "exasperated"; instead she said "ex-, ex-, ex- ... exasperated," which could be read as an insistence (albeit unconscious) on the degree to which she was exasperated at having been "dumped" by the man she was talking about—at having become his *ex*-lover.
- Words are often begun in the wrong place. One of my analysands started to say "my behavior," but dropped the "be" of "behavior." He caught and stopped himself just after he said something that sounded a lot like "my hate." Since this was a bit of a stretch ("hav," pronounced like the first syllable of "haven," being close in sound but not exactly the same as "hate"), I might not have punctuated it had the analysand not already made it clear that he had a good deal of resentment toward the person he was talking about. However, it worked very effectively to draw the analysand out regarding his minimally avowed anger with the man his behavior was directed at.
- Sentences are often begun but then trail off. One of my analysands was talking about his mother and said, "My mother is pretty, pretty, pretty ..." As he paused for quite some time (looking, as it turned out later, for the word *prosaic*), I simply stopped the sentence there by saying, "Your mother is pretty?" By stressing words and expressions the speaker had not stressed, we put a different spin on the very same text and

---

[2] Gill (1982, p. 63) defined neutrality as "giving equal attention to all the patient's productions"—that is, to everything he says or does in the course of a session. The focus here on the unconscious should make it clear how unsuitable the concept of neutrality is for productive psychoanalytic work. Gill himself gave far more attention to anything that smacked of transference, whether by way of allusion or resistance, than to other things (see Chapter 7), suggesting that his own approach is anything but neutral.

we encourage the speaker to pay attention to this different spin and elaborate on it.

Often the speaker will begin a sentence in a certain way and then do one of the following things:

- Break off in the middle of the sentence and begin a new one on a different subject (for example, "I really wanted to. . . . Anyway, the point is. . . ."). Here we must try to get the analysand to finish the first thought—it seems to have been avoided or censored by him, perhaps having met with his disapproval once he got part way into his discussion of it.
- Break off in the middle and reconstruct the sentence, presumably preserving the same thought, all the while avoiding what was to come next in the sentence as originally prepared in his mind (to whatever degree sentences are, indeed, prepared in advance in a speaker's mind). Once again, we must try here to get him to go back and complete the thought as initially formulated.

Obviously, there are people who almost systematically reconstruct their sentences as they speak, but this need not convince us that something other than avoidance is at work; avoidance and evasiveness are perhaps simply more endemic to their way of speaking than they are to that of other people.[3]

Indeed, as I mentioned in Chapter 1, the analyst must be vigilant in detecting all forms of avoidance in speech, whether that avoidance occurs through ellipsis (intentionally or unintentionally leaving out certain words in a sentence), circumlocution (using a convoluted form of expression instead of the word or idiomatic expression that came to mind), or any other rhetorical device.

Avoidance means that a part of the story is being left out, and it is our responsibility to ensure that missing parts are restored to the greatest extent possible. Although it is never possible to tell the whole story (to tell the "whole truth," as Lacan said, 1973, p. 8), it is nevertheless important to encourage the analysand to tell as much of the story as he is able to at a particular moment in time. Not to do so is a failure on the analyst's part to actively pursue all signs and traces of the repressed, which is ultimately tantamount to resistance on the analyst's part to the progress of the analysis; in this sense it can be understood as part and parcel of the analyst's countertransference (see Chapters 4 and 7).

---

[3] Certain American politicians have been known to chronically reconstruct their sentences as they speak, and this should perhaps be taken as a gauge of their forthrightness (or lack thereof).

Statements preceded by disclaimers like "here's a ridiculous thought for you," "the stupidest thing just came to mind," "I'm sure this has nothing to do with anything," or "this is totally irrelevant" should always be given the utmost attention (note that nonverbal cues, like yawns expressing boredom or an utterly flat tone of voice, can just as easily serve as disclaimers). Such disclaimers are often made when the analyst asks the usual "What's going through your mind?" after the analyst has highlighted something or made an interpretation and the analysand has lapsed into momentary silence. The analysand does not seem to want to reckon with what crossed his mind in the intervening moment and resorts to downplaying its importance. As soon as he terms an idea that has occurred to him "stupid," "irrelevant," "farfetched," "dumb," "trite," "absurd," or "out of the blue," the analyst can be sure that it is not. Lacan (1998a, pp. 11–13) went so far as to say that it is precisely with such stupidities that we do analysis. Such terms are defenses against thoughts that the analysand deems unseemly or off-topic and thus does not wish to mention.

Often a thought that initially appears to be a distraction or diversion from the topic at hand ("I was thinking about my boss again") turns out, upon exploration, to be absolutely germane—which is, no doubt, why it occurred to the analysand right after the analyst's punctuation or interpretation. Such disclaimers need not be viewed as suggesting "bad faith" or "deliberate" resistance on the analysand's part: The analysand is quite often duped by the seeming irrelevance of images, thoughts, and feelings that arise at specific moments in the therapy, and—following the conventions of everyday conversation—tries to stay on topic (a counterproductive habit of which the analyst must try to break him).

A similar strategy to that manifested by disclaimers can be seen in comments that are made in an offhand manner by the analysand so as to suggest that they are unimportant. A dream may be casually announced early on in a session as having been a nightmare, but no mention of any nightmarish qualities is forthcoming when the dream itself is described. It is only when the analyst reminds the analysand of the earlier remark that he specifies the nightmarish quality or recounts the nightmarish part of the dream that had been left out. It is as if the analysand adopts a strategy of telling the analyst something important and then attempting to distract her from it, as if to say, "Please don't make me talk about it!" In a word, the analysand seems to both want and not want her to notice something, and she must always side with the part of the analysand that wants her to notice (not with the analysand's defenses).

Sometimes the crucial association to an event or figure in a dream may come in the form of a stray or offhand remark made after the analysand has left the armchair or couch and is on the way out the door, when he thinks that it is too late to discuss it that day (those who practice the variable-length session might prefer to have the analysand sit or lie back down at that point and prolong the session; see Chapter 4). The analyst must not fail to remind the analysand of the comment at the next session should the analysand himself not mention it or seem to have forgotten it.

Parts of a dream that are left out when first recounted, and only remembered after the association process has begun during the session, are usually of particular importance to the understanding of the dream. Similarly, when the analytic work has proceeded beyond the initial stages with an analysand, the analyst—rather than having to actively encourage the analysand to associate to each and every element of the dream, which takes a good deal of work on the analyst's part and must often be kept up for many a month, failing which the analysand will likely take shortcuts in attempting to interpret his dreams—can confine her efforts to encouraging the analysand to associate to those elements of the dream to which he did not spontaneously associate, thereby *emphasizing what has been left out* of his associative and interpretative work. It is this continual emphasis on what has been left out of the story (recounting a particular event, a family dynamic, a dream, a fantasy, or a daydream) that allows the analyst to keep targeting the repressed.[4]

Unprovoked Denials and Overemphasized Assertions

Negation is also a way of admitting something.
— Lacan (1974–1975, March 18, 1975)

Another kind of statement the analyst should usually punctuate is what I call the "unprovoked denial." In this form of denial, the analysand insists that something is *not* the case even when no one has claimed that it is. One of my

---

[4] Here I am speaking as though something left out of a story were actually repressed, whereas repression proper generally involves something far more encompassing: that it be something left out of *all* the stories the analysand tells, whether to the analyst or to himself. Nevertheless, I think there is some heuristic value to the notion that something left out of any particular sentence or story is repressed, just as a footnote bears a certain repressed relation to the text from which it has been extracted. Strictly speaking, however, *suppression* might be the correct term for this.

analysands once stated that since our last session a memory had come back to him, but he hastened to add, "I don't think it has anything to do with my sexual orientation." He then proceeded to tell me that when he was six his cousins insistently told him that very soon he would turn into a girl, claiming that previously they too had been members of the opposite sex and had changed from one sex to the other around his age. They swore him to secrecy, making him promise not to talk with his mother about this. It does not seem to be much of a stretch to simply remove the "not" in his unprovoked denial and read this as though he himself recognized at some level that this event, which he admitted to having found quite distressing at the time, played some role in his current sexual orientation.

In such cases of unprovoked denial, one can always ask why someone is taking the time and energy to deny something that no one in the context at hand (in this case, in the analytic context) has in any way suggested or affirmed. One could retort that given what he knows of psychoanalysts, the analysand is simply trying to forestall a conclusion that he assumes the analyst will jump to. True as this may be of certain analysts, the thought nevertheless occurred to the analysand first, in a rejected or projected form—in other words, it was attributed to the person he would be speaking with about it later—and, indeed, in the case of the analysand just mentioned, it was he himself who first put the idea into my head that this might well be related to his current sexual orientation (I had not yet even heard the story).

Such unprovoked denials are as common in everyday life as they are in the therapy context: The introductory remark "I don't mean to be critical, but . . ." is a blatant warning that your interlocutor means to be critical, just as the introductory remark "I'm not trying to be cruel, I'm just saying that . . ." is a clear indication that your interlocutor recognizes that he or she is in fact trying to be cruel, at least at some level.

Similar to unprovoked denials are what I call "overemphasized assertions." Here the analysand (or politician, business leader, or someone else) affirms something so forcibly and repeatedly that the listener begins to wonder why: If the speaker so fervently believes what he is saying, why does he feel the need to stress it so appreciably? One of my analysands said, "I absolutely, positively, clearly remember . . .," leading me to suspect that he perhaps was in fact not quite so sure he remembered what he was claiming to remember; there had been no display of incredulity on my part, since he had just introduced a new topic and I had no idea what he was about to say. Here again, the speaker seems to "protest too much."

Taken Out of Context

[Psychoanalysis is] a practice that is based upon the ex-sistence of the unconscious.
— *Lacan* (*1973–1974, June 11, 1974*)

An obvious way of punctuating someone's discourse is to repeat it back to him verbatim, thereby highlighting, underlining, or underscoring it, as it were. Sometimes simply hearing the exact same words repeated by someone else sheds new light on them, allowing them to be heard differently. At other times, it may be more helpful to repeat back only some of the words in the analysand's discourse, isolating just one or two words from their original context to highlight the fact that the analysand used, for example, the exact same locution to qualify his lover as he used several minutes earlier to qualify his mother.

Many idiomatic expressions have multiple meanings, and reiterating only the idiomatic expression used by the analysand in his statement may shed a very different light on the meaning of the sentence than the analysand had originally intended. When, for example, one of my analysands was describing a dream and said, "In the dream I was holding an object of some sort and I ran over to give it to her," I simply repeated back "give it to her," recalling, as I did, the importance of that phrase in the analysand's sexual fantasies (it being pronounced by someone who was not clearly identified in the fantasy, telling him to have sex with a woman). Isolating the expression allowed the analysand to dwell less on the enigmatic peculiarities of the object as it was presented in the dream (devoid as it was of qualities) and what it might mean to give it to someone as a gift, and instead to consider one of the figurative meanings of the expression.

In another dream, the same analysand saw a woman he knew and noticed she was wearing a red blouse. He then looked down, "as if I wanted to transfer the red from her upper body down to the lower half, as if I wanted to see red." To "see red" obviously also means to get angry, and it clearly made more sense to repeat only those polyvalent words and not the whole of the analysand's statement. (In this case, the analysand noticed the double meaning himself and it led to a considerable nexus of ideas.)

Sometimes it is not the idiomatic expression itself that is ambiguous but rather the way that it is incorporated into the grammar of the analysand's enunciation. For example, an analysand of mine was talking about his relationship with his wife and came out with the statement "I was trying to earn her keep." When I queried, "Her keep?" he realized that he had turned things around in such a way that it was not clear whether he was saying that he was trying to be kept by her or to pay for her. A short time later, the same analysand was talking about another woman and complained, "Her regard of me was withering." When I responded with "Withering?" he heard both the sexual connotation and his intended meaning (which probably only the context could have revealed) that her good opinion of him was waning. He subsequently realized that *regard* can also be understood as to gaze or look: To be looked at by her made him wither.[5]

When faced with the description of a long, complicated dream to which the analysand initially professes to have few or no associations, it is often useful to highlight words or phrases in the dream that can lead off in several different directions because of their polysemy. In a detailed dream with several scenes in it told to me by one analysand, there were at one point some monks sitting at a round table singing a happy song to each other, but it had "a false ring to it," he commented. "Round table" could obviously lead to a couple of different trains of thought, but it was the words "false ring" that, when I repeated them to the analysand, led to several sessions of material regarding his marriage, the external circumstances (visa problems) that had led to it, the sort of false ring he had bought for the occasion (silver instead of gold), its eventual replacement by a gold ring that was subsequently lost in a fire, and so on. "We weren't taking the thing seriously," he remarked. He indicated that he wanted to escape from the institution of marriage, which he associated with his father. Although his father was always saying that "you must be joyful," it did not ring true to the analysand—rather, it seemed to be a put on, a joyful

---

[5] Casement (1991) provided an interesting example of taking what the analysand says out of context:

> If a patient were to say, "My boss is angry with me," this can be silently abstracted as "someone is angry with someone." Who is angry with whom then remains unclear. . . . It could be a statement of fact, objectively reported; it could be a reference to the patient's anger, projected onto the boss; it could be a displaced reference to the transference, the therapist seen as angry; or it could be an oblique reference to the patient being angry with the therapist. (p. 37)

In essence, Casement has simply taken the word *anger* out of context, allowing it to be applied in as many possible ways as he can think of. I would add that when the analyst takes words and phrases out of context in this way and repeats them back to the analysand, the analysand often responds by saying something like "That's actually an expression my mother used to use. . . ."

Note that by taking words and expressions out of context, the analyst is simply reversing what the unconscious does in the course of dream formation. As Freud (1900/1958, pp. 165–188) told us, the dream takes "day residues," such as comments someone made or statements read somewhere the day before, and recomposes them in different fashions so as to disguise what is really at issue in the dream. When the analyst takes them out of the context of the dream's manifest content, she allows the analysand to recall their original source in the day residues, residues that may include the analyst but that should not be presumed to do so in all cases (it is but one possibility among others).

face "he put on for [the family]." For the analysand to become a husband was to become like his father, whom he characterized as asexual, domesticated, and a fine, upstanding member of the community who was devoid of desire. And, indeed, although the analysand's wife-to-be and he had been passionate about each other before the marriage, he was no longer as attracted to her afterward. Taking the potentially polyvalent words "false ring" out of context led to a great deal of previously undiscussed material, as well as to a discussion of his ideal of marriage as a pledge to "the one special person" who "would cure me, make me whole . . . I could relax into being who I was really supposed to be."

Welcoming "Incoherence"

There is nothing but rhetoric.
— Lacan (1974–1975, January 21, 1975)

Confining one's punctuations to manifestations of the unconscious is certainly the safest approach the analyst can adopt, in the sense that it minimizes the impact of her own agenda—such as wanting the patient to realize something in particular, get to a specific point, or accomplish a certain goal—and most faithfully adopts the analysand's unconscious as a guide for the course of the therapy.

Nevertheless, such manifestations sometimes do not suffice to get the ball rolling at the beginning of an analysis; certain patients make very few slips in the early sessions, and profess not to recall dreams, daydreams, or fantasies, giving the clinician precious little to punctuate and thus no obvious means of participation other than showing that she is listening attentively.

What, then, is the analyst to highlight, reiterate, or punctuate? Anything that suggests that the analysand is working hard to be coherent when speaking to the analyst. For example, the analysand may say, "but that's a long story," and then begin to change the subject, or may say, "but that's not what I was trying to get at." Such phrases indicate a drifting (perhaps unintended) in the patient's associations and thoughts toward certain areas of his life story that then get censored when the patient remembers the point he was trying to make. In such cases, a conscious intention to remain coherent and not get off on a tangent, to portray oneself to the analyst as clear and as capable of making sense, begins to override the "freer" direction of the patient's associations, and the analyst does well to encourage the patient to follow that drift—implicitly indicating that the analyst is not in any way requiring the analysand to appear coherent. It is the analysand's ego that seeks to force his thoughts and speech to be coherent, whereas it is his "free associations" (as unfree as they ultimately are, in a deeper sense) that allow us a glimpse of the repressed.

We do not assume that the analysand is of one mind—indeed, we assume that the analysand is inhabited by contradictory thoughts and desires, some conscious, some preconscious, and some unconscious—and we certainly do not want to be complicit with the analysand's ego when it attempts to impose coherence and consistency on what comes out of the analysand's mouth. We do not in any sense accuse the analysand of being inconsistent when inconsistencies appear (whether the analysand contradicts himself in discussing what he feels or what he wants in the course of a session or from one session to the next)—indeed, we strive to highlight the ways in which he is not of one mind, in which he is a "divided subject," as Lacan (2006, p. 693) put it.

The Analyst as Artist

[It is our task to bring] out from the start the three or four registers on which the musical score constituted by the subject's discourse can be read.

— Lacan (2006, p. 253)

A fine painter can be thought of as looking at "the same thing" other people look at, seeing something different, and making it visible to us: The painter reveals—renders perceptible—something we had not seen before. In the case of van Gogh, it might be the humanity in an old pair of shoes, in the case of Monet, it might be the shimmering colors in a garden under the influence of the hot summer sun. A photographer does something similar with light and textures: She uses films, filters, shutter speeds, and aperture settings to bring out something that is there—already there, waiting to be seen, as it were—but that is not seen without her help. A novice musician strives to play the notes written on the sheet music at more or less the correct speed, but the accomplished musician subtly brings out, by varying speed and stress, the multiple melodies or voices implicitly there in the very same notes (as in the fugue by Bach on the cover of this book).

That might be one fruitful way of thinking about what we as therapists do as well: We bring out something that is there—already there, waiting to be heard—but that is not heard without our help. As one of my analysands once put it, his desire was like a murmur, a heart murmur so faint no one had ever heard it before, not even him, until he began his analysis.

4

Scanding
(The Variable-length Session)

The ending of a session cannot but be experienced by the subject as a punctuation of his progress. We know how he calculates the moment of its arrival in order to tie it to his own timetable, or even to his evasive maneuvers, and how he anticipates it by weighing it like a weapon and watching out for it as he would for a place of shelter.

— Lacan (2006, p. 313)

OF ALL OF LACAN'S CONCEPTS known to the English-speaking world, *scansion* is perhaps the one that is both most well and least well understood. It is most well understood in the sense that many are aware that it refers to the act by which the analyst puts an end—in certain circumstances, an abrupt end—to a session (it is perhaps rare for so many readers to have grasped something essential about any one of Lacan's concepts). Yet, it is perhaps the least well understood in that few seem to be able to say why and how scansion is employed. Indeed, when I give talks at psychoanalytic institutes in the United States, regardless of the topic I present, the discussion invariably veers off toward the topic of the variable-length session and occasionally dwells there until I ask if anyone in the audience has a question on something other than scansion.

In this chapter I will try to explain a few aspects of the why and wherefore of scansion. Let me begin by trying to clear up a few misconceptions. Varying session length does not necessarily imply that the session becomes shorter than whatever amount of time is standardly practiced by other clinicians in the same country, whether that be 30 minutes, 40 minutes, 45 minutes, 50 minutes, or 55 minutes. All of these session lengths are considered standard by different practitioners in different parts of the world (and often by different

47

practitioners in the same country or even in the same city), yet no one seems to express surprise at this kind of variability.[1]

In theory, at least, varying session length allows the analyst to prolong a session beyond any established session time (as Freud, 1913/1958, pp. 127–128, indicated that he himself sometimes did) in order to continue work that is progressing in a very useful direction; to complete, at least to a relative degree, the interpretation of a fantasy or dream; to foster the analytic work with an analysand who speaks particularly slowly for whatever reason (whether because a native speaker of another tongue, because of advanced age, because of regional speech patterns, or simply out of personal habit or ability) or takes a long time to warm to the subject at hand; or, in a rather different vein, to disconcert an analysand who systematically prepares large quantities of material for sessions so that nothing unplanned, spontaneous, or surprising can occur or who makes her most significant enunciations only on the way out the analyst's door. In the first few weeks of an analysis, I myself rarely end a session before 45 minutes have gone by, and the first several sessions often exceed an hour and a quarter so that I can get as complete an overall picture as possible of the analysand's life (allowing me to determine quickly whether I think we might be able to work together and how to orient the treatment, and allowing the analysand to quickly get a taste of the kind of work we might do together). As the analysis progresses, session lengths do tend to decrease to some degree (more with some analysands than with others), but sessions longer than 45 minutes do occasionally occur.

A second misconception that I have sometimes heard voiced is that Lacan recommends that the analyst end (or "scand," this being the verb form of *scansion* that I have adopted, modeling it on the French *scander* because the verb *scan* in English has so many other unrelated meanings) sessions arbitrarily or randomly. On the contrary, Lacan recommends ending sessions on the most striking point, when possible—that is, when the analysand articulates the most striking statement or question of the session. That should not be taken to imply that the point, statement, or question need be self-evident, transparent, or obvious in meaning. Often the statement or question on which the analyst scands the session can be understood in several different ways, and the analysand is left to ponder all of them in the time between that session and the next one. Scanding the session at such a point is designed to put the analysand to work, whether consciously or unconsciously, during the time between sessions. Not only does one remember best what one heard (oneself say) last, but an

---

[1] No doubt, as long as each practitioner adopts a standard and sticks to it, the devotees of the therapeutic frame are satisfied.

unfinished task often occupies the mind far more than a finished one (this is known in psychology as "the Zeigarnik effect"). A polyvalent, ambiguous, or enigmatic statement is often far more useful in making the analysis progress than an unequivocal, crystal-clear statement. The goal here is to ensure that the analysand does as much work as possible outside of the sessions, not just in them, for associations and interpretations that occur to the analysand herself are generally far more convincing to her than those made by the analyst.[2]

Scansion is merely an especially emphatic form of punctuation. When the analyst ends the session, he is effectively placing a period, exclamation mark, or question mark not just at the end of a sentence or at the end of a paragraph, but rather at the end of a section or chapter of text. Thus the question "How do you know when to scand a session?" is closely related to the question discussed in the last chapter: "How do you know what to punctuate in a session?"

By way of example, I will mention a couple of "emphatic punctuations" I have made. One was with an analysand who talked about someone she referred to as "a great guy" whom she had known for some 25 years. Earlier in the session—and, indeed, for several sessions prior to this one—she had been speaking about the importance to her of "loving somebody." After talking for quite some time about this "great guy" she said that between them "there's a familiarity, a contentment," only instead of "contentment" she said "contention"; she quickly noticed the slip and burst out laughing. I ended the session at that point to emphasize something we had discussed a bit in previous sessions: the competition and rivalry that characterized so many of her relationships.

---

[2] The push to make therapy into a shorter and shorter process—initiated in recent years above all by insurance companies and government-sponsored clinics and complied with more or less grudgingly by therapists of various ilks—almost inevitably short-circuits this process: The therapist is encouraged to "giv[e] insight through *interpretation*" (Malan, 1995/2001, p. 3) rather than to allow the analysand the time to formulate an interpretation herself. This prolongs the subject's alienation, in the sense that insight and knowledge continue to come from some other person than herself. Moreover, it generally neglects one of Freud's (1925b/1961, pp. 235–236) fundamental insights, which is that knowledge of something (of a connection between something in the present and something in the past or of a feeling that had been covered over or forgotten) does not necessarily constitute a "lifting of the repression"; analysands commonly say, "I know very well that x, y, and z, but I still feel the same way" or "but I still keep acting the same way." Just because one can articulate abstract or conscious knowledge of something does not mean that the problem has been resolved; as Freud (p. 236) said, "The outcome of this is a kind of intellectual acceptance of the repressed, while at the same time what is essential to the repression persists." There are different kinds of knowledge: Abstract knowledge of something is not at all like being able to feel it in one's bones, so to speak, to experience it in a new way. Freud (p. 236) indicated that we sometimes even succeed "in bringing about a full intellectual acceptance of the repressed; but the repressive process itself is not yet removed by this." Ferdinand de Saussure (1916/1959, p. 68) was getting at something similar when he said, "it is often easier to discover a truth than to assign it its rightful place."

Scansion may also be used in ways other than to highlight the most striking point; see, for example, Carrade (2000).

The slip she made involved saying something that was almost the exact opposite of what she had "meant" to say, and it was not the kind of slip whose meaning is quite unclear at the outset and that must be associated to and unpacked by the analysand at some length. Instead, her laughter indicated that she recognized that what she had actually said was diametrically opposed to the picture she was trying to paint of their relationship. I find such manifestations of the unconscious—which appear after a somewhat lengthy discussion of something—especially useful notes on which to end the session, for they tend to incite the analysand to ponder the contradictions within herself.

In a different case, an analysand who sought therapy so that he could come to some decision about his relationship to Buddhism as a spiritual practice and as a lifestyle (which he found clashed with his sexual practices in particular) was reminding me after several months of analysis that his "excuse," as he put it, for starting analysis was to become a better Buddhist, "to tame [his] mind." In saying this, he slipped and said "to time," which is identical in sound to "two-time." When I repeated back to him the words "to/two-time," he paused for a moment and then said, "So now I'm two-timing Buddhism with you . . . or is it you with Buddhism?" I ended the session there, leaving the analysand to ponder the very question he himself had raised; indeed, he did ponder it, bringing it up at the beginning of the very next session.

There are so many different kinds of points in sessions that make for suitable scansions that it is impossible to list even a small percentage of them (for further examples see the later section entitled "The Internal Logic of the Session"). In the examples I have given, I have obviously provided only the barest outline of the work going on in the analyses at the points in time in question. Since no amount of explanation of any individual case could convince some readers of the suitability of scansion, let me turn to the more general issue.

Scansion and the "Therapeutic Frame"

The neutrality we manifest in strictly applying the rule that sessions be of a specified length obviously keeps us on the path of nonaction. But this nonaction has a limit, otherwise we would never intervene at all—so why make intervening impossible at this point, thereby privileging it?

— Lacan (2006, p. 314)

Although all analysts punctuate in one way or another (obviously, they do not all employ the exact same punctuation techniques), and although I have never heard any analyst object to Lacan's notion of punctuation as such, many analysts take serious issue with scansion. While most of them invoke the importance of the "therapeutic frame," to which I will turn in a moment, many have expressed to me a concern that they themselves would wind up scanding sessions when bored, tired, exasperated, or just wanting to do something else, expressing thereby what strikes me as distrust of their own motives when they intervene *in any way* in the analyses they conduct. They spoke of the fixed-length session as tying their hands in a salutary way, as if they felt that they could not be trusted to wield a punctuation of that magnitude and that their analysands needed to be protected by a mutually binding law from their own untrustworthiness. One might wonder about their faith in their own ability to punctuate other potentially important parts of the analysand's discourse if they have so little faith in their ability to end sessions at points that would be likely to further the progress of the analysis.

I suspect that their lack of faith in their ability to effectively punctuate, whether in a small way or a big way, is related to a sea change in contemporary analysts' view of how and why analysis is curative: Rather than emphasizing the filling in of the gaps in the analysand's history and self-understanding, as Freud (1916–1917/1963, p. 282) did, or emphasizing that it is only the symbolic dimension that cures, as Lacan did, contemporary analysts often endorse the idea that it is the relationship itself that the analysand has with the analyst that is curative (the relationship often being included under the heading of "nonspecific factors" or "common factors"),[3] not anything in particular that the analyst says or brings the analysand to say.[4] Attention is thus diverted from the work of symbolization in the therapy, and what is considered to be of genuine importance is a secure, well-structured, protective relationship. This approach was already catching on in France in the 1950s: Lacan quoted one of his colleagues as having said that "the analyst cures not so much by what he says and does as by what he is."[5] It is the emphasis placed on the analyst's personality and on the relationship—as opposed to the work done by the analysand and the analyst to articulate the analysand's history and desire— that led to the ever-growing importance placed by clinicians in the latter half

---

[3] The notion of "nonspecific factors" seems to have been introduced by Rogers (1951) and includes such characteristics in the therapist as empathy, warmth, and genuineness.

[4] This idea is supposedly bolstered by studies (such as Frieswyck et al., 1986, Gaston, 1990, Goldfried, 1991, Castonguay et al., 1996, Ablon & Jones, 1998) comparing different forms of psychotherapy. These studies purportedly show that, regardless of the therapeutic technique adopted by the therapist, patients generally claimed to have found therapy most helpful when they said they had a good relationship (a good "therapeutic alliance") with their therapist. See my comments on this later in this chapter and in Chapter 7.

[5] Sacha Nacht (1956, p. 136), cited by Lacan (2006, p. 587) in "Direction of the Treatment." Such notions often go hand in hand with the belief that the analyst should provide the analysand with "emotional reeducation" or a "corrective emotional experience" (Alexander & French, 1946), or serve the analysand as a "good enough mother" (Winnicott, 1949/1958a, p. 245, 1960/1965a, p. 145).

of the 20th century and the beginning of the 21st century on the "therapeutic frame."[6]

Winnicott (1954/1958b, pp. 279–289) was a staunch supporter of protective boundaries in the analytic situation, believing that a secure, reliable, predictable setting was especially crucial for psychotic patients. With his developmental model suggesting that psychotics need to regress to certain earlier stages to correct a kind of natural developmental process that has been blocked and must be unblocked,[7] Winnicott felt that a secure frame was necessary for patients to trust the therapist enough to engage in this kind of regression. I do not believe that he himself always rigidly adhered to fixed-length sessions (see Margaret Little's 1990 account of her analysis with Winnicott, in which certain sessions seem to have lasted far longer than others), suggesting that a secure frame is not necessarily incompatible with variability in session length. Whether one accepts Winnicott's belief in the importance of regression or not,[8] it seems quite possible to establish trust with psychotic patients without rigidly adhering to a fixed session length.

What should be stressed here is, rather, that Lacan quite explicitly formulated scansion—involving at times abrupt endings to sessions—for work with neurotics, not psychotics.[9] Indeed, I would venture to claim that he did not consider it suitable for the analyst to make polyvalent, ambiguous, and enigmatic statements with psychotics at all or to emphasize the ambiguity in their own statements, much less consider them suitable points at which to end sessions

---

[6]The "frame" metaphor was, it seems, first introduced by José Bleger (1967) to describe the background ("non-ego") context of the analytic situation, not to describe analysis as a "holding environment" à la Winnicott, but Bleger's metaphor has clearly taken on a life of its own.

Marion Milner (1952, p. 194) used the word "frame" still earlier, but did not conceptualize it. She wrote the following: "As [the patient] becomes able to tolerate more fully the difference between the symbolic reality of the analytic relationship and the literal reality of libidinal satisfaction outside the frame of the session, then he becomes better."

[7]See my comments on developmental models in Chapter 9.

[8]Note that Winnicott's (1954/1958b) somewhat narrow definition of regression in psychoanalysis came, as usual, to be vastly broadened. Here is what he had to say about this broadening:

Incidentally I think it is not useful to use the word regression whenever infantile behavior appears in a case history. The word regression has derived a popular meaning which we need not adopt. When we speak of regression in psychoanalysis we imply the existence of an ego organization and the threat of chaos. (p. 281)

Winnicott (p. 290) also restricted regression to psychotics, for the most part, and stated that "there are no reasons why an analyst should want a patient to regress, except grossly pathological reasons." For some of Lacan's comments on regression, see Lacan (1998b, p. 426, 2006, pp. 617–618).

[9]Regarding work with neurotics, Winnicott (1955–1956/1958c, p. 297) said the following: "Where there is an intact ego and the analyst can take for granted these earliest details of infant care, then the setting of the analysis is unimportant relative to the interpretive work. (By setting, I mean the summation of all the details of management.)"

(this is, at least in part, due to the absence of the usual sort of "button ties" in psychosis, as we shall see in Chapter 10). The goal with psychotics is to recon-struct meaning, not deconstruct it, and the technique of scansion is explicitly designed to shake up, call into question, or deconstruct a neurotic analysand's self-conception. It would seem that the use of all striking or abrupt techniques has diminished vastly with the gradual disappearance of the distinction in many analysts' minds between neurosis and psychosis and the gradual formation of a kind of analytic technique that is supposedly suitable for both neurotics and psychotics. If all diagnostic categories of patients are to be treated using the same techniques, then clearly scansion—and even many forms of punctuation in its gentler guises—must be ruled out.[10] Lacan, however, maintains a firm distinction between neurosis and psychosis (even if in practice it is not always easy to make the distinction), and formulates widely differing approaches to treatment for these two different diagnostic groups.

Scansion as a Mini-castration

I am not the only one to have remarked that [scansion] bears a certain resemblance to the technique known as Zen. . . .

Without going to the extremes to which this technique is taken, since they would be contrary to certain of the limitations imposed by our own, a discreet application of its basic principle in analysis seems much more acceptable to me than certain methods of the so-called analysis of the resistances, insofar as such an application does not in itself entail any danger of alienating the subject.

For it shatters discourse only in order to bring forth speech.

— Lacan (2006, pp. 315–316)

Lacan occasionally refers to scansion as a "cut," and most clinicians—whether they end their sessions precisely after a fixed amount of time, vary by a minute or two, or systematically practice a variable-length session—are aware that analysands sometimes feel like they are being cut off by the analyst when he ends the session: cut off mid-sentence, perhaps, or in the middle of a thought or story, and/or suddenly cut off from the analyst who is now turning his attention to other patients. Analysands sometimes refer to scansion as a mini-castration, and the scansion of the session can be used in certain cases to effectively foster castration in neurotics who suffer from what might be termed "insufficient

---

[10] Note, however, that even McWilliams (2004)—an analyst who proposes one form of technique to be used with all diagnostic categories of patients (p. xi)—admits to varying session length by a few minutes for at least some of the reasons mentioned here (p. 113).

castration" (see Fink, 1997, pp. 66–71, 184–193).[11] For psychotics, however, no castration has occurred and abrupt scansions designed to strongly emphasize or call into question certain statements are likely to simply anger the psychotic analysand or throw her into a panic. It would seem to make far more sense in cases of psychosis to end sessions thematically—that is, after discussion of a certain event, experience, or dream has been more or less completed, rather than in the middle of such discussions. I suspect that even clinicians who claim to practice fixed-length sessions find themselves ending sessions a minute or two early or late with psychotic analysands in order to avoid abrupt endings. They implicitly understand that ending a session based on the movement of a second hand can be experienced as a harsh act, and whether they think of it as related to castration or not, they have learned by experience that it is far more bearable by neurotics than by psychotics.[12]

Another argument often made in favor of fixed-length sessions, even with neurotics, is that it limits the field in which the analyst's countertransference can have free range. The analyst might, it is thought, bring the session to a close at a particular moment owing to his own state (involving fatigue, disgust, confusion, a sense of inadequacy or failure, or whatever), rather than to that of the analysand. "If a knife does not cut, it cannot be used for healing either," Freud (1916–1917/1963, pp. 462–463) reminded us, and "no medical instrument or procedure is guaranteed against abuse." What is not clear is why misuse of the technique of scansion should be considered more serious than misuse of any other technique in the analyst's black bag, such as interpretation, suggestion, or so-called confrontation (Greenson, 1967). Will not the analyst's countertransference, if the analyst has not learned to deal with it adequately, express itself in those techniques at least as much and as dangerously as it would in that of scansion? It seems that, rather than exclude what is by a great many accounts a particularly useful technique, what is more important is that the analyst learn to deal successfully with his own countertransference.[13]

---

[11] Another way of saying this is that they continue to derive certain satisfactions from activities and symptoms that at the same time cause them a great deal of dissatisfaction. Scansion can be an effective technique for separating them from such ambivalent satisfactions (that is, from such "jouissances," to use the consecrated Lacanian term) and can be experienced as a painful and yet salutary castration of incestuous and other symptomatic satisfactions.

[12] Note that Winnicott (1954/1958b, p. 285) characterized the ending of sessions after a fixed length of time as an expression of hate on the analyst's part.

[13] Freud (1910/1957, pp. 144–145) said the following about countertransference: "We are almost inclined to insist that he shall recognize this counter-transference in himself and overcome it. . . . We have noticed that no psycho-analyst goes further than his own complexes and internal resistances permit."

Consider what Lacan (1991) had to say about the analyst's stance and what it might mean that it be characterized by neutrality or what he refers to here as "apathy":

> The better the analyst is analyzed, the more it will be possible for him to be frankly in love with or repulsed by his [analysand].
>
> What I am saying may seem a bit excessive, in that it bothers us. If we feel that there must, all the same, be something to the requirement of analytic apathy, it must clearly be rooted elsewhere. . . .
>
> If the analyst achieves apathy, as in the general public's conception of him . . . it is to the extent that he is possessed by a desire that is stronger than the other desires that may be involved, namely, to get down to it with his patient, take him in his arms, or throw him out the window.
>
> That happens. I dare say that I wouldn't expect much from someone who has never felt such desires. But apart from the very possibility of that happening, it shouldn't become a regular thing.
>
> Why not? Is it for the negative reason that one must avoid a kind of total imaginary discharge of the analysis? . . . No, it is [because] the analyst says, "I am possessed by a stronger desire." He is grounded in saying so as an analyst, insofar as a change has occurred in the economy of his desire. (pp. 220–221)

Lacan suggests here that the analyst need not feel nothing toward the analysand, need not have no desire whatsoever to either embrace or defenestrate the analysand. For, assuming the analyst has been sufficiently analyzed, his feelings and desires for the analysand will be superseded by a properly psychoanalytic desire: a desire for the analytic work to proceed and for the analysand to speak, associate, and interpret. Lacan (2006, p. 854) referred to this properly psychoanalytic desire as "the analyst's desire" and it should be clear that it does not require the analyst to have killed in himself every other desire by which he may be inhabited, but simply to have learned how to set those other desires aside during the analytic work itself.[14] A change must

---

[14] Other discussions of the analyst's desire can be found in Lacan (1978, pp. 156, 160–161). As I have put it elsewhere (Fink, 1997):

> Lacan's expression "the analyst's desire" does not refer to the analyst's countertransferential feelings, but rather to a kind of "purified desire" that is specific to the analyst, to the analyst not as a human being with feelings, but to the analyst as a function, as a role, a part to be played and that *can* be played by many extremely different individuals. "The analyst's desire" is a desire that focuses on analysis and only on analysis. . . . "The analyst's desire" is not for the patient to get better, to succeed in life, to be happy, to understand him- or herself, to go back to school,

have occurred in what Lacan refers to as the analyst's "economy of desire"—a change that can only occur if the analyst undergoes a thorough analysis of his own.

Although the modern American psychological establishment allows all kinds of people to practice psychotherapy without ever having been in therapy themselves—a true travesty, I think, as many would agree—a therapist's best training comes from his or her own therapy. And the more in-depth that therapy, the better the therapist's training. Several months of counseling with a religious counselor, drug and alcohol counselor, social worker, school psychologist, behavioral psychologist, analyst, or psychiatrist is of little value to the therapist in transforming her "economy of desire." It is not until one has plumbed the depths of one's own torturously complicated pleasures, desires, and suffering that one is in any way prepared for the variety and "perversity" of the pleasures, desires, and suffering one's analysands must be brought to explore, and the variety of feelings, desires, and displeasures one is likely to experience in listening to them.

Although Lacan himself draws no distinction between a personal analysis and a training analysis—believing that any personal analysis can become a training analysis, and that if a training analysis is not personal then it is no analysis at all—he clearly believes it important to reverse the old practice whereby, in the early years of psychoanalysis especially, training analyses were very often shorter than "personal analyses" (Lacan, 2006, p. 231). Such short training analyses may have been justified in the early part of the 20th century by the need for trainees to leave their home cities and countries to undergo analysis with Freud or one of the other early pioneers, something that could usually be done for only a few short months. Nevertheless, the tradition of short training analyses seems to have persisted well beyond that early stage, and even now many institutes require only four years of analysis at about three sessions per week. Anyone who has stuck with analysis beyond that point will tell you that an awful lot more can happen to your economy of desire in the later stages of an analysis. Although Lacan (1976, p. 15) proposed that an analysis has gone far enough when the analysand is "happy to be alive," he nevertheless draws a distinction between the "therapeutic" aim of analysis and the beyond of therapeutics required "to create an analyst" imbued with the analyst's desire (Lacan, 2006, p. 854). The therapeutic successes of an analysis

---

to achieve what he or she says he or she wants, or to say something in particular. . . . It is an enigmatic desire that does not tell the patient what the analyst wants him or her to say or do. (p. 6)

are not necessarily sufficient to allow one to work felicitously as a psychoanalyst oneself, to be imbued with a desire to conduct analyses oneself.[15]

One's own analysis, no matter how far-reaching, is nevertheless not sufficient in practice to allow the analyst to eliminate all traces of his or her countertransference, especially in the area of theoretical blinders, so to speak. Lacan (2006, p. 225) included many things in his definition of countertransference as "the sum total of the analyst's biases, passions, and difficulties, or even of his inadequate information, at any given moment in the dialectical process."[16] Although one's own analysis may have a great impact on one's passions, it may have a lesser impact on one's biases and a still lesser impact on one's "information"; this means that the analyst must engage in a continuous process of self-analysis (to whatever degree that is possible; see Chapter 7), regularly review cases, study myriad areas of human experience, and continue to seek out supervision for many years. This seems far more likely to limit the possibly nefarious effects of the analyst's countertransference than strict adherence to some fixed session length.[17]

Time's Money, Money's Time

Curiously enough, as the objectives of analysis lose their importance, ritual forms of technique become more highly valued.

— *Lacan* (2006, *p. 464*)

The fixed-length session can be criticized for rigidly adhering to a fundamental principle of capitalism: Time's money, money's time. However, time and money

---

[15] Although Lacan (2006, p. 324) is perhaps best known for his statement that "cure [is] an added benefit of psychoanalytic treatment" rather than a direct aim, he does not in any way disregard the therapeutic benefits of analysis. Consider his comment about neurotics: "They have a difficult life and we try to alleviate their discomfort" (Lacan, 1976, p. 15). It should be clear that it is not enough for the analysand to remark on one single occasion that he is happy to be alive, for he may—as did one of my analysands who said those very words one day—change his tune quite radically at the very next session! It should be a general sense that endures, not a fleeting feeling.

Although Freud is perhaps best known for putting the "scientific aims" of psychoanalysis before the therapeutic aims, he sometimes maintained the contrary: "The scientific results of psycho-analysis are at present only a by-product of its therapeutic aims" (Freud, 1909/1955, p. 208, footnote), and "cases which are devoted from the first to scientific purposes and are treated accordingly suffer in their outcome" (Freud, 1912b/1958, p. 114).

[16] See also Lacan (1988a, p. 23).

[17] To my mind, contemporary analysts' fixation on a standard session length smacks of obsession and might be understood as part of the obsessive strain in psychoanalytic theory itself (see Lacan, 2006, p. 609). Unfortunately, this fixation often renders analysts incapable of foiling the obsessive neurotic's own strategy in therapy: waiting for the Master to die (see Lacan, 2006, pp. 314–315).

cannot be equated, in any simple or direct manner, with the reality principle, and yet it seems to be utterly and completely confused with the reality principle by many analysts, who thereby seem to believe that there is no other possible relationship between time and money (and who perhaps are unaware that the equation of time and money is quite a recent one in many parts of the world). And even if this principle of capitalism could be equated with the reality principle, the notion that the analyst's job is to bring the analysand into line with the reality principle is a misguided one, encouraging him, as it does, to impose his own view of reality onto the analysand, as we shall see in Chapter 9.

The fixed-length session gives analysands the false impression that in coming to see the analyst they will be paying for a service like any other, a service whose conditions are regulated by a kind of contractual agreement in which analysands can be quite sure of getting exactly what they intend to pay for. This allows them to think of themselves as customers or "clients"—a term now consecrated by American psychological usage—who have the right to make specific demands upon the analyst.

This opens the door to a fundamental misconception about what they can expect in analysis; virtually all analysts agree that it is important to frustrate many, if not the vast majority, of the analysand's demands or requests, because (1) satisfying the analysand's demands does not ultimately help the analysand, (2) the analysand often demands things that the analyst cannot provide, and even if he could, they would destroy the therapeutic relationship, and (3) people often demand things that they do not really want. Indeed, Lacan (1965–1966, March 23, 1966) formulated the complex relationship between demand and desire by saying that the human predicament is such that "just because people demand something from you doesn't mean that's what they really want you to give them." To give me what I say I want (that is, what I request or demand) will not actually satisfy me because what I say I want is not the same as what I desire (and human desire is such that it cannot be satisfied with some specific object or action).[18]

As I have put it elsewhere, "in therapy the therapist sidesteps the patient's demands, frustrates them, and ultimately tries to direct the patient to something he or she never asked for" (Fink, 1997, p. 9), to discovering his or her own desire. This project is not suitable to the kind of exchange that occurs between service providers and customers in an economy in which time and money are equated, in which one receives so many minutes of a service (a massage,

---

[18] As Lacan (1966–1967, June 21, 1967) put it, "It is of the very nature of desire not to be satisfied."

for example, or a legal consultation) for so many dollars. This explains why Lacanians charge by the session, regardless of its length, not by the number of minutes that the session lasts. Not surprisingly, perhaps, American analysts I have spoken with often assume that the cost of each session must depend upon its length (were that the case it would almost ineluctably lead to ever longer sessions).

The fee is tied to the analytic work that the analyst manages to get the analysand to do during the sessions but also in the time between sessions—assuming the analyst manages to put the analysand's unconscious to work (for example, dreaming, fantasizing, and associating)—not to some specific number of minutes that elapse while they are in each other's presence (which, in any case, does not include time for reading over notes before sessions, note taking after sessions, case conceptualization, supervision on the case, and so on). It is not clear to me what makes the disconnect between time and money seem like such an unthinkable notion to certain people specifically when it comes to psychoanalysis: There are, after all, plenty of fields in which one is paid for doing a particular job, or some part of a job, regardless of how long it takes, whether that job (performed alone or in concert with others) is teaching a class, writing a song, running a corporation, cooking a meal, preparing an ad campaign, crowning a tooth, removing a gallbladder, drafting a newspaper story, renovating a home, or any of many others. Such jobs may go quickly on certain occasions and painfully slowly on others, requiring different amounts of preparation and research in different cases, unforeseen obstacles potentially arising when least expected. Furthermore, different people will complete the same job in widely different amounts of time (not to mention with widely different degrees of success). What would stop the relationship between time and money in psychoanalysis from obeying such widely accepted principles and constrain it to follow the model proposed by those members of the legal profession who bill strictly by the hour? Isn't it what gets accomplished in the session that is primordial?

Parisian Misuses

There's many a slip 'twixt the cup and the lip.
                                                        — Proverb

The variable-length session may be credited with making psychoanalytic treatment more affordable for many people in the countries in which it is widely practiced. Since sessions with analysands who have been in analysis for some time are often shorter than the standard 45- or 50-minute hours practiced by the majority of non-Lacanians, Lacanians are often able to see more than one analysand per hour and thus to charge less per session (they are also likely to have more broadly sliding fee scales than other clinicians, in my experience).

As virtually all things are taken too far by some, certain practitioners have been known to take scansion so far that the variable-length session invariably means "short session" in their work, leading them to compress ever further the time allotted to each individual session. Lacan himself and a number of his prominent followers were sometimes said to have seen (and some still are said to see) fifteen or even more analysands per hour, compressing session time to the point at which few dreams of any length could reasonably be recounted and associated to in the course of one and the same session. While this approach clearly forces the analysand to do the lion's share of the work of association and interpretation in the time between sessions and could theoretically be effective for certain people, one must seriously wonder about the effectiveness of having nothing but four-minute sessions for an entire analysis, even at a frequency of five sessions per week.

In my own analysis, I hardly felt that the longest sessions were necessarily the most useful, and often even found very short sessions the most productive (indeed, they were no doubt so short precisely because they had been so productive, building extensively on the work I had done in the time between sessions). Still, in my own practice, such extremely short sessions are something of a rarity; I, like many other Lacanians I know, find few reasons to systematically scand sessions after only a few minutes.[19]

The Internal Logic of the Session

The indifference with which ending a session after a fixed number of minutes has elapsed interrupts the subject's moments of haste, can be fatal to the conclusion toward which his discourse was rushing headlong, and can even set a misunderstanding in stone, if not furnish a pretext for a retaliatory ruse.

— *Lacan* (2006, p. 314)

Each session can be understood to have its own internal logic, in a manner of speaking. The analysand may announce a foreboding in the first words of the session that only becomes clear or articulated at the very end; she may describe

---

[19] Certain Lacanians provide some intriguing reasons for this, however, in two issues of the journal *La cause freudienne* (Ecole de la Cause Freudienne, 2000, 2004).

her father as "pigheaded" in the first few minutes of the session, only to repeat that exact expression in relation to her boyfriend 25 minutes later; she may fail to have any associations to the "stool" that appeared near the bar in a dream she told early in the session, and then come round to speaking about how much enjoyment she has been taking lately in her bowel movements shortly before coming to her consultations with the analyst, and so on.

The session sometimes comes full circle, contradicts what it began with, ends by building precisely on the conclusion of the preceding session, or ends by debunking the conclusion of the preceding session, and so on, establishing landmarks and turning points in the dialectical movement of the analysis. In this sense, each session may serve as another chapter in a particular story—a story that is rarely linear in its telling, moving instead at times from the strong assertion of one point of view to the equally strong assertion of a virtually opposite point of view (much like Dostoevsky's different voices in *The Brothers Karamazov*, for example), provisionally ending up somewhere else altogether, in a place that could not have been foreseen in advance by any but the most clairvoyant. Each session here serves as a kind of articulation or joint (as, for example, in a finger) linking things together and taking them in new directions at the same time. Each session has a kind of internal logic in relation to the work that has already been done in the prior sessions.

In the following sections I will provide some examples of how a certain series of sessions functions as articulations in a story, beginning first with examples of sessions from the early stages of an analysis and then giving examples of sessions from the end of an analysis. Given the amount of material the analysands presented in each session, which would fill many pages, I provide only a schematic account of each session here (all names and other identifying information have, of course, been changed).

The Internal Logic of the Early Sessions

We tell the truth as best we can—in other words, in part. The problem is that the way it presents itself is as a whole. And therein lies the difficulty: We must bring the analysand to sense that this truth is not whole, not true for everyone, not general, not valid for all.
—Lacan (1976, pp. 43–44)

The early sessions often involve a kind of planting of mile-markers or preliminary signposts along the road of a life that had previously seemed to be lacking in them or defined rather by external facts—"objective" events like changing schools, moving from one town to another, marriage, divorce, and the like. The brand new analysand often considers her life to be quite opaque, and what may immediately strike the analyst as important turning points in her life have never been thought of as such by her. She perhaps realizes at some level that she is no longer the happy-go-lucky girl she had been in her early years, but she does not seem to have a clue as to how she became the serious woman she is today who lives only to work. She does not know when things began to change or why they changed. Often the very first sessions lead to surprising connections, establishing links between a whole series of problems later in life and several specific earlier events that had never been given much thought. This leads to a first sketch of a life history where before there had seemingly been a life without history, history being understood here as recording the major symbolic turning points or mileposts along one's path, even before suppositions about cause and effect can be made. The analysand is often able to recall all kinds of "stray events" from her past, but they have never been connected to each other; they have never been related to each other in her thinking about her life, never put into any kind of chronological order or thought about in terms of patterns or causality. All of this changes once the analysis begins.[20] As an analysand of mine put it after just two sessions, "I have the sense of different parts of my life getting connected, getting connected as part of me."

In the case of one of my analysands (I'll call him Al), the first few preliminary meetings gave an intriguing sketch of his early history but included nary a mention of any siblings. Al recounted his relationships with members of the opposite sex from his earliest girlfriend at age seven to his current partner, one of his primary complaints at the outset of his analysis being his fixation on certain body types. He had tried in various ways to put a stop to this fixation, but it had always come back. He was even aware that he had dated certain women simply because they looked like other women he had been interested in or involved with, and he stated that his fixation on certain women bordered on the insane, leading him to go to crazy lengths and spend exorbitant amounts of money to see them. (In his late twenties he had gone with the same complaints to see a female counselor eight times who gave him assignments like "wake up tomorrow and decide to have a healthy relationship," which he did not feel had done him any good!) He described his love for certain women as "addictive," indicating that his father had been an alcoholic and that he himself had gone to Alcoholics Anonymous meetings for many years.

---

[20] These stray memories can be likened to a whole series or swarm of S_2s, as Lacan called them (2007, pp. 11–12, 35), which are finally given order and shape by the intervention of an S_1 that is introduced by the analytic process. The latter retroactively structures "random memories" into a more or less coherent history.

In the fourth session, Al began talking about something that at first struck me as a side issue or distraction: a distant relative who had become a kind of mother figure for him some years back and whose adopted daughter had made a pass at him. In the fifth session, he made it clear just how painful it was for him to talk about the scenario he had orchestrated with the mother and daughter; he had felt compelled to go out with the daughter and sensed that he was trying to get at her mother through her, an incestuous scenario that he was not a little ashamed of. He had, in fact, had nightmares involving this mother and daughter pair for years after that.

In the fifth session he also mentioned for the first time that he had an older sister; this came up merely in passing in relation to his own mother's attempts to get chummy with and sound out his teachers as he was growing up, something that she did not do with his sister's teachers. Regarding his relations with his sister he simply said that they fought a lot as kids (partly because his mother made it so clear that she preferred Al to his sister and his sister resented him for that), had hardly spoken throughout their teenage years, but had been getting along a bit better as of late. He then went back to his story about the mother figure and her daughter. Up until this point, the sessions had been of varying lengths, but all rather long; I would end them when he seemed to have gotten to the end of a series of stories about or associations to a particular facet of his life (relations with his mother one day, girlfriends another, and so on).

In the sixth session, he talked about his recent fascination with a woman he had seen who seemed oblivious to the fact that her body could have an effect on anyone—he could not "get her out of [his] head." We discussed some suicidal and homicidal thoughts that seemed to be involved in his fears of his car exploding (while his current partner was in the passenger seat) and the idea he had toyed with at various points in his life of shutting the rest of the world out of his life so as not to think about women and their bodies. I scanded the session when he said that he realized that his interest in cutting himself off from everyone was motivated by a wish to stay away from life and sex.

In the seventh session, Al spoke at length about aggression, indicating that he had realized that in his fears/fantasies he imagined his car exploding because it was rear-ended (rear ends played an important role in his fantasy life), and he talked about various ways in which he expressed his aggression toward women. He talked more about the body types he was attracted to and I asked him (in a very obvious move) to describe his mother. At first he talked only about her present looks, so I asked him to talk about her looks earlier on. I ended the session when he indicated that she was "curvy and round," for at the end of the third session he had said that the rear ends he was attracted to had a "bubble" quality to them, a formulation he had returned to in the sixth session. (In the second session he had not been able to describe the rear ends he was attracted to when I first asked him to say something about them.)

In the eighth session, Al turned more directly to the topic of his sister, indicating that although they had gotten along fairly well up to a point, their relations had taken a turn for the worse at around seven or eight years of age. Why? He did not know. She excelled in everything, did better than he did in school, was superior at sports, and beat him at every single game they played. At one point Al slipped and called her his "brother" instead of his "sister" and I asked him what he made of that. Was she perhaps a bit masculine, to his mind? He affirmed that he at times would have preferred to have had a brother rather than a sister. He added that, to this day, he refused to play games, because games with his sister would end in him having tantrums: "I'd go out of my mind." I ended the session at this expression of the conflict and tension between Al and his initially unmentioned sister.

In the ninth session, the importance of his sister truly began to come into focus: The first two crushes he had had involved girls who looked a lot like his sister and his first real girlfriend at around age 19 greatly resembled his sister. He had realized since the last session that it was "the sister connection that [made him] fetishize a girl." He recalled that at 15 he had written a poem praising his sister and had wanted to know and be friendly with (if not go out with) her girlfriends. At 20 he had written a virtual love letter to her in his journal, idealizing her using almost religious imagery. I scanded the session when he mentioned that as a child he would try to get a rise out of her, but she would remain cold and oblivious, which would annoy him all the more and get him very excited and worked up.

In the tenth session, Al began by talking about the fact that he had heard something in the apartment next to his, which he had at first taken to be child abuse, only to realize that it was his neighbor moaning during lovemaking. He felt compelled to listen for hours after that, just as he had felt compelled to listen to his parents fighting as a child: They would get louder and louder until his mother broke down and cried, at which point her voice would become shrill and she would become incoherent ("speaking in tongues"). That was the payoff for his listening, to his mind: He had to listen until things got to that point, a point that he did not really understand but that he felt his father had driven his mother to—his father had been able to do that to his mother. I queried, "Something you couldn't do to your sister?" I ended the session when he said "yeah" with a somewhat startled, deer-in-the-headlights look on his face.

In the eleventh session, he started by indicating that he realized that al- though his current partner sometimes moaned like the woman he heard in the apartment next to his, it had absolutely no effect on him. After quite a lot of discussion on everything he felt compelled to do (listen to a woman moaning, look at porn, masturbate, and so on), he came back around to the topic of the kind of effect involved in that moaning, and—mentioning that he had been thinking about what he had said in the previous session about sometimes wanting to get worked up and lose control himself in front of people—he postulated that what he seemed to want is not to have that effect on a woman but for her to have that effect on him. I ended the session there without trying to point out that this suggested that he had identified (at least in part) with his mother during the fights between his parents in which she got all worked up and lost control. There seemed to me to be no reason to do so: He was quite capable of drawing such conclusions himself.

Despite my highly schematic account here, in which I have obviously left out numerous details and side developments (what the novelist or scriptwriter might call "secondary plot lines"), I hope it can be seen how the scansions of the sessions keep the analysand's focus on the work at hand without totally determining its direction. At times the sessions seemed to alternate in focal point from his mother to his sister and back again (I left out most of the material related to his father and other father figures here to simplify my exposition), and different points of view were explored without any of them being set in stone: for example, that he wanted to have the kind of effect on his sister that his father had on his mother (and all the Oedipal implications of wishfully putting himself in his father's shoes, the father too having beaten him at every game they ever played), that he wanted to be like his mother at the mercy of his father (or his brother-like sister), or, as only time will tell, neither, both, or some combination of the two.

The analysand obviously felt free to bring in material from his current life (fear of his car exploding or overhearing his neighbor) and to launch into a wide variety of topics (his current job, relations with men, hobbies, and so on). He brought in new dreams and old nightmares and asked questions (such as whether or not he should prepare for his sessions or read psychoanalytic works), yet he was still able to lay down some preliminary signposts along his path in life and distill a few preliminary articulations. Separate time did not need to be devoted to building a "therapeutic alliance"[21] a good working

---

[21] Elizabeth Zetzel (1956/1990) introduced this term, but she attributed the concept of it to Edward Bibring (1937). Bibring argued (pp. 183–189) that the analyst appeals to "the conscious, uniform and rational ego" and pedagogically appeals to "reason, experience and morals." Zetzel (p. 138) took this to constitute a "therapeutic alliance between the analyst and the healthy part of the patient's ego."

relationship developed naturally alongside his elaboration of the material. This is typical in my experience: *If I attend carefully to the material brought forward by the analysand, the relationship (or alliance) takes care of itself.* Al did not seem to have any need for each session to be exactly the same length in order to settle in and talk to me. I have found the same to be true with the vast majority of patients, whether they know anything about the variable-length session or not prior to coming to analysis. Only those who have already worked extensively with therapists who adhere religiously to a fixed-length session have asked me about

---

Ralph Greenson (1965/1990) seems to have been one of the first analysts to stress the importance of striving specifically to get the patient "to develop a reliable working relation with the analyst" in certain unusual cases in which a positive alliance did not develop on its own. He dubbed this relation the "working alliance," characterizing it as the "relatively non-neurotic, rational rapport which the patient has with his analyst" and proffering that "patients who cannot split off a reasonable, observing ego will not be able to maintain a working relation and vice versa" (p. 152). Note that in Greenson's account, it is only in a few rare cases that the analyst must specifically strive to build such an alliance. See my comments later in this book regarding the dubious value of the "observing ego" in analytic work with neurotics. Note too Bibring's and Greenson's use of the term *rational*, as if the ego or a relationship could in any way be described as "rational" (on the unjustifiable use of such terms in psychoanalysis, see Chapter 9). Note that Brenner (1979/1990, pp. 185–186) did "not agree with Zetzel that an alliance is distinct from the remainder of the patient's transference nor with Greenson's less sweeping formula that working alliance and transference neurosis are to be distinguished from one another even though they are closely related." Brenner systematically demonstrated that none of the examples Greenson adduced involved anything new in the way of psychoanalytic work. For an example of the dangers of stressing the importance of building a "therapeutic alliance" with patients, one can simply consider the disastrous relationship Greenson built with the most famous of his patients: Marilyn Monroe (see, for example, Spoto, 1993).

Freud (1905a/1953, p. 117) indicated that in certain cases "hysteria may be said to be cured not by the method but by the physician," but he was referring to treatment by suggestion (under hypnosis) that took place in 19th-century mental institutions where, at times, the doctor's personal influence sufficed to bring about a curative effect, one which was, however, limited in duration. He certainly did not believe that the curative effects of psychoanalysis were due to the "person of the analyst" or to the rapport between analyst and analysand.

In my experience, most analysands feel they have a good rapport with their analysts when the work is going well. The rapport essentially "builds itself" when the work they are doing together is advancing, and there is no need to devote special attention to so-called rapport building. Contrast this view, however, with that of Malan (1995/2001):

> It is one of the most important characteristics of a therapist that he should be able to sense the degree of rapport existing at any given moment in a therapeutic session. Anyone who has this capacity can set it up as a kind of thermometer between him and the patient, and can use the moment-to-moment fluctuations in the level of rapport in order to gauge the appropriateness of what he has just said. It is of course going a bit far to say that then he *cannot go wrong*, but as a way of conveying an important principle the exaggeration is worth it. (p. 21)

A few lines earlier the same author goes so far as to say that the *"deepening of rapport . . .* is as near as one can ever get to scientific proof that the [therapist's] interpretation was correct" (p. 21). The reader should be able to infer the degree to which I disagree with such a point of view from what I say in Chapters 5 and 7.

the practice and I can only think of one person I have seen in my 20 years of clinical work who has chafed at it.

In a short space of time (eleven sessions), it became clear how important a role Al's sister had played and continued to play in his erotic life, even if most aspects of that role remained to be teased out. And while his initial discussion of his mother focused almost exclusively on her intrusiveness in his life and schoolwork, other facets of his relationship with her could now be seen on the horizon. Although he initially situated the shift in his relationship with his sister as having occurred at seven or eight years of age and as being based on his being a "screw up" at school while she was a "star student," it was already clear that this was a kind of "screen history"—a story he had told himself for many years but that was belied by facts he recalled after just a few sessions of analysis. In fact, the shift in his relationship with his sister had occurred at least two years earlier, although he did not know why. A great many doors were now open, a great many questions were already on the table, and Al was eager to go further.

It should be obvious that the early sessions of an analysis do not aim at "fixing" anything ("fixing" is quite foreign to the psychoanalytic project in general) and may, indeed, as Lacan (2006, p. 596) indicated, lead to a crystallization or systematization of symptoms.[22] The most important aims of the early sessions are to intrigue the analysand, to put the analysand—and above all her unconscious—to work (the analyst must make it clear by his comportment in the therapy that he is there to guide things to some degree but not to lead), and to encourage the analysand to sketch a preliminary picture of her life. Although these early sessions may have some salutary effect on certain kinds of symptoms analysands complain of when they first come to analysis— depression, lack of energy, anxiety—they may well have the opposite effect insofar as certain problems that had been swept under the rug are dragged out in the open. The analyst can only hope that the analysand gets enough out of the unique libidinal relationship with the analyst and the unheralded type of work they do together to bear the worsening of symptoms that sometimes occurs.

---

[22] See also Freud (1914a/1958, p. 152) and Lacan (2004):

> The symptom is only constituted when the subject notices it, for we know from experience that there are forms of obsessive behavior in which the subject has not only not noticed his obsessions, he has not even constituted them as such. In this case, analysis' first step— and Freud's passages on the subject are famous—is to constitute the symptom in its classical form, failing which there's no way to go beyond it for there's no way to talk about it. (p. 325)

The Internal Logic of the Late Sessions

Truth shows itself in an alternation of things that are strictly opposed to each other, that have to be made to go around each other.

— Lacan (2007, p. 127)

Let me turn now to an example of what a series of scansions might look like in the late stages of an analysis, in this case, that of a young woman who had been in analysis for many years. Without going into much detail about her complex and tumultuous history, I can safely say that the majority of the work of the analysis involved her attempts to separate from a mother with whom she was morbidly enmeshed and to become a woman in her own right. The mother was probably psychotic and, under the guise of the purest motherly love, was full of hate and anger at her daughter, who was doted on by the men in the family and unmistakably preferred by them to the mother herself.

Although many aspects of the relationship with the mother had been slowly worked through over the course of the analysis, the analysand, whom I shall refer to as Zee, still remained somewhat wrapped up with her (i.e., libidinally attached) in what she found to be an unbearable way toward the end of her analysis and kept trying to figure out why. Her mother had communicated to her that there was no room for her in the world—above all, as a woman who could enjoy being adored by and surrendering herself to a man—by criticizing her virulently, especially whenever she showed any interest in a man who displayed interest in her. Zee asked herself why she had obeyed her mother's wishes, hidden her resentment, and pretended not to see what was quite evident: that her mother was extremely jealous of her.

Zee eventually realized that a longstanding fear she had that her mother would "flip out" because of something she did was actually her "greatest fantasy"—to see her mother go to pieces, to watch her turn to dust. Was that, she asked herself, what she needed to do to finish her analysis: destroy her mother? Did she, she wondered, need to verbally reduce her to rubble? What then of forgiveness: "What is it that I haven't forgiven her for?" she asked.

At the next session Zee wondered why she had pretended not to see her mother's jealousy. Was it because she herself *wanted* to be angry and that if she recognized her mother's jealousy she could no longer justify her anger toward her? It seemed to her as if she had made a choice to be angry, as if anger was what was most precious to her, the part of her that she was most attached to. I scanded the session at that point, it having been obvious for quite some time that she had long derived her principal "enjoyment" in life—her main jouissance (that paradoxically disturbing form of satisfaction)[23]—from stewing in anger and resentment.

At the next session she proffered a formulation that she herself did not fully understand but nevertheless felt to be true when it came to mind: She had adopted the strategy of not existing in order to stop her mother from existing. She had sensed from an early age that her mother most fully existed when she was viciously, passionately criticizing her daughter; Zee had thus opted to give her mother the fewest possible opportunities to criticize her by virtually disappearing. Zee had restricted herself, had restricted so many of her own activities in life (spending an inordinate amount of time sleeping, sabotaging her studies and relationships, and curtailing her very movements in space through the development of numerous symptoms), so as not to leave herself open to criticism. She had throttled herself out of resentment for her mother, squeezing her own life out of herself in order to get back at her mother, in order to deprive her mother of the incredibly violent jouissance she so obviously thrived on. I ended the session after this discussion of Zee's self-mortification and self-immolation.

At the next session Zee tied some of these points to the symptoms she had struggled with through much of the analysis but that had started to fade as of late; at the session after that she said that seeing her mother as jealous (not just abstractly entertaining the idea but really experiencing her as jealous) was empowering. Her mother had convinced her since she was a little girl that they were victims, that they were powerless compared to everyone else, and Zee had been left to merely dream of having power over others, something she never felt she had. She suddenly felt that this was no longer true! I stopped the session after that declaration.

---

[23] *Jouissance* refers to the kind of enjoyment or satisfaction people derive from their symptoms, about which Freud (1916–1917/1963, pp. 365–366) said, "The kind of satisfaction which the symptom brings has much that is strange about it. . . . It is unrecognizable to the subject, who, on the contrary, feels the alleged satisfaction as suffering and complains of it." It is not a "simple pleasure," so to speak, but involves a kind of pain-pleasure or "pleasure in pain" (*Schmerzlust*, as Freud, 1924/1961, p. 162, put it) or satisfaction in dissatisfaction. It qualifies the kind of "kick" someone may get out of punishment, self-punishment, doing something that is so pleasurable that it hurts (sexual climax, for example), or doing something that is so painful that it becomes pleasurable. Most people deny getting pleasure or satisfaction from their symptoms, but "outside observers" (those around them) can often see that they enjoy their symptoms, that they "get off" on their symptoms in a way that is too roundabout, "dirty," or "filthy" to be described in conventional terms as pleasurable or satisfying. Lacan even went so far as to say, "jouissance bothers the hell out of us!" (Lacan 1973–1974, November 13, 1973). Jouissance is not necessarily something one deliberately seeks out or decides to go out and get. A good deal of our jouissance simply happens to us, often without our knowing why, as if handed to us on a silver platter by Providence or God's grace, coming when we least expect it and not coming, on the other hand, when we most expect it. For further discussion of the term, see Fink (1997, pp. 8–9).

At the next session Zee reiterated that making her mother flip out was her fondest fantasy but that something stopped her from enacting it: Was it that she could only know she was a woman if her mother was suffering? If her mother were put out of her misery—destroyed—what then? If her mother were no longer there to hate her, how could she know she was worth being jealous of—that is, truly of interest to men? I scanded the session when she wondered if her sense of herself as a woman was so precarious that she needed her mother to stay alive and could not even allow herself to fantasize about her mother being totally destroyed.

In the next session she said that she thought she had stopped herself from pissing her mother off in order to piss her off all the more surely. She was not entirely certain how she had done that, but she had long suspected that her mother's greatest pleasure in life was to complain and crush her daughter. When Zee would retaliate, her mother would get all the more worked up, visibly enjoying herself all the more. It was only by not retaliating that Zee could deprive her mother of something. In thinking back to the time when her mother had regained custody of her after several years' absence, Zee wondered why she had allowed herself to be roped into her mother's game when she had done no such thing with other women. It struck her that if she had allowed herself to be reeled in, it was in order to hurt her mother: Zee had in fact *baited* her mother. I ended the session when she postulated that the point was not to destroy her mother or cast her in the gutter but just to choose something else, something outside of her mother.

In the next session she recounted a dream in which her mother tried to impale her with the kind of skewers used to roast a chicken; rather than baiting her or fighting with her, Zee simply left the premises and dropped the whole thing. This quite short session ended when she commented that that was exactly what she would like to do but has never done before.

"What is the point of retaliating?" Zee asked at the next session. She had been seeking justice, wanting her mother to pay for her horrendous behavior, but to want to kill her mother was to remain bound up with her as before, enmeshed with her. What she now wanted to do instead was simply to exist, to be herself, and speak the truth. She would serve justice best by simply existing, by letting herself be.

This short description of a series of sessions toward the end of an analysis, as abbreviated and decontextualized as it is, hopefully gives a sense of the way each session builds on the previous sessions—not in the way that one puts one block on top of another in usual forms of construction, because certain sessions destroy or dislodge the block put in place in a prior session—following a nonlinear, dialectical sort of logic that at times swings back and forth from one extreme to another until the analysand finds her own path.

The scansions allowed each specific movement to be punctuated—in the best of cases, at the precise moment of its fullest, most emphatic expression—instead of being buried under "filler," material that would not necessarily have been crucial to the analysand's progress at that stage in the work. None of the sessions summarized here lasted more than 25 minutes, and some were probably closer to ten. Could more of these movements have been accomplished on any one day had I employed a 50-minute session? I sincerely doubt it: Each session already contained the crux of hours of work the analysand had done, dreaming and associating, between one session and the next, the intervals between the sessions having been no more than a day or two. This particular analysand worked harder than certain other analysands outside of her sessions, doing the bulk of the work in the time between sessions, but she was hardly totally atypical in this respect. Her sessions were not entirely thought out in advance and I continued to punctuate and ask about elements of her dreams that she had not already associated to. That said, at this stage in her analysis I did not need to do much more than punctuate and scand—she was more than capable of interpreting on her own!

Since analysands often feel obliged to speak for the entire duration of their fixed-length sessions, they are led to search for "filler," in a sense: They may well be aware that the important work of the session is the dream they had the night before that picked up on the precise theme they had been talking about in the previous session, but they may also suspect that it will only take ten or 15 minutes to discuss. Hence they are led to "pad" the session with 30 or more minutes of details of everyday life or thoughts they had, which they consider less important, just so that they will be able to fill up the time and "get their money's worth." Indeed, it is a common strategy on the part of analysands to "leave the best for last" (just as it is of public speakers of many ilks); they too are aware, at some level, that what they hear themselves say last is what is most likely to stick with them.

Since analysands who have variable-length sessions do not know when their sessions are going to end, they are more inclined to bring up what they consider to be most important right at the outset (of course, repression is such that sometimes what they consider to be the most important will not necessarily later strike them or the analyst as having been the most important) for fear of not having the opportunity to bring it up later. This helps combat what I will somewhat jokingly refer to as Parkinson's law as applied to psychoanalytic sessions: "Session material tends to expand to fill up the time available."

At the end of Chapter 3, I suggested that we might think of the analyst as an artist or musician who, with his questions and punctuations, brings out something that is, in a sense, already there, waiting to be heard in the analysand's discourse: her desire, which may well be buried or lying dormant. Scansion brings to mind a somewhat different metaphor, albeit a perhaps problematic one: It has sometimes been said that Michelangelo simply freed David from the marble from which he was cut, that a sculptor simply chips away the parts of the block of stone that are obstructing our view of the figure waiting inside. It might be helpful to some to think of each scansion as cutting away a small amount of stone; most often the analyst simply clears away tiny portions at a time, but perhaps occasionally reaches the final depth, the final dimension of the figure at one spot, only to approach the exact same spot of the final figure again from an entirely different direction, little by little approaching each point on the surface of the final figure from multiple directions. That would, of course, seem to assume that there was some sort of predetermined final figure, whereas one hardly gets that impression at the beginning of an analysis, but does a sculptor really have a "final" figure in mind when he or she begins carving?

Scansion and Scheduling

One never knows until afterward.
— Lacan (1973–1974, March 12, 1974)

I am often asked how it is possible to schedule patients when one practices a variable-length session. Clearly, if one allows ample time for the longest session one can imagine (personally, I try to block out about an hour and half for the first few sessions with a new analysand), one will encounter no scheduling conflicts. Nevertheless, practitioners usually find that the majority of the sessions they have with a particular analysand fall within a specific range. They can then take the average, add time for note-taking and a short pause, and schedule that amount (keeping in mind that they may need to always schedule more time for certain analysands, as I mentioned earlier), assuming that if a session goes longer than average with one analysand, it may well go shorter than average with the next and everything will even out. This may mean that analysands occasionally wait ten or more minutes for their sessions to begin, but such waits hardly seem unreasonable. This is just another way in which analytic work can be dissociated in the analysand's mind from more typical American business practices where being ten minutes late is often considered terribly bad form.

Quite a few additional examples of scansions I have made in my own practice are provided in later chapters in the context of descriptions of work with dreams, daydreams, fantasies, transference, and so on.

5

Interpreting

We often get the impression that, to borrow the words of Polonius, our bait of falsehood had taken a carp of truth.

— Freud (1937/1964, p. 262)

It takes off from the subject's own words in order to come back to them, which means that an interpretation can be exact only by being . . . an interpretation.

— Lacan (2006, p. 601)

PRIOR TO COMING TO psychoanalysis, most of us probably intuitively consider the goal of interpretation to be accuracy. And, in certain realms of human endeavor, a strong case can be made for accuracy being among the primary criteria of a good interpretation. Yet few psychoanalysts or analysands with several years of therapy under their belts would be surprised at the notion that interpretation in the analytic situation aims less at accuracy than at having a certain kind of impact.

In the human realm one of the first questions that arises is: To whom are we assuming that the interpretation seems accurate or truthful? The spontaneous response would likely be that the interpretation must seem accurate to the analysand. However, most analysands can probably recall interpretations their analysts made that struck them as wrongminded initially (and that they perhaps attempted to refute or even railed against), but that struck them as quite true later, sometimes much later. Most analysands can probably also recall interpretations they themselves arrived at or that their analysts made that really struck them at the time, but later seemed superficial, incomplete, or off base. Thus, if we are to adopt the criterion that an interpretation must seem accurate to the analysand, we would have to add the words "sooner or later" to the formulation.

74

Yet in certain cases analysands may come to realize that they were willing and even pleased, at one point in time, to embrace specific interpretations because they supported cherished views they held of themselves (whether positive or negative). Later in the analysis they begin to call those cherished views into question and find those interpretations lacking in truth value. In such cases, even the analysand's initial sense that the interpretation hit upon the truth seems undermined after the fact.[1]

The Truth Is Always Elsewhere

There is no truth that can but be said half way, just like the subject it brings with it. To express it as I have stated it before, the truth can only be half-said.
                                                        — *Lacan* (2005b, p. 30–31)

To the analysand, truth seems less than stable. When he says something in a session that he feels genuinely reflects his life, relationships, or way of being, by the next session that particular "truth" may, at times, no longer seem quite so truthful, quite so striking, quite so on target. On the other hand, certain statements, whether made by himself or by the analyst, may continue to seem absolutely true for long periods of time, constituting thresholds, turning points, "button ties,"[2] or major mile-markers in his analysis; indeed, he may view the sessions at which those statements were made as crucial moments of change for decades to come. But many other statements are likely to be viewed as

---

[1] Analysts often proffer interpretations that seem to them to be on target in the heat of the moment, in the context of the words the analysand has just uttered, but which they may well come to think of later as only very partial or even off the mark. This does not make such interpretations useless, but it does create something of a temporal conundrum as regards accuracy. What seems accurate at a certain moment in the session may not seem accurate several minutes later after the analysand has recounted other memories and associations. But those other memories and associations might never have been recounted had the inaccurate interpretation not been made. One might say that it is the very inaccuracy (or partial accuracy) of the interpretation that allowed the analysis to move forward, for in many instances the analysand does not mention certain thoughts or memories until he hears the analyst's blundering interpretation.

Often the analysand does not even realize the effect that the interpretation has had on him, but unwittingly returns to it in the subsequent session from a new angle, indicating that it has had an impact in a dream, daydream, or just in his thoughts about what to talk about next. It had an impact without his knowing it. Indeed, should the analyst mention it, he sometimes barely recalls the interpretation consciously, but the impact has nevertheless been real.

Perhaps most commonly, the analysand does not even recognize what the analyst has said as an interpretation. Either it blends in so smoothly with what the analysand had been saying or is so brief and cryptic that it does not fit the analysand's preconceived notion of what an interpretation is.

[2] For a description of "button ties," Lacan's *point de capiton*, see Chapter 10 and Fink (2004, pp. 111–116).

absolutely untrue shortly after they are made, then perhaps as partly true and partly false, and then perhaps as superceded altogether in a thoroughly new way of seeing things.

Truth has a funny kind of temporality in psychoanalysis. The analysand sometimes has the sense that he is saying something absolutely fundamental at the very moment he is saying it,[3] but once that truth has been articulated, it may no longer have the weight of truth for him. Perhaps more often he does not feel the impact of what he has said until afterward: In my experience, analysands often remark in one session how struck they were after the last session by something said in that last session. But the subjective conviction they had of its importance in the interval between the sessions is often lost by the subsequent session, and they sometimes feel they can no longer even explain what made it seem so striking, so relevant.

Truth, as experienced by the analysand in the analytic context, has to do with what remains to be said, with what has not yet been said. What has already been said often seems empty, whereas what is being said now for the first time is what has the potential to shake things up, is what feels important, truthful. To the analysand, *the truth is always elsewhere*: in front of him, yet to be found.[4]

Insofar as it concerns "what remains to be said," truth in psychoanalysis has to do with the experience of symbolizing what has never before been put into words. With Lacan, I refer to "what has never before been put into words" as "the real" (it can also be referred to as "the traumatic real"). Interpretation by the analyst, then, quite obviously seeks—at one level, at least—to inspire or to provoke the analysand to engage in the process of symbolization, to put

---

[3] In the early 1950s, Lacan was taken with the notion of "full speech," a kind of speech in which the analysand feels the weight of the truth while speaking; truth, in such cases, seems far more closely linked with enunciation (that is, the act of speaking) than with the enunciated (the statement thus made—in other words, the content). Later, the temporality of truth struck Lacan as more complex, since it is caught up in a future anterior tense: It is not quite true yet when he thinks it in between sessions, and it is no longer altogether true by the time he reports it at the next session (indeed, it may even seem ridiculous to him by the time he recounts it, its truth value no longer being there). All we can say is that it *will have been true* for him. In the 1970s, Lacan (1973, p. 6) offered the following formulation: "[enunciation] ex-sists with respect to truth," suggesting that truth and enunciation do not altogether coincide or line up with each other. On Lacan's notion of ex-sistence, see Fink (1995, Chapter 8). On his later views of full speech and empty speech, see Bruno (1995).

[4] Consider, in this connection, Freud's (1937/1964, p. 263) comment regarding interpretations that are not accepted by patients: "A 'No' from a person in analysis is quite as ambiguous as a 'Yes.' . . . A patient's 'No' is no evidence of the correctness of a construction, though it is perfectly compatible with it. Since every such construction [that is, a kind of overarching interpretation] is an incomplete one, since it covers only a small fragment of the forgotten events, we are free to suppose that the patient is not in fact disputing what has been said to him but is basing his contradiction upon the part that has not yet been uncovered."

into words what has never before been put into words. Interpretation aims to hit the real[5]; I use the term *hitting* here to indicate the degree to which what must be put into words may not be easy to get at and may require more than a simple prod or query—perhaps something more along the lines of a jolt. The idea here is not that interpretation should fall on the analysand's ears like a bolt from the blue—it being preferable to wait, as Freud (1913/1958, p. 140) recommended, until the analysand is but one short step from something before interpreting it and is thus ready to hear it—but rather that the interpretation need not, and at times must not, mesh nicely with what has been said up until that point. Often it must startle, perplex, or disconcert the analysand. The element of surprise can be very important here: Interpretations that have the most impact are rarely ones that the analysand is expecting, whether temporally (for example, if the analyst gets into the habit of providing interpretations at the end of the session) or conceptually (the analyst regularly harping on the same thing).

It should be clear that "truth," as I am using it here, is not so much a property of statements as it is a relationship to the real; to hit the truth is to alight upon something that had never before been formulated in words and to bring it into speech, however haltingly or insufficiently at first. For it is in the impact that speech is able to have on the real that lies the power of psychoanalysis. Left to its own devices, the real does not change over time; like a traumatic war experience, it persists, insistingly returning in nightmares or even waking life (leading, at times, to what I would be tempted to call "intruthive thoughts"). It is only by symbolizing it in words—and in many cases it must be articulated a number of times in different ways—that one can begin to shift positions with respect to it.

If there is some criterion of accuracy or truth in psychoanalysis beyond the analysand's subjective sense, sooner or later, that something he or the analyst said is true (and beyond the analyst's subjective sense, sooner or later,

---

[5] My expression here, "hits the real," is a loose adaptation of something Lacan (1973, p. 30) said: "Interpretation . . . targets the cause of desire." In this case the cause of desire is equated with the Lacanian real. We might think of the real here, alternatively, as the unsubjectified knowledge, the knowledge without a subject, that is found in the unconscious: It is there pulling the strings, so to speak, unbeknown to the analysand (see Fink, 1995). The analyst can garner a pretty good idea of what that knowledge is because of everything the analysand denies knowledge of: "I have no idea why I did that," "I have no idea what happened next," "I have no idea why I said that." Such statements about what the analysand does not know slowly sketch out an absence; they point in the direction of a gap in the analysand's knowledge that can only be occupied by a small number of possible things; as Lacan (1968a, p. 21) put it, "What is not known is organized like the framework of knowledge." If we listen carefully to what is left out of the analysand's discourse and what he claims not to know, we can discern what is likely known in the unconscious, unbeknown to him. Interpretation aims to hit that gap in his knowledge.

that something she or the analysand said is true), what would it be if not the changes that actually occur for the analysand: the disappearance of recurrent nightmares and preexisting symptoms, the ability to do things he was unable to do before (in a word, a change in "subjective position")? Such changes occur not, as the current wisdom would have it, because the neurotic analysand has found a new way of relating to people that is modeled on the "more perfect" relationship he has managed to form with the analyst,[6] because he has regressed and been reparented by the analyst,[7] or because he has learned to imitate the analyst in establishing firm boundaries for himself in his everyday life.[8] Rather, they occur because the real (what he had never before articulated) has been transformed: What was unconscious has not simply become conscious—it has been radically transmogrified.[9] The analysand need not be able to consciously formulate exactly what it was that had been unconscious, or precisely what was said that made things change, but he knows that he is no longer the same as before.

One of my analysands told me that he had noticed he was no longer putting so much pressure on his chalk when writing on the blackboard that it would break, which he had been wont to do for some time when standing in front of his class (much to his embarrassment). This change apparently occurred after I had rearranged a few of his words, saying something like "pressure at the board" (referring to pressure he had felt as a child when called on by teachers to perform at the blackboard, and to pressure he was putting on himself to fail for a whole variety of reasons). He had not given my phrase any thought at the time but realized a couple of weeks later that he was no longer breaking chalk, even though he was not making any special effort to ease up and did not know why he had stopped. Although this is just a micro-symptom, it points to the fact that the analysand need not even become conscious of what had been unconscious for a symptom to disappear,[10] as long as enough of it is verbalized by the analyst, the analysand, or the two together building on each other's words.

---

[6] McWilliams (2004, p. 17) wrote, "The therapeutic alliance is assumed to be internalized as a new model of relationship."

[7] For a discussion of reparenting, see, for example, Guntrip (1971).

[8] See, for example, McWilliams (2004, pp. 258, 289).

[9] Lacan (1977b, p. 14) at times even equated the unconscious with the real: "The real as what is impossible to speak." For the analysand, the truth is always elsewhere insofar as he manages to speak some of what was unconscious (what was once real because it was impossible to talk about at that point) and can thus move on to what still remains unconscious.

[10] It also points to the fact that the analyst need not know that what she has said has had an effect—I would not have known if the analysand himself had not told me a few weeks later.

Many analysts have, however, concluded that the main goal of analysis is to teach the analysand to observe himself in the same way that the analyst observes him in the course of the therapy. The idea here seems to be that when the analyst brings the analysand to an awareness of a pattern of behavior that he engages in unconsciously, the analysand can learn to try to consciously stop himself from engaging in it. Hence the importance to such analysts of fostering what they refer to as the "observing ego" in the analysand.[11] This has always struck me as a poor substitute for genuine change: If analysis could offer one no more than the possibility of learning to constantly observe oneself and consciously check one's own impulses, it would be hard to muster much enthusiasm about its benefits.

Although the promotion of the "observing ego" may be of some value in the treatment of psychotics, it is quite counterproductive in the treatment of neurotics, leading as it does to the further alienation of the neurotic subject (as I will explain in a moment). If conducted in the proper manner, psychoanalysis can help to actually eliminate the very *temptation* to engage in certain patterns of behavior.

Many of the analysands who have gone into analysis with me after working with practitioners who employ current mainstream approaches have had the same complaint, which was expressed in the initial sessions as follows: "I know what I'm doing now but I'm having a very difficult time stopping myself." The effect of such approaches to treatment seems quite clear in this complaint: Although an observing ego has been fostered in the analysand (at times making the analysand very sophisticated in employing the latest "psychobabble"), the real, drive, or repressed that is motivating the behavior has remained untouched and intact.

The goal of interpretation in many mainstream approaches is to bring an unconscious pattern to the analysand's attention, in the hope of allowing him to "catch himself in the act" in the future and stop himself before he repeats the entirety of the pattern. In these approaches, interpretation is generally designed to convey a simple, direct piece of information to the analysand. Ambiguous phrasing is avoided by the analyst, for the point is to convince the analysand of something, get the analysand to see something precisely as the analyst sees it, and indeed encourage the analysand to incorporate, internalize,

---

[11] The term "observing ego," often juxtaposed to "experiencing ego," derives from Richard Sterba's (1934) notion of "therapeutic ego-dissociation." For examples of its use in contemporary work, see Casement (1991, pp. 30–32) and McWilliams (2004, p. 211). As we shall see in Chapter 7, Casement goes a step further when he asks the analyst to split himself in much the same way into engaged analyst and "internal supervisor."

or assimilate the analyst's viewpoint (in effect, to set up in his own psyche a permanent observing ego of his own modeled on the analyst's ego).[12] In such interpretations, meaning is given primacy. The goal is to convey a meaning—a connection the analyst believes to exist between the analysand's relationship to his older brother and his earlier relationship to his father, for example—in such a way that the analysand comes to understand it precisely as the analyst does.

Impact Versus Meaning

Interpretation is an enunciation without an enunciated.
— Lacan (2007, p. 58)

It is false to think that an analysis comes to a successful dénouement because the analysand consciously realizes something. . . . What is at stake is not a move from an unconscious level, plunged in darkness, to the conscious level, the seat of clarity, by some mysterious elevator. . . . What is at stake is not, in fact, a move to consciousness but, rather, to speech . . . and that speech must be heard by someone.
— Lacan (2001, pp. 139–140)

Can interpretations in which meaning is given primacy hit the real? Can they have an effect on the unconscious? In the analytic setting, interpretations that aim at tying down a single meaning that is clear and distinct commonly shut the analysand down, in a sense, putting a stop to his discourse and stemming the flow of his associations. Such interpretations may well suffer from banality and merit no further comment, closing doors instead of opening them. The more convincing they seem to the analysand, the more likely they are to concern things that he has in fact already discovered or thought about himself. And even if they are new to the analysand, he is likely to simply latch on to the ideas expressed in them and incorporate them into his thinking about himself instead of taking them further. In a word, one might say that the analysand's thinking (or his ego) recrystallizes around easily graspable interpretations, whereas the goal of psychoanalytic work with neurotics is to thwart such crystallizations.

The neurotic very often comes to analysis with all kinds of preformed understandings of his situation—understandings that block his ability to see what

---

[12] Freud (1940/1964, p. 175) warned against this: "However much the analyst may be tempted to become a teacher, model and ideal for other people and to create man in his own image, he should not forget that that is not his task in the analytic relationship, and indeed that he will be disloyal to his task if he allows himself to be led on by his inclinations. If he does, he will only be repeating the mistake of the parents who crushed their child's independence by their influence, and he will only be replacing the patient's earlier dependence by a new one." This mistake is, nevertheless, repeated by numerous practitioners who believe that it heralds an "alliance" between the so-called healthy part of the analysand's ego and the analyst.

he is contributing to the situation and what his real stake in it is. The goal is not to get him to substitute the analyst's understandings for his own understandings (that is, to internalize her point of view) but rather to get him to become suspicious of all meanings and understandings insofar as they partake of rationalization and fantasy.[13] If he is happy to view things in a certain way, he likely has an investment in seeing them that way, for this way of seeing things props up a certain image he has of himself, whether positive or negative. The analyst's concern is to emphasize the partiality of that image—in other words, the degree to which that image includes only a part of himself. Her concern is not to provide a new meaning of his predicament, but rather to unpack, unfold, and in a sense deconstruct the meanings he is inclined to attribute to it. Should she provide a new meaning (or "signified," as Lacan often called it), he is likely to seize upon it and stop thinking for himself; while this might make sense in certain desperate circumstances where the analysand is at the end of his rope and contemplating doing something rash, it is hardly conducive to pushing back the boundaries of his ego to encompass ever more of what he has repressed.

An interpretation that conveys a meaning that one can easily understand is simply not a psychoanalytic interpretation, strictly speaking.[14] It is, rather, tantamount to suggestion. The point of a psychoanalytic interpretation, like that of so many of the other psychoanalytic techniques I have mentioned in previous chapters, is not to give the analysand some specific meaning to latch on to but rather to put him to work. Questioning, punctuating, and scanding are all designed to elicit, unfold, and at times explode the meanings implicit in the analysand's speech, impelling him to strive to put into words what he has never before said.

Meaning and the Nefarious Power of Suggestion

An interpretation cannot present just any old meaning.
        — Lacan (1978, p. 250)

Analytic interpretation is not designed to be understood; it is designed to make waves.
        — Lacan (1976, p. 35)

Interpretations that provide a single, readily graspable meaning should be understood as suggestions because they offer a specific way of thinking or seeing

---

[13] As Spotnitz (1999, p. 260) said, "Understanding alone doesn't help anyone get well."
[14] Lacan (1966, p. 13) provided the following ancillary thought: "An interpretation whose effects one understands is not a psychoanalytic interpretation."

things. If the analysand has a great deal of faith in the analyst, he will take the meanings conveyed in her interpretations very seriously, which will reinforce his position of dependency upon her. It was often remarked in the early days of hypnotic treatment involving suggestion that patients had to return time and again to the doctor to have the latter renew his suggestions; this indicates that suggestions are only as effective and long-lasting as is the patient's faith in the hypnotist. That faith tends to dwindle when contact with the hypnotist is broken off, implying that it is only the hypnotist's personal influence that is responsible for the admittedly spectacular improvements sometimes made after treatment by suggestion. We might say that the patient's conviction that he can do certain things is never internalized in the course of treatment by suggestion; he must always be convinced anew by the hypnotist—that is, by some other person.

The goal in psychoanalysis is quite different: Since people generally find ideas that they themselves arrive at far more convincing than those provided by others, and do not need to have such ideas constantly validated by other people, the analyst tries to bring the analysand to seek out answers on his own.[15] Although we have a tendency in our culture to think of the analyst as someone who provides answers, her primary purpose is to transform as many of the analysand's requests for answers from her into a will to find them for himself (this is why she, like the legendary Jew, "answers" so many of his questions with a question). Of course, he is not alone in his quest to find them, for the analyst assists him in his explorations, but she does her best to remain a discreet collaborator, a "silent partner" in many ways. To ensure that the finds and accomplishments of the analysand feel like they are his own to the greatest extent possible, the analyst generally chimes in only when he is but one short step from saying something that he seems to be circling around without being able to say it.[16] Her job is not to feed him with the

---

[15] There are, of course, people who at least initially are far more inclined to believe ideas proposed by others than ideas they come upon themselves.

[16] As Lacan (2007, p. 130) said, "The interpretation that the analyst provides is not the knowledge found in the subject but what is added to that knowledge in order to give it a meaning." This statement made by Lacan in 1970—and others made later, such as "Far too many analysts are in the habit of never opening their mouths" (Lacan, 1974–1975, February 11, 1975) and "Analysts often believe that their profession involves staying silent. . . . It is a mistake, a deviation, when analysts say so little" (Lacan, 1976, p. 42)—suggests to me that Lacan by no means considered interpretation to be "dead," as has been recently claimed by certain of his followers. Serge Cottet (1994) seems to have inspired this claim when, at a meeting in June of 1993, he referred to "the decline of interpretation," which was then taken up and amplified by others, in particular by J.-A. Miller (1996, p. 13), who declared that "interpretation is dead." Examination of their comments on the subject, however, indicates that they simply mean that the old "classical" form of interpretation in which the analyst directly tells the analysand the meaning of something (a slip, dream, or symptom) is dead, not the newer Lacanian

proverbial fish of her interpretations, but rather to help him learn how to fish.[17] Note that psychoanalysts of many non-Lacanian persuasions still cleave to the idea that the analyst, in interpreting, offers the analysand a specific signification; Lacanians, however, strive to interpret in such a way—as we shall see shortly—that the analysand finds the significations himself, or comes face to face with the fact that what he has been saying makes no sense at all. (This is not to say that the analysand, in this form of psychoanalysis, quickly gets to the point where he can dispense with the analyst altogether, for the presence of an other to whom one speaks remains crucial for all analysis insofar as we all continue to rationalize and to keep certain ideas out of mind indefinitely.)[18]

Dispensing a specific meaning invites agreement and at times even gratitude, reinforcing the analysand's dependent, infantilized position—for if he needs the analyst to provide such meanings, he must be unable to come up with them himself. Such specific meanings can also be intensely gratifying to the analysand, for they give him a validated way of thinking about himself, perhaps a new and satisfying identity for himself (this is one of the reasons why Lacan, 2001, p. 551, emphasized the sound of the French word *sens*—in English, "sense" or "meaning"—in the French word *jouissance* by writing it *jouis-sens*, which literally means "enjoy(s) meaning"; see also Lacan, 1990, p. 10). But in work with neurotics, new identifications should not necessarily be encouraged, since the enjoyment they bring (which may at times lead to results that the analyst herself considers desirable—in other words, "good" for the analysand—and that the analysand finds therapeutic) tends to put a stop to the work of the analysis, in effect short-circuiting the process of examining what is behind all such ego identifications.

---

form of interpretation, which is oracular, equivocal, "half-said," and more likely to cut off or destabilize meaning making than to try to tie down some specific meaning. Lacan (1973, p. 252) also indicated (in his French postface to Seminar XI, not included in Lacan, 1978) that psychoanalysts have "a duty to interpret."

There may well be a place for certain kinds of interpretations very early on in the analyst's work with certain analysands—indeed, at times, a somewhat startling interpretation may be the only thing that will allow certain people to become analysands in the first place. Nevertheless, I would recommend that such early, unexpected interpretations be given only by quite experienced analysts when they have a fairly good sense, after having conducted many analyses, that someone is not engaged and not likely to become engaged in the analytic process without a jolt of some kind.

[17] Analysts often feel compelled to give ("feed") the analysand interpretations at certain times when he insistently asks for something—some even refer to it as "demand feeding" —but it is generally sufficient to ask a question of one's own. Winnicott probably initiated the "feeding frenzy" among analysts with his oft repeated quote from one of his analysands: "Good management such as I have experienced during this hour is a feed" (see, for example, Winnicott, 1960/1965a, p. 141).

[18] For a similar point of view, see Casement (1991, p. 7): "Nobody can know his or her own unconscious without help from some other person."

Alternatively, dispensing a specific meaning may invite disagreement and suspicion of the analyst's perspicacity, leading to what is at times sterile intellectual debate and a likely waning, albeit temporary, of the analyst's ability to occupy the place of what Lacan calls "the subject supposed to know" (see Fink, 1997, pp. 28–33). Briefly stated, "the subject supposed to know" refers to the fact that the analysand tends to assume that the knowledge about what ails him—which is in fact located, loosely speaking, in his own unconscious—is located in the analyst.[19] It is this projection of his unconscious knowledge onto the analyst that allows the analysand to seek out his own truth via the analyst, but this projection (which is often of capital importance almost to the very end of a long-term analysis) can be jeopardized if the analyst repeatedly provides very specific interpretations that the analysand considers to lack credibility. This is one of the reasons why analysts, whether early on in their careers or later, so often proffer interpretations in the form of questions; they seem to believe that the analyst's position as someone who is supposed to know is less likely to be jeopardized by a question like "Do you think there is any kind of connection here with what you said earlier about your father?" than by a direct assertion like "Just as it was with your father" (a declarative, assertive, asseverative, or apophantic claim)[20]; I will examine the veracity of that belief later on.

The analyst must occasionally proffer specific meanings—for example, when the analysis has gotten bogged down due to a certain kind of transference that the analyst is unable to work around. In these cases the analyst must hazard an unambiguous interpretation of the transference (which I otherwise generally do not advise; see Chapter 7) with the understanding that she is likely to be off base but that the analysand will set her straight in word or deed (see Lacan, 2006, p. 225; Fink, 2004, p. 6). A flood of such straightforward interpretations could well jeopardize the analysis, but assuming some good work is being accomplished, an analysis can usually stand rocky moments like that from time to time (Freud, 1937/1964, pp. 261–262).

Nevertheless, in the interest of putting the analysand to work, interpretations should generally be polyvalent—that is, susceptible of at least two meanings, the analysand being given the task of exploring all of them. Should the analysand inquire of the analyst which meaning was intended, the analyst

---

[19] The analyst, of course, "knows he is not" the subject who knows (Lacan, 1966–1967, June 21, 1967).
[20] For a discussion of the term *apophantic*, see Lacan (1973, p. 30). *Apophantic* comes from Aristotle's *On Interpretation* where one finds the term *logos apophantikos* (meaning "declarative discourse"), which Heidegger (1975/1982, p. 180) glossed as follows: "discourse that has the specific function of showing, exhibiting, displaying, which in English is called assertion, statement, proposition."

can respond by turning the question around: "Was there one that you assumed I intended?" This response is likely to elicit facets of the transference that may not yet have been elucidated—thoughts the analysand has about himself that he has projected onto the analyst.

In the interest of polyvalence, the analyst does well to use common idiomatic expressions that she extracts from the analysand's discourse, since they often have multiple meanings, as well as prepositions that in current American English have come to mean virtually anything (such as *with*). In working from the analysand's own words in this way, and in eschewing clarity as an objective,[21] the analyst may find that her interpretations are still more polyvalent than she thought when she first enunciated them, resonating with yet other aspects of the analysand's experience that she had not consciously had in mind when she spoke. This makes her utterances both richer and harder to pin down.

If the goal of interpretation, then, is not to provide meaning but to have an impact of a certain sort, what kind of impact do we have in mind?

New Material: Spurring Along the Analysis

Interpretation is not the testing of a truth that would be decided by a yes or a no; it unleashes the truth as such.
                                                      — Lacan (1970–1971, January 13, 1971)

King: "Will you hear this letter with attention?"
Berowne: "As we would hear an oracle."
— Shakespeare, Love's Labor's Lost, I, I

As Edward Glover (1931) indicated long ago, interpretation aims to be *productive* in the therapy, that is, to elicit new material. Lacan (2006), discussing this viewpoint some three decades later, wrote:

Everyone acknowledges in his own way that to confirm that an interpretation is well founded, it is not the conviction with which it is received by the subject that counts, its well-foundedness instead being gauged by the material that emerges afterward.

---

[21] In this sense, the analyst is like Alan Greenspan, former chairman of the Federal Reserve Board, who once said, "I worry incessantly that I might be too clear."

But psychologizing superstition has such a powerful grip on our minds that people always seek out the phenomenon of well-foundedness in the subject's assent, entirely overlooking the consequences of what Freud says about *Verneinung* [negation] as a form of avowal—to say the least, negation by the subject cannot be treated as equivalent to drawing a blank. (p. 595)

The analyst's goal in interpreting is not to say something with which the analysand is likely to agree (although the beginning therapist is sometimes inclined to provide such interpretations to prove to the analysand that she is giving him something he will find worthwhile). As Freud (1937/1964) put it:

A plain "Yes" from a patient is by no means unambiguous. It can indeed signify that he recognizes the correctness of the construction that has been presented to him; but it can also be meaningless, or can even deserve to be described as "hypocritical," since it may be convenient for his resistance to make use of an assent in such circumstances in order to prolong the concealment of a truth that has not been discovered. The "Yes" has no value unless it is followed by indirect confirmations, unless the patient, immediately after his "Yes," produces new memories which complete and extend the construction. (p. 262)[22]

Indeed, cases in which the analysand disagrees with the analyst's interpretation may be of more value to the analysis ultimately,[23] assuming his disagreement is vehement rather than simply indifferent. The more adamant or fervent the denial, the more likely it is that the interpretation hit a nerve, so to speak. Although it may not be possible to explore that nerve there and then, the analyst can make a mental note of it, in the hope of returning to it at some later date, albeit perhaps indirectly or in different terms. Recall Freud's (1905a/1953, p. 46) insightful maxim, "A reproach which misses the mark gives no lasting offence," which we might reformulate for the analytic situation as: "An interpretation that misses the mark does not provoke endless denials and refutations."

Nevertheless, the more important point here is that the value of an interpretation must be judged by what it leads to—that is, by whether it furthers

---

[22] On the difference between construction and interpretation, Freud (1937/1964, p. 261) said, "'Interpretation' applies to something that one does to some single element of the material such as an association or a parapraxis [that is, a slip or bungled action]," whereas a construction is something that covers a large swath of analytic material.

[23] For some interesting remarks on the analysand's disagreement with the analyst's interpretation, see Freud (1937/1964, pp. 262–263).

the analysis or not (Freud, 1937/1964, p. 265).[24] In certain cases it may lead to an immediate abundance of associations, while in others it may have a more delayed effect, spurring dreams, daydreams, or ruminations for some time after the session in which it was proffered. In still others it may fall flat, leading to no new material (whether tending to confirm or invalidate the interpretation) in the short term or the long term. Of course, it is a complicated matter to determine what ultimately furthers the analysis and what does not. Certain sets of associations may seem very encouraging at first but ultimately grind to a halt, leading to an impasse. Certain lines of thinking sparked by an interpretation may seem productive at first only to be rejected as missing the point later. Nevertheless, one often has the impression that many such lines of thinking need to be explored and in some sense exhausted before more durable, farther-reaching lines can be found. One does not always hit on the best line of thought right away, nor was Rome built in a day.

The concern with generating new material led Lacan to at times characterize interpretation as a kind of "oracular speech."[25] Much like the Delphic oracle, the analyst says something sufficiently polyvalent that it *resonates* even though it is not understood, arousing curiosity and a desire to divine why the analyst said what she said. In the best of cases, the analysand is set to work not primarily at a conscious level—where we might find him commenting at the next session, "I was thinking about what you said last time, and I agree in one sense, but on the other hand . . ." (a kind of commentary that is discouraged by the very polyvalence of oracular interpretation)—but at the unconscious level, where it might lead to unexpected images, dreams, fantasies, or thoughts not prompted by conscious speculation.

Oracular speech is not speech that strives to demonstrate mastery of meaning—to demonstrate that it fully understands the analysand's discourse—but rather is evocative speech, equivocal speech, speech that one must project meaning onto, speech that one must work to attribute meaning to. As Lacan (1975a, p. 16) put it, "the oracle neither reveals nor hides: $\sigma\eta\mu\alpha\acute{\iota}\nu\epsilon\iota$, it makes a sign." And a sign—for example, the trajectory of a swallow's flight over the water or the appearance of a sacrificial animal's entrails—has to be read, has to

---

[24] This is not to say that just because the analysand goes on "blathering" after an interpretation, that the interpretation was useful. As Lacan (1966–1967, June 21, 1967) put it, "If interpretation were merely what yielded material—I mean, if one radically eliminates the dimension of truth—interpretation would be nothing but suggestion."

[25] For a discussion of analytic interpretation as oracular in nature, see Lacan (1970–1971, January 13, 1971, 2006, pp. 106, 588, 1973, p. 37, 1975a, p. 16). See also Stéphanie Gilet-Le Bon's (1995) fine commentary on the oracle.

be interpreted. It has no inherent meaning; it is up to the observer to give it one. The Greek σημαίνει also means "indicates," "shows," or "points to"; when someone points to something—say, a tree—we cannot know a priori whether she is trying to get us to notice its species, its shape, its bark, its color, its leaves, or the bird's nest in it, among other possibilities. Interpretation must have the virtue of being "allusive," Lacan suggested (2006, p. 641), equivocation being one of the most productively provocative instruments in the psychoanalytic toolbox.

Interpretation Does Not Provide a Metalanguage

Interpretation . . . points to desire, to which it is, in a certain sense, identical. Desire is, in sum, interpretation itself.

— *Lacan (1978, p. 176)*

If there is a cardinal law of psychoanalysis, it is to avoid talking nonsense, even in the name of analytic categories. No wild analysis: don't throw out words that have meaning only to the analyst.

— *Lacan (1976, p. 34)*

For many decades, psychoanalytic theory served as the basis of a great many interpretations made by analysts; the Oedipus complex was the great template, the overriding grid through which the analysand's experience was seen. The language of analytic theory was considered to be the perfect language within which to express the analysand's experience—in that sense it could be thought of as a metalanguage with respect to the language spontaneously employed by the analysand—and it was sometimes even thought that it sufficed to reduce his experience to analytic theory for the analyst's work to be done, so to speak. Once the analysand's life had been formulated in the language of the theory, it was believed that his symptoms should disappear. By the 1920s, Freud had already noticed that interpretations based on theoretical constructs like the Oedipus complex were no longer effective: Patients coming to see analysts had already read several analytic texts, had already framed their own experience using psychoanalytic concepts before ever lying on the couch, and would proffer statements like, "My problem, Doc, is that I'm still in love with my mother and that's why I hate my father." Oedipal formulations had become so commonplace as to no longer have any effect when used as the basis for interpretations. As additions were made to the theory—whether they were later Freudian concepts such as the id and the superego, Abraham's partial object, or Klein's good and bad objects—analysts often tried to translate their analysands' experience into those; such translations may have had some impact at the outset, but their effect soon wore off as later psychoanalytic concepts were again assimilated by the public.[26]

Rightly enough, analysts like Casement (1991) objected to this form of interpretation because it overlooks the particularity of each analysand and tends to look at patients only from the perspective of what they all have in common: supposedly universal conflicts like the Oedipal complex, or supposedly universal developmental phases like the depressive position. As Casement (pp. 206–209) indicated, we cannot immediately assume that silence on the analysand's part signifies resistance just because analytic theory suggests that it might on certain occasions; in many, if not most cases, its meaning is far more complex than that.

But we must take our critique of the notion of interpretation as a kind of perfect metalanguage further still (Soler, 1996). Translating the analysand's experience from one idiom to another—from his quotidian language to psychoanalytic jargon—cannot change his experience; it simply puts a theoretical meaning on it. He may well be satisfied with that meaning, for he feels that by providing it, the analyst is initiating him into psychoanalytic theory and taking him to be a serious candidate for analytic training or a serious analyst-in-training. His satisfaction with it, however, is likely to serve as an obstacle to him going further, and he is likely to feel that a theoretical formulation is the last word: It provides a final explanation with which he should be content.

This can lead to a short-circuiting of the psychoanalytic process, which, in its fullest expression, involves facing the fact that there are no such final explanations or ultimate answers. Although the analysand repeatedly wonders about the why and wherefore of his direction in life—about why he sided with one parent against the other, why he believed his parents wanted that certain something above all else from him, why he accepted to be humiliated by someone, why he complied with someone's every wish, why he did things that in retrospect were very harmful to himself and seem to have blocked his progress in life—and although he comes up with myriad reasons that explain in part what seem to have been choices that he made at different crucial moments or turning points, something always remains unexplained and, indeed, unexplainable. The further back in time his explorations go, the less discernible his motives seem to become. Rather than try to fill in these holes in his explanations or gloss over these enigmatic decisions with theoretical accounts or

---

[26] In this respect, it might be thought that analysis was a victim of its own success. This assumes, however, that translation into theoretical terms is a valid form of interpretation in the first place.

normalizing comments ("everyone has to do something like that to separate from his parents and individuate"; see Chapter 9), *the analyst must aim to bring this lack of explanations to the fore.*[27]

There is no ultimate answer or final explanation why one is a certain way or did a certain thing. There are certain constructions one can arrive at regarding one's life direction, but in the final analysis it just is, and *one must come to accept that.* One must come to own the decisions or choices that do not seem to have been decisions or choices. Just as a child's endless questions (Why is the sky blue? Why does light refract? Why does light take the form of waves? etc.) sooner or later lead to something unanswerable—and it is not always even clear that the child's true motive is to know the answer—the analysand's endless pondering leads to an imponderable, something ultimately unknowable that must simply be accepted.

There is always something for which an answer cannot be provided. The parents, when questioned by the analysand regarding the why and wherefore of early events, cannot provide anything other than their own points of view, assuming they even recall the events in question; nor can the analyst propose anything other than a series of possible reconstructions, none of which may acquire the force of conviction. None of these possible repositories of knowledge has the answer, meaning that knowledge itself is flawed in some respect. The Other (with a capital O) as the repository of all knowledge—that is one way of understanding Lacan's term—is lacking, is incomplete, and there is nothing to be done about it except to accept the predicament.

This is one way of talking about what Freud called "castration," something that applies to both men and women and involves our all-too-obvious limitations: We are not immortal, our days being numbered; we do not know when we will die; we cannot do all things, become proficient in all areas, or master all fields; and there are limits to our knowledge. Just as Freud (1937/1964, p. 252) said that the analyst must lead the analysand to confront the "bedrock" of castration (suggesting that the analyst can do no more than lead him to that point, it being up to the analysand to accept or reject the fact that he is castrated), Lacan argued that the analyst must lead the analysand to confront the lack in the Other and find a way to help him accept that lack or limitation and go beyond it.

---

[27] Lacan refers to this "lack of explanations" as the "lack in the Other" or "barred Other" ($\cancel{A}$), and to the analysand's encounter with this lack in the Other through his speech in the analysis as S($\cancel{A}$), which designates "the signifier of the lack in the Other." The fundamental fantasy (see Chapter 6) is what usually covers over this lack for the analysand and it is only when the fundamental fantasy comes into view and begins to be shaken up that the analysand is forced to grapple with this lack in the Other.

A stubborn insistence upon finding the final answer suggests a libidinal investment in continuing to blame one's predicament on circumstances or on other people, whereas in the vast majority of cases, circumstances and the actions of others can only explain so much and the analysand must finally accept that he himself played a part, indeed a very important part, in the way his life unfolded.

That libidinal investment implies a certain fixation in the way that the analysand finds enjoyment (or jouissance, a kind of satisfaction that the analysand does not necessarily experience as pleasurable or enjoyable per se) in life, as well as an unwillingness to find enjoyment in other ways. Yet this fixation is precisely what the analysand most often complains about when he first comes to analysis: He is not enjoying himself in life (perhaps he used to enjoy himself more or senses that others around him enjoy themselves more), his way of life is making him suffer instead of giving him pleasure, and he does not seem to be able to break out of this pattern of making himself miserable. I have referred to this elsewhere as a "satisfaction crisis" or a "jouissance crisis" (Fink, 1997, pp. 8–9), in which the analysand's former ways of enjoying himself (whether in an explicitly sexual manner or otherwise) have broken down and he comes to analysis asking the analyst to help him restore them to their former efficacy. The analyst, on the other hand, hopes to bring the analysand to enjoy himself in a new way, in a way that does not involve investments in seeing the world as he had before and blaming others and circumstances for his predicament.

Should the analyst fill the gaps in his explanations with explanations of her own, she will leave the analysand where he started instead of inspiring or provoking him to go beyond that. He will have a new way of seeing things, a new way of understanding his life, but he will continue to suffer as he did before, and he will continue to get "enjoyment" in the same ways that were insufferable to him prior to beginning analysis.

This is one of the reasons why Lacan (1977b, pp. 15–16) asserted that "interpretation need be no truer than it is false. It must be on target, which in the final analysis means that it stanches the call for meaning, in a situation in which meaning seems instead to be stirred up," this situation being one in which something has been repressed and "an inexhaustible flow of significations is called upon"—significations (indeed, rationalizations) that "throw themselves into the hole repression has produced." Lacan's approach to interpretation aims at something beyond inciting the analysand to bring forth ever more new meanings, although that is obviously important at the beginning of an analysis; later on, the emphasis goes on bringing about a change in "subjective position," a change in the way the analysand gets enjoyment in life, a change that puts an end to the attempt to endlessly try to explain what is ultimately unexplainable.

Examples of Equivocal Interpretations

It is only through equivocation that interpretation operates. There must be something in the signifier that resonates.

—Lacan (2005b, p. 17)

The effects of an interpretation are incalculable even if they are calculated.
—Aparicio (1996, p. 55)

In many cases, an interpretation can be constructed simply by citing something the analysand himself has said that was equivocal, for the analysand often has not heard the ambiguity in what he has said. In the case of an analysand of mine in the prime of life, who had remarked on several occasions that he was not in the position in the corporate hierarchy he should normally be in by his age and who often complained about bosses and other people in his life who tried to act with him like father figures, I simply repeated back to him a few of his own words when he said, "I've always stumbled on my own ascent to power." When I echoed, "ascent to power," he realized that the sounds composing *ascent* could also be understood as *assent*, and he began wondering about his refusal to assume power, his unwillingness to take any power in work situations, delegate responsibility to others, and so on. That allowed our discussions of power to leave the abstract plane of a generalized critique of authority as such (enlightening though it had been at the outset) and turn to his own suppressed or covertly expressed wishes to dominate others, lord it over others, and act aggressively toward others.

Interpretations based on citations of the analysand's speech are perhaps the most common and often the least shocking to the analysand; in my experience, analysands generally do not even think of them as interpretations.[28] Nevertheless, selective citations and citations taken out of context play on ambiguities in the analysand's discourse, ambiguities that the analyst considers to be of some

---

[28] This is one of their nice features, in that they allow for confusion about who authored them. As we shall see in Chapter 7, interpretations are often heard by the analysand as coming from the person he transferentially projects the analyst to be (a critical figure from his past, for example), making them difficult for the analysand to hear or accept. Interpretations that take something the analysand said—perhaps repeating something someone else said—out of context have the virtue of skirting this transferential conundrum (see Lacan, 2007, pp. 39–40).

importance (in certain cases, there are so many ambiguities in the analysand's speech that the analyst must pick and choose only a few of the most promising among them), calculating—albeit perhaps in a split second—that they will be of some use in opening up new avenues of discussion. The ambiguity in this case was a simple homophony: *ascent* sounds just like *assent* in most (if not all) forms of contemporary spoken American English.

In another case, the homophony was not as complete: I deliberately repeated an analysand's "We were both riding" (riding bicycles in a dream he had just told me) in such a way as to make "riding" sound like "writing" (which is quite easy to do in American English), for he had been talking for several sessions about his writing. Shortly after that I varied it by spelling aloud the word "righting," insinuating that his writing was perhaps tied up with the project of righting certain perceived wrongs, setting certain things or people straight.

In still other cases, the ambiguity in the cited portion of the analysand's speech is grammatical or idiomatic.[29] An analysand, whose older brother engaged for several years in a very specific sexual practice with him while the younger brother pretended to be asleep, talked for a number of sessions about how repugnant he found the idea of paying for sex. Although he had occasionally been tempted to pay for it, he would always "push it away," worried that the potential paid partner would see him as a "beast," "a repulsive presence," adding, "and I wouldn't know it." This was a fair summary of what he thought about his older brother, who had dominated him in numerous contexts, making him pay, in so many different ways, for his submission, and whom he would have liked to make pay in kind—that is, in suffering and humiliation. It sufficed for me to isolate the words "pay for it" for him to connect money, domination, and suffering and to realize that for him to pay someone else to have sex with him would mean assuming his brother's role in relation to him, at least at some level—something he was loath to do. Beyond this somewhat straightforward connection, his more general interest in making other people pay soon came to the fore. Here it was the multiple idiomatic meanings of the verb "to pay" and of the idiomatic expression "to (make someone) pay for something" that provided this very simple interpretation with a certain richness.

---

[29] Lacan (1973, pp. 48–49) proposed that, in interpreting, the analyst plays on three different types of equivocation: homophony, grammar, and logic. As an example of logical equivocation, consider the following statement relayed to me by an analysand: "Nothing is better than something bad." The speaker's ostensible intent was to say that it is better to be left with nothing than have something bad happen, but it can obviously be heard as praising tragic events (grammatical and logical equivocation obviously come together here, grammar being so crucial to logic in its everyday—that is, unformalized—usage).

The goal in this case was obviously not to reveal a specific "hidden meaning," but rather to get the analysand to wonder what he meant by "paying for sex," for what he meant was more enigmatic than he initially thought. Indeed, analysands often respond to analysts' citations of their equivocal speech with comments like "What did I mean by that anyway?" or "What does that even mean?" (Aparicio, 1996, p. 53).

Naturally, not all interpretation is strictly confined to citation of the analysand's speech. In the case of an analysand who, in discussing her frequent nausea in her adult life, recalled going into her parents' bedroom on several occasions when she was five or six to ask for Alka-Seltzer™ because she was nauseous, I recalled that her favorite sibling was six years younger than her. Although a great many things went through my mind very quickly, including the thought that she had likely seen her mother nauseous during pregnancy and probably wanted to be pregnant like or instead of her mother, imagining herself having daddy's baby, I simply asked if she had seen anyone else take Alka-Seltzer. She indicated that she had seen both parents do so on occasion, recalling first her father's hangovers and then her mother's sporadic morning sickness. The analysand then added that, as a child, she would make her stomach hurt by overeating (something she still sometimes did as an adult), at which point I proffered: "As if you were bringing on morning sickness." The words morning sickness were her own, but I added a few to them; and not forgetting that the sounds that compose morning can also be spelled mourning, I paused slightly between the words "morning" and "sickness" to see if she would hear "bringing on mourning" too.

We had talked about mourning the loss of various people in her life in prior sessions, but her responses to this interpretation went far beyond anything I might have imagined at that instant: mourning the loss of her mother's attention as her younger siblings were born (this one was predictable); her mother's mourning of her own lost youth, having given the analysand the distinct impression that having children was the source of all of her misery; and the analysand's decision early in life to never bear a child herself. Perhaps her periodic stomach aches over several decades were a reminder that she had never fully accepted that decision and had never fully mourned the children she might have had if she had gone through with her two pregnancies. Prior to making that interpretation, I had had no idea that she had ever been pregnant, much less twice. To paraphrase Lacan (1966 p. 13), an interpretation whose effects can be predicted completely in advance is not a psychoanalytic interpretation.

An important aim of this interpretation was to highlight the analysand's participation in the process—she was actively making her stomach hurt by repeatedly overeating (perhaps imitating or rivaling her mother's hearty appetite during pregnancy and making herself feel sick like her mother)—and to elicit discussion of whatever desire or longing was presumably behind it. Although the analysand was aware that she had entertained the idea of adopting a child, she was quite unaware of any wish she might still have to bear a child herself, despite her conscious decision earlier in life not to do so. In this sense, the interpretation managed to hit something she had never before contemplated, something ostensibly repressed: a desire.

Since virtually all speech (if not absolutely all speech) is ambiguous, the analyst cannot always think through every possible meaning of an interpretation before she enunciates it. Even if she had the time to do so—which she does not given the importance of striking while the iron is hot, most interpretations relying very significantly on a highly specific speech context that differs markedly from moment to moment—she could never foresee every possible way her speech could be heard by the analysand, at least in part because the analyst is inclined to understand what she is about to say on the basis of her intended meaning(s) and can only hear it as if she were another person once it has been enunciated. Thus the interpretation she provides often turns out to be polyvalent in ways that she had not expected: Although her interpretation was calculated (she had foreseen some of the possible meanings and effects of her speech), she may get more than she bargained for, so to speak, the effects of her speech being in some sense incalculable.

This perhaps accounts for at least some of fledgling analysts' "interpretation anxiety"—a variation on writer's block, writers sometimes fearing that they will have no control over things once they put them down on paper—and their marked preference for couching anything bordering on an interpretation in the form of a question. They soon learn, I suspect, that interpretations framed as questions are just as likely to open an unpredictable (and unpredictably long) series of doors as interpretations that are framed as assertions. In many cases, they are also afraid of saying something the analysand will find stupid and reject, and they feel they are taking a safer course by casting their interpretations in the form of queries. But such interpretations are taken to include just as many unfeeling or absurd insinuations by certain analysands as interpretations that are proffered apophantically, and analysts generally gain little by hedging their bets in this way. Such interpretations lose much of their potential surprise factor: Their ability to startle the analysand in a productive way is compromised and their force is attenuated, for it is as if the analyst were saying, "Don't pay too much attention to what I'm saying, it's only a speculation." Moreover, there is something fundamentally dishonest about the analyst presenting something of which she is quite convinced in such a syrupy, watered-down way. She is likely to become more insistent should the analysand not take the interpretation as seriously as she had hoped, but she has only herself to blame for she herself invited him to take it with a grain of salt by framing it as a question.

Brevity Is the Soul of Wit

Where words are scarce, they are seldom spent in vain.
    — *Shakespeare,* Richard II, *II, I*

It is insofar as an apt [juste] *interpretation extinguishes a symptom that the truth can be specified as poetic.*
                                        — *Lacan* (1976–1977, *April 19, 1977*)

I hope it is clear from the several examples I have provided here that provocative, productive interpretations need not be long-winded. Like long, involved questions that tend to lose or confuse the analysand, verbose interpretations often become diffuse, and difficult, if not impossible, to respond to.

Consider the following example from the psychoanalytic literature: Casement (1991) transcribed an interpretation he made with a patient who was prone to falling silent for long periods of time during sessions, even though she was obviously distressed. One day, after a prolonged silence, she stammered, "I am sorry, but I can't help being difficult like this." Casement, connecting this with the fact that her mother would often accuse her of being difficult when she was silent and would turn away from her when she tried to speak to her, replied,

> Perhaps it is precisely this difficulty, in communicating what you are feeling, that you need to convey to me now; but you expect me not to be prepared to stay with you if I actually experience some of that difficulty, so you feel that you must apologize. (p. 209)

Perhaps Casement did not say all of that at once to his analysand, and simply put it together like that for the purposes of his exposition, but if not there seem to be too many separate threads here leading off in too many different directions at the same time. Given the analysand's response to this interpretation, as Casement reports it, he seems to have conveyed what he meant to convey— that she was expecting him to be like her mother, who could bear neither her silence nor her speech, hence her apology. But he opted neither for economy of expression nor polyvalence, both of which are, of course, more easily found in hindsight than in the heat of the moment. It seems to me to be a good general principle—if one is going to provide specific meanings at all—to avoid interpretations with so many moving parts, so to speak, so many separate ideas.[30]

Just as brevity is the soul of wit, the punchier the interpretation, the better. And interpretations need not be devoid of wit, although one would hardly know it from the incredibly earnest, heartfelt, and even mournful tone of much of the work and of many of the interpretations reported in the contemporary psychoanalytic literature, which offers a striking contrast to the often playful and witty tone of the literature from the 1920s and 1930s (see, for example, Silberer's 1921 book *Der Zufall und die Koboldstreiche des Unbewussten,*"Chance and the Impish Pranks of the Unconscious"). I suspect that this is not primarily because analysts are seeing ever more severe cases of psychopathology, but rather because, having largely turned their attention from exploring the unconscious to developing a parenting relationship between themselves and their analysands, they have little experience with the wit involved in unconscious formations like dreams, daydreams, and fantasies.

Although humor is not called for at most times in the majority of sessions, it can occasionally be a useful way (and sometimes the only way) to get through to certain analysands. Moreover, there is no reason why analysis should not be fun, at some level, for both analysand and analyst; as Lacan (1988a, p. 77) said, "The closer we get to psychoanalysis being funny, the more it is real psychoanalysis." Indeed, moments of fun may be the only thing that keeps certain analysands coming back when the going gets tough.

An obsessive patient of mine, whose desire was tied up with impotence, emasculation, and ineffectiveness at the outset of his analysis, repeatedly talked at one point about the conflict between his work with computers and his academic and literary writing. He spent a couple of sessions talking about his "obsession with UNIX," the computer operating system. When I indicated that the sound of the word could be spelled differently, like *eunuchs*, he laughed hysterically and at the next session told me that I had "killed" his obsession with learning computer languages. The unconscious, like the small child (and even many adults), takes "pleasure in nonsense" (Freud, 1905b/1960, p. 125) and makes connections between homonyms (like *UNIX* and *eunuchs*) that bear

---

[30] Other such long-winded interpretations can be found elsewhere in Casement's work (1991; see, in particular, pp. 43 and 45), even though use of his "internal supervisor" or of "trial identification" (see my discussion of these in Chapter 7) would theoretically have led him to avoid interpretations to which it was so difficult to respond (p. 41). Freud (1937/1964, p. 261) referred to such extensive interpretations as "constructions" as opposed to "interpretations," but that does not make them any more palatable to the analysand.

no semantic relation to each other. Symptoms often disguise their meaning and origin by taking advantage of such homonyms to form "verbal bridges" between one idea or wish and another that is seemingly unrelated (Freud, 1909/1955, p. 213).

Another analysand of mine was loath for some time to complain about her mother, even though there seemed to be plenty of things one might complain about. One day she told me that when she was young she often played a game in which she imagined herself as a certain Professor Betwick (I have changed the name here), "a mad scientist doing experiments in the basement." We talked about various aspects of the professor's personality and then turned to the name itself. To *wick* she associated *witch*, *wicca* (a sort of witch religion), and then *wicked*, immediately volunteering the expression "No rest for the wicked," which was often used in her household. I asked, "Is that why you work so hard?" for she had often indicated that she was a workaholic; perhaps she considered herself wicked and was paying for it by working all the time. After a little laughter on her part, there ensued a long discussion about work, evil spells, "the wicked witch of the west," the fact that she occasionally thought of herself as a witch, and so on. We then turned to the first part of the name: *Bet*. Although nothing came to mind at first, she eventually associated it with a shortened nickname form of her mother's first name: Elizabeth. The mother almost always went by Elizabeth, but there were a few people who called her Betty, Beth, and even Bet. At this point I said, "wicked Betty," and then, "Betty the witch," at which point the analysand burst out laughing.

I ended the session there and the next session led to discussion of a few of her mother's more wicked aspects and of why the analysand had given her favorite persona such a name: Was it to make fun of her mother without realizing it (neither she nor her mother nor anyone else in the family had made the connection, perhaps partly because she pronounced the first part of the name like *bate*, instead of *bet*)? to locate in herself the evil she saw in her mother? to protect herself from her mother's malevolent side? It was no doubt all of these and more. My interpretations, "wicked Betty" and "Betty the witch," had not closed the door to any of them and had instead opened the door to a multiplicity of them, leading to a lot of associative material. Moreover, insofar as there was probably a certain modicum of aggression and ridicule in her unconscious choice of this sobriquet (Betwick), my formulation allowed her to enjoy that aggression, to enjoy ridiculing her mother, something she never overtly allowed herself to do. Laughter permitted an expression—an expression that I rendered socially acceptable in the analytic setting—of some of her aggression, allowing her to see, in a nonpunishing, nonthreatening way, that she was inhabited by longstanding aggression toward her mother (and perhaps even by a wish to bait or bate her). Her unconscious had, in a manner of speaking, formulated a witticism of its own that satisfied some of her aggressive drive, a witticism that I simply spelled out. It was, I believe, an amusing experience for both of us.

In our quest to get at what is repressed, we must encourage verbal expression of drives that the neurotic carefully keeps under lock and key, so carefully at times that he has forgotten there was anything in the safe at all or even where he last buried the safe. This requires that we know whether we are working with neurotics or psychotics, and that we thus situate such expressions at the proper level. When a severely inhibited neurotic analysand of mine told the analyst whom he was seeing before he began seeing me about an aggressive fantasy he had involving her, her first reaction was to assess whether he was actually thinking of enacting that fantasy with her. Although such fantasies could be a sign of danger ahead in specific circumstances with certain psychotics, this analysand had given her ample proof of his considerable inhibition in life and of his general tendency to punish himself for everything rather than lash out at other people. By taking up his fantasy at the level of "reality," as if it were something of which she considered him capable, she effectively stopped him from ever mentioning any other aggressive fantasies again, which soon defeated the analysis. For neurotics there is a serious barrier between thought and deed, between thinking and doing, and one can quite safely encourage the verbal expression of the drives, no matter how violent. With psychotics this is not always the case, hence the importance of being able to distinguish between neurosis and psychosis. Indeed, with neurotics we must entertain all aspects of dreams and fantasies in which drive components show themselves, since they are aspects of the real that have likely never before been brought into speech and that often lead to repetitive behavior until they are articulated in as many ways as possible.

Rather than trying to assess whether her analysand was planning on enacting his fantasy with her, this analyst would have done well to verbally embrace the aggression in the fantasy by repeating the most libidinally charged words he used. When, in his analysis with me, he produced a dream in which there was a dying horse, a horse he associated with me, I repeated with some warmth, "Dying!" thereby punctuating and emphasizing the aggression behind it and simultaneously conveying to the analysand that even if he was afraid of what he would like to do to me, I was not. I did not see it as aimed at me as a living, breathing human being, but as an ordinary part of the transference— that is, as aimed at someone or something other than or beyond myself (see Chapter 7).

Further examples of interpretations, which always require one to supply enough of the rich text of the analysand's discourse in any one session, as well as a glimpse of the larger backdrop, to make them comprehensible—ideally one would present the entire analysis to make any one interpretation comprehensible, but this is rarely feasible—are found in the chapters that follow.[31]

---

[31] As I have not yet introduced Lacan's concept of object *a* in this book (see Chapter 8 for a brief account of it), I have not discussed interpretation here in terms of the way in which the analyst, especially in later stages of an analysis, works to isolate object *a* in the fundamental fantasy (mentioned in Chapter 6) and to separate the analysand from it through various kinds of scansions and other interventions that do not always easily fall under the heading of interpretation. (For commentary on these techniques, referred to by some as "the flip side of interpretation," see especially issue 32 of the French journal *La cause freudienne* (École de la Cause Freudienne, 1996), entitled "Vous ne dites rien.") Nor have I yet introduced Lacan's notions of the master (or unary) signifier S_1 and of the binary signifier S_2 (see Chapter 10 for a brief discussion of them); hence I have not discussed interpretation here in terms of the way in which the analyst at times cuts the analysand off before he can provide an S_2, a meaning to something (an S_1) that is purely and simply nonsensical, reserving that for a more advanced book on technique where the drives and jouissance can be treated in detail. Regarding this latter approach to interpretation, see, for example, Soler's (1996) comments:

> This other [form of] interpretation . . . does not say anything either: it detaches what Lacan for a long time called the signifier that is asemantic, outside of the chain, empty of signification, but full of jouissance. . . . This cut does not make one understand anything but rather reduces signification, I could almost say that it castrates signification, not for the benefit of meaning but for that of the detaching of the signs to which the subject is subjected. (p. 30)

The English reader can find some good commentary on Lacan's later notions of interpretation in Nobus (2000, Chapter 4).

6

Working with Dreams, Daydreams, and Fantasies

Within an analysis far more of the repressed is brought to light in connection with dreams than by any other method.

— *Freud* (*1923a/1961, p. 117*)

No one can practise the interpretation of dreams as an isolated activity: it remains a part of the work of analysis.

— *Freud* (*1925a/1961, p. 128*)

THE LION'S SHARE OF THE material of an analysis is usually provided by dreams and fantasies. Why is that? Because through its oneiric creations, the unconscious "joins in" the analytic work by, at one level at least, supplementing the story of the analysand's life told by the analysand, alluding to memories the analysand left out. In some cases the analysand may simply have failed to recall these memories when she first provided the broad outlines of her life story at the beginning of the analysis but is easily able to remember them when they are evoked by dream elements (that is, they were preconscious). In other cases, the analysand may have actually forgotten (that is, repressed) them. The unconscious *alludes* to such omitted memories; dreams, daydreams, and fantasies usually do not present memories directly but rather provide snippets of scenes or elements associated with scenes from the past: names, places, colors, sounds, smells, and so on. It is quite rare for such scenes to be directly reproduced in them; instead, they are usually conjured up in a new way, in a wishful way, allowing us to arrive at ideas about those scenes that might not have been evoked had the scenes come to mind in another way. This kind of creative (re)presentation of scenes from the past in the analysand's oneiric

101

productions permits us to divine other motives, intentions, or desires in the scenes they allude to than we might have if the analysand had simply reported them in her ordinary discourse about her life.

How are dreams, daydreams, and fantasies to be put to good use in analysis? While the analysand is likely to spontaneously try to read a dream as a whole— as a story that, with a few substitutions, can be more or less quickly applied to her life (reading, for example, a dream of jump-starting a shabby yellow convertible in terms of what she is trying to do in her relationship with a man she recently met)—the analyst must elicit associations to virtually every word and phrase in the analysand's verbal account of the dream without rejecting out of hand her rough and ready global interpretation: "Shabby?" "Yellow?" "Convertible?" he must query. Her associations to those elements may well lead far afield from the analysand's budding relationship. Alternatively (or in combination with the former method), the analysand may spontaneously try to "decode" the dream by replacing one or two elements with other elements, just as Joseph did when he interpreted Pharaoh's dream of the seven fat cows and the seven lean cows as referring to seven years of plenty and seven years of famine. The first tack that the analysand spontaneously tries corresponds to what Freud, in *The Interpretation of Dreams* (1900/1958, pp. 96–97), characterized as the "symbolic" method of dream interpretation; the second tack corresponds to the "decoding" method. These are the two methods that predominated in prepsychoanalytic times.

Far more illuminating, however, is Freud's method of taking every single word or expression in the analysand's account of a dream, daydream, or fantasy as a potential point of departure for a whole series of thoughts related to the analysand's life and fantasies. An analysand of mine once recalled a very powerful scene from his past (a scene he professed not to have thought about in a very long time, perhaps not since it occurred) simply by associating to the color of an object that appeared in a dream he had, which he initially described as "blue or green." Following Freud's advice that we take both elements of an alternative ("blue or green") as terms to associate to,[1] even though the analysand felt he was correcting the former with the latter, I encouraged him to associate to both of them. He eventually concluded that the color of the object in the dream was the same as that of the "powder blue" carpet in his dining room

---

[1] Freud (1900/1958, pp. 516–517) made this advice quite general: "In analysing a dream I insist that the whole scale of estimates of certainty shall be abandoned and that the faintest possibility that something of this or that sort may have occurred in the dream shall be treated as complete certainty. . . . Doubt produces this interrupting effect upon an analysis that reveals it as a derivative and tool of psychical resistance."

growing up. He suddenly recalled that one day he had been lying on that carpet and heard sounds coming from the next room; he went and looked through the louvered doors between the dining room and the family room to see his mother and brother having sex on the floor, their bodies being visually cut into odd horizontal slices by the louvers. Having recollected that scene thanks to our associative work on the dream, the disturbing images he had been having around that time of partial bodies engaging in sexual acts tapered off. The scene alluded to by this dream element ("blue or green") could hardly have been guessed at from the manifest content of the dream, which involved selecting a notebook in a shop. Nevertheless, it seems to have been one of the latent thoughts that went into the construction of the dream.

As I mentioned in Chapter 2, no dream is too short to be dismissed out of hand as being unproductive for an analysis. Even if the analysand remembers nothing more than "something about a raincoat," useful work can often be done, assuming the analyst insists that the analysand associate to it. Analysands are often quick to consider short, vaguely remembered, or obscure dreams as obviously useless; they are lured into thinking that only somewhat elaborate and distinctly remembered dreams can serve any analytic purpose because they spontaneously look to interpret the *manifest content* instead of trying to find the *latent content*, the latter being the whole series of thoughts, memories, and feelings that are evoked by each of the different dream elements. Nevertheless, the fact that an analysand has forgotten the majority of a dream may well suggest that it dealt with a topic that was highly unpleasant to the analysand, a topic that is subject to repression, giving us all the more reason to try to work with the little she did remember. *Forgetting is, after all, a sign of repression.* So too, when an analysand announces that she has only a dim or faint recollection of a dream, our ears should perk up to the fact that it may have been more powerfully charged than other dreams, which is precisely why it is more difficult for her to remember.

One of my analysands once mentioned a long dream, the only details of which he could remember were the name Chrysippus and the vague sense that in the dream he was looking for his works. Although he was initially reluctant to ponder such a "skimpy dream," he provided the following associations when I prompted him to say whatever came to mind about Chrysippus: He was a Stoic philosopher, and the analysand had been "boning up" on Stoic logic recently. It occurred to him next that he had read somewhere that "Chrysippus was as great as Aristotle," though because his works were lost it was hard to substantiate that claim. After a pause he added that, as he had not yet published his own work, I must be like Aristotle to him whereas he is like Chrysippus, suggesting a certain wish to be as "well published" as I am. "If not better!" he added. As abbreviated as his recollection of the dream was, it brought up a whole nexus of thoughts and wishes about the analysand's ambitions and his rivalry with me, the latter being a topic about which he was initially loath to speak.

Early on in an analysis the analyst often need do no more than elicit the analysand's associations to the different dream elements; the memories recalled in this process help fill in the story of the analysand's life and generally convince the analysand that there is a lot more going on in dreams than she was at first inclined to think. There is no need to have the analysand associate to absolutely every element in a dream, for some of the associations are likely to lead in important directions and are worth pursuing for their own sake.

For example, an analysand once told me a highly elaborate dream, which I have shortened here for my present purposes:

> He was in a store after closing and had the sense that two other men were there, both from 2001: A Space Odyssey. He turned and saw Darth Vader, who had killed the other two men. (It must, he said while recounting the dream, be Star Wars, not 2001). Darth Vader said he was going to kill the analysand, who stalled for time, saying he had to go to the bathroom. Darth Vader followed him into the bathroom; as he went to the urinal, he heard Darth Vader draw a gun, and then felt it on the back of his neck. Suddenly he had the sense that he had been shot in the back of his head, and he wondered why he did not hear it. "If I had, I'd be dead," he reasoned. He reached up and felt a hole in his head. "So this is what it's like to be dead," he said to himself.
>
> He went back out to the store and his family was there; he tried to talk to his sister but she could not hear him. He stood in front of her and she bumped into him—he was invisible!
>
> In the next scene he was in a lobby. His friends were there too, and he tried to talk to them, but they could not hear him.
>
> Then the scene shifted and he was in a car with three or four other people. He realized that they were on their way to a meeting but that they did not know how to get to the meeting place. He knew how to get there but they could not hear him when he gave them directions. He climbed into the driver's seat and started driving. "Look, the car's driving itself," someone said.
>
> They arrived at their destination and he walked around the house, thinking it was Conan O'Brien's house; he went into the bathroom and peed in the toilet. A woman walked in whom he thought must be Conan's wife. She looked at the toilet water and said, "Oh, that's odd." She could not see him but could see the water. He thought with jubilation, "I'm having some effect on the world after all! I'll try to get her attention." He grabbed her breasts

and she giggled. "I've finally gotten through to someone," he thought and then woke up.

There were so many scenes and so many details in this dream (which I have already shortened) that we would obviously have been hard-pressed to go into all of them in a single session. Our discussion of the dream in the session in which he recounted it focused on just a few main points (which are further condensed here), and he returned to it in later sessions, but never in an exhaustive way. He began by saying that he had been feeling that he was having little effect on the world, that he was invisible, but that the dream offered a ray of hope. The whole key to *Star Wars*, he said, is that Darth Vader is Luke Skywalker's father; the dream, he continued, was about how you survive in the world after you have been killed by your father. He paused.

"While peeing?" I asked. He responded that peeing was a form of competition: He had once said regarding his brother, "I'm not going to get into a peeing competition with him." The partners were equal in a brotherly contest, but not between father and son. A (peeing) competition between father and son would, he implied, not be futile, as it would be between brothers.

Regarding Conan O'Brien, the analysand indicated that Conan took over David Letterman's show when the latter moved to CBS. Conan was unknown at the time and repeatedly apologized for his performance during his early years on the show. The analysand mentioned that he would get very worked up when he heard Conan's apologies, feeling that Conan should not apologize because he was very good. He professed not to know why he got so worked up about this. I ended the session there, thinking it more useful to end with something he did not understand about himself than to unfold all of the strands of the dream at that time (I also knew that we had another session the very next day).

At our next meeting, the analysand reported that he had thought more about the dream, especially the point on which I had scanded the session. He said he realized he identified with Conan and that, like Conan, he should stop apologizing for his "early work." The work he had been doing was "not so bad," he opined, "in fact, it's good." Interestingly enough, during the night between these two sessions he had had his first ever dream about having sex with his own wife (he usually dreamt about everyone else's wife but his own). This was perhaps not unrelated to his burgeoning acceptance of the validity and quality of his own work and his own accomplishments. Although we did not explore every nook and cranny of the dream or every possible wish fulfilled in it, a number of important articulations were located and the dream contributed to the overall movement of the analysis.

An analysand may be intrigued enough by a certain dream to return to it in future sessions, providing further associations to it. However, even when the analysand does not return to that particular dream, the analyst need not worry that the material the analysand did not have time to associate to will be lost forever. As Freud (1911b/1958) told us:

> We may rest assured that every wishful impulse which creates a dream today will reappear in other dreams as long as it has not been understood and withdrawn from the domination of the unconscious. It often happens, therefore, that the best way to complete the interpretation of the dream is to leave it and to devote one's attention to a new dream, which may contain the same material in a possibly more accessible form. (p. 92)

As I indicated earlier, it is generally advisable to allow the analysand to take the lead in starting off sessions and bringing up different subjects to discuss instead of regularly directing the analysand to associate to a dream recounted in the previous session (or to return to any particular topic the analyst found especially interesting or important in prior sessions). The analyst who worries that a certain opening or crucial association may be lost if he fails to return to it in the next session may find that he has lost a lot more by usurping the analysand's role in the therapy: The analysand may well come to feel that she is there simply to answer the analyst's questions and follow his line of inquiry, as opposed to raising her own questions about her life and taking the reins of the analysis in her own hands.

Once an analysis is well underway and the analysand has taken up the analytic project as her own, the analyst can, of course, briefly take the lead once in a while; more generally, the analyst can point out verbal or thematic connections between the material the analysand brings up in the next session and the discussion of a dream in the previous session—often simply by underscoring (that is, punctuating) an idiomatic expression or adjective that was used in both or by saying something as minimal as "like in the dream last time?"

Although Freud (1911b/1958, p. 92) once said, "The amount of interpretation which can be achieved in one session should be taken as sufficient and it is not to be regarded as a loss if the content of the dream is not fully discovered," there are certain dreams that bother or intrigue analysands to the point that they become emblematic of certain parts of their analyses, being returned to from time to time over a period of months or years. At least parts of several sessions may be devoted to their analysis at the outset, and there is no reason to exclude discussion of them at later points in time. Dreams should be considered potentially inexhaustible, there being no predetermined stopping point to their interpretation and thus no such thing as a "complete interpretation" of a dream. The analysand spontaneously ceases to speculate about the meaning of a dream when it stops inspiring her to do so, when it no longer bothers, perplexes, or intrigues her, or when other more pressing material comes to the fore.

One of my analysands once had a rather detailed dream about being on a plane that was forced to make an emergency landing. She was concerned in the dream about getting her luggage out of the overhead compartment, and the pilot came into the main cabin to help her with her bag, which turned out to be a carton of milk. Her initial discussions of the dream revolved around the role played by the pilot in bringing the plane down safely, since for many years she had imagined planes plunging into the ocean and had had panic attacks during flights; she had found it hard to trust men and to accept assistance or love of any kind from them. She remained perplexed, however, by the carton of milk that comprised her carry-on luggage, and it was not until several months later that she turned directly to the theme of motherhood evoked by it, elaborating on the role of a man in her thoughts about having children, something she was quite conflicted about. The several-month-old dream served her as a very useful jumping-off point for exploring her thoughts and feelings in this realm, and it led to interpretations of the dream that differed in some respects from the interpretations she had initially come up with.[2]

Devoting more than one session to the interpretation of a dream can be especially useful when things have gone beyond the stage of simply eliciting associations to all the different elements of the dream, as this is when an exploration of the possible wishes that may be found in the dream begins. Many analysands will spontaneously start the process of associating to their dreams before recounting them in sessions, an indication that they are taking upon themselves much of the work of the analysis, and at that point the analyst can focus his attention more on listening for those elements of the dream that the analysand has not associated to, has left out of the associative process, or seems to have given short shrift (which is not to say that the associations the analysand has while thinking about the dream on her own are identical to the ones she has when she talks out loud about the dream with the analyst, for additional dynamics then come into play: addressing another person and imagining what he will think, as well as hearing herself pronounce words aloud, which may allow for multiple readings). But few analysands will begin to spontaneously try to fathom the wish or wishes fulfilled in the dream, and this is where the analyst must often work the hardest.

---

[2] Such dreams sometimes become useful starting points for broader constructions of the type briefly mentioned in Chapter 5.

Finding a Wish in a Dream

The full interpretation of such a dream will coincide with the completion of the whole analysis. . . . It is the same as with the elucidation of a single symptom (the main symptom, perhaps). The whole analysis is needed to explain it; in the course of the treatment one must endeavor to lay hold first of this, then of that, fragment of the symptom's meaning, one after another, until they can all be pieced together. Similarly, no more can be expected of a dream occurring in the early stages of the analysis; one must be content if the attempt at interpretation brings a single . . . wishful impulse to light.

— Freud (1911b/1958, p. 93)

Articulating the wish or wishes enacted in a dream is often no mean feat, and there are no hard and fast rules about how this is done.[3] Sometimes a wish can be discerned somewhat directly. For example, if an analysand dreams of missing a train, and the dreamer's association to the train is to an upcoming trip to visit her mother, it would seem that she is inhabited by a wish (although it is probably not her only wish) not to visit her mother. She may consciously tell herself she is excited about going to see her mother, but her dream would seem to tell a somewhat different story. What it does not immediately tell us is why: Is she afraid of her mother? angry at her mother? ashamed of her mother? afraid of her own attraction to her mother? The analysand must be led here to entertain the idea that something in her does not want to go and must be encouraged to explore what that might be. The harder it is for her to imagine why she might not want to go, the more likely it is that the dream has touched on something repressed, whether that be an unconscious wish to punish her mother, an identification with her father, who regularly failed to show up when he had promised the mother that he would, or any of a number of other motives. While the wish in such a relatively straightforward dream can be expressed quite simply—a wish not to go—a fuller statement of the wish can be quite complicated. If, for example, the analysand associates missing the train with the expression "missing the boat," the wish fulfilled in the dream could be a wish to confirm her father's belief that his daughter could never do anything right or be there for anyone when she was genuinely needed; she might thereby be siding with her father against her mother. The relative simplicity of the dream as recounted should not be taken to imply that the dreamer's wish(es) must therefore be straightforward or transparent.

---

[3] Note that many analysts have long since given up looking for wishes in dreams, whether conscious or unconscious (see, for example, Segal, 1964, pp. 18–20).

Sometimes a wish grows out of a sequence of scenes, each of which makes up a part of the thought in which the wish is expressed. For example, consider a rather simply constructed dream in which the analysand's mother—who is in no way ill in real life—dies in the first scene and the analysand finds herself free, pursuing and achieving her most cherished goals, in the second scene. At the most basic level the dream could be read as saying something like, "If my mother were to die I would finally be free to be myself," and the wish therein could be formulated as something like, "I wish my mother would die so that I could finally be myself." At least in the early stages of the analysis, the analysand is not likely to put the two scenes together in this way, but rather to express perplexity at the juxtaposition of scenes in which something that struck her as so distressing upon waking was followed by something so exhilarating. The dream itself does not provide the "if . . . then . . ." clause necessary to connect the two scenes (if my mother died then I would finally be free): The analyst must often supply it (see Freud, 1900/1958, pp. 310–326).

It should be clear here that the wish or wishes implicit in a dream are not necessarily incredibly complicated or downright ineffable. As Freud (1923a/1961) told us:

> It is only too easy to forget that a dream is as a rule merely a thought like any other, made possible by a relaxation of the censorship and by unconscious reinforcement, and distorted by the operation of the censorship and by unconscious revision. (p. 112)

The thought expressed in a dream may, on many occasions, be remarkably like other thoughts the analysand expresses in the course of her analytic sessions. We need not be looking for something terribly highfalutin, abstruse, or opaque.

Sometimes multiple wishes can be discerned fairly easily, and those wishes may be complementary or contradictory, canceling each other out as it were. An analysand of mine dreamt that we were having a session in person (whereas virtually all of our sessions had been conducted by phone) and he was standing up. He suddenly realized how awkward it was to be standing like that, and he sat down in a comfortable armchair nearby. In discussing the dream, he indicated that there was something independent and almost defiant in his attitude in doing so, for he did not ask me if he could sit or where he should sit, but just went ahead and did as he thought fit. At the same time, his decision to take a seat in the comfortable armchair struck him as indicating that his attitude toward the analysis was changing, that he was letting his guard down: When he was standing, he was more alert and could leave the room in a flash if he so desired, just as he had for many months stayed on his guard, prepared to quit analysis at any moment. He expressed concern that the armchair was almost too relaxing, too intimate: It would take a lot more work to raise himself out of an armchair if he suddenly wanted to leave.

The dream thus struck him as paradoxical in that it seemed to express a wish to assert himself, to act independently without any concern for what I might want, and, on the other hand, a wish to allow himself to settle into the analysis, to become more intimate and less guarded with me. He was also struck by the twofold meaning he attributed to standing before me: He saw it as both a position of deference (as if he were standing before his old headmaster at school or a superior officer) and one from which he was able to look down on me. To sit was then both to stop being so deferential but simultaneously to stop looking down on me, his attitude up until that time being characterized by a curious admixture of deference and scorn, of feelings of inferiority and superiority.

Although the meanings and wishes implicit in such a dream might seem somewhat contradictory, they must all be taken seriously: No attempt should be made to reduce them to a single consistent meaning or wish. To do so would be to do violence to the complexity of each different analysand's attitudes, motives, and wishes. There is no a priori reason to think that people are consistent in their attitudes toward any one person or thing, and it would be foolish to try to artificially bring about some sort of consistency.

In certain instances, finding a wish in a dream is a bit like finding a needle in a haystack. Whether one ultimately concludes that not every dream fulfills a wish—disagreeing with Freud's sometimes absolute (Freud, 1900/1958, p. 121), sometimes tempered assertion (Freud, 1920/1955, p. 32, 1923a/1961, p. 118)—or simply that one has been unable to carry the analysis of the dream far enough, the important point is to keep an eye out for potential wishes when working with dreams.

Counterintuitive Wishes

There is a knowledge you understand in dreams that has nothing to do with what you are left with when you are supposedly awake. That is why it is so important to decipher dreams.
—Lacan (1973–1974, December 18, 1973)

One obstacle frequently encountered in bringing analysands to look for wishes in dreams, daydreams, and fantasies is that the wishes expressed in them are often quite counterintuitive to the analysand in her waking life, in many cases being the exact opposite of what she consciously thinks she wants. Many dreams fulfill wishes for punishment, for relationships or jobs to go awry, or for failure at any number of life projects. An analysand's first instinct is rarely to say, "I must want to fail at school—I wonder why," and to go on to speculate that perhaps she is unconsciously trying to prove her father right when he said she would never amount to anything or trying to show the world that she is not part of her supposedly perfect, successful family. When presented with such possible motives, the analysand is likely to respond, "Why would I want to prove him right? What good would that do me?" But, of course, just because it would not do her any "good" in the simplistic, commonsense way does not mean she is not unconsciously trying to prove him right anyway. Perhaps what she is getting out of it is something that is ultimately "bad" for her, but some motive is making her pursue it anyway. We mortals pursue all kinds of things that, in our more considered judgment, we think are bad for us. Freud (1900/1958, p. 476) was initially content to explain dreams that seem to involve self-punishment as satisfying "masochistic impulses"; as we shall see, however, these do not account for all such dreams.

There is often a considerable difference between the *apparent wish* enacted in a dream—say, a dream of waking up late for an important examination and being unable to get to the room where the examination is being held—and the more overriding or lifelong wish or wishes that underlie it: wanting, for example, to thumb one's nose at certain authority figures or to cry out for help to parents experienced by the analysand as overly demanding. Analysands are likely to simply be distressed by such dreams and fail to look for any wish in them because of their apparent masochistic strain; over the course of time the analyst must try to get them to look beyond the surface.

Freud (1920/1955, p. 32) later provided another way of thinking about "punishment dreams": He suggested that they often "merely replace the forbidden wish-fulfillment by the appropriate punishment for it." For example, a dream of being thrown in jail may satisfy the wish to commit the crime for which one would be thrown in jail. An analysand of mine had a rather detailed dream in which he was trying to avoid detection, having just escaped from prison. He saw a man dressed in a black coat (he later commented that his father had a coat just like that) and overheard the man say to a young boy, "There are many different types of perverts. You have to watch out for them; if you find them, you have to kill them." The man and the boy suddenly noticed the analysand, pulled out knives, and ran after him; the man stuck a knife into the analysand's neck, which caused the analysand to wake up in an extreme state of anxiety.

The anxiety he experienced successfully diverted his attention away from the comment made by the man in the dream regarding perverts; the punishment he received in the dream (being stabbed in the neck) might be understood here as signaling that the analysand had carried out what he himself considered to be a perverted act. In that sense, the dream fulfilled his wish to act as he thought a "pervert" would, but rather than staging the accomplishment of the "perverse act" in question, it staged the accomplishment of the punishment he felt he should receive for engaging in such an act. (As we shall see in a moment, it is also quite possible to imagine that the dream fulfilled a wish to be punished by a father figure for engaging in such acts—a wish for a father figure to limit his antics and force him into line.)[4]

Conscious Versus Unconscious Wishes

One must become accustomed to a dream being thus capable of having many meanings.
                                                            — Freud (1925a/1961, p. 130)

Contemporary practitioners rarely seem to pay attention to Freud's distinction between the conscious wishes and the unconscious wishes that are expressed in dreams. Freud urges us to take note of the conscious wishes but to pursue our work on the dream, when suitable in the context of the analytic treatment as a whole, in search of unconscious wishes. The latter are, after all, what dreams are most useful for helping us get at.

An analysand of mine once told me that he had had a dream the night before our session but had forgotten it. At our next session he told me that he had remembered the previously forgotten dream, which went something like this:

> He was having a heart transplant. There was a Ziploc plastic bag in which his heart was going to be put, either to be disposed of or to simply sit there in a sterile medical environment while the operation was performed and then be put back in his chest. He overheard some nurses talking, saying that he might be having a bypass instead of a transplant. He wanted to change his mind but it was too late. He wanted to just get up and walk out but it was too late.

---

[4] Lacan (1988b, pp. 127–129) discusses a dream (based on material found in Raymond Queneau's novel, *On est toujours trop bon avec les femmes*) of a man who in waking life wanted to publicly denounce the King of England as an ass, or *con* (Queneau may well have based this on Freud's comments in the case study of the Rat Man, Freud, 1909/1955, p. 179). Since doing so was illegal in the kingdom and punishable by death, the man instead dreamt that he was having his own head cut off. The punishment staged in the dream represented (in a displaced manner) his wish to call the King an ass.

Several of my analysands have recounted "intruthive" thoughts in which they imagined their own heads (and other body parts) being cut off for different, albeit related, reasons. Others have reported repeated punishment dreams and daydreams related to the fact that they felt that they should have been punished early on in life for precocious sexual behavior with a sibling, sexual behavior that was discovered by at least one parent but that went unpunished at the time, owing apparently to the parent's belief (during a particularly liberal era) that it was "perfectly natural" or to a wish to hide it from the other parent who might "go ballistic." In all such cases, the failure to receive punishment for something that they knew was generally considered wrong led to considerable, and indeed sometimes life-impeding, anxiety.

He said that upon awakening he immediately associated the dream with analysis: Through analysis he was getting a new heart. He did not think of himself as "big-hearted," which to him meant emotional, warm, and connected to other people. To get a new heart would be to become warmer and more connected to others.

Continuing to discuss the dream, he commented that he had had doubts about analysis since the beginning of the treatment, the analytic approach seeming to him to conflict with his spiritual beliefs and practices. At times he would have a "change of heart" about the analysis and contemplate leaving it. Nevertheless, he referred to analysis as "the latest link on the chain" of his spiritual path, but he slipped when saying "the latest link" and instead said "the last link." It was as if he felt that analysis was somehow his last chance. Although in the prime of life and in good health, he had recently begun to imagine he had Alzheimer's or a heart condition, and he was preoccupied with thoughts about death.

During the session, we did not get to his associations to nurses and Ziploc plastic bags—work for a future session perhaps, I thought—for it seemed more important to me to highlight the fact that the dream emphasized the inevitability of the operation: The analysis could not be stopped even if he wanted to stop it. I said, "A wish that it be impossible to stop." "Yes," he said, "that it be too late to back out of it—I'd feel guilty if I did and I know you'd talk me into staying. . . . [It being impossible to stop] would put an end to my doubts and dithering. All I could do is go along with it."

This, we might say, was at least one of the analysand's *conscious* wishes that was expressed in the dream. An *unconscious* wish showed its face in a discussion of the verbal phrase "to be forced," which the analysand used a number of times in recounting and associating to the dream: It turned out that he often fantasized about having a woman force him to do many different things and had in fact contacted a dominatrix at one point. Being forced played a role in a number of his sexual fantasies, and in his everyday life nothing elicited conflicting feelings in him like having the sense that he was being forced to do something: It made him feel rebellious and yet secretly satisfied; he bridled and chafed at it and yet orchestrated certain situations in such a way as to feel forced. He found it difficult to make decisions—especially important life decisions—and wished that someone or something would force him to make them, rendering inoperative his doubts and misgivings. One might suggest that it was as if in the dream he wished his doctor (that is, his analyst) would force him to go through with the operation.

None of his prior "spiritual masters" had forced him to make a commitment to a certain practice and he had eventually left them all, one after the other, with a sense of disappointment. His attitude toward them was never so subservient that he felt he could not leave, and thus he had always managed to avoid (that is, "bypass") the operation he felt he so badly needed. A new heart would allow him to make decisions, but the catch-22 was that he would be unable to make the decision to acquire a new heart until after he had already acquired it!

The unconscious wish would then seem to be to be forced by the Other to do what he wanted to do and knew he needed to do (and to be rendered incapable of avoiding doing so by leaving). The paradox here is that it was by being thus castrated, so to speak (losing all autonomy), that he believed he could overcome the kind of castration he experienced in his lifelong inability to make decisions and act on them, to accept that the decision to do one thing necessarily cuts off other possible avenues, thereby limiting one's ability to do and be anything and everything. That is, he needed to be castrated (submit to the heart-change operation) in order to overcome castration. Indeed, he often complained that his father had not taught him "how to be a man"; the implication seemed to be that his father would have taught him how to be a man had he demonstrated to his son what it meant to have the balls to castrate him, figuratively speaking. The unconscious wish, then—and it is an extremely common one, as I indicated in Chapters 4 and 5, although practitioners tend to turn it a blind eye—is that the father/doctor/analyst will provide the longed-for castration, the castration the analysand's biological or adoptive father failed to provide.[5] This was not a wish that I discussed with the analysand during that session; I simply made a note of it for future reference, feeling that the analysand might be scared off were I to enunciate such a seemingly outrageous wish (better to let him come around to formulating it himself, I surmised, which he later did in his own vocabulary).

Daydreams and Fantasies

> *What is fantasy if not* . . . ein Wunsch, *a wish, a rather naive one at that, like all wishes.*
>   — Lacan (2004, pp. 61–62)

> *No one ever talks about sexuality anymore in psychoanalytic circles. Analytic journals, when you open them, are the most chaste journals imaginable.*
>   — Lacan (2005a, p. 29)

Daydreams and fantasies seem to be more difficult for most people to remember than their nocturnal productions. Beyond the time of adolescence and early

---

[5] His sense was that the Other's desire was (or should have been) to castrate him, and his desire at some level was to (let himself) be castrated.

adulthood, when many people spend a great deal of time daydreaming, often deliberately embellishing their daydreams and steering them in certain directions, few people seem to even realize that they continue to daydream—no doubt at least in part due to the counterintuitive nature of their daydreams. The thoughts that flash through their minds strike them as unpleasant or downright atrocious, and they do not even think of them as daydreams, which in common parlance are supposed to be so pleasant, so wish-fulfilling. They do their best to forget them as quickly as possible.

Once in analysis, people have to be encouraged to pay attention to the fleeting thoughts, images, and scenarios that run through their minds (and that may take the form of "intruthive thoughts," as I called them in Chapter 5). The only ones they may think of as fantasies, strictly speaking, are the sexual thoughts, images, and scenes that occur to them, but it is surprising how few sexual fantasies most people tend to remember, even when such fantasies are repeatedly summoned up or indulged in during frequent masturbation. It is as if the moment orgasm is reached, the fantasies that accompany masturbation are not given a moment's further thought and indeed often "evaporate" from consciousness altogether.

Many an analysand is hard-pressed to recall a single masturbation fantasy, especially when such fantasies conflict so palpably with the ways the analysand thinks of herself during waking life.[6] One analysand, for example, could only come by imagining her male boss watching her be stimulated by another man, whereas during her waking life she thought of herself as a modern career woman who established equal relationships and partnerships with men. Another analysand would imagine the woman in whom he was interested having sex with another man while he watched, whereas he thought of himself as wanting a "total relationship" with a woman: She would be his lover, best friend, soul mate, and intellectual alter ego—in short, someone with whom he could share everything. It is not surprising that fantasies that so utterly contradict

---

[6] In numerous cases, the analyst must ask every few sessions whether the analysand remembers any masturbation fantasies (so the analysand realizes the analyst wants her to pay attention to, recollect, and talk about them) or, should that seem an overly charged term, any sexual fantasies. Asking once is rarely enough! And even when the analysand does mention such fantasies, she is likely to describe them in the vaguest of terms; the analyst often has to ask myriad "indiscreet" questions to get any genuine sense what the fantasy involved. The analysand may be still more disinclined to talk about such fantasies than about other aspects of her life, feeling that her secret enjoyment (that is, jouissance) of them will be taken away from her or somehow ruined if she talks about them. The analyst must not resist the effort required to overcome the analysand's resistance to talking about such things, for otherwise he allows his own resistance to steer the therapy away from sensitive topics. Analysands' symptoms are always related to sexuality in some way, and a full and open discussion of what turns the analysand on must come sooner or later in every analysis.

what one thinks one wants in everyday life are so swiftly forgotten. Since the 1950s, many an analyst seems to have taken that forgetting as license to ignore the murky, counterintuitive realm of sexual fantasies, which speaks volumes about the degree to which analysts have given up on getting at the repressed.

While the analysand is likely to at least view such sexual thoughts and images as fantasies, she is less likely to think of aggressive thoughts and images that flash through her mind as fantasies; they strike her as bizarre and annoying, and perhaps as inexplicable, but certainly not as fantasies per se. If she is carrying her infant and imagines slipping and dropping the child down the stairs, she will do her best to brush the thought away in horror, to put the loathsome image out of her mind so completely as to never recall it again if possible. If a noise awakens her in the night and she begins to imagine getting a baseball bat out of the hall closet, creeping downstairs, surprising an intruder, and beating him senseless with the bat, over and over again—the brutality of it suddenly making the scene dissolve, bringing her back to consciousness sweating profusely and with heart pounding—she is hardly likely to think of that as a fantasy! She will be far more inclined to think of it as akin to a nightmare (indeed, we seem to have no real word for such horrific scenarios that go through our minds when we are awake, *daymare* seeming to be the only appropriate one) and utterly disinclined to see any possibly wishful impulse in it.[7] It might be said that in our times, in which sexuality permeates popular culture—which has taken over the interest in sexuality formerly shown by the majority of psychoanalysts—analysands are more likely to disavow any wishful component to their aggressive impulses than to their sexual impulses, the latter currently being more acceptable (at least in the United States) than the former to the popular mind.

It is often forgotten that daydreams and fantasies are just as capable of disguise as dreams are and that they too must be associated to if they are to be interpreted. One of my analysands once recalled that he had had a fleeting "nasty thought" about his brother and then imagined himself having a "nasty accident." It struck him as typical of the way he punished himself for any aggressive impulses he might have toward others, and he quickly catalogued it among his oh-so-common "masochistic tendencies." He never for a minute considered that the initial fantasy, so to speak, had been that his brother was in a nasty accident and that the substitution of himself for his brother was a disguise, something that would render the fantasy more palatable to his

---

[7] She will also hardly be inclined to see any possible connection between her state of arousal in the "daymare" and sexual arousal.

partly waking consciousness. When I said, "To imagine your brother having an accident . . ." he responded, "Now *that* would be a daydream!"

Sometimes elements in dreams, daydreams, and fantasies have to be construed as meaning the opposite of what they seem to mean to discern any meaning in them (see Freud, 1900/1958, pp. 245–246, 471). One woman I worked with, whose mother had made it clear to her that she (the daughter) was not allowed to have a man of her own, had sexual fantasies in which her male partner had a whole harem of which she was but one member. Although ostensibly satisfying her mother's prohibition against having a man of her own, the fantasy nevertheless, at one level at least, simply substituted polygamy for monogamy: It satisfied a disguised wish for an exclusive relationship with a man (or we might say that it fulfilled her wish for an exclusive relationship with a man in a disguised form). She also had fantasies in which she was catering to the sexual whims of an ugly old man; at one level, these fantasies staged her obeying her mother's wishes that she entice and be available to all men, no matter how repellent, and yet at another they simply replaced the young, good-looking man of her dreams with a decrepit letch.

It is often difficult for the analysand to fathom how wishes that seem to be expressed in "her" fantasies are in any sense her own; they seem not to be her own as much as those of other people she has known (and often hated with a passion). One of my analysands recalled and recounted a masturbation fantasy in which he heard in his mind the words, "Okay, let's get her started"; he suddenly realized these were the very words his father used to utter in talking about his car.[8] The analysand commented that, just as his father had spoken of his car as if it were a woman, the analysand was talking to his own penis as if it were a woman (his father's woman). At some level it seemed that it was his father's desire (to get something started) that was being enacted in the fantasy. I scanded the session there and at the next session the analysand reported that our discussion of the fantasy had served as a sort of an exorcism—he felt as if his body were no longer his mother's body: "I have one of my own," he said, "I'm fully equipped."

Man's Desire Is the Other's Desire

The motive forces of fantasies are unsatisfied wishes, and every single fantasy is the fulfillment of a wish.

— Freud (1908/1959, p. 146)

---

[8] This apparently simple fantasy illustrates Miller's (1996, p. 11) claim that "fantasy is a sentence that is enjoyed, a ciphered message that harbors jouissance."

When the analysand finds herself having fantasies that seem not to be her own, she is likely to feel intruded upon, alienated by the very desires that she finds inhabiting her. Yet it is an inevitable fact of life that we assimilate other people's desires, taking them into ourselves, and our fantasies often enact other people's desires in a disguised or not-so-disguised form. As Lacan often put it, "man's desire is the Other's desire" (see Lacan, 2006, p. 628, for example), a formulation that has several meanings, the most germane to our discussion here being that we come to want the same thing that others want.[9] Still, the analysand is often reluctant to recognize the things that go on in her fantasies as expressing wishes at all because they do not feel like her own wishes. Nevertheless, that reluctance must be overcome if she is ever to discern the desires that inhabit her and either arrive at a point where they feel like her own or go beyond them to others. Insofar as one's desires are so closely tied to other people's desires, it is foolish, strictly speaking, to talk about "one's own desires"—as if one could *own* desires, as if one could be the sole proprietor of desires—and yet it is important for the analysand to reach a point at which she can feel at one with or at peace with the desires that inhabit her.[10]

An analysand of mine had a long series of sexual fantasies that she found especially revolting and shameful. In these fantasies, one woman was licking the sexual parts of another woman, one of whom was often considerably older than the other. Sometimes it was clear that the analysand herself was doing the licking, but often it was not clear who was doing it to whom. In the course of the analysis it became clear that licking was associated in her mind with healing a wound (as, for example, when a dog or cat licks a sore) and, by extension, making something all better. It was as if, in the fantasy, she was trying to heal her mother's wound, her mother having made it amply clear to her through her attitudes and discourse that she felt deprived of a penis, that she felt sorely lacking in the genital realm, and that she expected the analysand to compensate her for this, to make it up to her (as if the daughter were to blame for the mother's "castration").

The analysand did not initially feel that she had taken it upon herself to compensate or heal her mother at the genital level (which was not unproblematic for the analysand herself either), but she did recognize that she had long done everything possible to make her mother's life as easy as she could, to stay out of trouble, and to obey her in every respect. Making the necessary

---

[9] For other meanings of it, see Fink (1997, pp. 54–56, 2004, pp. 26, 31–32, 119).

[10] As Freud (1933/1964, p. 80) put it, and as Lacan so often repeated, *"Wo Es war, soll Ich werden* (where it [that foreign desire] was, I must come into being)" (Lacan, 2006, p. 801).

sacrifice on her mother's altar was the daughter's way of getting her mother off her back: It was only once she had satisfied her mother that she felt she could rid herself of her mother and think about satisfying herself. In these fantasies, she ensured her mother's satisfaction, making herself the instrument of her mother's jouissance ("the Other's jouissance," as Lacan put it), and we could in some sense say that these fantasies enacted "the Other's desire" (Lacan, 2006, pp. 823–826), even though they were also designed to preserve the analysand from being "swallowed up whole" by her mother. The number of meanings and motives involved in these fantasies was far greater still (I cannot go into all of them here),[11] but they illustrate the degree to which it is often hard to say where, in a fantasy, the subject's own desire leaves off and the Other's desire begins. Once the various meanings and motives were unpacked, these fantasies, which had persisted for many years, vanished altogether and were replaced by sexual fantasies of a very different tenor.

A male analysand told me of recurrent sexual fantasies he had in which there was both a woman and another man with a big penis—the latter was the one who was sexually gratified in the fantasies, at least explicitly. The analysand associated the big penis with his father, recalling having been impressed as a child with his father's "enormous penis" (this comparison by the young boy of his penis with his father's adult-size penis is, in my experience, the virtually constant source of men's concerns that their penises are too small), and he associated the fact that the father figure in the fantasies was the one who was gratified with a number of facets of the relationship between his father and him that we had been discussing for some time. He realized that he had, in a manner of speaking, been propping up his father, sensing that his father needed the son to get things wrong so that the father could set things right and show his son how things should be done. As the analysand put it, "[I have been] situating myself as a problem for him to solve."[12] This allowed the father to show his prowess in many areas and propped up the father's image of himself as a capable, competent man compared to his son. Regarding the fact that the father figure was the one who had sex in the fantasies, the analysand commented, "Maybe that'll shut him up!" The father spent a lot of time and

---

[11] I'll just add here that their satisfactions were still further linked: The daughter felt she could not obtain more satisfaction for herself than her mother obtained, for otherwise the mother would feel "gypped" and let her know it in no uncertain terms. Note that, as the analysis was conducted in French, the other meaning of the English word *licking*—beating or punishing—was not germane.

[12] In fact, he slipped when he said this and actually said, "[I have been] situating myself as a problem for him to be solved," regarding which he remarked, when I prompted him to think about what that might suggest, that for him, his father was a problem to be solved, a problem he himself had to solve.

energy criticizing the son and the son could never find the words that would silence his father; perhaps sex would?

Discussion of these fantasies led to an extended number of sessions that each touched on the fact that the analysand always blamed himself for being a "screw up"—for doing badly in school and getting in trouble in one way or another—and would never attribute any blame to his father (who would, moreover, make fun of him when he was a child if he complained about his father's treatment of him). Yet he found himself heatedly commenting, regarding a relative of his who seemed to be "screwing up" in much the same way he had as a kid, that the relative's parents must have pushed him too hard and treated him like a problem child (just as the analysand's own parents had treated him) and that the relative must be taking revenge on them. Perhaps much of his own "bad behavior" as a kid had been secretly motivated by the wish not only to prop up his father's image of himself as superior to his problem child, but also to drag his father's good name (the family name) through the mud.

In his sexual fantasies, the analysand ensured his father's satisfaction, making himself the instrument of his father's jouissance: He complied with what he felt his father demanded of him—that he be a screw-up, incapable of making love to a woman properly—and with what he felt his father wanted (to feel superior to his son by outcharming him in relation to all women). Yet, even though these fantasies enacted "the Other's desire," they simultaneously involved the father in a "sordid" scenario with homosexual overtones and a background tinge of adulterous rape (these were details of some of the fantasies that I did not mention). Even though the analysand acted in these fantasies to prop up his father—that is, he acted as "the Other's guarantor" (Lacan, 2006, p. 824)—he simultaneously undermined his father, striking out at him. Discussion of these fantasies in the context of his life helped bring out some of the analysand's anger at his father, which was prone to showing up in displaced forms as anger at others around him or at me, and shed light on certain aspects of his stance in life vis-à-vis the Other (that is, certain aspects of his "fundamental fantasy," a concept I discuss further on).

Anxiety Dreams and Nightmares

Freud indicates that a dream wakes us up at the very moment at which it might release the truth.

—Lacan (2007, p. 64)

There is a class of dreams that are so disturbing that it seems out of the question that there may be a wishful component to them. Certain dreams bring so much anxiety that they awaken the dreamer and are experienced as nightmares. Freud (1900/1958, p. 580) hypothesized that, in such cases, the censor has been unsuccessful in its attempt to disguise a wish that is highly unacceptable to the preconscious and the dream is abruptly terminated; the dream has thus failed to protect sleep, to allow the dreamer to go on sleeping. Twenty-five years later he proposed a slightly different explanation: He hypothesized that, at least in many such cases, the censorship involved in dream formation has not done its job properly—it has failed to disguise the wish enacted in the dream, which is likely to be reprehensible to the dreamer's moral sense—and introduces anxiety in a last-ditch effort to confuse the dreamer, who will be inclined to notice only the anxiety generated by the wish that is enacted in the dream and not the satisfaction found in it (Freud, 1925a/1961, p. 132).

One of my analysands recounted a dream in which he was ardently making out with one of his female subordinates in a public space at work where he could be seen by many of his colleagues. He was extremely anxious at the thought that he might be seen by someone—which would lead to him losing his job and his wife finding out why he had been fired—and he repeatedly tried to get the subordinate to go into his private office with him, to no avail. The anxiety was foremost in his thoughts about the dream, leading him to neglect for the most part his attraction to the specific woman he imagined making out with in the dream and the pleasure he was taking in the act of making out in public. In that sense, anxiety served to disguise from him a very obvious wishful impulse expressed in the dream. It also served to obscure a possible wish for his wife to find out about his philandering so that she would force him to put a stop to it and punish him for his unfaithfulness (with which he was quite uncomfortable even though he persisted in it).

Another man told me a very detailed dream in which he was supposed to meet his wife at a certain time and place, but things kept happening in the dream to thwart him and he woke up anxious about keeping his wife waiting. When I commented that the dream staged him keeping his wife waiting and asked if there was any sense in which he might want to keep her waiting, he immediately indicated that he had been thinking that he tended to satisfy her every request too quickly and neglected to just let her want him, to keep her desire for him alive, something he felt he was not terribly good at. (Other elements in the dream and his associations to them suggested a link between his wife and his mother and brought out how much he enjoyed as a schoolboy deferring as long as possible his return home, where his mother was waiting for him.) His anxiety at the end of the dream served as an effective screen, preventing him from recognizing a wish that the dream had blatantly fulfilled: to keep his wife waiting.

The appearance of anxiety in a dream is thus very often a lure: Anxiety serves to disguise or divert attention from wishes in many dreams, indeed, many more dreams than people are likely to suspect. Nevertheless, Freud also made room for dreams that do not at all fit into the wish-fulfilling category.

In *Beyond the Pleasure Principle* (Freud, 1920/1955), he introduced the notion of repetition compulsion ("a compulsion to repeat") and outlined a class of dreams in which the dreamer repeatedly relives a traumatic experience in the hope of introducing some anxiety into a situation for which she had in reality been unprepared, anxiety being associated by Freud with a kind of preparedness or first stage of readiness for a problem. For example, someone who is in a train wreck for which there was no warning may find herself repeatedly dreaming of the moments before the wreck and the wreck itself, hoping to somehow prepare or brace herself for the impending crash, as if the fact of being prepared or braced would have spared her the trauma (if not the physical injury owing to the train wreck, at least her traumatized reaction to it). It is as if she were retroactively trying to introduce some anxious expectation, some readiness, into the earlier event. Freud (p. 32) hypothesized that the psyche spontaneously tries to "master the stimulus" and continues to strive to do so in such overpowering cases even though the attempt is futile.

In my experience, all the clinician can do in such circumstances is to encourage the analysand to speak exhaustively about all of the material around the trauma—her relationships with all of the people involved, her life at the time, and the consequences of the event—until all the libido attached to the trauma is drained away. In the case of one of my analysands, who for some two decades had repeatedly had nightmares about a car accident she had been in that had led to the death of her best friend, it took several years of analytic work to tease out all of the threads of her relationship with her best friend, her connection with all of the other actors involved in the accident, her life at the time, and so on. Her nightmares eventually ceased and have not returned for several years thus far.

Lacan (2006) offered a way of thinking about nightmares that do *not* take the form of a simple repetition of an earlier event: Their nightmarish quality derives, he suggested, from the fact that it is not one of our wishes (that is, one of our "desires" in his terminology) but rather one of our demands that is satisfied in such dreams.

> It is, in any case, a fact of experience that when my dream begins to coincide with my demand (not with reality, as is improperly said, which can safeguard my sleep)—or with what proves to be equivalent to it here, the other's demand—I wake up. (p. 624)

In his view, we often demand from others things that we do not even want them to give us, in a sense, for if they did give them to us it would lead to the extinguishing of our desire, our desire (which as he understood it is always a desire for something else, something more) being what is dearest to us, we being far more concerned with having and experiencing desire than with satisfying it. For it is the having and experiencing of desire that makes us feel alive, not its satisfaction. In general, we prefer not to get what we demand—even if we express dissatisfaction when we do not get it—so that we can go on desiring. Lacan theorized that we awaken in horror from dreams in which our demand is about to be satisfied because that will entail the crushing and extinguishing of our desire; such dreams threaten to jeopardize our very being as beings of desire, desire being what is most precious to us (far more precious, in many cases, than satisfaction).

One analysand reported a dream that she experienced as a nightmare in which she asked her boyfriend to move with her to another city and he agreed to do so. On the face of it, it seems as if she got what she wanted in the dream, but her discussion of her situation with her boyfriend made it clear that although she had thought about asking him to move with her, her fondest wish was for him not to be like her father who was always quick to compromise, not to be flexible with her when she knew full well that he did not want to move to that city. Her most cherished desire, we might say, was that he not give up on his desire! When he did in the dream, her desire for him to be a certain way, to be a certain kind of figure for her, was crushed. It was as if she were being deprived of her desire for a certain kind of man: a man who knew what he wanted, who did not bend over backwards for her, who was, to her mind, phallic.

The Fundamental Fantasy

The unconscious is the fact that being, by speaking, enjoys, and . . . wants to know nothing more about it.

— Lacan (1998a, pp. 104–105)

Although analysands often present a plethora of different fantasies in the course of even just a few years of analysis, Lacan hypothesized that virtually all of these particular fantasies stem from one and the same structure: a "fundamental fantasy" (see, for example, Lacan, 2006, p. 614) that defines the subject's most basic relation to the Other or stance with respect to the Other.[13] The myriad

---

[13] For what may be his earliest use of the term, see Lacan (1988a, p. 17).

scenarios that run through the analysand's mind, daydreams, and masturbation fantasies were considered by Lacan to be permutations of the fundamental fantasy, usually presenting one facet of that fundamental fantasy, albeit in a disguised form. Or, to put it differently, the myriad scenarios, daydreams, and masturbation fantasies all boil down to a "single" fundamental fantasy, a fantasy that plays an important role in structuring the analysand's relationships with significant others in her life.

I will not discuss the fundamental fantasy at any length here, as I have already done so elsewhere (Fink, 1995, pp. 61–68, 1997, pp. 56–71; see also some further remarks in this book in Chapter 9), but I would like to point out that the general idea is that the analysand's fundamental fantasy at the outset of the analysis is experienced by her as insufferable: She cannot bear the thought of the fantasy that gives her satisfaction—she cannot bear to think about what gives her enjoyment—for she finds it so reprehensible, so contrary to everything she feels she is and stands for. She "wants to know nothing . . . about it" (Lacan, 1998a, p. 105). If her fundamental fantasy involves, for example, being scorned and criticized by a man (scorn and criticism having been the major forms of attention she received from her father), and she orchestrates things with every new man she meets such that he begins to scorn and criticize her (or selects men who already have that propensity), this is likely to leave her satisfied at the level of fantasy but dissatisfied in terms of her ideals and goals for herself. And the more relationships she "contaminates" by subtly or not so subtly inducing them to conform to the image of her fundamental fantasy, the more insufferable she is likely to find that fantasy. The analyst's goal, in asking her to recount and associate to so many of her dreams, daydreams, and fantasies in the course of her analysis, is obviously to bring her to modify that fundamental fantasy, to reconfigure or "traverse" it, as Lacan (1978) put it.

It is not easy to detect and articulate one's fundamental fantasy; it may take many months, if not years, of analysis. Indeed, my sense is that by the time an analysand has brought out most of the elements of a fundamental fantasy such that it can be clearly and convincingly articulated, it has already begun to change and give way to something else: a new fantasy. This is a regular feature of psychoanalytic work: The analysand is far more able to articulate something that no longer has the same hold upon her than to articulate something that she is still currently in the grips of. For example, the aforementioned analysand whose father regularly appeared, albeit in a disguised form, in his sexual fantasies was able to elaborate many of the facets of his fundamental fantasy (involving the simultaneous propping up of his father as superior to him in every way and dragging his father's "good name" through the mud to "fix him") when certain conflicts in his life had come, as it were, to a head, but also when, after several years of analysis, he was ready to move beyond this stance in relation to the Other that was so problematic for him—that is, when he was on the verge of reconfiguring his fundamental fantasy.

Since reconfiguration of the fundamental fantasy is something to work toward in the later stages of an analysis, I will leave fuller discussion of it to an advanced book on technique (interested readers can find primarily theoretical discussions of it in Fink, 1995, 1997).

7

Handling Transference and Countertransference

[Transference] remains, with the sticking power of common consent, identified with a feeling or a constellation of feelings felt by the patient, whereas by simply defining it as the kind of reproduction that occurs in analysis, it becomes clear that the greater part of it must remain unnoticed by the subject.

— Lacan (2006, p. 461)

Recognizing Transference

IN THE CONTEMPORARY psychoanalytic literature, the term *transference* has come to designate virtually everything that transpires in the analyst's office. Freud (1905a/1953, p. 116) introduced the term *Übertragung*—which has been translated as *transference*, but literally means transmission, translation, transposition, or application (from one idiom or register to another idiom or register)— to refer to "new editions or facsimiles of the impulses and phantasies which are aroused ... during the progress of the analysis" and which "replace some earlier person by the person of the physician. To put it another way: a whole series of psychological experiences are revived, not as belonging to the past, but as applying to the person of the physician at the present moment." These translations or transpositions can take several different general forms:

- At the perceptual level—whether visual, auditory, olfactory, tactile, or other—some feature of the analyst reminds the analysand of a parent (or of someone else of importance in his past), such as the sound of her voice, the color of her eyes, hair, or skin, her build, her sweaty or cool palms when she shakes hands with him at the beginning and end of sessions, and so on.

At times, it suffices for the analyst to simply *have* a nose—regardless of its actual shape or size—for the analysand to "see it" as like his mother's nose (he may indicate that it was only when he saw it from a certain angle or in a certain light, for example, that it reminded him of hers). In other words, it is not that some real feature of the analyst reminds him of his mother, but rather that he projects onto her something about his mother that he is grappling with at that particular moment, something that is associated with that specific facial feature. He "sees it in her," as it were, as if in a perceptual register.

- Some "coded" feature of the analyst or her entourage or environment reminds the analysand of a parent (or of someone else of importance in his past), such as her age; her style of dress (clothing, jewelry, makeup, and accessories), which may suggest a particular socioeconomic class or the attempt to create a certain kind of look (professional, casual, ethnic, disheveled, bad girl, preppy or Sloan Ranger, etc.); her vocabulary, grammar, and general way of speaking (which again may indicate something about socioeconomic class or aspirations, educational level, country or region of origin); or her choice of office type, location, and decor (all of which situate her in various socially, linguistically, or semiotically coded contexts).

    These features involve *sign systems* of one kind or another—sign systems that have evolved within a specific culture and linguistic group (even if more than one language is spoken and even if more than one culture is represented within that group).[1] As always, the analysand is "free" to read the analyst's dress, way of speaking, and so on as meaning something that is in no wise intended by the analyst; after all, we cannot control or determine the meaning of our own speech, dress, or actions— other people determine their meaning (Fink, 2005b, pp. 574–575).

- Some expression of emotion on the analyst's part may remind the analysand of a parent (or of someone else of importance in his past), such as embarrassment manifested in flushed cheeks at certain moments during the therapy; nervousness manifested in a wavering or tremolo in

---

[1] Note that many of these semiotic features of transference involve both perceptual and linguistic components. For example, the analyst's exact age may be known to the analysand from a variety of official or unofficial sources, but the analysand may get a distinctly different impression of her age from seeing, hearing, or being with her. Similarly, the analyst's style of dress involves both perceptual and semiotic components: The former include, for example, the color, cut, and feel of the fabrics, as well as the general appearance this style of dress gives the analyst; the latter include things like brand names, price ranges, social group connotations, and whether the clothing is stylish, out of style, or altogether unfashionable (although some of these arguably involve both perceptual and semiotic components).

her voice, fidgeting of hands, squirming in her chair, or crossing and uncrossing of legs; anxiety reflected in panicked looks, blood rushing from her face, or stiffness of posture; suppressed anger reflected in an obviously controlled tone of voice, brusque gesture, displaced peevishness (e.g., speaking angrily to someone who calls on the phone while presumably angry with the analysand), and so on. All of these detectable emotions, which may recall such emotions seen by the analysand in other people from his past, can be placed under the heading of *affective effects*; they involve libido instead of images or signs per se.[2]

   Indeed, the analyst need not actually feel or manifest any emotion for the analysand to "sense" a particular emotion emanating from her: In many cases, the analysand projects onto her emotions that he sensed in his mother—emotions that disturbed him and that he is still grappling with.

Although I do not believe that Freud ever spelled out all of the different features—perceptual, semiotic, and affective—of the analyst (and his surroundings) that could serve as fodder for transferences, he certainly never limited transference to the succession of positive and negative feelings that the patient has toward the analyst. This is, however, arguably the most widespread understanding of transference—Malan (1995/2001, p. 21), for example, admitted that "the word has gradually become more loosely used for *any* feelings that the patient may have about the therapist." Perhaps it would be better to say that it is the most widespread *mis*understanding of transference, for transference is far more complicated than that.

Transferential Configurations

We soon perceive that the transference is itself only a piece of repetition, and that the repetition is a transference of the forgotten past not only on to the doctor but also on to all the other aspects of the current situation.

— Freud (1914a/1958, p. 151)

I prefer to leave the notion of transference its empirical totality, while stressing that it is polyvalent and that it involves several registers: the symbolic, the imaginary, and the real.

— Lacan (1988a, pp. 112–113)

---

[2] Note, though, that the analysand often becomes aware of the analyst's emotions through visual and auditory channels, and that there is thus a perceptual component involved here as well. Furthermore, should the analyst's vocabulary change when she is agitated, there may be a linguistic component too.

What happens when an analysand encounters a trait in the analyst that reminds him of something from the past?[3] Let us suppose that the analyst occasionally wears glasses, and that her glasses are similar to those of the analysand's mother, even though analyst and analysand are about the same age. If the analysand's feelings about his mother have always been positive, we might expect him to transpose some of those positive feelings onto the analyst and to work cooperatively with her in the sessions. If, on the other hand, the analysand's feelings about his mother have always been negative, we might expect him to transpose some of his negative feelings onto the analyst and be hostile to her in the sessions.

But while transferences may sometimes become evident to the analyst in the form of feelings the analysand expresses in one way or another, whether intentionally or unintentionally, to the analyst, they perhaps become evident even more often in other ways: The analysand whose relations with his mother were quite sour might remain openly warm and ostensibly cooperative during the sessions but secretly have no faith whatsoever in the eyeglass-wearing analyst, even vowing to himself to keep all his best insights from her. He may strive to convince the analyst that he is taking her interpretations seriously, all the while ridiculing them in his mind and doing whatever it takes to render her work as useless as slippers are to fish. He may let nothing emotional transpire and may be quite unaware of any negative feelings he has toward her; nevertheless, he adopts a stance toward her that likely reflects a similar stance he adopted toward his mother, a position involving furtive protest and rebellion.

Let us now imagine a still more common case: The analysand says and would like to believe that his relations with his mother were fine, whereas much of his activity or inactivity in life suggest just the opposite (for example, he never follows her advice, never pursues any of the women she approves of, prepares for none of the careers she recommends, and so on). Indeed, it often takes quite some time before analysands can go beyond their initial assertions that everything is fine in their families: Repression is often such that they are consciously convinced that relations with a parent were hunky-dory when they were anything but, and yet they find themselves adopting an oppositional stance toward that parent, a stance whose origins are mysterious to them.

When such an analysand sees the analyst wearing glasses that resemble his mother's, his transferential oppositional stance is not likely to find expression in

---

[3] Ferenczi (1909/1990, p. 18) likened the analysand's sense that the analyst is like an important figure from his past when he locates a single trait in the analyst (name, hair color, etc.) that reminds him of that figure to the rhetorical trope known as *synecdoche* (pars pro toto, the part taken for the whole).

dirty looks or some kind of emotional outburst; it may, however, eventually lead to recurrent latenesses, long silences, early departures, absences, and vacations, all of which the analysand justifies with perfectly plausible sounding reasons (his boss keeps making him work late, he is exhausted from working so hard, he has to dash off to medical appointments, his junky car keeps breaking down, and so on). And in doing so he is not necessarily acting in bad faith: He is giving the reasons of which he is aware, and they may well be the only reasons of which he is aware.

It makes little sense to say here that the analysand has "unconscious feelings of anger" toward his mother and thus toward the analyst, for something is not, strictly speaking, a feeling if it is unconscious: *It has not yet become a feeling; it can only become a feeling when it is felt.*[4] Nevertheless, the repressed aspects of the relationship with the mother are manifesting themselves in the creation of a rebellious stance on the analysand's part, of which he himself may be unaware.

Transference is thus in no way, shape, or form confined to the field of affect alone: Just as an analysand's symptoms may reflect a whole family structure, the transference may involve a repetition of a highly complex structure of the same kind. Consider the following case that I briefly supervised. The analysand would fall into numerous protracted silences, and her analyst was at the end of her rope. Both the analyst and I assumed at the outset that the analysand felt that the material she needed to articulate was too shameful to speak about, or possibly that since she had never spoken about it to anyone, the real events themselves she had lived through were resisting symbolization—that is, were resisting being put into words. It soon came out that the analysand had once been raped by a male practitioner; she had remained silent in his office during the rape, even though she knew that her mother was close by in the waiting room. At this point her analyst and I began to wonder whether she was experiencing the therapy as a kind of rape, even though her analyst was female—in other words, we hypothesized that she had transferred the frightening figure of her former male practitioner onto her current female analyst.

Discussion of this possible link did not, however, do much to loosen the analysand's tongue. She remained silent—as if stubbornly so—and yet was clearly uncomfortable during her sessions, anxious outside of them, but nevertheless eager to come to them. Slow, tedious work on a few fragmentary

---

[4] As Freud (1915b/1957, p. 178) put it, "Strictly speaking . . . there are no unconscious affects as there are unconscious ideas"; and, again, "We cannot assert the existence of unconscious affects in the same sense as of unconscious ideas" (Freud, 1916–1917/1963, p. 409). He does, however, occasionally make an exception for guilt.

dreams and scant associations finally brought to light that for a couple of years when the analysand was a child, her father would touch her sexually when her mother was out of the house. He threatened that she would be sent away from home should she ever breathe a word about it to her mother, and she had never told a soul about it for decades. *The family situation that she was reproducing in the analysis thus turned out to be extremely complex*: Her prolonged silences were a way of protecting and remaining faithful to her father, of reliving her no doubt frightened and yet aroused state while lying silent as her father touched her, of keeping secret from her mother/analyst her bewildering victory over her mother in the quest for her father's attention, of sparing her mother/analyst the twofold shock of the father's perfidy and of the daughter's complicity, and, undoubtedly, of accomplishing other things as well.

Such complex transferences are often very difficult to detect and perhaps account for why most clinicians view transference simply as the way the analysand feels about the analyst at a particular moment in time.[5] One might even postulate that their difficulty detecting complex transferences has led them to engage in what might be referred to as "affect hunting," constantly asking the analysand, "How did that make you feel?" *as if feeling were the key to all things* (transferential and otherwise), which it clearly is not.[6] Contemporary clinicians

---

[5] Ralph Greenson (1967, p. 155) did a bit better when he defined transference as the "experience of feelings, drives, attitudes, fantasies, and defenses toward a person in the present which do not befit that person but are a repetition of reactions originating in regard to significant persons of early childhood, unconsciously displaced onto figures in the present." Lacan (1988a, p. 273) once provided a rather more poetic "definition" of transference, in the allegorical vein of the era of Romantic painting: "Error taking flight in deception and caught by misunderstanding."

[6] Affect may help us locate repressed material, but ultimately we are guided by repression first and foremost, not by affect. Affect and thought (or desire) are usually connected to each other at the outset, but when subjected to repression they have a tendency to become detached from each other, the one being found without the other: The analysand is angry but does not know why, or vividly remembers an incident from his childhood but recalls no feelings he had at the time. As Freud (1916–1917/1963, p. 409) argued, "The most immediate vicissitude of [an] affect [tied to an idea that undergoes repression] is to be transformed into anxiety." In other words, when we encounter anxiety we can assume that some thought (a wishful thought) has been repressed and the affect associated with it, regardless of its original tenor, has been set adrift, so to speak; it no longer seems to be connected in the analysand's mind to any event, circumstances, or thought and transforms into anxiety, anxiety being "the universally current coinage for which *any* affective impulse is or can be exchanged if the ideational content attached to it is subjected to repression" (p. 403–404).

In this sense, affect often is a lure: It inclines us to think that the analysand is extremely upset by something that he may instead be extremely pleased by, at least at one level, or extremely worried by something that he may instead be wishing for, in at least one respect. Anxiety is a pretty sure sign of repression, but it does not tell us where to look for the repression or what the initial affect was. And other affects can serve as lures as well: The analysand may feel sad but is secretly ecstatic, or may act upbeat when he is actually mourning the loss of an unacknowledged love object.

Perhaps contemporary clinicians are constantly in search of affect because, taking "rapport" between themselves and their patients to be the be-all and end-all of psychotherapeutic treatment (like Malan,

also have a nasty tendency to attribute intractable silences, and many other treatment difficulties as well (e.g., lack of associations, inability to remember dreams or daydreams, tardiness, cancellations, no-shows, and so on), to a willful resistance to the treatment on the analysand's part instead of looking at the larger picture. Such treatment difficulties generally arise (1) from the fact that it is not easy to articulate what has never before been articulated, (2) from the repetition of an earlier situation, which may be very complex and hard to elucidate, or (3) from something the analyst is or is not doing, for example, refusing to help the analysand articulate what has never before been articulated (indeed, allowing both the analysand and herself to avoid that difficult task) or not striving to figure out what earlier situation the analysand may be repeating.[7]

This is why Lacan (2006, p. 595) decided to adopt a point of view diametrically opposed to that of many contemporary clinicians when he said, "There is no other resistance to analysis than that of the analyst himself," [8] the idea being that when analysts are inclined to conclude that the analysand is resisting, it is often their own failing, not his. In other words, treatment difficulties tend to arise when the analyst herself adopts what Freud (1900/1958, p. 639) referred to as the "ostrich policy," sticking her head into the sand so as not to see. Since "whatever interrupts the progress of analytic work is a resistance" (p. 517; see also Freud, 1915a/1958, p. 162), it makes perfect sense to characterize the analyst's obstruction of the treatment as a resistance.

Transference Is Everywhere

Even if we assume that we must consider transference to be a product of the analytic situation, we can say that this situation could not create the phenomenon from scratch, and that, in order to produce it, there must be, outside of the analytic situation, preexisting possibilities which the analytic situation combines in what is perhaps a unique way.

— Lacan (1978, pp. 124–125)

1995/2001, pp. 84–85), they feel that the stronger the affect expressed in a session, the greater the rapport. Privileging rapport leads therapists to privilege affect above all else. Lacan (1988a, p. 57) criticized this excessive privileging of affect back in 1954: "The slightest peculiar, even strange, feeling that the subject professes to in the text of the session is taken to be a spectacular success. This is what follows from this fundamental misunderstanding." For a somewhat more detailed discussion of affects in psychoanalysis, see Fink (2004, pp. 50–52).

[7] Note the term "situations" in Freud's (1920/1955, p. 21) comment that "patients repeat all of these unwanted situations and painful emotions in the transference."

[8] See also *Seminar III*, where Lacan (1993, p. 48) said, "The patient's resistance is always your own," and *Seminar XXIV* (1976–1977, January 11, 1977), where he said, "Resistance finds its point of departure in the analyst himself."

The kind of transposition from one register to another found in transference in the analytic situation can be found in many other situations as well. Most of us have had the experience of taking an instant liking or disliking to someone we have just met simply because she resembles someone else we like or dislike, has the same name as someone else we like or dislike, or has some other feature (appearance, profession, voice, etc.) that reminds us of someone else we like or dislike.

Such transferences may make us do stupid things, for example, immediately trust people we should not trust, avoid people we might have a great deal in common with, and even fall in love with someone who has only the superficial qualities of the people we have loved in the past, not their more profound qualities. (One of my analysands told me that at age seven he developed an instant crush on a girl he met the first day of summer camp who looked almost exactly like his sister.) Indeed, the very process of falling in love and the experience of being in love owe a tremendous amount to transference: The more intensely one is *in love* at the outset, the more likely it is that a "case of mistaken identity" like that found in transference is at work, the more likely it is that a "false connection" (Freud & Breuer, 1893–1895/1955, p. 302) has been made between a beloved earlier figure and the current beloved.[9] The most passionate forms of love generally involve a total misrecognition of the otherness of the other person and a massive projection of all kinds of desirable qualities onto someone about whom one knows very little. The object of such massive projection sometimes even protests that she or he wants to be loved for her- or himself, not put on a pedestal or idealized. In many cases, people begin to fall out of love precisely when the other's actual qualities begin to come into view and the perfection that had been projected by the lover onto the beloved proves to be illusory.[10]

Similarly, transference often plays a considerable role in students' relations to their teachers. Students often quickly assume that their teachers have a great deal of knowledge and become enamored of them, only to later recognize the limits of their knowledge. At the outset they consider them to be virtually omniscient, which may well be what they thought of their parents when they were small children; and just as in the case of their parents, the limits of whose knowledge they eventually recognized, in due course they come to perceive the limits of their teachers' knowledge, often becoming a good deal less enamored of them in the process. The teacher is at first seen by them as a kind of "subject

---

[9] As Freud (1915a/1958, p. 168) said, "This is the essential character of every state of being in love."
[10] A whole book could be written on this topic; since it is my next writing project, I will not comment on it any further here.

supposed to know" (see Chapter 5) who elicits the student's love, and then ultimately falls, to a greater or lesser degree, from that pedestal, leading to disappointment, disillusion, or even despair—this sometimes occurs only after quite a few years. The analysand's love of knowledge, knowledge that he hopes to find in the analyst, plays an important role in an analysis almost right to the very end. Like Socrates' disciples, who believed Socrates had a great deal of knowledge even though he professed to have none (except regarding love), and were able to seek knowledge precisely because of their belief that he possessed it, analysands are able to engage in the arduous task of seeking knowledge about themselves precisely because of their belief that the analyst possesses it. Indeed, Lacan considered this belief to be the indispensable motor force of analysis with neurotics.

However, although transference can be found in many facets of life and can assume many different guises (warm feelings toward one's accountant, ever more brazen shoplifting,[11] taunting highway patrolmen, scrupulous compliance with conventions, etc.), not everything one encounters in the psychoanalytic situation is transference.

Not Everything Is Transference

Transference is the putting into operation of the unconscious.
— Lacan (1978, p. 267)

The former analyst of an analysand of mine was apparently ten or more minutes late to virtually all of their fixed-length sessions. The analysand did not feel particularly neglected by either of his parents or complain, for example, that one of his parents was always late in taking him to school or picking him up after extracurricular activities. Hence when he eventually expressed annoyance with his analyst for repeatedly showing up late, one could have hardly considered it to be a transference per se: He was annoyed with her the way he might have been annoyed at anyone else for acting as though her time was far more valuable than his. He may, of course, have been more upset with her than with a plumber, say, who did the same thing, because of the importance she had taken on in his life partly as the result of other transferences, but his annoyance with her repeated latenesses should not, in and of itself, be termed a transference.

---

[11] Several of my analysands have made very clear links between the kinds of trouble they got into as teenagers and their intense, but displaced, anger at their fathers.

Nor should it be assumed to reflect the way he reacts to everyone around him—that he must be quick to think that everyone acts as though they value their time more highly than his, for example—as clinicians are often so quick to presume. We must not jump to the conclusion that the way the analysand reacts to the analyst is necessarily the way he reacts to everyone else in his daily life, as if there were no specificity to the way the analysand behaves with different people.[12] After all, the analyst presumably presents herself to him more as a blank screen or "mirror" (Freud, 1912b/1958, p. 118) than most other people in his life do, which presumably allows him to project and repeat more aspects of relationships and situations from the past with her than he is able to with colleagues, friends, and lovers who make no pretense of being "the woman without qualities" (to paraphrase the title of Robert Musil's unfinished novel). Although transference can be found in all facets of life—people obviously project and repeat in the workplace and at home—they still generally have several different ways of relating to others in their repertoires, being friendly and cooperative with some, obsequious with others, and rivalrous and uncooperative with still others, for example. To suggest that the analysand must act in the same way with everyone else as he does with the analyst is quite a stretch: It is an abduction, in Pierce's sense of the word (see Eco, 1984), not a deduction!

There are, of course, cases in which an analysand presumes that people are always trying to humiliate him or convey to him that he is worthless, and anything the analyst does will be read as confirming that. But often enough, as in the case of the analysand mentioned earlier whose analyst was always late to sessions, it is not the analysand's "habitual way of being" or his "inferiority complex" that is at work (via so-called projective identification or anything else), but rather the analyst's "habitual way of being" or countertransference that is making her systematically late.

While it is often useful to see if there is more than meets the eye in the analysand's annoyance at such things, analysts must recognize their own contribution to such situations. This does not mean that they should unburden themselves to their analysands, exploring with them in the session their own possible reasons for being late, but that they should articulate a commitment to being on time in the future and work through in supervision or in their

---

[12] This is, nevertheless, "an underlying premise of dynamic psychotherapy," according to Bauer & Mills (1989/1994, p. 200): "Patients interact [with their therapists] in a way that is generally consistent with their characteristic modes of functioning." Curiously enough, this very premise contradicts another of their presumptions: The therapist's "real behavior," which is highly individual, has a big effect on the patient's attitudes and behavior vis-à-vis the therapist. It would seem that one cannot have it both ways.

own analysis whatever unconscious motives are at play. Perhaps the analyst has grown to dislike the analysand; perhaps she feels he is laid-back and that she can easily run a few errands before sessions without him being fazed; or perhaps he has subtly encouraged her latenesses by not complaining about them because he enjoys feeling superior to her or having a legitimate beef with her. Many other things could, of course, be at work as well, but they have at least as much to do with the actual relationship between the analyst and the analysand as individuals as they do with transference; indeed, in many cases transference may have nothing to do with them, countertransference playing the leading role.[13]

It should hopefully be obvious that countertransference is no simpler than transference: It too may involve the repetition of an earlier or parallel situation (as, for example, when the analyst brings a problem from home into the office, or a problem with one analysand into the work with another analysand) with imaginary, symbolic, and real components. As I mentioned in Chapter 4, Lacan (2006, p. 225) defined countertransference very broadly when he characterized it as "the sum total of the analyst's biases, passions, and difficulties, or even of his inadequate information, at any given moment in the dialectical process" of analysis (see also Lacan, 1988a, p. 23).

This broad definition allows us to see that even the analyst's perspective on psychoanalytic theory can function in a countertransferential way; if she believes in the existence of "projective identification" she may well (as we shall see later in this chapter) view the aforementioned analysand's annoyance with her repeated latenesses as at least partially his fault: She may be inclined to think that he has "projected into her" his belief that everyone puts their wishes before his or takes advantage of him and has ended up *making* her fulfill his expectations! Analysts may not only have "inadequate information" insofar as they fail to study significant psychoanalytic literature, but also insofar as they embrace psychoanalytic concepts that conveniently shift the onus for difficulties in the treatment from the analyst to the analysand. Countertransference includes the

---

[13] Winnicott (1949, p. 70) has, in my view, confused matters regarding countertransference by introducing the term "objective countertransference," which he defined as "the analyst's love and hate in reaction to the actual personality and behaviour of the patient, based on objective observation," which is then distinguished by certain authors (see, for example, Spotnitz, 1999, p. 229) from "subjective countertransference." I suspect that we would be hard-pressed to find any two analysts who could agree in any but the most approximate manner upon "the actual personality and behaviour of the patient" based on their "objective observation" of him or her, and that any attempt to distinguish subjective from objective in matters of countertransference is destined to quickly founder. Lacan (1976–1977, November 16, 1976) claimed that at the end of one's analysis "the unconscious remains Other," meaning that the analyst is still quite capable of misunderstanding and misrecognizing her own motives, feelings, and reactions.

analyst's own theoretical biases and blinders, regardless of the form they take: whether the analyst refuses to take any theory into account and finds herself unable to see anything in the case other than what her preexisting notions and the pop psychology she has learned from the media allow her to see; reconceptualizes the case every week depending on what she happens to be reading; relies excessively on theory in sessions, such that she is unable to hear what the analysand is actually saying and tries to squeeze what is happening in the sessions into the framework of a cherished theory; or tries to use the case to prop up her own recently formulated theories, fitting the "facts" to her own framework. All of these can, in my view, be usefully thought of as part and parcel of the analyst's countertransference.

How to Handle Transference

If psychoanalysis is a means, it situates itself in the place of love.
— Lacan (1973–1974, December 18, 1973)

Having said a little now about how to recognize what in the analytic situation is owing to transference and what is not (owing instead to countertransference),[14] let us now turn to the so-called *handling* of transference.

Although the parameters of transference that I have thus far outlined may strike the reader as abstract, the experience of transference is anything but, whether considered from the vantage point of the analyst who is on the receiving end of it or from that of the analysand who is in the grips of it.

Positive Transference

I would say that positive transference is when the person in question, the analyst in this case, is in our good graces; negative transference is when we keep an eye on him.
— Lacan (1978, p. 124)

In certain cases, the analysand finds himself thinking about the analyst a great deal of the time, wondering about her life, and perhaps even trying to find out more about her; in a word, he has become enamored of or even somewhat

---

[14] Note that even the basic constraints of the analytic situation itself, such as meeting at scheduled times in a specific location, making regular payments, and so on, can be fodder for transference, since analysands who refuse to be part of the "system" may rebel against such constraints as representing Establishment, authoritarian values and hold the analyst personally responsible for them.

obsessed with someone he barely knows and who very likely has few if any of the characteristics of the women who have been of interest to him in the past (if indeed any women have been of interest to him in the past). The analyst may not be physically attractive to him, may be several decades older or younger than he is, may dress in a manner he finds unflattering or indicative of a cultural or class milieu that is repugnant to his sensibilities, and yet for some reason he may find himself feeling very enthusiastic about her and eagerly looking forward to each of his sessions with her. (This kind of infatuation often occurs among analysands who are of the same sex as their analysts as well.)

The analysand feels he has found someone who truly listens to him, can understand him, and may possibly be able to help him in his time of need. She strikes him as knowledgeable—as already knowing or likely to know what his problem is and how to solve it. In a word, he sees her like a positive figure from his past, like someone who, at least at one point in time, seemed open to him and willing and able to help. Nevertheless, *he does not experience his transference as transference.* He does not say to himself, "The only reason I feel this way about my analyst is because she reminds me of the way my mother was when I was little and she still acted like a mother to me." Instead, he experiences it as a strong feeling for this particular person, right here, right now. He is caught up in it, not observing himself at a distance from it: His passion for his analyst feels very real to him.

As long as his transference takes this form and does not interfere with the work he is doing in the therapy, *there is no need to intervene in any way to temper his enthusiasm.*[15] Psychoanalysis harnesses the kind of excitement (libidinal energy) generated by the analytic situation and the case of mistaken identity that it fosters; it does not try to neutralize or dissipate it as certain other forms of treatment do. When one of my supervisees said she was troubled by the fact that a male analysand of hers had told her, "Sometimes I think the only reason I get on the bus to come to therapy is because you're good looking," I replied, "At least you've got that going for you." She later indicated to me that it was very helpful to her and to the therapy as well to realize that whatever aesthetic or erotic interest brought her analysand to therapy was fine, as long as it inspired him to engage in the work of exploring and changing his life. When the analysand has this kind of positive transference to the analyst, the analyst

---

[15] As Freud (1916–1917/1963, p. 443) said, we "need not bother about [the transference] so long as it operates in favour of the joint work of analysis." According to Gill (1982, p. 81), Ferenczi, Rank, and Reich all maintained that "a strong positive transference, especially near the beginning of analysis, is only a symptom of resistance which requires unmasking"; hence *they* would presumably argue that it *is* necessary to intervene in such a way as to temper the analysand's enthusiasm. Reich, in fact, believed that positive transference always hides a more fundamental, primordial, negative transference.

strives to get the analysand to begin the laborious process of the analysis out of love for her, to begin recalling certain parts of his past, as well as daydreams and fantasies that he usually pays no attention to, and to begin associating to them. This is hard work, and the analysand needs all the motivation he can get.

Recall that psychoanalysis began with a love story: Anna O. (whose real name was Bertha Pappenheim) came up with the "talking cure" out of love for Joseph Breuer, the attentive young doctor who made housecalls morning and night to work with her for hours at a time. He was the only person whose presence she would notice and the only person she would speak with during certain phases of her treatment (Freud & Breuer, 1893–1895/1955, pp. 21–47). In the beginning (of psychoanalysis) was love. And her love was inspired by a man who, whether she found him good-looking or not, was a well-respected physician whom she could assume knew something about her condition and how to heal her (even though, as history shows, she was the one who had virtually all the knowledge and he was simply smart enough to follow her lead). Even though the parties to the love story from which psychoanalysis was born did not live happily ever after together, the fact remains that love, inspired by a belief that the other party possesses knowledge, was the mainspring of the treatment Anna O. invented.

Many of the graduate students in clinical psychology whom I supervise are quick to try to dispel a patient's belief that they have considerable knowledge of what ails him. They often do so in the interest, so they say, of honesty and to assure the patient that he has as much power in the relationship as the clinician. As laudable as their goals may be—and it is indeed the patient who has the lion's share of the knowledge, the practitioner having very little, especially at the outset of the treatment—they often end up undermining the patient's faith in their ability to help him. Rather than "empowering" him, they end up disempowering him, making him feel dejected and despondent. He feels that he has no knowledge that is of any use in this domain; if he did, he would not be in the predicament in which he finds himself in the first place. It is often very important for him to believe that someone else has the knowledge that can help him; dispelling that belief is to take away his last shred of hope. Hence, this attempt to intervene in the patient's transference of knowledge onto the analyst can lead to despair.

Trying to convince the patient right from the outset that he has as much, if not more, knowledge than the clinician is most likely to succeed when the clinician herself is young and working in a training facility where all the therapists are either seeing their very first patients or have only a year or two of experience. For in such cases, patients are usually aware that they are getting what they are paying for, so to speak—that their therapist has comparatively less "expertise" than other therapists they might seek out in the community who have been practicing for many years.

Nevertheless, in numerous cases the patient simply feels that the clinician "doth protest too much" and is just being modest or trying to spare his feelings of inferiority. Socrates's claim to know nothing (except about love) never convinced his disciples, who continued to believe that he was a veritable fount of knowledge. This points to an extremely important facet of psychoanalytic technique: The attempt to dissipate or "liquidate" the analysand's transference is doomed to failure, because the analyst's disclaimer—for example, "I can't possibly know what the problem is, you're the one who has the knowledge here"—is heard by the analysand as coming from the person whom he projects her to be: a very knowledgeable person (otherwise, he asks himself, why would she be a clinician in the first place?). The attempt to mitigate some of the more cumbersome aspects of the transference by commenting on or interpreting it from within the transference (that is, when one is the object of the analysand's transference as opposed to a third party, such as a friend, colleague, or consulting physician) is generally doomed to failure for the very same reason. Should, for example, the analysand have the sense that the analyst is angry at him and the analyst deny any such anger, her denial will nevertheless be heard by the analysand as coming from someone whom he presumes to be angry; indeed, he may take the denial itself as a sign of anger!

Nevertheless, the majority of analysts seem to have fallen in with Freud's (1913/1958) point of view that we must interpret the transference whenever it begins to lead to resistance:

> So long as the patient's communications and ideas run on without any obstruction, the theme of transference should be left untouched. One must wait until the transference, [the handling of] which is the most delicate of all procedures, has become a resistance. (p. 139)

They seem not to have realized that an interpretation of the transference that comes from the transferential object herself, the analyst, is not a way out of the transference but simply reproduces the transference; for, as Lacan (2006, p. 591) said, "The analyst's speech is [always] heard as coming from the transferential Other." If, for example, the analyst has become associated with a critical parental figure, her interpretation will be heard as critical; if she has become associated with a seductive maternal figure, her interpretation will be heard as seductive. We do not achieve some sort of metaposition outside of the transference by interpreting it (the claims of therapists like Levenson, 1995, p. 88, that we can "metacommunicate" notwithstanding). We remain up to our ears in the transference. As Lacan (1967–1968, November 29, 1967) said, there is "no transference of the transference," meaning that—just as there is no position outside of language that allows us to discuss language as a whole without having to rely on language itself in our discussion—there is no way in which we can step completely outside the transference situation in order to discuss what is happening in the transference itself (see also Lacan, 1998b, p. 428). The interpretation of transference is a vicious cycle!

Analysts have tried to get around this vicious cycle by dividing the analysand into two parts: the "experiencing ego" and the "observing ego" (Sterba, 1934). The trick, in their view, is to invite the observing ego, which they consider to be "rational," to step outside of the transference (which is presumably engaged in by the experiencing ego alone) into some kind of metaspace, a space outside of the transference where analyst and analysand can meet as "reasonable" observing egos and agree upon what is happening between the irrational, unreasonable, experiencing egos who are caught up in the transference/countertransference.[16]

It may sound like I am being ironic here, but many authors speak in precisely these terms, as if "rational," "irrational," "reasonable," and "unreasonable" were simple, serviceable categories[17] that could be unproblematically associated

---

[16] To the degree that the interpretation of transference is successful, presumably by fostering the development of an "observing ego" in the analysand, it generally leads, as Lacan (1967–1968, November 29, 1967) said, to "the elimination of the subject supposed to know"—that is, to the elimination of the motor force of the analysis. Nevertheless, many analysts agree with Gill (1982, p. 73) that "allusions to transference" and "transference resistances . . . are present all the time" in analysis and should be "consistently" (p. 27), if not constantly, interpreted. Not surprisingly, their goal is generally "to help [analysands] understand themselves" (p. 66)—in other words, to foster the development of an "observing ego" in them, which amounts to a sort of conscious subject in them, not who is supposed to know, but who actually knows.

[17] If there is one thing one could hope that analysts learn from their study of and experience with psychoanalysis, it is that there are many different forms of reason and many different logics (including, at a minimum, propositional logic, modal logic, and intuitionist logic). If nothing else, there are various forms of rationality associated with the different diagnostic categories. For example, there is an obsessive form of rationality (highly correlated, in so many ways, with our contemporary form of capitalism, with its equation of time and money), a hysteric form of rationality (which runs counter to the former in numerous ways), and so on. See Lacan's (2007, 1998a) work on the four discourses, as he calls them, and my discussion of them (Fink, 1995, Chapter 9). "Reason," one might say in another vein, is but the sum total of the prejudices of one's time and place. As Macalpine (1950/1990, p. 196) put it, "It is particularly unfortunate that the antithesis, 'rational' versus 'irrational,' was introduced, as it was precisely psychoanalysis which demonstrated that 'rational' behavior can be traced to 'irrational' roots." See my comments in the footnotes to Chapter 4 on the role granted to the "rational observing ego" by many 20th-century theorists.

It might be postulated that whereas neurotics operate according to an either/or logic, perverts operate according to a both/and logic, and psychotics operate according to a neither/nor logic. Either/or logic is familiar to us from most ordinary forms of philosophy and mathematics; it implies that if A is B, A is not not-B (if, for example, Socrates is mortal, he is not immortal). When there is a logical contradiction in neurosis (that is, when one asserts that Socrates is both mortal and immortal) one proposition is conscious whereas the other is unconscious (the neurotic man, for example, may consider himself to be male consciously but female unconsciously; he can usually only consciously consider himself to be both after a good deal of analysis). The pervert, following a both/and logic (A can be both B and not-B), need

with one or another of the psychical agencies, and as if—even if an agreement
as to what is going on could be reached between reasonable, "dispassion-
ate," observing egos taking a "time out" from the hothouse of the transference
relationship—it would change anything when they return to the hothouse
(apart from encouraging the analysand to suppress any and all transference
reactions in the future). The analysand is likely to remain just as hypersensitive
to criticism as he was before, for example, but he may begin to "talk himself
down" from his high dudgeon when he remembers his discussion with the
analyst to the effect that he constantly felt criticized by his father as a child,
which is the origin of his hypersensitivity to criticism today. The upshot is that
he will still get very angry but will learn how to suppress his anger after the fact
instead of acting on it. Or he will still experience women's comments to him
as invariably seductive but will learn how to "reason with himself," reminding
himself on each occasion that he experiences their comments that way because
of things that occurred with his mother. Such is the usefulness (or uselessness,
as the case may be) of enlisting the aid of the analysand's observing ego![18]

---

not locate the contradictory assertions in different agencies and can quite consciously affirm both the
male and female aspects of himself and others (see Fink, 2003). The psychotic, following a neither/nor
logic once a psychotic break has occurred, and prior to the possible construction of a delusion that
may restore meaning to his world, finds that A is not equal to A because words fail to remain attached
to things, sliding off them instead (see Chapter 10). Thus he can affirm neither that A is B nor that A
is not B. This somewhat speculative and off-the-cuff characterization of the different logics operating
in the different diagnostic categories will hopefully at least make plausible to the reader my assertion
here that there is no single form of rationality.

[18] For further discussion on the interpretation of transference and the "observing ego," see Fink (2004,
pp. 5–9). The "observing ego" is also considered by many analysts to be the "healthy part of the ego"
with which they hope to form an alliance. Lacan (2006, p. 591) sarcastically referred to this part of the
ego as "the part that thinks like us"—that is, the part that thinks like the analyst thinks. Gill (1982, pp.
9–15) associated the "cooperative," "observing ego" with what he called the "facilitating transference,"
and the "experiencing ego" with what he called the "obstructing transference."

Those who try to foster development of such an observing ego in the analysand believe that psychoanalytic treatment should proceed by dispensing knowledge to this observing ego. However, as
I mentioned in Chapter 5, the point is not for the analysand to acquire knowledge about what he is
doing, but rather to change, and knowledge is not necessarily the key to change—indeed, it may well
impede change. Such an approach often leads analysands to make comments like that noted earlier:
"I know very well what I'm doing now but I'm having a very difficult time stopping myself." Although
an observing ego has been fostered in the analysand, the repressed that is motivating the behavior has
remained untouched. As Freud (1937/1964, p. 233) said, "We have increased his knowledge, but altered
nothing else in him."

Lacan (1978) commented on this as follows:

> To appeal to a healthy part of the subject, who is supposed to be in touch with reality and
> capable of judging along with the analyst what is going on in the transference, is to misrec-
> ognize that it is precisely this part of the subject that is caught up in the transference—to
> misrecognize that it is this very part [the ego] that closes the door, or the window, or the
> shutters, as you like, and that the beauty [the unconscious] with whom one would like to
> speak is behind them and is asking for nothing more than that the shutters be reopened.
> (p. 131)

Gill (1982) is one of the foremost proponents, in the non-Kleinian analytic world (I will discuss Klein later in this chapter), of the systematic interpretation of transference, yet he acknowledged something (which he appeared to view as a simple anomaly or curiosity, even though he repeated it numerous times in the course of his book) that seems to corroborate Lacan's view that it is generally pointless to interpret the transference. Gill indicated that in the transcripts of complete sessions he provided in volume 2 of his work, one can see "how regularly the analysis of the transference has its own repercussions on the transference—often repercussions which result in an enactment of the very patterns of interactions to which the interpretations refer" (Gill & Hoffman, 1982, p. 8; similar remarks are made on pp. 4, 105, 170). He indicated, for example, that when the male analyst working with a man whom Gill called "Patient E" made an interpretation to the effect that the patient was worried that there was an intimate, homosexual component to his relationship with the analyst, the patient heard the interpretation "as a homosexual approach" or come-on (p. 105). The analyst in that case had apparently been sensed for some time by the patient to be encouraging the patient to form a homoerotic bond with him, and the analyst's interpretation was taken by the patient as confirmation of his preexisting sense. Another analysand, whom Gill referred to as "Patient G," had obviously felt for some time that he was in competition with his analyst and perpetually losing the contest. When his analyst commented at length on this, the patient "experience[d] every interpretation as an enactment of the competition. Even interpretations that [were] about that very thing"— for example, the analyst proffered, "My saying that you have experienced it as a competition in which I am besting you is yet another move in this game of besting you"—were "experienced as aloof, one-upmanship" on the analyst's part (p. 170). When his analyst told him he seemed to be seeking the analyst's approval, the patient concluded that this was just one more way he was messed up and failing. When the analyst commented that the patient felt the analyst was putting him down, the patient took the comment as another put-down (pp. 162–164). The analyst's speech is heard as coming from the person the analysand imputes the analyst to be, not as coming from the person the analyst thinks he is or would like to be, or as coming from some objective outside observer. In this sense, interpretation of the transference, which is allegedly engaged in so as to "resolve" or "liquidate" the transference, ends up merely feeding the transference, making it still more intense and unwieldy.[19]

---

[19] As Glover (1955, p. 130) put it, "The transference-neurosis in the first instance feeds on transference-interpretation." His interest, however, seems to have been in deliberately interpreting the transference in order to make the transference neurosis more intense. Strachey (1934/1990, p. 79, footnote 31)

This is one of the reasons why Lacanians will often proffer very short interpretations that omit the subject of the statement (avoiding, for example,
"I think") and that consist essentially of the analysand's own words—perhaps
strung together in a slightly different order—such that it is not entirely clear
to the analysand *who* authored them. This makes it more difficult for such interpretations (see Chapter 5) to be experienced and rejected "as coming from
the transferential Other."

Despite an entire volume of theoretical considerations on the interpretation
of transference and a second volume of transcriptions of sessions purporting to
show the reader how to detect and interpret transference, Gill provided little
if any evidence that the interpretation of transference led to enduring change
in the analysands he presented. The possible sources and evolution of Patient
E's fear of intimacy and homophobia were never even broached, nor were the
probable causes of Patient G's competition with authority figures. Both of these
patients made it quite clear that fear and competition characterized many of
their relationships with others, yet the reader was never given so much as
a glimpse of their connection with the patients' histories. As important as it
may be for analysts to be attuned to "allusions to the transference" (Gill, 1982,
p. 21) in stories analysands recount during their sessions, and as important
as it may be to get analysands to elaborate on such allusions in detail, virtually every direct interpretation of the transference in the sessions Gill and
Hoffman collected led to a quandary, a messy soup that the analysts whose cases they presented extracted themselves from only with
the greatest of difficulty. Unwittingly, Gill and Hoffman appear to
have provided ample evidence that *it is counterproductive to interpret the
transference.*

Although one cannot see any great benefit accruing to the patients they
presented, one *can* see that the attempt on the part of some of the analysts
whose sessions were included in the volume to find allusions to the transference everywhere and to systematically interpret the transference led them to
overlook the most basic facets of psychoanalytic technique:

- They overlooked *slips of the tongue* (Patient G said, "my being angry with
  me" instead of "my being angry with him," implying something very
  different, indeed; Gill & Hoffman, 1982, p. 174).

---

believed that the most effective interpretations (which he referred to as "mutative interpretations")
are transference interpretations, and he attributed this to the fact that "in the analytic situation the
giver of the interpretation and the object of the id-impulse interpreted are one and the same person."
I would argue instead that this is precisely why transference interpretations are often the *least* effective
interpretations.

- They failed to notice *mixed metaphors* (Patient G said, referring to the upcoming end of the therapy, "Time is running out. The crystal ball with the sand ends July 21st," obviously meaning "hourglass" instead of "crystal ball," and thus referring quite transparently to his view that his analyst was, or at least believed he was, clairvoyant—if not a fortune teller; p. 156).
- They rarely asked their patients to *finish their sentences*, allowing their patients to censor an astonishing number of thoughts, many of which seemed to begin with a direct allusion to a thought or feeling about the analyst (for example, "You really—," p. 170; see also pp. 152, 160, 163, 169, and 176), leading one to suspect that these analysts would not have needed to work nearly so hard to draw out indirect "allusions to transference" if they had simply devoted a little more effort to getting their patients to *free associate* (perhaps they were looking for transference in all the wrong places).
- They paid no mind to the *specificity of their analysands' use of language* (Patient E used the word *homosexual* to refer to specific sexual acts alone, whereas his analyst used it as he saw fit, as if he were the one who determined the meaning of words; pp. 104–105) and they allowed extremely ambiguous formulations uttered by their patients to go unnoticed, as if they were perfectly comprehensible.[20]
- They let their patients drone on interminably about the minutiae of their week instead of encouraging them to talk about something more relevant, seeming to pick up on "allusions to transference" as a last-ditch effort to get them to say something of significance during their sessions (Gill, 1982, pp. 21–22; Gill & Hoffman, 1982, p. 149–154).

It seems to me that the analyst is far more likely to remain attuned to the transference in all its varied forms if she follows the general principles outlined in the preceding chapters than if she focuses exclusively on the transference (or anything else for that matter) and tries to understand everything the analysand says in terms of what it means about her and her relationship with the analysand. The latter will likely lead her to skid into the imaginary register and take her eye off the symbolic ball, so to speak.[21]

---

[20] Indeed, this approach to language seems to be quite common for Gill (1982), who quoted plenty of ambiguous formulations by Freud and other analysts without seeming to notice that these formulations were open to multiple interpretations. He even went so far as to say at times that he knew what the analysts he cited really meant, even though they did not say in so many words what he thought they meant.

[21] Interestingly, Bauer & Mills (1989/1994, p. 198) noted that "an important impetus for development in the here-and-now use of transference comes from the burgeoning field of short-term psychotherapy"—

Overly Positive Transference

We have no right to dispute that the state of being in love which makes its appearance in the course of analytic treatment has the character of a "genuine" love.

— *Freud (1915a/1958, p. 168)*

As noted earlier, as long as the analyst is able to channel the analysand's enthusiasm for the analysis and infatuation with the analyst into genuine psychoanalytic work, she need do nothing in particular except avoid undermining the analysand's belief that she possesses knowledge of what ails him and of how to help him. Let us now suppose, however, that the analysand reaches a point where his infatuation goes so far as to lead him to come to his sessions not to work but simply to bask in the analyst's marvelous, luminous presence. If it does no good to interpret his love as not really being for the analyst but for someone else,[22] what is to be done? For here the transference has become a resistance to the work of the analysis: "anything that interferes with the continuation of the treatment may be an expression of resistance" (Freud 1915a/1958, p. 162).[23] What concretely can be done, since interpretation is either bound to fail or to alienate the subject by appealing to an observing ego that is assumed not to be in love?

In general, the best policy is to do the strict minimum required to get the analysand back to work. The analyst should avoid accusing the analysand of being in love with her; it may be sufficient to simply give the analysand less eye contact and attention when he is saying nothing, show signs of boredom when he seems content to just be there, or ask about dreams, daydreams, and fantasies. If need be, she might draw a link between the current situation and scenes the analysand has already reported from his past in which something analogous occurred (for example, those happy moments of his childhood in which he lay contentedly on the floor in the kitchen while his mother baked bread, relishing the warmth of the oven and the lovely smell). This keeps the emphasis on the similarity of situation without explicitly pointing to the

---

in other words, from practitioners (and the insurance companies who pressure them) who hope to find a way in which the longer-term project of exploring the patient's past can be bypassed. Bauer and Mills made regular use of such concepts as "mature" and "maladaptive" behavior, suggesting that they and their colleagues in "dynamic" or "psychodynamic psychotherapy" are primarily concerned with getting their patients back to "normal functioning," an approach I criticize at length in Chapter 9.

[22] This is what Socrates did with Alcibiades when he said that Alcibiades was not really saying what he was saying for Socrates's sake but rather to win over Agathon (Plato's *Symposium*); see Lacan (1991).

[23] Freud's (1913/1958, pp. 139, 144) term for transference that takes the form of resistance is *Übertragungswiderstand*, which is translated by Strachey as "transference-resistance." See Lacan's (1978, p. 130) comments on the term.

analysand's love, which the analysand may not be really aware of, proud of, or eager to avow.

In any case, the analyst should concern herself primarily with a different question altogether: Why is such a manifestation of transference love occurring at the present time? Especially when the transference love has arisen not right at the beginning of the analysis (intense love that arises right at the beginning of the analysis may suggest a diagnosis of psychosis, not neurosis) but later on, what has usually happened is that, when faced with the virtual impossibility of talking about something, of putting some traumatic experience into words, the analysand has had his attention diverted to something about the analyst herself. He has become frustrated in his attempt to recall or formulate something and his attention has shifted to the only other person there with him in the room: the analyst. He may flash on something about her that bothered him (for example, the way she shook his hand that day, what she was wearing, a new piece of art in her office, or some comment she made in a recent session), or he may suddenly recall something positive about her (for example, her smile upon greeting him, her gait, or her presence).

In such cases, the transference has not become a resistance, as it was in the earlier example in which the analysand simply wished to bask in the analyst's presence; on the contrary, the *resistance* to the work of symbolization put up by the traumatic real *has given rise to transference* as a diversionary tactic, as a way of diverting attention away from the "pathogenic nucleus" (Freud, 1912a/1958) of the problem the analysand is trying to tackle, and onto something that is not transparently linked to it.[24] As Lacan (1978, p. 145) put it, "Transference is both an obstacle to remembering and the rendering present of the closing up of the unconscious, which results from the failure to hit the spot at just the right moment." In other words, transference arises at the very moment at which the analysand finds himself unable to approach (with or without the analyst's assistance) that pathogenic nucleus any more closely, unable to "hit the spot."[25]

The analysand certainly need not be conscious of creating a diversion. Indeed, he probably is rarely conscious of it in such cases: He is as duped by the diversionary maneuver as the analyst is. If the analyst is able to recognize transference here as a diversion, she will realize that they were getting close

---

[24] As Lacan (1988a, p. 36) put it, "Resistance is the inflexion [or detour] discourse makes upon approaching this [pathogenic] nucleus." See my detailed discussion of this topic (Fink, 2004, pp. 25–26, and footnote 24, pp. 170–173).

[25] Lacan (1978, p. 130) also put it as follows: "Transference is the means by which communication of the unconscious is interrupted, by which the unconscious closes up again. Far from being indicative of the signing over of powers to the unconscious, transference is, on the contrary, the shutting down of the unconscious."

to the pathogenic nucleus and try to find ways to help the analysand continue to hone in on it. Transference arises so consistently at such moments that we should, indeed, probably always presume that a particular transference is a *product* of resistance (understood as the real's resistance to symbolization and as the analysand's reluctance to say certain things out loud to the analyst for fear of the analyst's reaction, whether that be criticism, moral censure, loss of esteem in the analyst's eyes, or whatever) rather than assuming that the transference *itself* has become a resistance. After all, if it was not one before, why would it suddenly become one now?

Not-so-positive Transference

In and of itself, transference constitutes an objection to intersubjectivity.
— Lacan (1968a, p. 18)

When it arises as a diversion from the difficult work of symbolizing the real, transference is not always especially positive. When the analysand is frustrated with the difficulty of the task, he may experience the analyst as not helping or even as *deliberately* not helping, for she is believed to know the answer he is seeking, and if she refuses to give it to him, she must be deliberately withholding something from him! Since, however, she most likely does not actually have the answer, the best she can do is avoid taking whatever negative thought about her that sprang to the analysand's mind at the time at face value and try to help the analysand with the work at hand.

This requires a highly counterintuitive stance on the analyst's part: She must keep foremost in her mind that the majority (hopefully the vast majority) of the analysand's positive and negative thoughts about her and reactions to her have nothing to do with her as a person, as a living, breathing human being with her own personality, likes and dislikes, values, and so on. They are, rather, related to the preexisting position in the analysand's psychical economy that she has come to occupy. This is precisely why we call them transferences! This, nevertheless, seems to be the easiest thing to forget, and clinicians have an almost incurable tendency to fall into the trap of thinking that it is about them when it is not (and of thinking that it is not about them when it is, as we shall see later). *Insofar as the analyst has managed to keep her own countertransference to a minimum, the analysand's thoughts about her and reactions to her are related to the work they are engaged in and not to the analyst as an individual.*

As Lacan (1968a, p. 18) reminded us, the very existence of transference "constitutes an objection to intersubjectivity." The analytic situation is not a forum in which two different individuals encounter each other as subjects, because the party of the first part (so to speak) lends herself to any and every projection drummed up by the party of the second part. This means that something essential about her own subjectivity fades in the encounter, stays on the sidelines. Even though Lacan was a proponent of the idea of intersubjectivity in the 1950s, he came to see that to talk about the analytic situation as an intersubjective one is to overlook the existence of transference.[26]

---

[26] Much of the literature on the so-called intersubjective, interpersonal, and relational approaches to psychoanalysis and psychotherapy seems to adopt some variant of a subject-to-subject perspective. As seductive as these approaches may be when it comes to critiquing power relations in the therapeutic setting, one wonders whether the kind of equality between analyst and analysand that some theorists seek is not the same as what was already experimented with by Sandor Ferenczi in the early part of the 20th century, when he and his patients would take turns analyzing each other on the couch. Ferenczi abandoned the experiment when it quickly proved ineffective.

Note that Bollas (1983), who is referenced by many relationalists, tried to co-opt Lacan's term *Other* by situating the Other in himself as analyst. He wrote, "It is a feature of our present day understanding of the transference, that the Other source of the analysand's free association is the psychoanalyst's countertransference" (p. 3). This reduces the triad Lacan presented as crucial to the analytic situation— the analysand's ego, the Other (as the analysand's unconscious), and the analyst's ego—to a dyad, which amounts to a collapse of the symbolic dimension into the imaginary. For example, rather than simply ask his analysand "Helen" why she thought she often lapsed into silence (or what was going through her mind at such times, to see if anything had occurred to her from the Freudian "Other scene" known as the unconscious—the "anderer Schauplatz" that Freud, 1900/1958, pp. 48 and 536, borrows from Fechner—or if anyone had ever lapsed into silence like that with her in the past, to see if the pauses were related to her history) Bollas responded to her by saying that it must be difficult for her "to speak to this stranger (the analyst) and . . . to entrust the simplest things to him" (p. 13). This total presumption on his part is based on his own sense of what it must be like to talk to someone new (many of my analysands, for example, have no such trouble at the outset). Moreover, this interpretation, like several others he made based on his countertransference, had little if any effect, and Helen's silences only seemed to stop when they were connected to her experience of her mother—that is, her history with her mother. Note that this is probably what she would have told him at the outset (that is, approximately a year earlier) had he simply asked if anyone had ever lapsed into silence like that with her in the past, since it was her mother who had done so. The detour he took via his own subjectivity—that is, his attempt to understand her experience through his own experience of himself with her in the analytic setting—seems quite sterile, requiring him to make a series of guesses based on his own personality and countertransference, none of which really seem to hit the mark. And this detour (this attempt to fathom her subjectivity on the basis of his own subjectivity) is necessitated by his failure to ask one of the most elementary questions imaginable. (Regarding other such uses of the countertransference, see my comments about Renik's work in the notes to Chapter 8.)

Ogden, another analyst associated with the relational and intersubjective approaches, also tried to make a virtue out of long detours via his own subjectivity. He even dubbed his own distracted thoughts and daydreams, which evidently took up the lion's share of a session with one of his patients (Ogden, 1994, pp. 464–467) "the analytic third," painstakingly finding (one might say inventing) a relationship between what was going on for his patient and his own thoughts about not being recognized, his mechanic treating him unfairly, and so on. Apart from recognizing the fact that he confused things by using the word *third*—which is generally reserved in psychoanalysis for the oedipal triangle and, in more Lacanian circles, for the symbolic dimension that interrupts the imaginary, dyadic relationship between mother and child or analyst and analysand—we should note that one can generally find a connection between any two things if one looks hard enough and is inventive enough. Furthermore, Ogden would have had no need to so thoroughly analyze his own bored "reverie" if he intervened with his patients in such a way as to get them to do productive work during their sessions, instead of

It is counterintuitive for the analyst to constantly bear in mind that the lion's share of the analysand's thoughts and reactions that seem to be about her actually have nothing to do with her, because in everyday life most of us are inclined to take what others think and say about us very personally. But even in everyday life we would often do well to realize that people think and say all kinds of things about us that have little if anything to do with who we are as people and have a great deal to do with their own current struggles and conflicts (whether they feel neglected or inadequate, are jealous of those around them, are angry with everyone, or whatever, leading one to wonder whether a subject-to-subject relationship is ever possible). And, although in our love lives many of us tend to take criticism leveled at us by a lover at face value, given the prevalence of transference and projection in relationships we would often do better to realize that the criticism in question concerns

---

allowing them to drone on and on about the same things or lapse into 15- to 20-minute-long silences (p. 478).

In the case of Mrs. B (pp. 477–83), for example, Ogden rather unbelievably allowed her to avoid talking much about her parents for two years (at a rate of five sessions per week) because she felt she could not give a "fair and accurate" (p. 479) account of them! She was obviously inclined to give an "unfair" account—that is, to complain about them, to present them as the pains in the neck she experienced them to be growing up—and she could no doubt have been quite easily induced to give unfair and inaccurate accounts (isn't every account unfair or inaccurate in some way?) by simply asking, "You might be tempted to give an unfair account?" or "You're concerned you might dupe me as to who your parents really were?" Or by simply saying, "It is nevertheless of the utmost importance for you to tell me about them." Instead, he allowed her to talk endlessly about everyday matters, an experience that not surprisingly became mind-numbing for both of them (she was increasingly unable to think of anything to say, he having accepted her statement that "she would tell [him] about them when she found the right way and the right words to do so" [p. 479], a rather obvious refusal to free associate). Having given up on the use of speech to learn something about her history, as a last resort Ogden combed through the minutia of his personal fears and ruminations about his health during sessions (which, granted, may have been different than his fears and ruminations during sessions with other patients) to try to find some interpretation of what was going on in the analysis, an interpretation that hardly surprises the reader based on the little we are actually told about the patient herself. Rather than see the analyst's thoughts and feelings here as somehow caused by the patient, or by some creation of the analysis (the so-called analytic third), I would suggest that Ogden was rendered ill by his own technique and was finally rendered ill enough to pay attention to the patient's predicament in the analysis in a way that tied it to her history (she resented her analyst, no doubt, as a man who, like her own father, seemed to take little or no interest in her, perhaps at least in part because he did not require her to talk about what she may well have known she needed to talk about). Rather than see his "intersubjective" reaction as reflecting a heightened attunement to his patient, much less as some sort of guarantor of the objectivity of his interpretations, I would be inclined to see it as an illness brought on by his own failure to encourage his analysand to speak about matters she did not want to speak about and to interpret her relationship with her father. If he had viewed the articulation of her history—that is, the symbolic dimension—as the "third" that needed to be summoned up, as opposed to some sort of transferential/countertransferential third, I suspect that the analysis would have preceded far more quickly and with far less distress for both analysand and analyst—the latter suffered what he quite astonishingly referred to as a "somatic delusion" (p. 481). Perhaps he complained "that we are each trapped in our own subjectivity" (p. 470) precisely because he failed to work with what could take him outside of himself, so to speak.

someone else in the lover's life (whether someone from his or her past or the lover him- or herself).

Useful as it is in everyday life to learn not to see ourselves as the actual target of others' criticism (or jokes, sarcasm, or disparaging remarks) and even of others' praise, it is more useful still in the analytic setting. Insofar as the analysand does not experience transference as "merely a projection" and instead takes his annoyance at the analyst as verily and truly about her, *the analyst must make a special effort not to take criticism in the spirit in which it was given or respond in kind*. If she does, she will end up debating the analysand's criticism ("I have *too* been trying to help"), objecting to his accusations ("but I gave you two new interpretations yesterday"), retorting with criticism of her own ("you're the one who's been uncooperative"), or simply getting angry. She must instead try to situate herself at a different level: She must learn how not to react as though she were the genuine target of the criticism, remembering at all times (at least trying to) that she is dealing with transference.[27]

Her goal in her communications with the analysand is not to accuse him of projecting horrible things onto her when she is such a fine person, requiring him to somehow keep totally separate in his mind the figures from his past with whom he is furious and the well-intentioned analyst who is a person in her own right. For were he to become successful in keeping them totally separate, he would no longer be able to project things onto her. That would quickly jeopardize the therapy as a whole because when analysands are unable to remember certain facets of their past relations with others, they are often led to repeat them with the analyst, which means that the analysis can nevertheless gain access to them, albeit in a disguised and somewhat unwieldy form. One of my analysands, whose ability to remember often required the detour of repetition, was once talking about what things were like when he lived with his father before his family situation changed dramatically. He recalled sitting with his father at the dinner table but could not imagine what it had been like. It suddenly occurred to him that I was angry at him, allowing me to hypothesize *not* that his sense that I was angry at him was related to something I had done or said earlier, but rather that his father would sometimes be angry at him at the table. He confirmed this by saying that his father was always yelling at him to "eat his meat," which the analysand often found quite disgusting as a child. His father's anger at him thus emerged first in the transference projection and only then as a memory.

---

[27] Reacting in kind is what I have referred to elsewhere (Fink, 2004) as being caught up in the imaginary transference, whereas situating oneself at a different level, bearing in mind that one is dealing with transference, relates to the symbolic transference.

Should such repetition have been truly thwarted—had I, for example, systematically disputed the analysand's sense that I was angry, jubilant, or skeptical whenever he sensed that I was (so that he would have a more "reality-based" view of me, for example, and not confuse me with other figures)—the analysis would have lost one of its principal sources of information about the analysand's past. As Freud (1920/1955, p. 18) put it, "The patient cannot remember the whole of what is repressed in him, and what he cannot remember may be precisely the essential part of it." To thwart the repetition of what he cannot remember, then, is to jeopardize the therapy.[28]

The analyst must thus accept any and all projections. She cannot, for example, tell the analysand, "You are confusing me with your mother but I am nothing like her." For this would be to assert her own individuality and would thwart future projections of this kind. She must thus walk a fine line: She cannot reject the analysand's projections, and yet she cannot respond to his overtures or attacks with overtures or attacks of her own (something she might be inclined to do in everyday life). To respond in kind, to do unto others as they do unto you, to engage in tit-for-tat as little children do (or quid pro quo as many adults and nations do), is to become hopelessly mired in the imaginary dimension, where "feelings are always mutual" (Lacan, 1988a, p. 32, 1973–1974, November 13, 1973), love in one party eliciting love in the other, hatred in one party eliciting hatred in the other. The analyst must be, not exactly "above that," but situated in a different dimension: the symbolic dimension.[29] She must point not to the simple fact of projection (she must

---

[28] Lacan (1978, p. 128) proposed that at the crux of repetition is "the ever avoided encounter" with something, "the missed chance": We repeat something because at the last second we veer away from it, we miss our aim. And "if transference is nothing but repetition, it will always be repetition of the same missing (or failure) [ratage]" (p. 143).

[29] Winnicott (1960/1965c, p. 161) seems to have meant something quite similar when he referred to "the analyst's professional attitude" and "the work he does with his mind": "The professional attitude is rather like symbolism, in that it assumes a distance between analyst and patient. The symbol is in a gap."

Szasz (1963) provided an intriguing account of the origin of the concept of transference, suggesting that Anna O. and Joseph Breuer had gotten caught up in a person-to-person (ego-to-ego) relationship that became too hot to handle (Breuer became so engrossed in her treatment that his wife became jealous of his patient; when Breuer finally acknowledged to himself the nature of his feelings toward Anna O., he felt terribly guilty about them and broke off the treatment, at which point Anna O. suddenly produced an hysterical pregnancy). One could easily characterize this relationship in Lacanian terms as an imaginary one, for the parties to it related to each other as one living, breathing individual to another living, breathing individual. Freud, who was not a party to the relationship and was therefore not caught up in it, was able to formulate that Anna O. would have been likely to fall in love with any doctor who had treated her so assiduously, visiting her morning and evening day after day for years. She came to love Breuer, Freud hypothesized, not for his own personality and quirks, but as a symbol, as a stand-in for earlier figures who loved her. Szasz, in suggesting that Freud's concept of transference implies that the analyst is not taken as an object—that is, like any other object—but as "a symbol (of another object)" (p. 442), came close to formulating what Lacan called the symbolic dimension, the

not say, "You're projecting!" or "You're really angry at someone else"), but find a way to direct the conversation back to the topic that was under discussion before the diversionary transference reaction occurred.[30]

Consider the following example: My work with a certain analysand went fairly smoothly at the outset, even though he had warned me that his previous analyses had bogged down in prolonged silences. For a couple of months he recounted his history and current predicament, but as time passed he began to bring very little to his sessions: a brief snippet of a dream, a fleeting thought, or a glimpse of a daydream. After offering up the snippet or glimpse he would lapse into silence, professing that he had given it no thought whatsoever prior to the session and had no associations to it during the session. I did my best to draw him out about the different details of the dream, thought, or daydream, but over the course of several months things worsened and he offered less and less material at each successive session

---

dimension that allows the analyst to realize that the patient's affections are less about the analyst as an individual than about someone else or something else. Szasz, however, seems primarily concerned with indicating that analysts accuse their patients of transferring things onto them in a defensive manner, telling themselves that such accusations are based on "neutral description" (p. 433). He saw this as a convenient way analysts have of letting themselves off the hook: "The patient does not really love or hate the analyst, but some one else. What could be more reassuring?" (p. 438). What he leaves out of account is the fact that the analyst can and should strive, as far as possible, to comport herself in the analysis like a blank screen so that whatever love or hate the patient feels for the analyst really is about someone else and not about her as an individual.

[30] Some analysts seem so concerned with not being associated by the analysand with the "bad parent" that they overlook sizable portions of the material presented by him. One of my analysands had been in therapies of various kinds for over 20 years, always with female therapists, and had been convinced for over 2 decades that all of his problems centered around his father. Within a few weeks of starting analysis with me, material surfaced that led to an at least temporary dialectical reversal of his thinking; he suddenly realized that, although he still had many problems with his father, he resented his mother terribly in certain ways and was sabotaging his own life to spite her. It would not be farfetched to hypothesize that his female therapists had wanted him to associate them with a positive figure in his life and had thus more or less unwittingly directed his attention primarily to the father—with whom they felt they would not be so easily conflated in his projections—allowing them to stay, to a high degree, out of the line of fire. (Curiously enough, within a few short weeks of working with me, his difficulty getting and sustaining an erection with his girlfriend abated substantially.)

On the other hand, many analysts strive very hard to find an "allusion to transference" in virtually everything the analysand talks about, not in order to avoid his projections but rather to encourage him to think that everything he discusses revolves, in one way or another, around the analyst. Gill (1982) provided an example in which a patient talked in his session about an angry outburst he had with his wife, and Gill encouraged the patient to consider that he might also be angry with his analyst. Gill entertained the possibility that "such an interpretation might be met by the rejoinder that it is his *wife* the patient is talking about, *not* the analyst" (p. 65). What Gill failed to realize is that it was precisely in this way that the analyst angered the patient, thereby bringing about confirmation of his interpretation; it is the interpretation itself that angered the patient! In such examples, it often seems more likely that it is not the analysand but rather the analyst herself who is angry or who is expecting the analysand to be angry at her for something she has done that she does not feel so great about. Insofar as "feelings are always mutual" (Lacan, 1988a, p. 32), the analyst finds a way to make the analysand as angry as she is or as she was expecting him to be.

He soon began missing sessions fairly regularly and could say no more about his no-shows than that he found sessions painful when he had nothing to talk about. He continued to pay for all his sessions, whether he showed up or not, and I did not become overly frustrated with his absences until they began to become more frequent than once a week, even though I knew they were not a highly auspicious omen. There were aspects of his history that inclined me to think that, at one level, he perhaps wanted me to rant and rave and tell him to get back to work. His father had been a somewhat weak, ineffectual figure who, when angry on one occasion with his children who were making a racket, put a chair through the wall in a room down the hall from the children's bedroom, threatening, "Next time it's coming the other way." It was not entirely clear to the analysand what that meant, but it never actually happened. The analysand nevertheless felt that he should have been punished for a large number of things he had done as a child and adolescent. The analysand's anger at his father (for not punishing him, it seems, which would have relieved the analysand of the burden of constantly punishing himself) was tightly under wraps, and his anger at me had only just begun to surface, in particular in a dream in which I appeared in animal forms, was virtually starved to death, and then revived by the analysand himself. His repeated no-shows may have been an unwitting expression of anger at me and/or an unconscious attempt to get me to provide the punishment he felt he deserved.

After a somewhat tumultuous period in which the analysand made a feeble attempt to break off the analysis, it occurred to me that he was perhaps repeating something that had transpired early in his childhood: At one point in his sexual play with his younger sister (which his mother had walked in on at one time but dismissed as "perfectly natural"—this was one of the episodes he later felt he should have been punished for), he had come up with the idea, apparently all by himself, that his erect penis "maybe is supposed to go in there [in her vagina]." He had apparently never seen her vagina before the day he proposed that he put his penis in it, and he characterized her vagina as looking "like a big red wound." She responded to his proposal by screaming "no!" and was never again willing to "play doctor." He identified quite strongly with her (even having a very erotically sensitive spot on his body just to one side of his male genitalia, which he himself described as a sort of mirror image on his body of her clitoris) and I postulated that he was repeating some aspect of this scene with the roles reversed: He was comporting himself in the analysis with me as she had with him—he would play along up to a certain point and then close down. He would respond somewhat to prying on my part but would then clam up, never going any further on his own.

It was in getting him to talk more explicitly about that particular scene and his whole array of thoughts and feelings about it that I was able to put a stop to the kind of "silent treatment" that was jeopardizing the analysis. One of the questions that seemed to have been plaguing him was whether he should have forced his sister to go further. At some level he seemed to think that if he had done so, he would not have become so deathly afraid of vaginas, which he never again looked at after that scene with his sister. Insofar as what was going on in the analysis was a repetition of that scene, he seemed to be wondering whether I would force him to go further—in other words, would I do to him what he himself had not done to his sister?

It was, it seemed, the difficulty the analysand encountered in attempting to formulate this almost unthinkable question ("Should I have raped her?") that seemed to be diverting his attention to the relationship with me: imagining me to be critical of him, thus making it difficult for him to come to sessions and talk; wanting me to punish him for something (a thought? a wish?) and yet at the same time hoping to escape punishment. We were able to go beyond this moment of stasis in the analysis by returning to what I hypothesized to be the source of the repetition, not by my suggesting to him that the predicament in which we found ourselves in the analysis (me prying and him shying away) was similar to his former predicament with his sister, a speculative comparison at best which would have simply amounted to giving him a piece of knowledge about something going on in the analysis and would not have changed anything related to *the repressed that was bringing about the repetition in the first place*. Rather than interpreting his transference reaction, which took the form of prolonged silences and no-shows, I focused on what it interrupted: a fuller discussion of that early childhood scene.

Acting Out

> But if, as the analysis proceeds, the transference becomes hostile or unduly intense and therefore in need of repression, remembering at once gives way to acting out.
>   — Freud (1914a/1958, p. 151)

Just as the analyst must accept the analysand's projections, whether flattering or unflattering, since they may provide the key to certain aspects of the repressed, so too must she accept his "acting out." "Acting out" is a genuinely psychoanalytic concept which has in recent decades come to mean no more than "acting badly" or "acting inappropriately" in common psychological parlance (see Chapter 9 on the latter term), but Freud introduced it to refer to actions that the analysand engages in outside of the consulting room that seem to express in a displaced manner something the analysand has not been able to express in the consulting room, not necessarily through any fault of his own or of the analyst. In describing it, Freud (1914a/1958) said:

> The patient does not *remember* anything of what he has forgotten and re-pressed, but *acts* it out. He reproduces it not as a memory but as an action; he *repeats* it, without, of course, knowing that he is repeating it. (p. 150)

Insofar as the patient I just discussed managed to miss one or more sessions a week, we might say that he was acting out something that he could not remember: the painful silent treatment his sister had given him and his desire to perhaps force her. (Some contemporary analysts might refer to his long silences during sessions as "acting in," since it was an expression of the repressed in the sessions that took the form of an act, that of remaining silent.)[31]

The analyst can try to encourage the analysand to talk, even to talk vocifer-ously, instead of acting, to express his anger verbally instead of breaking things or punching someone, but if she tries to prohibit all action on his part she is likely to end up truncating the analysis of one of its possibly important sources of information. What is more, acting out can serve as a kind of corrective to the analyst: just as kids sometimes engage in destructive or self-destructive activity outside of the home when they feel that their parents refuse to listen to them, analysands sometimes engage in self-destructive activities outside of the con-sulting room when they feel that their analyst is refusing to hear something they are trying to convey or is refusing to take something they are saying seriously. In other words, the analysand's acting out should serve as a word to the wise.[32]

Downright Negative Transference

> *I have often been asked to advise upon cases in which the doctor complained that he had pointed out his resistance to the patient and that nevertheless no change had set in; indeed, the resistance had become all the stronger, and the whole situation was more obscure than ever.*
> — *Freud (1914a/1958, p. 155)*

Faced with persistent, overt negativity on the analysand's part, the analyst should consider several different possibilities—apart from the obvious choice

---

[31] See, for example, Ormont (1969). Certain analysts, like Sterba (1940/1990, p. 85), have used the term *acting out* indiscriminately for any form of action taken by the analysand, whether in or outside of the session.

[32] Note that it may be fitting at times to refer to "acting out" in situations that Lacan (2004, p. 148) called "transference without analysis"—for example, when adolescents play out with teachers what they cannot express at home. See also Lacan (1998b, pp. 420–421). For a commentary on Lacan's many discussions of acting out in a case reported by Ernst Kris, see Fink (2004, Chapter 2).

to begin working with a good (or potentially with a new) supervisor, ongoing supervision being essential to all analytic work.

If the analyst has been punctuating the analysand's speech and attempting to make interpretations, and her punctuations and interpretations have done nothing but infuriate the analysand even though she has introduced them gradually and at a point at which it seemed the analysand was ready to hear them, she should first and foremost consider the possibility that she has misdiagnosed the analysand: Perhaps he is psychotic, not neurotic, and she has to completely reorient herself in the treatment (see Chapter 10). Working with a psychotic as though he were a neurotic can very easily lead to seriously negative transference; I have supervised cases in which many things that would not be taken as persecutory by a neurotic—such as punctuating, interpreting, abruptly scanding, note taking, and even requesting to tape-record or videotape the sessions (something that is often suggested by the therapist's supervisor in certain training programs, with no regard to the patient's level of paranoia)—have led to terribly negative reactions on the psychotic analysand's part and at times even to the termination of the therapy.

If the analysand's transference began in an at least slightly positive way but slowly but surely became stubbornly negative, and if attempts on the analyst's part to connect that negativity to figures from the analysand's past and to reconceptualize the case (with the help of a supervisor) bear no fruit, the analyst must consider the possibility that she has become so closely associated in the analysand's mind with one of the analysand's parents or caretakers with whom he is terribly angry or bears an undying grudge that she can do nothing further at the present time: The only course of action open to her is to refer the analysand to another analyst, preferably one of the opposite sex.[33]

Although there are too many other reasons why persistent, overt negativity on the analysand's part arises to address in an introductory text like this, the next section may help clarify and go beyond at least some of them.[34]

---

[33] See Grete Bibring-Lehner's (1936/1990) useful discussion of this point.

[34] For a discussion on negative transference, see Miller (2005), which takes up the few direct comments Lacan made about negative transference and offers the following ideas/speculations: (1) Insofar as analysands often enter analysis feeling they know nothing and are empty or lacking in many respects, they grow angry with their analysts, whom they believe know everything or are full, ideal figures (the analysand's want-to-be is pitted here against the analyst's being; pp. 33–34); (2) Negative transference is produced whenever a repression is lifted (pp. 90–92), at least in part because the analysand does not want to know anything about what has been repressed (perhaps also, I would add, in part because if the analyst makes an interpretation that leads to the lifting of a repression, she has proven to the analysand that he could not free himself from the repression by himself, which is especially irksome to the obsessive).

158   Fundamentals of Psychoanalytic Technique

Dealing with Transferential/Countertransferential Impasses

In self-analysis the danger of incompleteness is particularly great. One is too soon satisfied with a part explanation, behind which resistance may easily be keeping back something that is more important perhaps.

— *Freud (1935/1964, p. 234)*

True self-analysis is impossible; otherwise there would be no [neurotic] illness.
— *Freud (1985, p. 281)*

Analytic work bogs down at different times for a wide variety of reasons. Many of these reasons can be attributed to countertransference in the broadest sense of the term—that is, as "the sum total of the analyst's biases, passions, and difficulties, or even of [her] inadequate information, at any given moment in the dialectical process" (Lacan, 2006, p. 225). The analyst has come to conceptualize the case in a particular way and consequently comports herself toward the analysand in a particular way (these two are in fact theoretically inseparable), and this conceptualization and stance—as useful as they may have been at one point in the analysis—are now standing in the way of further progress.

How is the analyst to proceed? If we understand the analyst here as having gotten stuck in a particular imaginary relationship to the analysand—as having made a certain investment in her image of the analysand and of herself with the analysand—we have to acknowledge that she has become deaf to things that may not fit into her conceptualization and blind to any other way of formulating the case. This conceptualization has become precious to her and she has, to some degree, consolidated her own sense of who she is as an analyst around this conceptualization. In a word, she has fallen out of her role as symbolic Other and as real cause of the analysand's desire, and has become locked in an ego-to-ego stalemate—"ego-to-ego" because she herself has hypostatized or reified the analysand as an ego through her rigid conceptualization of the case.

The obvious solution here is to let in a breath of fresh air, the kind of air provided by the symbolic. The symbolic landmarks and parameters of the case need to be reconsidered, and this is extremely difficult, if not downright impossible, to do by oneself. Just as it is very difficult for one to recognize and change the symbolic (that is, unconscious) coordinates and determinants of one's own symptoms and repetitive patterns without the help of an analyst—which is why full-blown self-analysis is impossible (those who think that it is possible are deluding themselves as to what analysis is and can accomplish)—it is well nigh impossible to step back from a case both personally and conceptually and reformulate it from a thoroughly new point of view without the help of someone else: a supervisor.

The supervisor is never in the consulting room with the analysand whom he is being consulted about, and thus he cannot be taken with or turned off by the analysand, as he might otherwise be (when Freud, for example, commented that one of his female analysands was beautiful and charming, you can be sure that he put his countertransferential foot in his mouth with her). Nor is the supervisor likely to feel that he is in the line of fire—that is, to feel put out by the analysand's demands or tempted to satisfy them. The supervisor is unlikely to fall into the trap of associating the analysand with someone from his own past based on looks, style of dress, tone of voice, gestures, and the like. In other words, the supervisor is automatically placed in a position in which he is immune to a great many imaginary pitfalls. Of course, his own more or less rigid theoretical perspectives may well make him blind to certain things, but at least *his blindnesses are not likely to overlap with the analyst's own blindnesses.* The supervisor is presented only with the analysand's words, insofar as they are more or less faithfully reported by the supervisee. In other words, the supervisor is able to situate the analysand at the symbolic level immediately, without becoming mired in the imaginary (there are, of course, some imaginary effects that enter into supervision between supervisor and supervisee).

The supervisor is thus able to hear much more of the analysand's discourse than the analyst herself may have heard, owing not necessarily to his years of experience or "extraordinary powers of insight" but to his distance from the many facets of the imaginary register that are unavoidable in the consulting room. Many of my graduate students are surprised that their fellow therapists-in-training are able to provide so many new angles on a case and make so many connections in the symbolic material that they themselves had not noticed, and they are inclined to think that their fellow students must be far more insightful than they are—until the shoe is on the other foot and they find themselves in the supervisory role, astonishing their fellow students with their own powers of insight.[35]

---

[35] Lacan (2006) commented on this as follows:

> Young analysts, who might nevertheless allow themselves to be impressed by [certain analysts'] impenetrable gifts . . . will find no better way of dispelling their illusions than to consider the success of the supervision to which they themselves are subjected. The very possibility of that supervision would become problematic if viewed from the perspective of contact with [the analysand's] reality. For in supervision, instead [of coming into contact with the patient's reality], the supervisor manifests a second sight . . . which makes the experience at least as instructive

It is the virtually direct access to the symbolic material of a case that makes supervision, whether by a senior analyst or by a group of earnest colleagues, so productive in reframing a case.[36] This is true even when one has been in practice for a very long time, and suggests the utility and importance to even the most senior of analysts of regularly presenting cases to groups of colleagues (two—or more—heads are better than one). Supervision is best viewed as a lifelong endeavor, not something one does only during a few short years of training.

In my many years of being supervised and supervising other people's work, I have been able to see and experience the benefits of the supervisory process at both a micro- and macro-level, so to speak. At the micro-level, we often find that something present at the symbolic level in a session is not heard by the analyst, even though it is included in the analyst's notes. On one occasion, a patient made a slip of the tongue that his therapist did not recognize as a slip until she repeated it in supervision with me (the patient described himself as being the kind of guy who is "in short demand" when he evidently meant to say "in short supply"). On another occasion, a fairly direct symbolic connection went unnoticed between a patient's statement that she was "tired of letting people feed off of" her and a dream recounted in the same session in which she was living inside a refrigerator. In a third case, it was a patient's repeated use of the metaphor of having "nothing underneath" and of having "no rod"—by

---

for him as for his supervisee. And the less the supervisee demonstrates such gifts—which are considered by some to be all the more incommunicable the bigger the to-do they themselves make about their secrets regarding technique—the truer this almost becomes.

The reason for this enigma is that the supervisee serves as a filter, or even as a refractor, of the subject's discourse, and in this way a ready-made stereography is presented to the supervisor, bringing out from the start the three or four registers on which the musical score constituted by the subject's discourse can be read. (pp. 252–253)

Lacan proposed that, in the best of cases, the supervisee can learn to situate himself in the symbolic position in which the supervisor is automatically placed, even when the supervisee is in the consulting room with the analysand:

If the supervisee could be put by the supervisor into a subjective position different from that implied by the sinister term *contrôle* (advantageously replaced, but only in English, by "supervision"), the greatest profit he could derive from this exercise would be to learn to put himself in the position of that second subjectivity into which the situation automatically puts the supervisor. (p. 253)

This is obviously an ideal position that can never be completely achieved; hence the need for ongoing supervision.

[36] The use of videotapes of sessions for supervisory purposes may compromise the supervision, since video has imaginary effects upon supervisors and colleagues that may at times overshadow the symbolic material, giving them the false impression that what *really* goes on in therapy is what one sees with one's eyes: body language, for example (see Chapter 8).

which she apparently intended to convey "no backbone"—that went unheard by a therapist otherwise well attuned to castration anxiety.

At the somewhat more macro-level, I can cite a case in which I was fairly easily able to propose a dialectical reversal of the analyst's conceptualization of a case on the basis of a dream she reported to me. The analysand had repeatedly presented herself to the female analyst as having been the victim of inadequate mothering, and the analyst had been feeling that she was unable to dislodge the analysand from her constant demands to be mothered by the analyst (the latter also seemed to be having trouble setting limits regarding the analysand's demands for contact with her outside of the sessions). In a dream the analysand recounted, she found herself on a bus surrounded by several women, each of whom was holding a large pile of diapers. After some discussion, I suggested to the analyst that it was not, perhaps, so much that she felt that she had been severely neglected by her mother as a child as that she had come to believe that she contained so much shit that she would be too much for *any* mother to handle. The analyst found this to be at an extremely useful reversal of her thinking about the case, and it relieved some of the pressure she had been feeling to give in to at least some of the analysand's multifarious demands.

Supervisors and colleagues of mine—whether in individual consultation or at more formal presentations—have provided me with similar reversals of perspective that have allowed me to take a fresh approach to analyses I have conducted. This should underscore the importance of talking with supervisors and colleagues about one's most difficult and troublesome cases, not just about the cases that are going well; the latter are the ones we are most inclined (or even encouraged) to showcase in our attempt to convey to others that we are doing a good job and that they should refer patients to us!

In certain instances, it has been clear from the material reported to me by supervisees that they have been following only one possible thread of their analysands' discourse (the only one they have been able to fathom or the one that most tickles their fancy, for some personal or theoretical reason) despite the fact that other threads are plainly visible and could suggest very different perspectives on the case. If one thread has exhausted itself or has led to a temporary stalemate, it is time to explore the others.

In other instances, it has been clear to me simply by the paucity of symbolic material—details about the family, early life events, schooling, first relationships, dreams, fantasies, and so on—that the analyst has gotten bogged down in the analysand's stories about everyday life and requests for help with current difficulties. The analysand has persisted in seeing the analyst as simply someone to complain to or as an expert who can solve his problems, and the analyst has allowed the analysand to fill up sessions with complaints (perhaps feeling that the analysand's life is or was especially horrendous) or has taken the bait (perhaps being flattered to be viewed as an expert) and has been providing answers rather than putting the analysand to work to elucidate his own problems.

Few analysts would, I think, disagree with me here about the importance of ongoing supervision. I would, however, like to comment on Casement's (1991) proposal of an apparent way around supervision, which he termed the "internal supervisor" (see especially pp. 30–32). Casement proposed that, in the process of being supervised on cases, the analyst comes to develop a sort of internalized supervisor: She imagines hearing the supervisor's voice or seeing things as the supervisor would see them, alongside her own voice and vision of things. Casement seems to believe that the development of such an internal supervisor allows the analyst to be engaged in the therapy and at one remove from it at the same time. He explicitly likened this split in the analyst to the split Sterba (1934) proposed fostering in the analysand between the "observing ego" and the "experiencing ego." I mentioned in Chapter 5 that such a split merely alienates the analysand still further, encouraging him to observe himself as if he were another person (in this case, the analyst) and to check his own impulses as if they were foreign to him. Casement would have us reduplicate or prolong this alienation in the analyst (it is "in their own experience of being a patient, that therapists establish the first roots of what later becomes the internal supervisor," p. 31) even though it may at times lead to "a preoccupation with a self-monitoring [that] can disturb the free-floating attention" (p. 51). There is plainly a sort of self-policing function that is filled here as analysts "learn to watch themselves [presumably as their supervisors watch them] as well as the patient" (p. 32). The supervisor also seems to be encouraged by Casement to shape the supervisee in his own image, as opposed to helping the supervisee find her own path and style as an analyst, the latter being the approach Lacan (1975b, p. 183) clearly advocated when he said, "Don't imitate me."

Although there may be a superficial homology between the "experiencing ego" and the analyst as caught up in the imaginary register, on the one hand, and the "observing ego" and the analyst as operating in the symbolic register, on the other, I think it is important to emphasize the degree to which the analyst does best to operate as exclusively as possible in the symbolic register and not to cultivate a split between her experiencing and thinking. Should the analyst find herself regularly experiencing what is going on in the analysis in the imaginary register of struggle, rivalry, seduction, and aggression, no amount of self-observation (of replaying her supervisor's voice over and over in her head—and that voice is, moreover, no more than what she *imagines* he would say, not what the supervisor would actually say if he knew the facts of the case) is going to mitigate that and the analyst needs to return to her own analysis.

Casement (1991) also seems to believe that he can adequately deal with many of the difficulties that arise in the transference by what he, following Robert Fliess (1942), called "trial identification," wherein the analyst tries to mentally imagine being in the analysand's place (in this way "he can monitor what it may feel like to be the patient," p. 34) and anticipate what the analysand's reaction to interpretations and other interventions might be.[37] This, he feels, prevents him on many occasions from making interpretations that, although "accurate," would likely be perceived as banal, formulaic, or predictable by the analysand (pp. 33–34). The limits of "trial identification" are, I hope, clear from my discussion of the imaginary in earlier chapters of this book: People differ significantly from each other and, unless we are incredibly imaginative or have unbelievably vast experience with people from virtually every walk of life, we will never be able to truly imagine what it is like to be someone else. It is not by empathically putting ourselves into another's shoes (assuming that other wears shoes) that we can determine what to say or do, but rather by working with the other's language and history. Otherwise we are more likely than not to end up deluding ourselves into thinking that we have successfully imagined how the analysand feels and experiences the world, and to cling blindly to our imagined formulation of his world.

Perhaps highly seasoned analysts can try to imagine what it must be like to be someone else and simultaneously stay open-minded enough to hear what the analysand says that does not fit into this imagined picture, but I suspect that they are few and far between. In any case, I would hypothesize that it is not because of especially well developed powers of empathy that such seasoned analysts are able to do so (if, indeed, they are), but rather because of their recognition of the specificity of the *symbolic coordinates of the analysand's existence*, and their acknowledgement that those coordinates are *fundamentally different* from their own.

If anything can help an analyst supervise herself, it is writing down a thorough formulation of the case—something I would recommend as a prelude to or preparation for supervision by another person. This formulation should include: (1) as much of the analysand's early childhood and later history as she has been able to piece together, laid out in chronological order; (2) what the analysand offered as his presenting problem as well as what appeared, in the

---

[37] Casement mentioned both Reik (1937) and Money-Kryle (1956) as forerunners of his own notion here.

course of the work, to be the problems that actually precipitated the analysand's entrance into therapy; (3) the major articulations of the work that has thus far been done, including important connections that have been drawn regarding the analysand's history and relationships, as well as any reversals in perspective that have been arrived at (for example, the analysand may have initially blamed all of the problems in his family on his father, later concluded that his father was actually but a victim and his mother was to blame instead, and still later arrived at a more nuanced picture of things); (4) all of the transitory and more enduring symptoms that have thus far been discussed and their possible meanings, with hypotheses about what repressed material led to their formation; (5) the fantasies (of all kinds) the analysand has recounted and their possible convergence on something like a fundamental fantasy, suggesting what his most basic stance toward the Other may be; and (6) diagnosis (if the diagnosis is not clear, the reasons for thinking that a certain diagnosis makes sense should be elucidated, as well as the reasons for thinking that a different diagnosis also makes sense).

Once the analyst has articulated in words (that is, via the symbolic) everything she would want to tell others about the case, including her own position in the analysis and her previous and current difficulties, and has made her account of the case coherent and understandable to others, she should go back and search for anything she has wittingly or unwittingly left out of her account. For when we try to tell someone a clear story about something, we (just like our analysands when they tell us stories about their lives) inevitably leave things out—things that may well turn out to be crucial. In my own work supervising analysts, I often find that details mentioned by the analyst in an offhanded manner (that were not included in her notes or intended to be mentioned by her, coming up only in response to a question I asked or in an impromptu discussion) are the ones that put an entirely different face on the case and allow us to rethink it in a productive new way. Similarly, when I write up my own cases for presentation, I often find that it is the details that I keep putting into footnotes, pushing to the back of my word-processing file, or writing on endless bits of paper that provide the most new insight into the case. I also find that I get a great deal out of my own case write-ups if I reread them a couple of weeks after I have written them so that I have some more perspective on them: By that time I am not so caught up in the process of constructing a good, coherent story, and I can read the stories a bit more as if I were someone else reading them.

Case formulation of this kind can be helpful because it requires us to think through and rethink the *symbolic coordinates* of the case and articulate them in words. We may suddenly realize that what we have written—whether it was our own words or a transcription of the analysand's words—can be understood in more than one way, and the mere fact of laying things out on paper or on the computer screen frequently allows us to make connections we might not otherwise have made (for example, that the names of two important people in the analysand's past were identical, or that the foreign name for a particular religious practice the analysand engages in is spelled exactly like his last name). Nevertheless, such case formulation should be seen as no more than a prelude to individual or group supervision: Only other people can help us see what we ourselves are not yet ready, able, or willing to see.

Our formulation of a case at any one moment in time becomes a kind of theory—a theory that simultaneously allows us to see certain things and blinds us to others and a theory that, as Kuhn (1962) taught us, we cling to and give up only with very great difficulty.[38] Just as scientists, when faced with data that do not initially seem to fit the current dominant theory, do not jettison their precious theory but instead tweak it here and there to accommodate the data (when they do not simply discount the data as artifactual), clinicians are inclined to bend over backwards at first to fit speech about previously unmentioned life events, dreams, and fantasies into a preexisting conceptual framework. It is only under the weight of overwhelming countervailing evidence that certain scientists are willing to give up their precious theory and seek out a new one; a sluggish, stubborn, stodgy temperament like that in the analyst will likely drive all but the most obsessive analysands to distraction and lead many an analysis to wrack and ruin. The analyst's own analysis and ongoing supervision, along with continued study, are our best guarantees against such an outcome.

Projective Identification

He who is not in love with his own unconscious goes astray.
    —Lacan (1973–1974, June 11, 1974)

No discussion of transference in our day and age would be complete without a discussion of "projective identification," a process to which negative coun-

---

[38] As psychosis teaches us, theories are also self-confirmatory. If I hear or conclude for whatever reason that my boss is in love with me (as in erotomania), I will interpret everything she says in that light and believe her to be speaking in riddles, toying with me, playing hard to get, or ignorant of her own deepest feelings should she deny being smitten with me. If I conclude that she is out to get me (as in paranoia), I will interpret everything she says in accordance with that conviction, as potentially implying some evil intent on her part. Just as we saw in the case of transference interpretations by the analyst, everything my boss says will be heard by me as coming from the person I impute her to be. Lacan (2006, p. 428) referred to this as the "paranoiac principle of human knowledge" (see also pp. 94, 96, 111, and 180).

tertransference is often attributed by non-Lacanian psychoanalysts of many different persuasions.

Insofar as analysts are inclined (as I mentioned earlier) to take the analysand's reactions personally, they often find themselves thinking rather negative thoughts and having rather negative feelings about the analysand. Instead of being encouraged to realize that they are erroneously situating themselves as the target of the analysand's anger and that they should try to situate themselves differently in the analysis, they are often encouraged to believe that they are experiencing "projective identification," a state of affairs in which the analyst supposedly experiences what the analysand would be experiencing but does not want to experience (he has projected it "into her"), or feels what the analysand is refusing to feel, that feeling being supposedly split off by him. (This account, as we shall soon see, is rather simplistic, but it will serve my initial purposes here well enough.) The analyst's countertransferential feelings do not, in this perspective, reflect either her personal idiosyncrasies or infelicitous stance in the therapy, but rather something "objective" about the analysand; as Paula Heimann (1950, p. 83) put it, "The analyst's countertransference is not only part and parcel of the analytic relationship, but it is the patient's *creation*, it is part of the patient's personality."

The first thing we should notice here is that, instead of being encouraged to think they are situating themselves incorrectly vis-à-vis the analysand, analysts are encouraged to think they have become *exquisitely sensitive* to something of which the analysand is not even aware. We should perhaps be suspicious of the fact that the analyst's negative reaction to the analysand is thereby magically converted into a virtue, a dialectical reversal of the situation being effected here not for the analysand's sake but apparently so that the analyst can have a clear conscience. If nothing else, the very fact that the analyst is let off the hook so thoroughly here, her *bad temper being transmogrified into divine sensitivity*, should put us on our guard. This alchemical transmogrification of something lowly—the dross of the analyst's confused countertransferential feelings and anger—into something worthy (the alchemist's gold) may well explain part of the popularity of the concept.

Seeing analysts embrace a concept that transforms countertransference into transference—that is, that places the onus on the analysand instead of on the analyst—we may be reminded of Lacan's (2006, p. 595) comment that "there is no other resistance to analysis than that of the analyst himself." Using, as Lacan himself did, psychoanalytic theory to analyze the history of psychoanalysis, I would propose that we entertain the hypothesis that the growing fascination with countertransference after World War II and its redemption in psychoanalytic theory might well reflect analysts' resistance to the psychoanalytic process itself. As we shall see, it certainly reflects a privileging of the imaginary register over that of the symbolic.

The Historical Development of the Concept of Projective Identification

We use language in a way that goes far beyond what is in fact said.
— *Lacan (2005b, p. 41)*

Projective identification is a highly complex concept, and it is used in different ways by different authors.[39] As so often happens in the history of psychoanalytic concepts, the term has taken on a life of its own, analysts attributing meanings to it that Melanie Klein, who coined the term, did not originally intend.

Klein (1946/1952) glossed the processes that she grouped under the term "projective identification" as follows:

> When projection is mainly derived from the infant's impulse to harm or to control the mother, he feels her to be a persecutor. In psychotic disorders this identification of an object with the hated parts of the self contributes to the intensity of the hatred directed against other people. (pp. 300–301)

It seems quite plain in the context of her article that Klein means that the infant or psychotic adult attributes his own aggressiveness, for example (one of the "hated parts" of himself), to the mother or some other person, "identifying" the other person as the aggressor instead of himself. He can then in good conscience hate the other person instead of himself, for his hatred is simply a response to the other's preexisting aggression.

There is actually nothing new in this formulation—it is a classic case of projection of one of one's own thoughts or affects onto someone else[40]—except

---

[39] As Joseph Sandler (1987) cautioned:

> [Projective identification] is a notion that is difficult to discuss from a non-Kleinian perspective. This may in part be due to the fact that those who use the concept tend to speak of it as a simple mechanism, while in fact it is one which (like so many others in psychoanalysis) shifts its meaning according to context. It has as a result acquired a certain mystique, with the unfortunate consequence that it is sometimes either dismissed entirely or thought to be understandable only with special "inside knowledge." (p. 14)

Ogden (1979), however, has tried to formulate it in a manner that frees it from its Kleinian metapsychological presuppositions.

[40] See, for example, Freud's (1911a/1958) famous comments on paranoia:

for the term *projective identification* itself. What the child mentally attributes to the mother has not literally or materially gone into the mother herself or in any way invaded the mother as a person—it has simply become part of the child's view (or representation or fantasy) of the mother.[41] Note that Klein here associates projections of this kind made by adult patients with *psychotics*, not neurotics.

In a presentation given in 1958, Heinrich Racker (1968) used Klein's term to refer to something further: According to Racker, the patient projects something onto the analyst and the analyst in turn identifies with the patient's projection. (Joseph Sandler, 1987, whose account of the history of the term *projective identification* I am following to some degree here, calls this stage 2 in the development of the concept.[42]) According to Racker (1968, p. 134), in

---

> The mechanism of symptom-formation in paranoia requires that internal perceptions—feelings—shall be replaced by external perceptions. Consequently the proposition "I hate him" becomes transformed by *projection* into another one: "*He hates* (persecutes) *me*, which will justify me in hating him." (p. 63)

According to Ogden (1979, p. 358), there is already something new in Klein's account: "First, there is the fantasy of projecting a part of oneself into another person and of that part taking over the person from within"; second—and here Ogden said that he was following Schafer (personal communication)—"the person projecting feels 'at one with' the person into whom he has projected an aspect of himself."
[41] This is clear from Klein's (1946/1952) account of what she calls "introjective identification," in which the child attributes to itself (or sees itself as having) certain features initially seen in the mother. The child here *thinks of itself* as having those traits but is not necessarily thought to have them by other people.

It is also clear from the footnote she supplies after she writes "split-off parts of the ego are also projected on to the mother or, as I would rather call it, *into* the mother"; the footnote reads as follows:

> The description of such primitive processes suffers from a great handicap, for these phantasies arise at a time when the infant has not yet begun to think in words. In this context, for instance, I am using the expression "to project *into* another person" because this seems to me the only way of conveying the unconscious process I am trying to describe. (p. 300)

Here as elsewhere in the text Klein made it clear that she was referring to *fantasies* the child has of putting something into the other person; she is not arguing that something is actually being put into the other person, where it might take on some sort of independent existence. (Note that, although certain authors make a distinction between phantasy with a "ph" and fantasy with an "f," in my usage here they are interchangeable.) Nor does she argue that in her other main article on identification (Klein, 1955; see especially pp. 311–312).

By way of an amusing final confirmation, Phyllis Grosskurth (1987, p. 449) reported that when Klein was supervising a young analyst by the name of Sonny Davidson, who told her, "I interpreted to the patient that he put his confusion into me," Klein replied, "No dear, that's not it, *you* were confused!"

Grosskurth (1987, p. 449) went on to say that Klein "was particularly worried about the 'fashion' for countertransference she saw developing. If a candidate tended to talk too much about how a patient made him angry or confused, she would remark pithily: 'Look, you tell that to your analyst. I really want to know something about your patient.'"
[42] Ogden (1979) indicated that other analysts, like Bion, extended the concept around the same time as Racker, whom Ogden does not mention in his 1979 account of the development of the concept.

the normal course of events, the analyst identifies with the analysand in order to understand him; indeed, she identifies "each part of [her] personality
with the corresponding psychological part in the patient—[her] id with the
patient's id," her ego with his ego, and her superego with his superego. These
"concordant (or homologous) identifications" are, Racker claimed, "the basis
of comprehension"; if the analyst does not identify with the patient at every
level, she will fail to comprehend the patient. The analyst may instead, however, identify at the level of her ego "with the patient's internal objects, for
instance, with [his] superego"—for instance, with a patient's internalized punishing parental figure—especially when such "internal objects" are projected
onto the analyst by the patient. Racker referred to this as a "complementary
identification." Complementary identifications indicate that the analyst has
failed to fully identify with the patient in the concordant manner, for in them
she identifies not with what the patient is but with what the patient projects;
she identifies with the kind of object the patient treats her as (p. 135). As
Racker put it,

> The patient's defence mechanism [projective identification] frequently really
> obtains its ends—in our case to make the analyst feel guilty—and not only
> implies (as has been said at times) that "the patient expects the analyst to feel
> guilty," or that "the analyst is meant to be sad and depressed." The analyst's
> identification with the object with which the patient identifies [her], is, I
> repeat, the normal countertransference process. (p. 66)

Whether or not one accepts Racker's notion that concordant identifications
are necessary if the analyst is to understand her patient—a notion I critiqued

---

Note that in his extensive discussions of projective identification, Ogden (1979, 1982) broke down the
phenomenon of projective identification differently than Sandler. In step one, "there is the fantasy of
projecting a part of oneself into another person and of that part taking over the person from within"
(Ogden, 1979, p. 358). Ogden differentiated this step from projection pure and simple, so to speak, by
postulating that one continues to feel "at one with" the person into whom one has fantasized projecting
a part of oneself, whereas in projection *stricto sensu* one feels removed from that person. In step 2,
"there is pressure exerted via the interpersonal interaction such that the recipient of the projection
experiences pressure to think, feel, and behave in a manner congruent with the projection" (p. 358). In
step 3, the projected feelings are "psychologically processed" by the recipient (mother or analyst), who
hopefully handles them "differently from the manner in which the projector has been able to handle
them" (p. 360). At that point (in step 4), they can be reinternalized by the projector. Ogden's account
is quite clear and exhaustive, yet it is full of implausible assumptions; nevertheless, Ogden (1982,
p. 148) admitted that "not all mental activity or feeling states of the therapist reflect the internal state
of the patient." Still, his accounts of his experience of projective identification are quite extreme: At
one point the therapist "felt that his body and speech . . . had been to some extent conquered and taken
control of by the patient" (p. 151).

at some length in Chapter 1—it is at least visible in Racker's account that there is some subjective involvement on the analyst's part in whether she identifies with the patient himself ("empathic identification," we might say) or with what he projects onto her ("projective identification"). In other words, it seems not to be an automatic or thoroughly objective process that happens without any contribution on the analyst's part. Indeed, it seems to suggest, in Racker's rendition, a failure by the analyst—a failure that presumably need not occur or that might possibly occur very infrequently (even though Racker refers to it as "the normal countertransference process").

Sandler (1987) maintained that stage 3 in the development of the concept of projective identification came with Wilfred Bion, who, in Sandler's view, one-upped Racker on this point: Rather than seeing the analyst as playing a role in identifying in either a concordant or a complementary manner—suggesting that the analyst's subjectivity is in some way involved—Bion (1962) described the analyst as an object of sorts (as opposed to a subject), as a "container" into which the analysand simply puts whatever he wants to, the analyst playing no part in either accepting or rejecting some or all of the analysand's projections (Ogden, 1982, p. 161, called the analyst "a receptacle into which unwanted parts can be dumped").[43] The effect of this reconceptualization is to take the

---

[43] At least one of the purported reasons the patient has for "putting feelings into another person" is that he is scared to death of them and feels compelled to make another person feel them first to see if they are safe to be felt; see, for example, Casement (1991, p. 71) and Bion (1959, pp. 312–313). Although I understand how the analysand can more easily accept some facet of himself when he sees that his analyst does not reject it, I do not see how the analysand could verify that his analyst has been made to feel exactly what he was afraid of feeling and thus that it is "safe to be felt." This strikes me as quite mysterious.

Note that Bion did not always speak of projective identification as involving something more than "the patient's phantasy" (see, for example, Bion, 1957, p. 268). Note too that Bion read his own conception of projective identification into Melanie Klein's aforementioned essay; regarding her brief discussion of projective identification, Bion (1957) wrote:

> By this mechanism the patient splits off a part of his personality and projects it into the object where it becomes installed, sometimes as a persecutor, leaving the psyche, from which it has been split off, correspondingly impoverished. (p. 266)

It is still open to question here whether Bion merely viewed the patient as *thinking* of that split-off "part of his personality" as installed in the thing or person he has projected it into or whether Bion viewed this as really having occurred.

What strikes me as amusing—and may similarly strike those who are familiar with Lacan's often-repeated statement that "there's no such thing as a sexual relationship"—is that Bion (1962, p. 90) used the typical sign for a woman (a circle with a cross coming out of the bottom of it) "for the abstraction representing the container" and the typical sign for a man (a circle with an arrow coming out of the top of it) "for the contained." In other words, Bion seemed to believe in the possibility of a direct relationship between container and contained, between the analyst and what is projected into the analyst, that is akin to some sort of direct, unmediated relationship between the sexes (indeed, some sort of "preestablished harmony").

analyst out of the equation, in some sense, suggesting that she cannot be in any way blamed or otherwise held accountable for what she is feeling and experiencing: Her "countertransferential feelings" are really not countertransferential at all, since they correspond directly and in some *unmediated* fashion to the analysand's transference.[44]

Note that, whereas Klein had already suggested in the 1940s that certain projective and introjective processes could be found not only in the psychoses, but even in severe neuroses, Racker and Bion blurred things considerably when they argued that projective identification occurs with all patients. Klein (1957, p. 69) maintained that such confusional states—projective and introjective processes—normally disappear after the working through of what she calls the "depressive position," "which is normally well on the way in the second half of the first year and the beginning of the second year" of life, leading to a considerable "decrease in projective identification." Racker, Bion, and many analysts in their wake extended the latter concept to virtually all ages and all diagnoses.

A Critique of the Concept of Projective Identification

Every form of expression of the emotions in human beings has a conventional character to it. There is no need to be a Freudian to know that the supposed expressive spontaneity of the emotions turns out, upon examination, not simply to be problematic but highly variable. What signifies one emotion in a region where a certain language is spoken can have a completely different expressive value in another region.

— Lacan (1998b, p. 429)

---

[44] An attentive reading of the paper Sandler purportedly based his account of Bion (1959) on bears out only a part of this account, for Bion (p. 313) made it clear that both mothers and analysts sometimes fail to "introject the [child's or] patient's projective identifications," "denying them ingress" because they cannot tolerate them, suggesting that a subjective factor persists. Nevertheless, the main point stands: Bion averred that certain patients strive "to force" parts of their personality into their analysts, and that the analyst, like the mother, needs to "serve as a repository" for their feelings. "Failure to introject [those feelings] makes the external object appear intrinsically hostile" to the patient (p. 314). It is not clear to me whether Bion viewed all countertransferential feelings as due to such projections by patients.

Winnicott's (1949, p. 70) concepts of "objective countertransference" and of "[hating] the patient objectively" do not function in exactly the same way but are equally pernicious, in my view, for novices and even for experienced analysts. I do not believe that there is any such thing as "objective observation" in the psychological realm, insofar as we all see "reality" through the lenses of our own fantasies, nor do I believe that it is possible for the analyst, in practice, to completely distinguish between love and hate for the patient that may be owing to her own susceptibilities and "love and hate in reaction to the actual personality and behavior of the patient, based on objective observation" (p. 70). The only form of objectivity we can aspire to in psychoanalysis is work based on the symbolic material: the analysand's speech and the symbolic coordinates it provides us with. That is, after all, what allows us to discuss our cases with other analysts and allows them to form their own opinions of those cases—opinions that may differ from our own. Their potential validity depends on the degree to which they explain the symbolic material of the case.

Let us note that analysts generally acknowledge that everything they know or suspect about their analysand's thoughts and feelings is interpreted or processed by them in some way: It is not "raw data," so to speak. The analysand's speech, which many practitioners consider to be the single most important medium of psychoanalytic work, must be interpreted if it is to be understood or otherwise worked with.[45] Similarly, as I argue in Chapter 8, so-called body language is not transparent, universal, or obvious in the way many people seem to think it is: At the very least, it does not mean the same thing for everyone, regardless of social and cultural milieu and background. Body language is something that the analyst may try to "read"—by which we mean interpret—but the only way the analyst can be sure she knows what the analysand's body language means is by asking him to talk about it, which takes us back to the medium of speech. The analysand's actions also tell us something about the analysand's thoughts and feelings, but they too must be interpreted, for they do not necessarily have the same meaning early on in the therapy as they do later, being dependent at least in part on what is going on in the analysis at the particular time at which they occur. Nor does a specific action necessarily have the same meaning for different analysands.

None of these things—the analysand's speech, body language, or action—can be transparently understood by the analyst. All of them must be considered in context—in the social, cultural, and political context, but also in the context of everything that has hitherto transpired in the analysis. This means that the analyst is always and inescapably part of the equation, insofar as she is the one who interprets all of these contexts and is palpably involved in the history of the analysis. Try as she might, she is not a transparent medium (like a medium who supposedly channels spirits and turns tables), a pure and simple instrument that contributes nothing to the situation, whose own neurosis and insecurities can be considered to play no role in the analysis. Even when she becomes quite adept at situating herself in a symbolic position, she is never able to completely eliminate imaginary interference.

But the concept of projective identification, as used since around 1960, suggests that the analyst can gain access to what is going on for the analysand in an unmediated way! The knowledge the analyst supposedly obtains here goes well beyond that provided by a well-developed sense of intuition or some exquisite sensitivity acquired through years of practice: The analyst is postulated here to be in direct contact with the analysand's mind and passions, as if in a kind of Vulcan mind-meld (the kind Dr. Spock was able to perform by

---

[45] It is not directly "grokked," to use Robert Heinlein's term from *Stranger in a Strange Land* (1961/1968).

touching a person or a creature from another galaxy on *Star Trek*). Such powers strike me as truly implausible. They are even harder to believe when we consider that, in at least one prominent and widespread way of thinking about projective identification, the analyst does not become in touch with what the analysand is thinking or feeling, but rather with what he is *not* thinking or feeling!

I will discuss this via some examples found in the literature, but first let me mention that a great many analysands would be likely to find such a mind-meld rather spooky, to say the least. In fact, they often find it scary to say their own thoughts and feelings out loud and are only willing to articulate them little by little in the therapy as they come to trust their analysts more and more; indeed, they sometimes take refuge in the fact that the analyst does not know about these thoughts and feelings at the outset, and that they can even withhold them at certain points if they are not yet ready to explore them or to let the analyst explore them. As Winnicott (1960/1965b) said,

> It is very important . . . that the analyst shall *not* know the answers except in so far as the patient gives the clues. The analyst gathers the clues and makes interpretations, and it often happens that patients fail to give the clues, making certain thereby that the analyst can do nothing. This limitation of the analyst's power is important to the patient, just as the analyst's power is important, represented by the interpretation that is . . . based on the clues and the unconscious cooperation of the patient who is supplying the material which builds up and justifies the interpretation. (pp. 50–51)

Small children occasionally believe that their parents know all of their thoughts without their speaking them (see, for example, Freud, 1909/1955, p. 164), but adults often take consolation in the fact that they can let other people know their thoughts and feelings only when they want to and that they can hide them, at least to some degree, the rest of the time. Even though many of us may at times wish we could have such an unmediated connection with other people, it is generally only the psychotic who believes that he does.

Sometimes, especially with analysands with whom I have been working for many years, I say something and they respond that that was exactly what was going through their minds—how did I know that? Of course, it was something that occurred to me based on the entirety of the context: their discourse that day, the sum total of things they have said to me in the past, the larger social and cultural context, and the expressions and formulations available to them in the language they speak. In other words, it is essentially a product of knowing a great deal about how they think and feel about things and of knowing their mother tongue very well. Such "mind reading," for example, happens less with my analysands whose mother tongue is French, which for me is a second language: I do not have at my disposal the full range of expressions that are likely to occur to them, as extensive as my knowledge of the language may be.[46] All of my access to their thoughts is mediated by my (conscious or nonconscious, intellectual or visceral) interpretation of their speech, gestures, and actions. And my interpretation is, of necessity, mediated by my entire background: my upbringing, education, and knowledge of the language we use to converse with each other. I cannot, for example, pick up on certain religious allusions analysands make if I have not familiarized myself to at least some degree with the tenets of their faith—I may, in the best of cases, ask about something I do not understand, but I may not even realize that an allusion was being made because I thought I understood the meaning that was intended, when in fact there was actually more than one level of meaning intended.

This is something I encounter all the time when I am asked to review the work of other translators: They often do not even realize that something is an idiomatic expression and should be looked up in the dictionary because it has a meaning that is very different from its literal meaning. Instead, they take it at face value because it already has a discernible meaning, even if it is not the one that was intended by the author. This is just a further indication that the entirety of one's cultural and educational background is involved in one's interpretation of another's speech, just as it is involved in one's interpretation of another's written text.

The first example of so-called projective identification I will discuss here is provided by Patrick Casement (1991, pp. 64–78), who classed projective identification among the various forms of what he called "interactive communication" or "communication by impact." He reported on a case conducted by a female therapist he presumably supervised, and I have chosen it for its brevity and clarity. A certain Miss G frequently missed sessions and would often remain silent at the beginning of sessions for long periods of time. Her female therapist felt "enormous pressure" to speak first during sessions and felt abandoned and uncertain as to what was happening when Miss G failed to show up for consultations. The only thing that we are told about Miss G's

---

[46] Of course, one never knows the full range of words and expressions available in one's mother tongue either, as there are simply too many (estimates for the English language range from 450,000 to about a 1,000,000 distinct words and expressions). The range of expressions one is familiar with depends largely on what country and what area within that country one was raised in, one's familiarity with people from other areas and other countries, one's reading, and so on. Early on in their work some of my supervisees are inclined to think that patients are employing neologisms when they are simply using words or phrases that the supervisees have never before encountered. These words and phrases may be particular to a region or subculture they did not grow up in (dialects and variant grammars), jargon from a field with which they are unfamiliar, citations from songs, poetry, novels, TV shows, or movies well known to people of a certain generation or education, and so on.

history is that she "had been traumatized as a child by her mother's repeated absences, in hospital with cancer, and (at the age of 4) by her mother's death" (p. 77). Casement's conclusion was that Miss G was trying to impress upon her therapist "how unbearable it must have been when she was so often left in this state of not knowing what was happening to her mother" (p. 78); in other words, Miss G was trying to make her therapist feel as abandoned and confused as she herself had felt as a small child. Miss G apparently sensed that she was unable to have this effect on her therapist with words (we are not told whether this was due to the fact that her trauma dated from such an early age that she could not express it in words or whether her therapist did not seem terribly attentive to her words) and thus was ineluctably led to try to have this effect with actions. When her therapist told her as much, "the patient was gradually able to acknowledge that this made sense to her" and eventually missed fewer sessions and spoke more easily at the beginning of sessions.

The patient was presumed by Casement to have cast her feelings of abandonment by her mother "outside of herself,"[47] and the therapist was presumed to have picked up on them unconsciously and "taken them in"—that is, identified with them (how one "identifies" with feelings that have never been expressed remains to be determined) or at least identified with the patient's predicament early in life.

There are, it seems to me, a number of different ways that we can think about Miss G's situation, only a couple of which I will discuss here. If, as Freud (1915b/1957, p. 178) put it, "Strictly speaking . . . there are no unconscious affects," only "unconscious ideas," it makes little sense to say here that the analysand has "unconscious feelings of abandonment" related to her mother. As I said earlier, something is not a feeling unless or until it is *felt*, even if it is felt in a displaced or disguised form—in the form, for example, of anxiety or rage. Miss G, who had obviously already conveyed to her therapist that she was traumatized by her mother's disappearances when she was a young child, had, I would propose, neither repressed her feelings (feelings being susceptible of suppression, but not of repression, in the psychoanalytic sense of the term) nor projected her feelings; indeed, she was afraid of getting close enough to her therapist to *feel anything* for her. Given her early childhood experience, we would be hardly reaching to suppose that Miss G generally avoided getting close to people—perhaps to women in particular—for fear that they would abandon her. Her goal was to feel as little as possible for her therapist and to want and expect nothing from her therapist. The moment she began to feel something

---

[47] We are never told how this projection of feelings outside of oneself, this casting out, is possible, a point I shall refer to at length later.

for her or want something from her, she went AWOL. She did everything possible not to actualize feelings of abandonment! Indeed, she may well have followed the oft-jilted lover's motto: "Leave them before they can leave you."

In this sense, her feelings were not somehow projected outside of herself; rather, she was numb and trying to stay numb. What the therapist felt was how she herself, as a person with her own particular characteristics and sensitivities, reacted to Miss G's silences and missed sessions. Other therapists, differently constituted, with their own particular characteristics and sensitivities, might have relished the silences as opportunities to reflect on other cases and might have viewed the missed sessions as time in which to catch up on their reading; or they might have become angry at the patient over the missed sessions; or they might have become neither angry nor worried but simply established a limit regarding what they were willing to tolerate in their work schedule by saying, "Two more missed sessions in a row and I won't be willing to keep this time open for you anymore." Many a supervisee has told me her analysand was projecting something into her and making her feel a specific way when it was pretty clear to me that I myself would not have reacted at all as she did, if nothing else because I have never felt that specific way with *any* of my analysands. I believe that this is because I situate myself in the therapy very differently than many others do, not feeling myself to be in the line of fire as they are wont to; but my sense is that even if I were to take analysands' digs, silences, or absences personally, I still would not take them in the same way as they do. Different therapists have very different personalities and react to their patients in a wide variety of manners, few of which should be attributed directly to the patients.

What Casement called "projective identification" here seems to be nothing more than (1) repetition of a style of relating on the patient's part—avoidance of closeness to stave off the potential for unbearable feelings of abandonment—which generally goes by the simpler name of *transference*, coupled with (2) a countertransferential reaction to this on the therapist's part. The latter's countertransferential reaction, while no doubt common, can hardly be said to have been *forced* upon her by the patient.

Rather than characterizing the patient as having a *need* to make the therapist feel what she once felt and will no longer allow herself to feel, we could, alternatively—were we convinced that the therapist's reaction to the patient's silences and absences indicated something significant about what was going on in the analysis—hypothesize that the patient was unwittingly repeating a situation from the past, with the caveat that the positions were inverted this time, the patient playing the part of the one who makes herself scarce. This might be understood, along the lines of Freud's (1920/1955, p. 16) discussions of repetition compulsion, as a repetition of a traumatizing situation in order to master it, to make oneself the agent instead of the passive recipient of the traumatic experience. In this case, too, there is no special need to postulate an attempt on the patient's part to make the therapist feel or do something in particular. We see here again that "transference is itself only a piece of repetition, and that the repetition is a transference of the forgotten past not only on to the doctor but also on to all the other aspects of the current situation" (Freud, 1914a/1958, p. 151).

A question I would raise here regarding so-called projective identification is as follows: If we assume (and this is a big assumption) that the patient is "trying to get rid of" certain feelings or is "projecting them outside of herself," why does her therapist "identify with them"—that is, feel them?[48] Is the therapist somehow obliged by the patient to feel the patient's feelings, as Casement (1991, p. 70) suggested when, in talking about a different patient, he said, "Mrs. T did much more than project her feelings onto me. She *made* me feel what *she* could not yet bear to feel consciously within herself"—or as Bollas (1987, p. 5) implied when he said that the analyst is "compelled to experience one of the analysand's inner objects"? If the therapist is *obliged* to feel the patient's feelings, *cannot help but* feel the patient's feelings, *cannot avoid* feeling the patient's feelings, how do we explain the fact that some therapists do not, in fact, feel them? Must we conclude that those who do not are simply insensitive brutes?

Perhaps there is a simpler explanation. To feel what another person is feeling is something that virtually all of us are familiar with in certain contexts, and it does not seem to require any special gift or unusual sensitivity: Laughter can, as they say, be "infectious," and the sadness of someone close to us can make us sad just as his or her joy can make us joyful. But this is not true in every circumstance, for a loved one's sadness can make us all the more determined instead to cheer that person up, and a loved one's joy can make us all the more depressed if things have not been going our way as of late. In other words, we must be *disposed* to laugh or cry, and perhaps even wanting and looking to laugh or cry for this to happen. Many of us can, at times at least, steel ourselves to a lover's pain, whether because we feel that it is a put-on designed to manipulate us, or we want to play the strong role, or we have decided to break up with that person. This suggests that for an analyst to be infected by (read: "identify with") her analysand's feelings, she must be disposed or predisposed to do so; she must—to return to our earlier example—be susceptible to feeling abandoned or prone to being worried about others (the latter is undoubtedly

---

[48] See Freud (1921/1955, Chapter 7) for a more rigorous discussion of the use of the term *identification* in psychoanalysis; see also Jean Florence's (1984) enlightening commentary on identification.

characteristic of a large number, though not all, of those who go into the so-called helping professions).

Not all emotions are contagious or infectious to everyone. When, for example, I take airplanes, I often see anxious people around me holding onto the armrests for dear life as the plane careens down the runway preparing for liftoff, but I do not become anxious for all that. Instead, I rather enjoy the plane's acceleration during liftoff. Similarly, I rarely feel anxious in sessions with anxious analysands; were I to become as anxious as they are, in any case, I think I would have great difficulty helping them with their anxiety. Perhaps, due to my own particular makeup, I am more impervious to people's feelings than other analysts (especially those trained in other traditions), but I suspect that it is rather that I have a particular conception of what my role is as an analyst, which is quite different from theirs, and that I tend to attribute whatever feelings I may have for the analysand and about the analysis to myself and not to the analysand.

Let us admit, however, for the sake of argument, that some analysts are less impervious to others' feelings and regularly feel abandoned when their patients feel abandoned, anxious when their patients feel anxious, depressed when their patients feel depressed, and so on (through no fault of their own—that is, not because they want to feel those feelings or are prone to feeling them). It is not clear to me of what value this may be to their patients, but at least we seem to be on somewhat firm ground here regarding the "communicability of affect" from one person to another in certain cases. What must be pointed out here is that the concept of projective identification (as currently used by many clinicians) goes much further than this, for *it postulates that the analyst feels what the patient does not feel.* In other words, it cannot rely on a notion like the "communicability of affect," for the presumption here is that the patient does not have the affect that the analyst is experiencing!

Emotion is generally a bodily experience or at least generally has a visceral component: When prey to strong emotions, we may feel them welling up in our chest, stomach, neck, face, and so on. A good actor learns how to produce such bodily signs when they are called for by his or her role, and the consummate politician learns how to suppress such outwardly visible bodily signs by adopting a "poker face" in front of a hostile public or reporters. Nevertheless, even the consummate poker player sometimes lets escape some facial or bodily manifestation of strong emotion (the twitching of a facial muscle, a nervous hand gesture, playing with hair, or something of the sort), referred to as a "tell" by the card player, and even the consummate politician tends to sooner or later make a slip of the tongue or slur his or her words in such a way as to divulge some heightened emotion.

Most of us can read these signs fluently in our loved ones, and experienced therapists can fairly easily read many such signs even in people they just met, see on television, hear on the radio, or speak with on the phone (see Chapter 8).[49] It seems notable, then, that analysts who embrace the notion of projective identification would say that they are *not* picking up on subtle signs of suppressed emotion in their analysands—indeed, they argue that projective identification is occurring precisely at moments at which there are no such signs to pick up on. They do not argue that we are dealing here with something along the lines of the classical Freudian notion of repression whereby the link between thought and affect is broken, affect continuing to exist and to be felt by the analysand, certain signs of it being visible to other people. In other words, they are not arguing that their analysand is feeling something but simply does not want to feel it, want to acknowledge it, know what to call it, know what it is due to, or know what to connect it to. Nor are they arguing that the analysand is deliberately or unwittingly suppressing his emotions. What they are arguing is that his emotions are "split off" in such a way that they are projected outside of his psyche and body altogether.

This strikes me as a rather incredible claim. When Freud introduced the notion of splitting, he suggested that in certain rare cases (like in fetishism) the analysand becomes of two minds, most simply stated. In his most important paper on the subject, Freud (1938/1964) stated that splitting involves a kind of both/and logic whereby the analysand *both* believes that women do not have penises *and* yet simultaneously cannot help but think that they do have penises. The analysand seems to be able to not merely entertain both hypotheses but genuinely believe both of them at the same time, even though they are contradictory. Nowhere does Freud suggest that one of those two thoughts—or that one of those two minds by which the analysand may be characterized, so to speak—becomes located in someone else or can be found in someone else, whether parent, sibling, or analyst. Splitting is something that, for Freud, occurs within one and the same person, and both sides of the split remain "within" that person, however approximately we must take terms like *within* and *without*, or *inside* and *outside*, in psychoanalysis.[50] And according to Klein

---

[49] A company called Business Intelligence Advisors has recently begun to study such tells, speech patterns, and other rhetorical strategies (such as those mentioned in Chapter 1) to determine when politicians and business leaders may be dissimulating (Laing, 2006).

[50] Although I generally think that we divide up the world into inside and outside in far too rigid a manner, saying that "something is all in our mind" or that "the outside world is telling us something," I usually think that theorists who embrace the notion of projective identification also use the terms outside and inside in an overly rigid manner when they talk about the child perpetually introjecting and projecting objects, as if the objects they are talking about were actually situated in some space that

(1946/1952), although a person may fantasize that he is not characterized by a certain emotion, and that someone else is instead, the split remains at the level of fantasy: The emotion has not left that person's psychical economy.[51]

I would argue that the burden of proof rests on the shoulders of those who believe in the most far-reaching version of projective identification (Bion's, corresponding to stage 3 in Sandler's account): They must (1) cogently conceptualize the mechanism by which emotions that are "split off" can be projected outside of one's psyche and body altogether; (2) tell us where these emotions "go" when they are split off—for presumably they are split off at many if not all times by the analysand, not only when the analysand is in the presence of the analyst (or are we to suppose that they flow back into the analysand at the

---

is clearly defined as me or not me. My sense is that there is no such clear-cut distinction for very young children, that time in childhood being characterized by what Lacan (1988a) referred to as "transitivism," examples of which are when one child falls down and the child watching cries, or when Paul hits Peter but says that Peter hit him (p. 169); see also Lacan (2006, p. 113). However, once the ego becomes more well-defined, through oedipalization (or, as Lacan formulates it, through the workings of the Name-of-the-Father, or more generally stated, the symbolic function), such transitivism disappears, being found in such a wholesale fashion in adolescents and adults only in psychotics (see Chapter 10). One adult psychotic woman, for example, proffered the following: "When someone close to me suffers, I suffer at least as much as him—I take his suffering from him" (Cambron, 1997, pp. 94–95).

Analysts who believe in projective identification would thus either have to claim that projective identification only occurs in work with psychotics—although the question would then arise why analysts themselves would be subject to transitivism just because their psychotic analysands are—or that transitivism continues in a more or less unrestricted fashion throughout our lifetimes, in a manner that never becomes mediated by language and custom. The latter strikes me as highly dubious: We do not all feel each others' feelings all the time, and if we did life would become incredibly confusing indeed! It would become even more confusing if we all felt what everyone is *not* feeling!

In any case, defenders of projective identification would still have to explain by what mechanism the analyst comes to feel something that is not being felt by her analysand.

[51] We are probably all familiar with disowning our own ideas at certain times: We tell our loved ones or analysts, "You're probably thinking that . . ." when that is precisely what just occurred to us, or "It sounds to me like you're angry that I . . ." when in fact we ourselves are angry. In other words, we project certain ideas and feelings onto others, presuming that they have them, seeing them in others instead of in ourselves. That in no way obliges those others to have such ideas or feelings! When one of my analysands lapses into silence and I ask him what he is thinking, he often says something like, "You must be thinking I'm the lowest of the low" or "You must be mocking me for being such a miserable wretch." I am generally very focused on the material he has just been discussing and not at all preoccupied with judgments of that kind. By conveying what he is thinking to me via speech, he obviously "puts the idea in my head," so to speak, but it does not thereby become a view I share with him: I do not think that he is the lowest of the low or mock him for being a miserable wretch.

Another of my analysands is quick to say that I sound angry at any and every moment—before the session has even begun or when we are in the middle of talking about something—when I am not feeling at all angry. At times it is because he is angry with me, and at times it is because he expects virtually everyone to be angry with him for everything. But I do not become angry with him for all that. Were he to become highly insistent and relentlessly insist that I must be angry with him, he might well anger me eventually, producing anger in me by accusing me again and again, but in such a case he could hardly be said to have split off his own anger.

end of the session?); and (3) elucidate how it is that they come to be felt by the analyst, when they are indeed felt by the analyst, for as we have seen they are not felt by all analysts. In the absence of compelling explanations of these processes, the notion of projective identification seems to rely on mechanisms or procedures bordering on magic. Few notions in psychoanalysis are, to my mind, fraught with more conceptual confusions and aporias.

For those who lend credence to Occam's razor—the principle that the best explanation is often the most concise explanation, the explanation that requires the fewest debatable hypotheses—I would recommend seeking an explanation of what the analyst is feeling first and foremost in the analyst herself, next in the relationship between herself and the analysand as it has developed over the course of the analysis, and only lastly—should all else fail—in something the analysand is not even experiencing.

Projective Identification as Normalization

The human tendency to twist the knife in the wound is universal.
— *Wodehouse (1933/1981, p. 536)*

The subtext of the notion of projective identification, as I read it, is often based on a specific conception of what the analysand *should be feeling* when he discusses certain things. I call it a subtext because it is rarely mentioned explicitly by analysts, and yet it seems to form part of the implicit backdrop to their commentary on cases. As I indicate in Chapter 9, notions of normality have come to play an ever larger role in psychoanalytic theory in recent decades, and analysts increasingly appeal to *what they think any human being would normally be feeling* in certain situations. In numerous supposed instances of projective identification, the analyst purports to be feeling what the analysand would be feeling were he not so disturbed, not so abnormal.

Consider the following example supplied by Casement (1991, pp. 68–70). Mr. and Mrs. T went to see Casement because, he said, of Mrs. T's frigidity. She told him that they "had spent the first five years of their marriage getting a house and decorating it, in preparation for beginning a family"; then a son was born who began to have serious medical problems when he was six months old—he died after she had cared for him for another nine months. She was seven months pregnant with their daughter at the son's funeral, where she "felt tearful but held it in"; she told Casement that she had never cried since then, feeling numb instead. The daughter died at the age of ten months "of the same constitutional brain disorder as had her brother."

Casement commented on this as follows: "What was most striking, during the telling of this terrible sequence of pain and loss, was that Mrs. T's face and tone of voice remained wooden and lifeless. . . . She showed no feelings at all. But my own feelings, upon listening to her, were nearly overwhelming me. I was literally crying inside" (p. 69). In wondering about his own response, he tells us that he knew he "would be moved by any account of a child's death,"[52] but instead of concluding that his reaction had primarily to do with his own makeup, he concluded, "What was producing this effect upon me had something to do with her inability to show any expression of her own feelings." Now what could allow him to know "her own feelings" when he had just met her for the first time? Isn't it just slightly possible that she was not a very feeling person? As much as I myself might well have felt as Casement did in the session with her, I certainly would not have arrived at his conclusion:

> Mrs. T. did much more than project her feelings onto me. She *made* me feel what *she* could not yet bear to feel consciously within herself. . . . I could see that it had been the patient's own lack of emotion that had been having the greatest impact upon me. As a result, I had been feeling in touch with tears which did not altogether belong to me. (p. 70).

Casement, like so many other analysts (as we shall see in Chapter 9), seems to rely on a taken-for-granted notion of what would be the "appropriate" type and quantity of affect for all people to display in such a situation. And from whence derives this notion? It would seem that it is from the affect he himself would be likely to display in such a situation.

Certainly, Mrs. T's lack of affect in telling her story would be striking to almost any Westerner in our day and age where it is more the exception than the rule to lose a child in infancy. Nevertheless, there are parts of the modern world where the infant mortality rate is extremely high—for example, half of all children die by the age of five in Haiti today (Arnst, 2006)—and it was not uncommon even in 18th-century England for women to lose the majority of their children before they reached the age of seven (the parents of John Law, often considered to be the inventor of paper money, lost ten of their 14 children to childhood illnesses). Contemporary Westerners would no doubt be shocked by the somewhat matter-of-fact way non-Westerners talk (and people from prior centuries write) about their lost infants, who number as many as one in five in the first year of life in certain countries even today, where, in the words of Thomas Hobbes, life often remains "nasty, brutish, and short."

---

[52] Casement would perhaps do well to recall Winnicott's (1949, p. 74) comment, "Sentimentality is useless for parents [and analysts too], as it contains a denial of hate."

However, their attitudes are not a sign of heartlessness, but rather reflect their harsh reality, stoicism, and at times a sense that it is God's will.

Casement's presumption that he "had been feeling in touch with tears which did not altogether belong to" him implies that *her reaction should have been the tears that he was crying inside.* If she was not crying, it was necessarily—according to his assumptions—because her sadness was split off and projected into other people. But isn't it at least theoretically possible that Mrs. T's feelings about the loss of her children might be very different from Casement's feelings upon hearing her story, whether because she came from a different culture, a different socioeconomic background, a different religion, a different family, or even a different diagnostic category than him? The assumption that the analyst is feeling what the analysand would be feeling if only she were in touch with her feelings very often rides roughshod over the potential otherness of the other, over the genuine differences among people, relying as it does on a presupposition that we are all fundamentally alike in our "basic humanity." A safer assumption might have been that Casement had yet to determine how Mrs. T felt during her children's illnesses and at their deaths, but that what *he* was feeling was his own reaction to the combination of such a story and so-called flat affect on the storyteller's part.

In any case, Casement could well hypothesize that Mrs. T had repressed a good deal related to her children, and perhaps her husband as well, insofar as she told him at the outset that she had been unable to have intercourse for the past 5 years due to medically unexplained "gynecological pain"—in other words, due, in all likelihood, to the formation of a symptom related to sex and reproduction. If we formulate this snippet of a case in terms of repression, it can be hypothesized that her "gynecological pain" had taken the place of her mental pain. *Her emotions had not left her body and gone into someone else; they were simply localized in her body in a disguised fashion.* What could be more classically neurotic, and indeed hysteric, than this? What could possibly lead us to appeal here to some improbable notion about feelings being projected through space or about a will on Mrs. T's part to make someone she had just met experience something so he would know what she had (not) gone through?

Rule of Thumb

Everyone knows that one must have squared things with one's own unconscious if one is not to be mistaken in detecting it at work in the material the patient supplies in the analytic artifice.
— Lacan (1977b, p. 11)

I would propose as a rule of thumb that analysts (especially beginning analysts) never presume that they are feeling what the analysand is feeling, or should be feeling, or does not want to feel, or has made her feel, and that notions like projective identification (and all of its more recent offspring, such as "projective transidentification" and "projective counteridentification") should be appealed to only as a last resort, when all other explanations have failed.

I would also propose that, if one is to rely upon such explanations, they be used only in discussions of psychosis—which is, after all, the realm of psychopathology they grew out of. A great many of the recent examples of projective identification in the literature, however, come from obvious cases of neurosis; Ogden (1979, pp. 368–369) went so far as to suggest that virtually everyone is employing projective identification all the time in analysis, including the analyst! The very notion of treating thoughts, feelings, and "parts" of the self as so many objects that can be moved about at will—a notion that is central to the concept of projective identification—smacks seriously of the kind of "concrete thinking" so often associated with psychosis. Perhaps this is why psychotics do not reject out of hand interpretations involving the moving about of such objects: Such interpretations mimic their own way of thinking about things. (Which is not to say that objects actually move about in that manner: To contradict Hamlet, thinking does not necessarily make it so!)

There are obviously complex interactions that occur between analysand and analyst; the latter are by no means isolated monads (in Leibniz's sense) that have no real effect on each other. For example, with the analysand whose case I discussed in an earlier section, it was no doubt my tendency to pry that encouraged his repetition with me of the particular scene that occurred with his sister as a child, leading him to fall silent more often, which encouraged my prying still further (which encouraged still more silence on his part, and so on). At times, the analyst pressures the analysand to act in certain ways, at other times the analysand pressures the analyst to act in certain ways, and a subtle, complex dance results from this.[53] The analyst clearly plays an important part in the repetitions that occur in the analysis: She is anything but a neutral or objective observer. An analyst who believed herself to play no role in what transpires in the analysis would be embracing a highly obsessive theory of psychoanalytic treatment indeed.[54]

---

[53] Ogden (1979, pp. 359–360) referred to a patient who "exerted terrific pressure on the therapist to conform to the projected fantasy" and described "an external pressure exerted by means of interpersonal interaction." One can easily accept the notion that people pressure each other into acting in specific ways without accepting the notion of projective identification as a whole. Let us note, nevertheless, that the more the analyst situates herself in the symbolic register, the less likely she is to experience such "terrific pressure" in the first place.

[54] One might even go so far as to say that, whereas one finds concepts like "the autonomous ego" in predominantly obsessive forms of psychoanalytic theorization, and concepts like "man's desire is

Note that the kinds of interpretations analysts make to their analysands when working within a conceptual framework that includes projective identification are not, strictly speaking, interpretations at all according to the criteria presented in Chapter 5. For something to be considered an interpretation, in the Lacanian sense of the term, it must be evocative and polyvalent. The kinds of things analysts tend to say regarding so-called projective identifications rarely play on the multiple staves of the musical score of speech and should instead be qualified as explanations—that is, statements that provide specific, concrete meanings. As we have already seen, these are the kinds of statements that should be avoided when working with neurotics, and, as we shall see in Chapter 10, these are the kinds of statements that make perfect sense when working with psychotics.

A Cautionary Tale

"You are putting sleepiness in the air."
— An analyst to an analysand

An exceptionally perspicacious therapist with whom I have worked for several years once told me that her first analysis, which lasted 3 years, came to grief when her analyst appealed to projective identification to explain the fact that he fell asleep during one of her sessions with him. Shortly before the session, her brother had begged her to commit suicide with him and she was, as she put it, in a state of crisis, blubbering, and not at her most articulate. In the midst of this, she noticed that her analyst seemed to be asleep but figured that he might just be looking down at his notes. When his head slumped over to the side and he awoke with a jolt and a loud snore, there was no longer any doubt in her mind that he had dozed off. He tried to act as if nothing had happened and asked her what she was thinking. "That you're tired?" she offered, mortified

---

the other's desire" in predominantly hysterical forms of psychoanalytic theorization, concepts like "projective identification" stem from predominantly psychotic forms of psychoanalytic theorization. In that sense, each such set of concepts may be understood to reflect not only the particular patient population they were designed to grapple with and elucidate but also to reflect the psychoanalysts who are attracted to each particular style of psychoanalytic theorization. Note that Lacan (1976–1977, December 14, 1976) at one point diagnosed himself publicly (perhaps tongue in cheek to at least some degree), saying, "In the final analysis, I am a perfect hysteric, that is, one without symptoms, except now and then."
    Curiously enough, what strikes me as one of the most boringly obsessive theoretical works in the psychoanalytic literature, Gill's (1982) *Analysis of Transference*, plays up the importance of the analyst's role in the analytic situation. We should no doubt always be mindful of what Mark Twain said in *Tom Sawyer Abroad* (1896/1996): "There's another trouble about theories: there's always a hole in them somewhere, sure, if you look close enough."

and shocked. He admitted that he was tired but proffered, "You are putting sleepiness in the air." He explained that she had unconsciously wanted him to abandon her and had thus *made* it happen.

The fact that this explanation did not at all tally with her own experience of the session and of the analysis did not lead her to break off the analysis immediately—she wondered about her own unconscious intentions and tried to explore them in future sessions. But whenever she brought them up, her analyst changed the subject and seemed unwilling to work through this incident. It was this, combined with some erratic countertransference reactions on his part involving him missing sessions, that led her to leave the analysis and find someone else to work with. Had he simply acknowledged his own tiredness or sleep deprivation, apologized for nodding off, and perhaps even rescheduled the session, none of that probably would have happened. It seems that it was the very existence of a theoretical concept like projective identification in his bag of psychoanalytic tricks that allowed him to deny his responsibility for falling asleep and to attribute the "sleepiness making" to his analysand—more stubbornly than many would have, no doubt, but with the blessing of the likes of Bion (1955, p. 226) who characterized one of his patients as speaking "in a drowsy manner calculated to put the analyst to sleep."[55] No one trained in a Lacanian approach to transference and countertransference could ever, it seems to me, have asserted that the analysand was responsible for the analyst's napping. As even Gill (1982, p. 63) said, "Countertransference can be rationalized easily in terms of a theory of therapy."

Not all appeals to the concept of projective identification are as naive and foolish as the one I have included in this cautionary tale, but I hope that it will dissuade practitioners from letting themselves off the hook for their own lapses.

Privileging the Imaginary

What we have here is only the effect of the analyst's passions. . . . It has nothing to do with countertransference on the part of this or that analyst; it has to do with the consequences of the dyadic [i.e., imaginary] relation, if the therapist does not overcome it, and how could he overcome it when he views it as the ideal of his action?

— Lacan (2006, p. 595)

---

[55] Such moves on analysts' parts incline analysands to believe that their doctors are nuttier than they themselves are and would do well to have their heads examined by other doctors who are not such fruitcakes. They are right when they say, as Joni Mitchell does in "Twisted," "My analyst told me/ That I was right out of my head/ But I said dear doctor/ I think that it's you instead." *Cave sanatorem:* Beware of the therapist!

The attempt to make use of imaginary-level reactions on the analyst's part (such as feeling annoyed, angry, bored, sleepy, rejected, abandoned, scared, and so on) to the analysand's projections encourages the analyst to situate her work in the imaginary register, thinking that the lion's share of the work occurs in the transference and countertransference. However, according to Lacan, transference reactions occur at moments at which symbolization fails—that is, when the analysand is unable to go any further in his articulation of the "pathogenic nucleus"—and countertransference is indicative of the analyst's failure to situate herself in the position of the symbolic Other, having become bogged down in the imaginary relation (that is, in the dyadic relation between two egos; see Fink, 1997, Chapter 3).

In other words, according to a Lacanian perspective, transference and countertransference occur at moments when the all-important process of symbolization breaks down, not when something productive for the analysis is happening. Transference and countertransference are thus diversions, imaginary lures, and are associated with moments of stasis, not moments in which something psychoanalytically important can be done. Direct work with the transference and countertransference may be satisfying to the analysand at some level, but it does not produce the kind of change that Lacanian psychoanalysis aims at.[56]

When Heimann (1950, pp. 83–84) stressed that "the analyst's countertransference is not only part and parcel of the analytic relationship, but it is the patient's creation, it is part of the patient's personality" and concluded that "the analyst's countertransference is an instrument of research into the patient's unconscious," she came perilously close to jettisoning the symbolic dimension. Clinicians are led to engage in theoretical acrobatics to separate the analyst's potential psychopathology—Spotnitz (1999, p. 229) called this the analyst's "subjective countertransference" —from the analyst's "objective countertransference" (which is supposed to be a pure, unmediated reflection or even product of the patient himself). However, even Ogden (1979, p. 367) recognized that "we are not dealing with an 'all or nothing' phenomenon here."

The underlying assumption—that the analyst knows herself so well that she knows what part of her reaction to the analysand is subjective and what part of it is objective—is fundamentally flawed. For the analyst continues not to know all of her own motives even after a very lengthy analysis—such is the nature of the unconscious. To emphasize, as Zetzel (1956/1990, p. 145) did, the "reality aspects of the therapist's personality" is to assume that the analyst is the one who knows what is and is not real in her personality. But analysands are, as has

---

[56] Miller (2003, p. 35) said, "What we see today is that countertransference is thought to be the royal road to the unconscious—not dreams, but countertransference."

so often been remarked, highly attuned to facets of the analyst's personality of which she herself may be blithely or stubbornly unaware! Hence Freud's recommendation (which he unfortunately did not follow himself) that the analyst be prepared to do another stint of analysis every now and then.

When the analyst is construed by Bion and his followers as a container (is it like the Danaides' leaky vessel or, rather, like a hermetically sealed Tupperware container, one might wonder?) into which the analysand puts whatever he likes without any mediation whatsoever, it seems that the symbolic has been altogether thrown out the window.

I have heard it said by a variety of different practitioners that one must be able to get at the same kinds of problems through the imaginary register as through the symbolic register, since analysts who work in very different ways all have a certain modicum of success, albeit varying degrees of success. I would not dispute that the analysts who work primarily on the imaginary level have some curative effects on their patients—above all on their psychotic patients, insofar as the imaginary is one of the levels that we must work with in psychosis (see Chapter 10). I would, however, argue—on the basis of many years of supervising analysts trained in psychoanalytic approaches that emphasize the imaginary almost to the exclusion of the symbolic, and of many years analyzing patients who had already done long (and often multiple) stints of imaginary-level work with other analysts before coming to me—that the type of cure aimed at in such practices is very different from the type of cure aimed at when one emphasizes the symbolic register, the former above all fostering the development of an observing ego that acquires knowledge of the analysand's "patterns"—patterns that often do not change (as I indicated in Chapter 5). Analysts are, of course, free to define transference and countertransference in ways other than Lacan does, but their work is then likely to be situated primarily at the imaginary level and at the imaginary level, the analyst's own personality takes center stage. As Lacan (2006, p. 587) put it back in 1958, "The more [the analyst's personality] is involved, the less sure he is of his action." Perhaps this explains at least part of the obsession in the contemporary psychoanalytic literature with discussions of the analyst's countertransference and with the attempt to find a way of arguing that it truly reflects the analysand at least as much as the analyst.[57]

---

[57] Ogden (1994), for example, saw it as something that is jointly produced by analyst and analysand. One even gets the impression that he has benefited far more from the analyses he has conducted than his patients have because he told us about the repressions of his own that were lifted (p. 471) and the "particular form of separation and mourning" (p. 483) he underwent in the course of them rather than telling us about his patients' repressions that were lifted.

8

"Phone Analysis"
(Variations on
the Psychoanalytic Situation)

Whether it wishes to be an agent of healing, training, or sounding the depths, psychoanalysis has but one medium: the patient's speech.

— Lacan (2006, p. 247)

ON AVERAGE, AMERICANS move every 18 to 24 months, sometimes "just across town"—which, in the metropolitan sprawl of an area like Los Angeles, might mean a two-hour drive from one's former residence—sometimes to a different city, state, country, or even continent. In my own practice, most of my analysands have moved at least once or twice during the course of their analyses, often to locations up to about 1,000 miles away; four of my analysands have left the North American continent for a year or more; and two have moved at least eight times in about eight years.

Given the mobility of the American population—a mobility that many people who are not American find difficult to fathom—analysts in America are faced with a thorny problem: how to sustain long-term psychoanalytic work with analysands. It is sometimes possible, of course, to refer an analysand to another analyst in the city to which she has been transferred, but often the analyst does not know the clinical work of any analysts practicing in that city well enough to confidently recommend someone. Moreover, a great many moves analysands make are for limited lengths of time, such as a three-month internship, a six-month sabbatical, a yearlong Fulbright, or a two-year stint at an overseas corporate headquarters. In these cases it is impractical to continue

189

analysis with someone else, given the virtual certainty of the return home in a fairly short space of time (not to mention the analysand's reluctance to "start over" with someone new and deal with possible language barriers), and yet the analysand's difficulties may be such as to require continued treatment during that space of time.

The analyst could, in theory, try to dissuade the analysand from making such short-term moves by trying to impress upon her the importance of continuing her analytic work in person, and in certain cases this might indeed be fitting. In many cases, however, the short-term move represents a very special opportunity not likely to present itself again, and in other cases it represents something of a forced choice, the analysand's employer saying, "Move to city X to help set up the new office or start looking for a new job" (job security in the United States is not what it is in much of Europe, for example, and the exigencies of life intervene in analysis in a way that they did not when analyses lasted only a few short months). Hence the importance of finding a way to allow the analytic work to continue during such virtually unavoidable absences.

Many years ago in my own practice, an analysand who had gone abroad for a year on a fellowship began calling me in distress. Even though we had agreed that she would resume her analysis upon her return, her distress was such that she felt she could not wait until then. After several such desperate calls, we agreed to schedule regular times for her to call (I do not think that unscheduled phone calls to "touch base" or talk briefly about one specific thought, association, or feeling make much sense, except in emergencies), and we worked over the phone until she returned to the United States. I noted very quickly that the work with her over the phone proceeded very much as it had proceeded with her on the couch, and when I was later led to leave the West Coast and accept a position in Pittsburgh (some 2,500 miles away), we resumed our phone sessions.

Little by little, I began including occasional phone sessions in my work with many different analysands, some of whom could not leave the house at times because of overwhelming anxiety, some of whom were ill or immobilized momentarily, and some of whom had simply been stranded when their cars broke down. It allowed certain people to continue their analyses when they might otherwise have spiraled down into deep depressions, others to continue when at their lowest points ever, and still others to continue when their fears of driving or of buses overturning might have prevented them from making it to their sessions. I also began to propose occasional phone sessions to analysands in the Pittsburgh area who called me to cancel their sessions due to torrential rains, tornado warnings, and snow and ice storms that made driving conditions extremely hazardous, as well as to partially disabled and elderly analysands who were not confident on their feet during harsh, wintry conditions.[1]

It soon became clear to me that phone sessions could usefully *complement* in-person sessions, but I hesitated for a number of years to take on analysands whose work with me would, due to distance and their financial circumstances (which precluded regular trips to Pittsburgh), be done almost exclusively over the phone. But after enough years working with my West Coast analysands by phone, I began to accept analysands who lived far away and had no other Lacanian analysts (or any analysts at all) to turn to in their areas.[2]

Imaginary Phenomena

[The analyst] must adjust himself to the patient as a telephone receiver is adjusted to the transmitting microphone.

— *Freud (1912b/1958, pp. 115–116)*

I was at first surprised to note that the analyses of these "telanalysands" (or "telysands") began much like any others and that I was often able to get them just as engaged in the analytic endeavor despite seeing them in person only rarely or sometimes not at all. I also noted that virtually all of the transference reactions I had become accustomed to from in-person work (expressions of love, infatuation, idealization, anger, hatred, fear of judgment, and so on) arose in phone work, the only thing missing being transferences based on my actual physical appearance or dress. Indeed, it might be said that the analysands whom I never saw in person projected things onto me all the more freely because they did not have a visual image of me in front of them. Much like the analysand on the couch, who is freed from looking at or being looked at by the analyst, the analysand on the phone is free to imagine me however she likes.

---

[1] The severity of much North American weather would surprise plenty of people from other parts of the world; the only obstacle to analysands making their sessions that is in any way comparable in Europe is, in my experience, public transit strikes which sometimes immobilize cities for weeks on end.

[2] Given their backgrounds, many of my analysands might never have gone into analysis with anyone other than a Lacanian. This is perhaps a peculiarity of my practice, but it seems to me to be an important point to consider: It is often only the analysand's positive transference to a certain theoretical framework or approach that allows him or her to go into analysis, and the practitioners of that certain approach may be few and far between. Some schools of psychoanalysis have a bad reputation in the U.S., especially among certain segments of the population, and many people would evidently prefer no analysis at all to analysis with practitioners from those schools. Referrals to non-Lacanian analysts are pointless in such cases.

Phone work in fact eliminates certain imaginary phenomena for the analyst as well; for we are all inclined to associate each new person we meet with others we have known who resemble the new person in one way or another, visual resemblance often predominating in such associations, and to react to the new person as we did to the old, at least at the outset (the better we get to know the new person, the more the differences between the two people we associate with each other come into view and our reactions tend to change accordingly). When the analytic work is conducted by phone, the analyst cannot be captivated by the analysand's appearance (Freud seems at times to have been so captivated by the beauty of his female analysands, like Dora, that he became a prisoner of his own infatuation with them) or be led to assimilate her to other women he has known (and loved or hated) or to other analysands he has treated.

The analysand, too, is freed from the tendency to instantaneously identify the analyst with some other person and from captivation based on visual images. Nevertheless, since it is the analysand who does the self-disclosing, not the analyst,[3] the latter remains something of a blank projection screen and the

---

[3] There are, to my mind, very few reasons for the analyst to self-disclose, far fewer than clinicians trained in other forms of psychoanalysis seem to find. Self-disclosure by the analyst allows his analysand to think of him as a flesh and blood person whose feelings she must not hurt; she begins to worry about him and does not want to upset him. If the analysand says to the analyst that he looks or sounds ill, for example, what is she likely to do if he says, "Yes, I am ill"? Will she feel sorry for him and not want to demand too much? Will she feel she should not take up his time? The analyst's self-disclosing response ("Yes, I am ill") situates the analysand's comment at the imaginary level by assuming that it is addressed to him and is in fact about him. When one of my analysands told me I sounded tired, I instead responded, "Tired?" After a brief pause, the analysand mused, "Maybe I always think people get tired of listening to me; I'm always sure I'm boring them." By not assuming that the comment was necessarily about me, and by avoiding self-disclosure, I was able to situate the analysand's comment at the symbolic level and get at something far more significant than helping her supposedly know when her perceptions about people are accurate or inaccurate (analysts sometimes seem to think that they should try to help their analysands improve their "reality testing" in this way, as if reality were such a straightforward thing; see Chapter 9). A simple reiteration here ("Tired?") allowed the analysand to articulate something important about the way she saw herself in relation to other people, indeed, in relation to the Other as such, whereas self-disclosure (assuming I had been tired) might well have made her focus instead on my state and try to go easy on me. (I am not suggesting that the analyst deny tiredness that is overwhelming; see the "Cautionary Tale" discussed in Chapter 7.)

Assuming the analyst's training has made him capable of handling the analysand's demands and anxieties, he should not encourage her to tailor her discourse to what she thinks he can or cannot stand. The more she perceives him as an actual person, the more likely she is to censor or downplay certain things that she has to say and the less likely she is to enact her "fundamental fantasy" with him. If he indicates that there has been a death in his family, she may feel unable to talk about a death wish she has had; everything the analyst reveals about his own state potentially stops her from saying something she had to say.

One of my analysands had been in therapy before coming to see me, and in that therapy he complained a great deal about his Catholic upbringing and his Catholic school. After a few weeks of this, his therapist told him she was Catholic; that shut him up and in fact led him to leave therapy with her.

analysand is likely to "see" in him features of other people based on his way of speaking, his tone of voice, his intonations, his cadence, and even his way of breathing (one of my analysands at times likened my breathing to her mother's).

The Analyst's Presence

It may be objected that the analyst nevertheless gives his presence, but I believe that his presence is initially implied simply by his listening, and that this listening is simply the condition of speech. Why would analytic technique require that he make his presence so discreet if this were not, in fact, the case?

— *Lacan* (2006, p. 618)

Both non-Lacanians (Zalusky et al., 2003) and Lacanians (Miller, 1999) have been known to argue that phone analysis is impossible, it being necessary that analyst and analysand be physically present to each other. What is it about

---

I hear stories like that all the time! Such a self-disclosure by the therapist was hardly productive for the analysand's progress; perhaps the therapist truly could not take hearing such complaints and so it was productive for her.

The point, in avoiding self-disclosure, is not to *deny one's own state*, whether it be one of fatigue, boredom, or anxiety. Such states should be noted by the analyst for his own information and contemplation after the session, not ignored, as they often say something about the way the analyst is positioning himself or failing to intervene in the analysis and should be learned from. For a more theoretical discussion of the disadvantages of self-disclosure, see Fink (1997, pp. 31–33).

Practitioners who attempt to justify the practice of self-disclosure, even only in specific circumstances, often find themselves in deep water, theoretically speaking. Consider, for example, the following comments by Malan (1995/2001):

It is so easy, in this kind of situation, to obtrude one's own personal feelings into what one says to the patient, which very quickly goes over into seeking sympathy rather than giving it. Patients are not interested in one's personal tragedies; certainly not when they are in the midst of their own. Thus the therapist's feelings can be shown, but must only be shown *objectively*, under complete control, entirely in the service of the patient. (p. 26)

Although Malan rightly cautioned the therapist against blithely interjecting his own experiences and woes into a patient's session, as this essentially amounts to asking the patient for sympathy (as Lacan said, all speech constitutes a demand for recognition and love, and the therapist's speech is no exception to the rule), he nevertheless sanctioned occasional self-disclosure with the untenable claim that this can be done "objectively"—an odd term to use under any circumstances in a discussion of therapy, which he then glossed as involving "complete control," as if there were such a thing (see Chapter 9).

Renik (1999) is one of the foremost apologists for the practice of self-disclosure. He argued not merely for what he referred to as "selective" self-disclosure (leading to "relative anonymity"), but for ongoing, thoroughgoing self-disclosure, which he called "playing one's cards face up." The goal of self-disclosure, according to him, is to level "the clinical analytic playing field" between analyst and analysand, *not* because that would be more democratic or postmodern, but simply "because it yields

physical presence that is supposedly so crucial? What is it that is supposedly missing from phone analysis?

Certainly it is not direct physical contact that is missing, for analysis rules out such contact (apart from such formal contact as the ritual shaking of hands at the beginning and end of sessions). As Lacan (1971–1972, June 21, 1972) put it, "From the moment one enters into analytic discourse, there is no longer any question of an encounter of bodies." Analyst and analysand need not touch each other for an analysis to proceed; for similar reasons, analyst and analysand need not come into contact with each other through the sense of taste.

Surely it is not thought that the analyst and analysand must be able to smell each other, although a comical episode, which Lacan commented on, did once occur at the Société Psychanalytique de Paris (SPP) in the early 1950s. In discussing the analysts of his time who seemed to believe that in order to understand their analysands they needed to look beyond language, to look beyond their analysands' speech, Lacan (2006) wrote:

> Nowadays, a young analyst-in-training, after two or three years of fruitless analysis, can actually hail the long-awaited advent of the object-relation in

---

better clinical results" (p. 523). Even Renik did not sanction forms of self-disclosure that will not further the analytic work with a specific patient (for example, he did not tell a patient that he had sexual feelings for her even though he did), but his examples show that he worked almost entirely at the level of the conscious, observing ego. He recounted in detail an interchange with a patient, whom he referred to as "Anne," that led her to *understand* many things about how she operated with her analyst and her husband as well, but he gave no indication that Anne changed in any durable way due to the new understanding she acquired. The simple fact that "she and her husband [went] on to have a very long talk" and "made love more intimately and passionately than they had in years" that night (p. 527) was adduced to prove the value of this approach to treatment! As Aristotle reminded us, "One swallow does not a spring make, nor does one fine day"—nor one fine night, for that matter.

Renik's self-disclosing approach clearly fostered changes at the level of the observing ego—changes in the analysand's thoughts about her own behavior patterns—but it hardly seems designed to foster change at a more fundamental level. Indeed, by talking so much about himself and his own way of seeing things, he quite explicitly tried to avoid having his analysands work out with him problems that they had in former relationships, thereby thwarting many different facets of the transference. For example, he said, "I was aware of not wanting to seem controlling like Anne's mother. The kind of presumptuousness that Anne felt she got from her mother was something I particularly dislike, so I was taking pains to be sure Anne experienced me differently" (p. 526). This implies that Renik deliberately tried to dodge Anne's likely transferential projections!

Another of Renik's analysands commented that she thought he had such a large "personal stake in not being seen as domineering and unfair" that when she saw him "that way, rightly or wrongly, [he was] quick to react and to try to sort it out"; she felt that this got "in the way of [him] being able to listen to [her] sometimes" (p. 532). In other words, when she confused him in her mind with someone from her past whom she felt to be domineering and unfair, he would use self-disclosure to wriggle out of the transference! The fact that Renik could recommend ongoing self-disclosure to all analysts in all cases suggests that he had jettisoned the lion's share of the concept of transference. There are other ways to go about "actively soliciting the patient's observations about the analyst's personal functioning within the treatment relationship" (p. 529) and thereby learning from the patient than through systematic self-disclosure.

being smelled by his subject, and can reap as a result of it the *dignus est intrare* of our votes, the guarantors of his abilities. (p. 267)[4]

In the episode Lacan referred to, an analytic candidate was enthusiastically admitted into the upper echelons of the SPP when he reported that his analysand had finally been able to smell him, an achievement of rather uncertain value, at best. This anecdote aside, I suspect that it is not the sense of smell that those who object to phone analysis are primarily concerned with. Nevertheless, I could easily counter with an anecdote of my own, in which one of my analysands suddenly said during a phone session, "I wonder if your breath smells right at this very moment." When I queried, "My breath?" he commented that his father would often come home from parties having smoked a cigar and eaten unfamiliar foods, things the analysand associated with "adult smells." It is not clear that the analysand could have smelled my breath even if we had been in the same room at that time; what seems clear is that olfactory projections and associations are not ruled out just because the analytic work takes place over the phone.

If it is thought that there must be visual contact between analyst and analysand, is it then impossible for blind people to undergo analysis or become analysts? I suspect most would say that it is not. Moreover, the use of the couch in psychoanalysis largely obviates visual contact, except at the very beginning and end of sessions. Would those who believe that even this highly limited visual contact is indispensable feel that video conferencing (video phones or "web cams") would effectively rectify the problem? The importance of seeing each other, however limited it may be, cannot be excluded out of hand due to its relation to the gaze (which I will return to a little later on); nevertheless, it should already be clear that it is not always indispensable, assuming one admits that the blind are analyzable.

What seems absolutely essential, to my mind, is hearing: Analyst and analysand must be able to hear each other speak. It is what the analysand says and how she says it that is of the utmost importance in analysis. As long as a good, clear phone connection (without background noise, echoes, delays, or interfering conversations) can be established, as long as the analyst and analysand can hear each other very well—well enough to hear each and every slip, stumbling, stuttering, hesitation, sigh, and yawn—the analysis can proceed.[5] Interestingly enough, certain analysands have mentioned to me that they feel our phone sessions are *more* intimate than our in-person sessions

---

[4] For further comments on the same episode, see Lacan (2006, p. 465, 1994, p. 79).

[5] Analyst and analysand must, of course, each have total privacy if they are to speak freely.

because they hear me speaking right in their ear and sense that I am even closer over the phone than when they are lying on the couch a few feet away from me.[6]

Body Language

While the subject's discourse could, possibly and occasionally, be bracketed in the initial perspective of an analysis because it may serve as a lure in or even as an obstruction to the revelation of truth, it is insofar as [his discourse] serves as a sign that it is now permanently devalued. . . . It seems that any other manifestation of the subject's presence will soon have to be preferred to it: his presentation in his approach and gait, the affectation of his manners, and the way he takes his leave of us.

—*Lacan* (2006, p. 337)

Analysts who rely a great deal on their "reading" of the analysand's body language are apt to find the use of the telephone problematic. But as I mentioned earlier, "body language" is not transparent, universal, or obvious in the way many people seem to think it is, and the only way the analyst can be sure he knows what the analysand's body language means is by asking her to talk about it (and even then, she may not know or want to tell!). Not many hand gestures have an unequivocal, universal meaning even in one and the same culture, and the same can be said for many of the body postures that I have heard clinicians claim to read.

Does, for example, an unusually erect body posture imply rigidity? some sort of phallic stance? Or might it rather be the incarnation of "uprightness," suggesting a grafting onto the body of a parent's moral admonitions or an identification with a parent's rigid ethical stance? Is, to provide another example, sitting hunched over invariably a self-defensive or self-protective posture? a sign of irritable bowel syndrome? Or might it occasionally stem instead from an identification with Quasimodo or with the hunchback of the rue Quincampoix (see Lacan, 2006, p. 422)? *Body language is not self-evident!* To understand it we have to ask the analysand what it might mean—we have to ask her to speak about it.

---

[6] Sharon Zalusky (1998) and Arlene Kramer Richards (in Zalusky et al., 2003) reported something quite similar (Dan Collins was kind enough to send me these texts). Phones have, of course, been used for decades by lovers for long, intimate conversations. And they have been used in more recent years for phone sex as well. I suspect, however, that no one would say that they automatically have more overtly sexual connotations than the standard analytic couch!

One of my analysands regularly placed his hands on his stomach when he told me emotionally charged stories. Some practitioners might have jumped to the conclusion that they were "gut-wrenching" for him or that he had an ulcer or some other problem of the digestive tract. When I asked him about it, he said that, in his culture, this was where the heart was conventionally thought to be located, and that he often felt a constriction or pressure in his heart—a kind of heartache that he characterized all women in his culture as having. The metaphorical meanings of the word for heart in his mother tongue were extremely important to him, and he once even said that he had "a hard rock in [his] heart that needs to be broken up." These were things that I, coming from a different culture and a different linguistic background, could never have guessed by attempting to "read his body language."

Human body postures and gestures cannot be read like animals' postures and gestures, which tend to have an unequivocal meaning for all members of the same species, based as they are on their genetic code.[7] Human body postures and gestures are affected by language, history, and culture and thus cannot be considered to have an unequivocal meaning for all humans or even all speakers of the same language; their meaning is often quite individual.[8]

Some analysts seem to be in search of something surer, more objective than speech, since speech can lie. They seem to assume that body language is not subject to pretense—that the body always tells the truth. But body language can "lie" like any other language; one need only consider how actors hide the truth by making certain gestures and adopting a certain body language to see this (and, indeed, all of us are actors on the stage of everyday life). The ability to see the analysand's facial expressions, gestures, and body postures may occasionally suggest to the analyst that there is a contradiction between what the analysand is saying and what she is feeling, but that contradiction cannot be taken at face value and the analyst must still ask what the analysand makes of the fact that she, for example, smiled while saying that her mother's death was a horrible experience for her. Furthermore, in my experience such possible contradictions can easily be picked up on in other ways, and, in any case, they must be brought into speech to have any therapeutic effect.[9] There simply is no getting around the use of speech in psychoanalysis.

---

[7] I am aware that this is something of an oversimplification and that ethologists might argue that postures and gestures in the animal kingdom are not as universal as we think.

[8] As Lacan (1988a, p. 255) put it, "A human gesture is closely linked to language, not simply to motor manifestations."

[9] Note that although Freud (1909/1955, pp. 166–167), in the case of the Rat Man, observed that when the analysand told him the story of the rat torture, "his face took on a very strange, composite

The absence of visual cues may even have a salutary effect, in that it thwarts the analyst's temptation to jump to conclusions about the analysand's body language.

In the end, the introduction of telecommunication technologies "press[es] us a little harder to examine [analytic] experience in terms of what is positive in it" (Lacan, 2006, p. 267), as opposed to what is "negative" or ruled out in it—that is, touch, taste, smell, and even sight (when the couch is in use).[10]

---

expression," and continued by saying, "I could only interpret it as one of horror at pleasure of his own of which he himself was unaware," he did not interpret this directly to the Rat Man, but simply made a mental note of it. We must be wary of jumping to conclusions about the meaning of anything in analysis, including the analysand's speech, facial expressions, gestures, and postures.

[10] It might be thought that, insofar as the gaze is one of the forms taken by object a in Lacan's work (for a detailed discussion of object a, see Fink, 1995, pp. 83–97), analysis cannot proceed without the presence of the analyst's gaze. Let me recall first that Lacan's list of the possible avatars of object a is quite extensive, including the voice, the gaze, the breast, the imaginary phallus, the turd, the urinary flow, the phoneme, and the nothing (Lacan, 2006, p. 817). Note that although many, if not all, of these objects are discussed at length in analysis, only a few of them are usually present, the turd and the urinary flow being among the rarest to be welcomed in the consulting room—except, perhaps, by people like Winnicott (1954/1958b, p. 289) who took "regression" in the most literal sense imaginable: "the couch gets wetted, or . . . the patient soils, or dribbles." Lacan (2006, pp. 617–618, 1998b, p. 426), on the other hand, suggested that "regression" in the psychoanalytic situation is best understood as referring to moments at which the analysand begins using little-kid expressions and baby talk, as opposed to some sort of "real" developmental regression or genuinely acting like a child.

Turning to another of the incarnations of Lacan's object a, note that no breasts need to be present for analytic work to occur, since analysis between two males of the species seems to be possible. Lacan nevertheless mentioned at least once that "the analyst must have breasts," in the sense that the analysand must at some point attribute breasts to the analyst, even if the latter is male, presumably because they are among the mother's secondary sex characteristics.

What seems clear is that virtually all of these objects (virtually all of the avatars of object a) enter into analysis not as "actual objects" but rather as part of the analysand's libidinal economy—indeed, one wonders how the imaginary phallus and the nothing could enter the analysis in any "actual" way. In my own experience, certain analysands for whom the gaze is a very important object a have reported imagining me watching them, looking at them from a variety of different standpoints and perspectives, and observing them interact with people, teach, masturbate, and so on. They have not failed to try to describe the quality and weight of that gaze, or to associate it with the gaze of one or both of their parents. In a word, all of the gaze-related phenomena that I have come to expect from in-person sessions have also arisen in phone sessions.

Miller (1999) stated that "in the session, the [analyst and analysand] are together, synchronized, but they are not there to see each other, as is clear by the use of the couch. Their mutual presence in flesh and blood is necessary, if for no other reason than to have emerge the sexual non-relation." It would seem that he thought that the fact that "there is no such thing as a sexual relationship" (Lacan, 2007, p. 134, 1998a, p. 57, and elsewhere) could not be brought home to the analysand unless she was faced with the paradox of being in the analysand's presence but not having sex with him. This strikes me as one possible way that the analysand can be brought to face this basic psychoanalytic truth, but certainly not the only way. Indeed, I do not believe that Lacan formulated this fundamental notion (see Fink 1995, pp. 98–125, for a detailed discussion of it) with the analytic situation itself explicitly in mind—it can be gleaned virtually anywhere.

Challenges Specific to Phone Analysis

Our effort is . . . a reconstructive collaboration with the person who is in the position of the analysand.

— Lacan (2007, p. 100)

All of this is not to say that analytic work by phone does not present challenges of its own. It sometimes can be difficult, for example, to know whether the analysand is laughing or crying (certain of the sounds we make at such moments can be quite similar), and the analyst cannot assume he knows which it is. In the preliminary sessions held face to face, the analyst can often guess by the look on the analysand's face whether she is being ironic, sardonic, joking, or serious (though his guess may well be wrong at times, especially when the analysand has a "poker face"). That is less possible over the phone—just as it is not always possible once the analysand has graduated to the couch[11]—and the analyst must pay extra attention to the fewer cues available to him such as subtle changes in breathing, short exhalations associated with laughing, and changes in an analysand's typical way of expressing herself. In short, the analyst must, as always, make the most of what is available to him given the constraints and parameters of the situation. Whereas in face-to-face work, a hand gesture or opening of the mouth may indicate that the analysand is about to say something and then stops herself, the only medium available in phone analysis is sound, so the analyst must be attentive to moments at which the analysand breathes in and seems about to say something and then stops. One might be surprised at how much one can pick up on once one becomes attentive to such things.[12]

Phone analysis is occasionally so convenient that it seemingly becomes too convenient: The analysand does not need to set aside a half-hour, say, before and after each session to travel to the analyst's office[13]—all she has to do is pick up the phone wherever she may be (at home, at the office, in her car,

---

[11] "Graduation" to the couch should not be rushed, but it often is, leading to an awkward situation I frequently hear about in supervision, in which analysands uninvitedly move back and forth between the armchair and the couch. Use of the couch should be deferred until a diagnosis (other than psychosis; see Chapter 10) has been pretty firmly arrived at and until the analysand has formulated a question of her own (see Fink, 1997, pp. 14, 25–27, 133–134). This often takes as long as a year at several sessions a week, and it is, in any case, better to err on the side of caution.

[12] The analyst must, of course, be just as attentive while on the phone as during in-person sessions. He must not take the fact that he is invisible to the analysand as license to read, daydream, or engage in any other activity that diverts his attention from his work with the analysand.

[13] In eliminating travel time, phone analysis also eliminates travel itself and therefore has the obvious benefit of being far easier on the environment than in-person analysis.

at a hotel, or wherever) and dial the proper number. The effort involved may for some be too small; without the added effort of coming to see the analyst, they may be inclined to view the analysis as a convenient way to "blow off steam" rather than as a venue for often difficult associative work. The analyst may wish, in such cases, that it were not so easy for the analysand, but the true problem lies elsewhere: if the fee for sessions has been set at a suitably high level and the analyst requests timely payment so that the analysand does not feel she is getting a free ride, so to speak, the problem cannot be solved by adding a half-hour drive each way to the analyst's office (an artificial way of making someone feel more invested in the process) but only by finding a way to get the analysand truly engaged in the analytic work. In other words, this is the same kind of problem that can arise in any analysis in which the analysand spends her time complaining, talking about everyday matters, or not knowing what to talk about at all. The analysand's engagement in the process cannot be augmented by adding hurdles; the analyst must find a way to inspire the analysand to raise a question or questions of her own.

Some analysands find the hurdles of phone analysis already challenging enough: One might be surprised how many analysands find it difficult to always have their phone line working, their phone operating without any shorts in it, their batteries charged,[14] a phone calling card that is activated, and the proper number to call in hand. One might also be surprised at how many fail to call at the agreed-upon time. Indeed, all of the resistances at work in in-person analysis also come into play in phone analysis: Anything that can go wrong will go wrong when resistance arises.

Some analysts seem to think that the analysand's resistances and transferences would be unable to express themselves in the more limited field of telephone analysis, but in my experience they *always* find a way of expressing themselves. Just as Freud said that we should not be concerned when we are unable to explore absolutely every facet of a dream during a single session because whatever was left unexplored in one dream will present itself in a future dream, whatever cannot be expressed to the analyst in one way due to the constraints of the situation (through visual or olfactory signs, for example) will be expressed in another way that *is* accessible to the analyst's senses.

If the analysand cannot give an unwitting gestural indication of exasperation with the analyst, she will "accidentally" drop the phone or move in such a way that she rips the phone out of the wall (I do not mean to suggest that the meaning of an act of any kind is immediately transparent; one still has to

---

[14] I discourage the use of cordless phones and cell phones at the present time since they usually do not provide the same clarity of sound as traditional wired phones ("land lines").

encourage the analysand to talk about its possible meanings). Although she cannot inadvertently try to open the door to the analyst's office with the key to her own house, expressing the degree to which she feels at home with the analyst, she will unintentionally give a potential date the analyst's phone number instead of her own. If her body posture cannot tell the analyst that she feels as intimate with him as with her own mother, she will inadvertently dial the analyst's number when she intends to call her mother and vice versa (this has happened in my practice on numerous occasions). If the analysand cannot show the analyst that she is loath to pay him by rummaging through all of her pockets and purse for five minutes before laying her hands on the check or cash, she will mistakenly put the wrong street number or zip code on the check she sends by mail, forget to sign the check, neglect to apply postage to the envelope, drop the letter in the mud or snow—you name, I have seen it!

The truth will out. The analyst can, assuming he has welcomed everything the analysand has to say and encouraged all that she is loath to say, be confident that the material will manifest itself in one way or another.[15] He simply needs to be attentive to everything that is accessible to him and not fail to inquire about things he thinks he hears but that may be initially glossed over by the analysand. The analysand can then usually be trusted to collaborate by indicating the moments at which her body is speaking unbeknown to the analyst, her hands trembling while recounting a dream in a manner devoid of affect, her head tingling while recounting an incident involving her father, her sharp pain in the gut while recounting a breakup, and so on. We rely on our analysands to tell us about myriad things that occur outside of our field of vision, so to speak—fleeting thoughts that come to them between sessions,

---

[15] As Freud (1905a/1953, p. 77) said, "He that has eyes to see and ears to hear may convince himself that no mortal can keep a secret." And as Lacan (2006, p. 386) said, "Repression cannot be distinguished from the return of the repressed in which the subject cries out from every pore of his being what he cannot talk about." The fact that "the truth will (come) out" perhaps accounts, to at least some degree, for the fact that analysts of very different persuasions seem to have at least some modicum of success, even when they seem to ignore the fundamental workings of dreams as conceptualized by Freud and Lacan, returning to prepsychoanalytic methods of dream interpretation. Numerous analysts make no use whatsoever of the particular signifiers their analysands use, and do not even solicit their analysands' associations to their dreams, relying instead in their interpretations on the "images" found in the dreams (as if those images were not conveyed to the analyst in words), as is common among Jungians, or on analogies that can be drawn between the stories told in the dreams (not that every dream tells a discernible story) and things going on in the analysis or in the analysand's life outside of the sessions (for an example, see Casement, 1991, p. 95). We might hypothesize that, insofar as such analysts nevertheless express their eagerness or willingness to listen to dreams and work with them, the analysand's unconscious finds a way to speak a language understandable to the analyst it is addressing. If the analyst will not pick up on the fact that the question "Why?" is being presented in a dream by a staircase that divides into the shape of the letter Y (Casement, 1991, p. 37, mentions this example proffered by Bion as an illustration of the notion of "reverie," rather than as an example of

daydreams, fantasies, dreams, nightmares, outbursts, crying jags, moments of joy, and so on—so why not bodily reactions during sessions as well? Do we think that we are the only ones capable of noticing them?

Phone sessions involve other challenges as well, of course. Phone lines occasionally go dead without any warning and analysts who practice the variable-length session must make it clear to their analysands that they do not end sessions by simply hanging up the phone but with something more like, "Okay, we'll stop there today. I'll speak to you tomorrow at three." Analysands should be asked to call back immediately should their calls be disconnected without any such prelude.

Insofar as the scansion of the session can be rather abrupt at times, analysts practicing it over the phone will notice a difference here from in-person sessions: The analysand is less likely to take an abrupt scansion as a punishment (it can be experienced at times, as I mentioned in Chapter 4, as a "mini-castration") when it is followed by a handshake at the door and a welcoming greeting at the next session than when it occurs by phone. Tone of voice can only do so much to mitigate that abruptness. Therefore, with certain analysands, the analyst may want to avoid such abrupt scansions (by adding, for example, "so long" or "good-bye").

Telephone analysis is undoubtedly not for everyone. Certain analysands may need the kind of libidinal connection with the analyst that can only be generated in person for them to become engaged in the analytic work, the absence of a visually based erotic transference leading to virtually no transference at all in their cases (this can be combated in certain instances by regular, albeit infrequent, in-person sessions). Other analysands may find the analyst's physical presence comforting, feeling a need not just for attentive listening but also for regular interested looks; such analysands often do not speak very

---

paying attention to the *letter* of the analysand's discourse, and listening for the homophonies and double meanings it plays on), then the unconscious will try to find other avenues by which to convey to the analyst the desire that is seeking expression in the dream. Indeed, as Lacan (2006, pp. 623–629) told us, a dream is designed not simply to fulfill a wish but to get a wish recognized by the person to whom it is addressed. Once a particular analysand has worked with a particular analyst for a certain period of time, the analysand's unconscious adapts its productions to its addressee's way of listening. If the analyst pays attention only to stories or allegories, the unconscious will produce stories or allegories; if the analyst primarily pays attention to images, the unconscious will produce images. This is something we might try to keep in mind when analyzing the dreams produced by other analysts' patients: We may be inclined to interpret them from our own unique perspectives, but then we overlook the fact that they were dreamt as they were dreamt because of the particular person for whom they were dreamt! One might argue, for example, that one of my analysands dreamt of a sore on his pelvis because his unconscious "knew" that I would be likely to read the word *sore* as a palindrome of *eros*, as well as an anagram for the word or name *rose*, and that another dreamt of *martial* arts when it was the anagrammatic *marital* arts that were plaguing him.

freely at the beginning of their analyses and seem to build trust in the analyst more on the basis of his virtually unfailing presence at their appointments and patient waiting for them to speak than on the basis of his attentive listening.

In any case, the use of the phone as a complement to regular in-person sessions seems to me far preferable to the common European practice of seeing analysands who live far away intensively once a month. For even when the analysand has four or more sessions in the course of a weekend stay in the analyst's city, the rhythm of the analysis is constantly broken by three- to four-week hiatuses, and it is hard to imagine how any real work ever gets done, the unconscious having a tendency to "close up," so to speak, when on vacation from analysis (Lacan, 2006, pp. 838–839).[16] Indeed, this is the very reason why analysts try to have as many sessions as possible per week with their analysands, as opposed to only one a week (the frequency adopted by much of the psychotherapy world); it is quite difficult to build on material from the previous session when a great deal of time has elapsed between sessions, and in my experience one is able to do far more intensive work at a frequency of three to five sessions per week than once a week, much less once every fourth week.[17]

A Common Practice

It is always the narrative of the dream as such—the verbal material—that serves as a basis for the interpretation.

— Lacan (1976, p. 15)

---

[16] See, too, Lacan's comments (1991, p. 390, 2006, pp. 333, 359). In both of these places, he referred specifically to the diminishing effect of making certain kinds of interpretations by around 1920. See, above all, Lacan (1978, Chapter 10).

[17] There are even a considerable number of analysands who only see their analysts every two to six months because they live on different continents and have to cross the ocean for sessions. Numerous South Americans, and even certain North Americans, fly, for example, to Paris every couple of months for a short stay during which they have several sessions a day. As helpful as this may be for them to get a sense of how people trained in a certain school work—and the only real way to get a sense of this in psychoanalysis is to do some analysis with them—it hardly seems to be a recipe for a full analysis. It would seem to provide, rather, but a taste or sample of what analytic work might be like with a certain analyst. For when the unconscious is not put to work on a virtually daily basis, the ego tends to reform and recrystallize around conceptualizations and positions that have already been arrived at, and it requires considerable renewed effort to reopen the unconscious and put it back to work in ways capable of once again shaking up the fixity of the ego. Freud (1913/1958), who generally saw his patients every day except Sunday—that is, six days a week—referred to this as the "Monday crust" (p. 127): he found that it was harder for analysands to set the unconscious back to work after just one day off!

Virtually every analyst is led, at one point or another, to talk at some length with an analysand by phone, whether due to an emergency hospitalization, panic attack, deep depression, or some other unexpected, unusual situation. Many analysts are uncomfortable doing so, feeling that it violates the therapeutic frame they have established, and they try to avoid phone conversations instead of using them as opportunities to continue the analytic work. My hope is that further discussion of what is "positive" in the analytic situation—that is, of the senses we do make use of in analysis that make it effective—will help them become more comfortable working by phone. In my view, it is above all work with the signifier as enunciated in speech (words as pronounced aloud during the session) that makes analysis effective, meaning that the phone provides all that is necessary for analysis to proceed. Some might argue that limiting oneself to the medium of the voice leads one to believe that work with the signifier is the only effective work in analysis—that it is, in other words, a self-fulfilling prophecy. However, in my own case, I began practicing with the premise that in psychoanalysis "the symbolic dimension is the only dimension that cures" and only stumbled upon the telephone as a medium much later. My understanding of Freud and Lacan suggests that they both attribute the success of psychoanalysis to a relationship established through speech and to work that proceeds via speech.

In the past few years I have learned that a great many analysts in America conduct analyses partially or exclusively by phone. Richards and Goldberg (2000) conducted a survey and found that over 85% of the members of the Division of Psychoanalysis (Division 39) of the American Psychological Association did at least some work over the phone and were satisfied with its effects.[18] It seems, however, that not many analysts have written about it, Sharon Zalusky (1998) in Los Angeles being a notable exception. Interestingly enough, she noted that in her first experience with phone analysis, she "was more present to hear the nuances of her [analysand's] associations . . . and was able to hear her differently." This strikes me as especially revealing, given her rather obvious focus on the nonverbal, affect, countertransference, the "holding environment," and so many of the other concerns of contemporary analysts.[19] I myself have

---

[18] See also Sleek's (1997) earlier article on therapy via videoconferencing.

[19] Zalusky's article sparked a good deal of controversy among analysts, a number of them agreeing with her that phone analysis can be a useful complement to in-person analysis. Those who disagreed with her did so primarily based on the importance they attributed to "containment" and "the holding environment" in the analytic setting (which I would consider to be far less important than many, especially in work with neurotics), to regression (see Chapter 4), and to "reading" the analysand's body language and body states. Interestingly enough, her objectors (see Zalusky et al., 2003) seemed to believe that the latter was so crucial to their work that phone analysis could not even be considered

conducted numerous analyses partially or exclusively by phone, with no greater or less variety of success than those I have conducted in person, and I supervise numerous analysts, Lacanian and non-Lacanian trained, who also do phone analysis. I have had a number of experiences in which analysands, who had previously done analysis in person with analysts who made a great deal of the "holding environment," countertransference, and body language and whose analyses had broken down, did far more effective work (in their own estimation) over the phone with me (of course, whether that should be attributed to my rather different approach or to the phone work—or both—is an open question). Many analysts can, of course, tell stories about successes they have had with analysands who came to them after unsuccessful analyses with analysts of other orientations. Perhaps my orientation lends itself better to the phone than others. It will be interesting to see over time how other analysts think phone analysis compares to in-person analysis.[20]

---

psychoanalysis! For more on this topic, see my case discussion of an analysis that proceeded entirely by phone (Fink, 2003).

Note that Winnicott's (1960/1965b) notion of holding has, as is so common in the history of psychoanalysis, been extracted from the context in which Winnicott developed it, that of the infant-mother relationship:

> I refer to the actual state of the infant-mother relationship at the beginning when the infant has not separated out a self from the maternal care on which there exists absolute dependence in a psychological sense. (p. 48)

Analysts have since applied the notion of holding to work with analysands across the diagnostic spectrum, whereas Winnicott himself limited it to work with psychotics. Note that it was also regarding "the treatment of schizophrenia and other psychoses," not of the neuroses, that Winnicott asserted that "the reliability of the analyst" was more important than interpretations—in other words, that the "therapeutic alliance" was more important than anything the analyst actually said (p. 38).

We have here yet another instance in which concepts and techniques forged specifically for work with psychotics have come to be used indiscriminately, there being little distinction in many clinicians' approaches between work with neurotics and psychotics. On the contemporary therapy scene, one size fits all.

[20] Some analysts have even experimented with e-mail and instant messaging, but the signifier and the written word are not the same: Speaking is our first and probably our primary mode as beings of language, and the jouissance involved in enunciating is an essential aspect of psychoanalytic work. Thus even though we tend to make significant typographical errors, my sense is that e-mail and instant messaging are overly restrictive media for psychoanalysis.

9

Non-normalizing Analysis

It should be obvious that analytic discourse does not in any way consist in making what isn't going well go away, in suppressing what isn't going well in ordinary discourse. . . . The discourse that proceeds only by true speaking is precisely what is disturbing. . . . It's enough for someone to make an effort to speak truly for that to bother everyone.
— Lacan (1973–1974, February 12, 1974)

THE NOTION OF normality has such a strong hold on us that many of us are relieved to be told that our demons, the urges and fantasies we struggle with, are "normal." McWilliams (2004, p. 212) provided a short case history of a neurotic woman she treated who, after a certain amount of time in analysis, began to speak about "masturbation fantasies, of which she was deeply ashamed, involving various kinds of masochistic subjugation." McWilliams reported that she remarked to her analysand "that such fantasies are common and not necessarily correlated with actual masochistic sexual behavior," for the analysand was concerned "that she was 'really' in some fundamental sense a sexual masochist."[1]

In characterizing the analysand's fantasies as "common" (another term for "normal" in many therapists' vocabulary), the analyst's approach here was to try

---

[1] McWilliams (2004) recommended elsewhere in the same book that the kind of work we do in analysis be related to the level of severity of patients' psychopathology:

> For those in the neurotic range, we can keep opening up questions and inviting exploration; for those in the borderline range, we expect a dyadic struggle that requires us to be active, limit setting, interpretative of primitive dynamics and focused on the here-and-now relationship; with those in the psychotic range, we need to be educative, normalizing, and explicitly supportive of the patient's capacities. (pp. 143–144)

Nevertheless, the patient with whom she made the normalizing remarks was, according to her own assessment, clearly neurotic, suggesting that once one opens the door to normalization it tends to affect how one practices with all and sundry.

to remove the patient's concern and alleviate her tension. Such an approach—which is so widespread in our times[2]—may provide momentary relief to certain patients (others may well find it annoying or patronizing to hear their fantasies characterized as "common," "normal," or "ordinary"), but we must consider the other likely short-term effects, as well as the long-term effects, of such interventions. In the immediate, such interventions can put a stop to the patient's exploration of her masturbation fantasies—after all, if they are "common" what need could there possibly be to articulate all the details of them and associate to them to figure out what they are about? If most everyone has them, why should the analysand bother to decipher what they mean to her in particular, especially when that deciphering process can be long, arduous, and humiliating? In the longer term, such comments by the analyst suggest to the analysand that the analyst, like most other people, believes that there is such a thing as normality and that one is okay if one is normal (and perhaps even that we should all try to be as normal as possible). This suggests a kind of *tyranny of norms* on the analyst's part—the kind of tyranny the analysand can expect from friends, relatives, guidance counselors, school psychologists, and the like (one hardly needs to see an analyst for this)—and, in order to show the analyst that she (the analysand) really is sick or abnormal in some way, the analysand may well go on to ask whether this aspect or that aspect of her life is normal until she alights upon something that the analyst cannot possibly characterize as normal.

McWilliams seems to have felt that she needed to assuage this particular analysand's misgivings before she would be able to even begin to discuss her masturbation fantasies (in other words, she presumed that the effect of her intervention would be to open the door to a discussion of these fantasies, not to close it), but in my experience it is usually enough in such cases to simply call into question the analysand's view that such things may not be normal—by saying something as simple as "They're not?"—without endorsing the notion of normality oneself.

When a male analysand of mine was concerned that the woman he had picked to marry resembled his sister in many ways, I could have told him

---

[2] Here is another example of such a normalizing approach. Basescu (1990) wrote:

> One woman [a patient] said, "I had a bad weekend. Other people are stable. I'm so up and down. I hide my rockiness." I said, "Don't we all." She: "You too?" I: "Does that surprise you?" She: "Well, I guess not. You're human too." I understood that to mean she also felt human, at least for the moment. (p. 54)

Here, in the guise of self-disclosure, the analyst implicitly suggests that he himself is normal and "human," so his patient must be normal and human too insofar as she is like him.

that it is quite normal for men to choose women who resemble their mothers or sisters, and he might have felt momentarily relieved at my saying so, but this would very likely have forestalled his realization that he could not enjoy his relationship with his wife because he felt that it was incestuous. While it is hardly unusual, statistically speaking, for men to choose women who resemble their mothers or sisters, making a remark to that effect would not have addressed the specificity of his incestuous relations with his sister many years before and their effects on his present relationship with his wife.[3]

Freud (1916–1917/1963) himself made less use of the notion of normality than people tend to think, and he indicated quite explicitly on several occasions that he saw no real distinction between normal and neurotic:

> If you take up a theoretical point of view and disregard the matter of quantity, you may quite well say that we are *all* ill—that is, neurotic—since the preconditions for the formation of symptoms [that is, repression] can also be observed in normal people. (p. 358)[4]

Lacan (2006, p. 394) made still less use of notions like normal and abnormal, roundly criticizing the "infatuation with normalizing analysis" he found in other analysts' work (see also pp. 263, 282, 488, and 730). In my view such notions are best left to statisticians, rightfully figuring only in discussions of things like normal distribution, the normal bell-shaped curve, and standard deviations from the mean. Such statistical uses always allow one to raise the question, "What is so great about being average (for example, about being of normal, average intelligence), like most everyone else?"

Despite the fact that Freud himself made scant use of the notion of normality, he nevertheless paved the way for a theory of normality and abnormality with his notion of specific libidinal stages—oral, anal, and genital—which he thought should unfold in a specific order and lead to a hierarchy dominated by the genital stage (he even went so far as to refer to the latter as forming

---

[3] For further remarks on the subject of the analyst judging the analysand to be normal or abnormal, see Fink (1997, pp. 35–38).

[4] Freud (1916–1917/1963) made the same point in greater detail further on in the *Introductory Lectures on Psychoanalysis*:

> We cannot deny that healthy people as well possess in their mental life what alone makes possible the formation both of dreams and of symptoms, and we must conclude that they too have carried out repressions, that they expend a certain amount of energy in order to maintain them, that their unconscious system conceals repressed impulses which are still cathected with energy, and that *a portion of their libido is withdrawn from their ego's disposal*. Thus a healthy person, too, is virtually a neurotic. (pp. 456–457)

See also Lacan's (1976, p. 15) comment: "I do not think one can really say that neurotics are mentally ill. Neurotic is what most people are."

a "well-organized tyranny"; Freud, 1916–1917/1963, p. 323).[5] Nevertheless, it was already clear to Freud that there were a great many cases in which, although a hierarchy did come into being, that hierarchy was not dominated by the genital stage; and over the course of time it has become clear that in other cases no hierarchy forms at all.

One conclusion that can be drawn from this is that there is nothing *inevitable* about the progression from oral to anal to genital; it cannot be considered to be a "natural progression" because it depends so significantly upon the child's relationships with its primary caretakers, and those relationships are such that things can take a turn (or "progress") in a different direction at many points along the way. It is perhaps only statistically that one could say that this is the "normal" or "natural" path of development (and it may well not even be true statistically, when we consider how few of people's most intimate sexual fantasies involve intercourse).

Nevertheless, many analysts set out to outdo Freud in this regard: They wanted to chart out the child's developmental processes in such a way that they could be viewed as natural, normal, and virtually inevitable *except when obstructed*. For them it was not enough to say that people often develop in such and such a way, or that in Western culture in the 20th century people tended to develop according to such and such a timeline: They wanted to find a clear telos of development, a clear best end state of development, often referred to as "emotional maturity" (see, for example, Spotnitz, 1999, p. 23), toward which the child's nature impelled it, assuming its caretakers did not impede its progress.

"Why did they want to?" one might ask. Such a solidly established developmental model would give them a specific image of the type of personality they were trying to mold and would justify all kinds of interventions that would move the analysand in that direction (as opposed to simply following Freud's recommendation to seek out the repressed). It would also provide a kind of map for them in the otherwise unwieldy long-term process of analysis, for they began to view analysis as a reparenting process wherein one brings the analysand back to each of the developmental snafus that has occurred during the otherwise normal "maturational processes" (Winnicott, 1977, p. 2) and leads him anew through each of the "maturational stages" (p. 3) that has gone awry. Conceived of in this way, the analyst was simply removing obstacles to the analysand's natural development, and she could shift responsibility for her

---

[5] In many psychology textbooks today this three-stage developmental model is (along with the id, ego, and superego tripartition of the psyche) virtually the only aspect of Freud's work that is discussed in any detail.

actions to the theoretical model itself. In other words, it was relieving to the analyst, for it told her what she *ought* to do given her assessment of the "stage" at which the analysand was stuck.

As seductive as such a notion may be for the formulation of a universally valid psychoanalytic theory, it relies on a monolithic, transhistorical, transcultural notion of human nature (Bowlby, 1982, p. 123, for example, makes it clear that he believes that his work is "fundamental for an understanding of human nature"). But the visions of human nature that have been formulated over the last few millennia diverge significantly, to say the least (as do the psychoanalytic visions of the last few generations, as we shall see in a moment). Virtually every philosophy that has grappled with the question "What should one do?" or "What is to be done?" has attempted to formulate a universally valid notion of human nature from which rights, obligations, and duties arise. It is as if philosophers were saying, "Tell me what a human being is and I will tell you what he or she should do." If, for example, humans are the only animals that can reason, then they *should* reason and act as reasonably as possible; if they are the only animals for whom their very being is a question, then they *should* be mindful of the question of being and of their "being toward death"; and so on. Normative models seem to grow like weeds from universalizing claims about what human beings are.[6]

Kohut (1984, p.187) approvingly cited King's 1945 definition of the term *normal* in biology as "that which functions in accordance with its design." It is as if Kohut thought it could apply equally well to the psyche and as if he thought it were so very clear what human beings are designed for! Joseph (1982), on the other hand, outlined some of the main attempts by analysts to define normality as an ideal state of mental health and his survey suggests that there is little overlap among the different definitions by Jones, Klein, Hartmann, Kubie, Money-Kyrle, and others—and that the criteria invoked by them are virtually impossible to verify.[7] I would argue that a close comparison of the different theories of human development put forward by just over a century of psychoanalytic speculation would show little overlap among them, inclining us to believe that no universally accepted notion of human nature is even vaguely in the offing.

---

[6] To such philosophical claims, the skeptic is always free to retort, "Why should I be reasonable or be mindful of my being toward death just because no other creature on earth can be? Does their inability to do these things oblige me in any way?" To similarly constructed developmental claims about the "normal" path of human development, the skeptical analysand can always respond, "Why be normal?" or "Why follow one's nature?"

[7] Joseph (1982) seems, however, to try to salvage the concept as a "process" that unfolds over time, a well-known form of "hand waving."

A Universal Theory of Human Nature?

The analyst [mistakenly] tries to normalize the subject's behavior in accordance with a norm, a norm that is coherent with the analyst's own ego. This will always thus involve the modeling of one ego by another ego, by a [supposedly] superior ego.

— *Lacan (1988a, p. 285)*

Although I cannot provide a detailed comparison of the different psycho-analytic theories here, I would like to suggest that some of the most basic notions found in them are probably very hard to reconcile (above and beyond the problems inherent in their attributing widely varying meanings to the same terms). Consider how difficult it would be to reconcile the following:

- For Freud (1923b/1961, p. 29), the ego does not exist at birth and develops over the course of time through a series of identifications with parents of both sexes and as a "precipitate of abandoned object-cathexes."
- For Klein a rudimentary ego already exists at birth and suffers from the outset from "persecutory anxiety" (characteristic of the so-called paranoid-schizoid phase endemic to the first three months of life; Klein, 1955, p. 309), which leads the infant to split one and the same object—the breast, for example—into two different objects (good and bad breasts) that are alternately loved and sadistically attacked (at first orally, and then urethrally, muscularly, and anally), introjected and projected (Klein, 1950, p. 249). In Klein's view, if all goes well, between three and six months of age the child will suffer from "depressive anxiety" (characteristic of the so-called depressive position), and by six months the child's ego will be relatively well consolidated (Segal, 1964).
- According to Lacan (2006, pp. 93–100), the ego first begins to form during the mirror stage between six and 18 months of age.
- For analysts starting from something of an ethological position (based on the study of animal behavior and development, perhaps like Bowlby, 1982), there would seem to be little if any reason to hypothesize splitting of the object; the infant may be content with the mother (or more specifically with her breast) one moment and furious with her the next without our needing to assume that the infant forms two quite separate representations of the mother (much less that he projects his own badness or anger into the bad breast or projects his own goodness or love into some other object in order to preserve it from his own internal badness—or that it makes any sense to talk about projection and introjection at a time in life when the boundaries between self and other are still so undefined).

- Mahler's (1972) notions of "separation" and "individuation" and the ages at which they occur bear little if any resemblance to Lacan's (1978) notions of the logical moments (as opposed to chronological moments) of alienation and separation. The latter—like Freud's notion of primal repression—are not only diametrically opposed in spirit but also conceptually incompatible with Winnicott's (1954/1958b, pp. 278–294) belief in the possibility of regression to earlier developmental stages, and indeed the necessity of such regression in the treatment of psychosis.[8]

I hope that I have at least rendered plausible my claim here that no widely accepted, solidly established model of normal human development can be drawn out of a century of psychoanalytic theorizing, the differences among the different schools of analysis (only a few of which I have included here) being far too great. Analysts have nevertheless not given up their hope of finding a theory of development that would be valid in all times and places, and they have turned to the "hard sciences" for inspiration and support, enlisting neuroscience to understand the "neural circuitry" involved in mother-child attachment, for example. The hope, apparently, is that neuroscience can provide an objective, incontrovertible definition of "optimal neural functioning" at the different ages of life, allowing us then to postulate what a child and its mother should have done by such and such a point in the child's life to achieve such functioning. The fact that we can still raise the question "neural functioning that is optimal for what?" indicates that the problem here is simply pushed back a notch, and

---

[8] The notion of "developmental processes" (Winnicott, 1977, p. 2) that naturally follow their predetermined course unless obstructed strikes me as one of the least well demonstrated notions in the contemporary psychoanalytic panoply. Still less well demonstrated is the notion that adult analysands can regress to virtually any point in the developmental process, "repair something," and move forward again. Such a notion implies that someone who has reached adulthood and has become psychotic can theoretically return to any and all missed developmental stages and turn out neurotic (or "virtually normal," that is, a subject split between unconscious and conscious) at the end of his analysis, something for which there seems to be little proof. Winnicott (1960/1965a, pp. 145,149), for example, argued that as long as there is a kernel of a "true self," the patient's "false self" can be worked through in analysis, and an obvious psychotic transformed into a neurotic. If a "true self" is there, it can, in theory, according to Winnicott, be uncovered and brought forward. Note that it does not take much for there to be a true self in the picture, in his view: "The True Self appears as soon as there is any mental organization of the individual at all, and it means little more than the summation of sensori-motor aliveness" (p. 149). In his view, psychoanalysis with psychotics involves gaining the patient's trust to the point at which he can regress with the analyst all the way back to the moments of the earliest dependency on the mother, and the analyst is able to correct the problems of mothering that the patient encountered with his own mother as a child. There seems to be no age limit regarding when this can occur—in principle, an 80-year-old could regress all the way to infancy and reconstruct his life from there, coming out neurotic instead of psychotic. Spotnitz (1999) endorsed similar views. From Lacan's perspective, it seems, rather, that if primal repression does not occur early on in life, it will never occur, and analytic work with adult psychotics must aim at something entirely different than it aims at with adult neurotics (see Chapter 10).

that different analytic schools will continue to have different ideas about what they think neural functioning should be optimized for.

Normal for Whom?

What is called a neurotic symptom is simply something that allows [the neurotic] to live.
— Lacan (1976, p. 15)

The sheer number of different developmental theories expounded by different psychoanalysts would, one would think, be enough to call into question the belief in our ability to find one satisfactory explanation for something as obviously complex as human development and a single path to "normal" development. At the very least, it would have to be admitted that what is normal (statistically speaking) for obsessives is hardly normal (statistically speaking) for hysterics. People who fall within different diagnostic categories operate in fundamentally different ways: The logic of the ways humans develop and live their lives differs very significantly from one diagnostic structure to the next (see my remarks on those different logics in Chapter 7, footnote 17).

Consider the extremely common remark made by men in the West (the statistical majority of whom are obsessive) that they do not understand women (the statistical majority of whom are hysteric): Women tend not to reduce sexual partners to body parts the way men do; women often feel a need to have their partners express desire for them regularly, whereas men often feel threatened or overwhelmed by their partners' expressions of desire for them; and so on. Men tend to feel that women have illegitimate wants, and they have managed to convince many women that their wants are illegitimate (to the point that the women often feel crazy for having them); indeed, perhaps the most common claim made by men is that women are illogical (and let us not forget that the vast majority of psychoanalysts during the 20th century were men, meaning that psychoanalytic theory often has an obsessive slant to it; see, on this point, Lacan, 2006, p. 609). But men would do better to realize that the logic of women's desire is quite different from the logic of their own desire. There is a logic to both, but *they are fundamentally different logics.*

Men often profess that they would like to get women to think like they do (as Rex Harrison famously put it, in *My Fair Lady*, "Why can't a woman be more like a man?")—in other words, eliminate their difference from men so that they would be the same as men. And analysts, who have mostly (though not exclusively) been neurotic, have often wished they could make psychotics into neurotics, reshape psychotics in their own image, make them like themselves.

Both of these projects involve the attempt to eradicate the Otherness of other people, to reduce whatever difference from oneself the other manifests to zero. They run utterly and completely counter to Freud's (1919/1955, p. 164) warning not "to force our own ideals upon [a patient who puts himself into our hands in search of help], and with the pride of a Creator to form him in our own image and see that it is good." Freud no doubt found himself succumbing to this normalizing temptation at times, which is precisely why he issued this warning to us.[9]

The point, in my view, is not to propose that we nuance our approach to normality by adding several new categories—"normal for women," "normal for men," and so on—but rather to propose that we jettison the notion of normality in general, because it is not only useless but often even harmful to our clinical work. Indeed, it blinds us to the fact that each person's neurosis (or major symptom) makes him or her operate in ways that seem "abnormal" to anyone else but that are utterly and completely "normal" to the person in question. One of my analysands, for example, does his best to never touch a doorknob, never shake hands with anyone, and never let anyone touch his books. Although this may strike many as bizarre, irrational, or even crazy (except perhaps during flu season), it is perfectly "normal" and "rational" to him given that these things are all connected for him with the feeling of being contaminated. He did not go into analysis because he thought these things "abnormal" but rather, at least in part, because more and more things had become connected over the years with the feeling of being contaminated and his ability to move around in the world was becoming distressingly limited.

What would it mean for such an analysand to become "normal"? That he never again be worried about being contaminated? That he be worried about being contaminated only in situations in which most other people would be worried? Or only in situations in which a "real" danger exists? If the latter, then a "real" danger as defined by whom—the scientist who says that a certain illness can be transmitted by an open sore on someone's hand or the scientist who says that it cannot be transmitted in that way? Pathways of transmission often are

---

[9] To paraphrase what La Rochefoucauld said of love, there are people who would never have worried about being normal but for hearing normality discussed. And to paraphrase what Lacan (1988a, p. 16) said of the ego, normality might well be said to be part of the contemporary "mental illness of man."

The logic of men's desire often involves hiding or rationalizing desire—that is, acting as though one were acting out of purely unselfish, "rational" motives when one is in fact doing exactly what one *wants* to do—whereas the logic of women's desire often involves placing desire center stage. It is easier in French to bring out the degree to which what is called "normal" is often male-centric, for the word itself is pronounced "nor-mâle," *mâle* meaning male, suggesting that the norm is a male norm; the word also contains *mal*, meaning evil or pain.

not understood for a long period of time and defy many scientists' expectations. An appeal here to "simple common sense" would be tantamount to an appeal to what "most other people"—read "most analysts"—would think, as opposed to some discernible standard by which to determine what is "reasonable" and what is not when it comes to fear of contamination.[10]

The analyst would do far better, I think, to keep her eyes and ears glued to the trail of the repressed than to fix them on any such elusive ideal as that of normality. This might allow her, in the present case, to try to locate the first appearance of such fears, which, as it turned out when I asked the analysand, was related to contact he had as a young man with someone who worked with lepers; this revived in his mind the warnings the analysand had received as a child from those around him not to have contact with the lepers who lived not far from his childhood home. It also revived his anger at his mother for endangering his health by inviting a possible leper into their home, and his anguish when his father died of a highly contagious disease when he was a young boy. Feeling guilty toward his father for having had, after the father's death, virtually unlimited access to his mother, he felt that he himself deserved to be infected and to die like his father had—indeed, his mother sometimes told him just that. His younger brother too had died of a highly infectious disease, and he felt guilty toward this brother as well; family members had sometimes commented that the younger brother was stronger and smarter than the older brother, and the older brother had at times wished that the younger brother would disappear. It also seemed that his fear of being contaminated disguised a wish to contaminate others whom he considered to be in his way, like his father and brother had been.

Once these and other related factors were elucidated, his fears subsided to such a degree that he rarely complained of them anymore.[11] Is there anything to be gained by labeling his earlier fears "abnormal" or "unhealthy" and his later absence of fear as "normal" or "healthy"? Is there any point in labeling his earlier fears "irrational" and his later absence of fear as "rational"? The use of terms like *rationality* and *normality* is one of the biggest shams—indeed, one of the biggest

---

[10] I once attended a case presentation in which the analyst presenting the case talked so much about his own fear of contracting AIDS from one of his patients that I came away feeling I knew a lot more about the analyst's neurosis than about his patient's!

[11] Note that the symptom in this case began when the analysand was a young man, even though many of its underpinnings dated back to his early childhood. In this respect, it illustrates Freud's notion of "deferred action" (also known as "ex post facto action" or "retroaction"): Twenty years after certain critical events had occurred (leading to no such symptom), a meeting with someone who worked with lepers led to the formation of a fear of contamination that lasted for decades thereafter. See, on the subject, Freud (1895/1966, pp. 353–356).

rationalizations—in current psychotherapeutic discourse. As Macalpine (1950, p. 196) nicely put it, "It is particularly unfortunate that the antithesis, 'rational' versus 'irrational,' was introduced, as it was precisely psychoanalysis which demonstrated that 'rational' behavior can be traced to 'irrational' roots."

It seems hardly coincidental that it is at the very moment in history at which we have become highly attuned to the differences in perspective that arise from people's different sexual, racial, religious, cultural, economic, and educational backgrounds, highly attuned to the way people's experience of the world and of themselves is affected by their origins, language, and social milieu, which in turn determines their views of reality (this attunement leading to an epistemological standpoint known as perspectivism, or perspectivalism, which postulates that there is no such thing as knowledge that is context-free, or perspective-free), that norms and normalization have become so important in psychology and psychoanalysis.[12] Having rejected many facets of Freud's theory that might have oriented them in their work in the face of attacks on traditional theories of knowledge, clinicians seem to be clinging ever more tightly to notions like normality to combat the kind of relativism that seems to grow out of recent developments in fields devoted to the study of culture, race, knowledge, and so on. Strict adherence to norms and to a teleological view of how all human beings should develop in order to reach some specified normal end state will not, in my view, help guide the practitioner's work but will simply further enforce the tyranny of norms. A far more useful guide for the perplexed clinician is to focus on the origins, workings, and consequences of repression in each individual case.

"Inappropriate Affect"

> [The] affects [of neurotics] are always appropriate, at least in their quality, though we must allow for their intensity being increased owing to displacement. . . . Psycho-analysis can put them upon the right path by recognizing the affect as being . . . justified and by seeking out the idea which belongs to it but has been repressed and replaced by a substitute.
> — Freud (1900/1958, p. 461)

Normalizing approaches can be seen day in and day out in clinics around the United States in the use of a number of ever more popular terms; I will begin

---

[12] Nor is it surprising that the drive to normalize is so strong in the "melting pot" known as the United States, where the pressure to become like everyone else begins in school ("peer pressure") and continues in psychotherapy.

with the terms *appropriate* and *inappropriate*. What could possibly make someone's affective state "appropriate" or "inappropriate"? And what is it that a person's affect is considered to be appropriate to or for?

"Appropriate" is presumably not meant in some Platonic sense as a universal, immutable quality or characteristic of an emotion; most practitioners who use this term would not claim, I suspect, that they are saying that manifesting a certain affect is inappropriate in every circumstance, in every single place on earth, in every culture, and in every historical era. And yet they seem to be claiming that, in their specific historical time and place on earth, certain affects are always inappropriate in certain circumstances—in clinics or hospitals, or in the therapist's private office. If an analysand becomes verbally aggressive during a session, many practitioners are quick to tax him with inappropriate behavior. But isn't it often simply an ordinary transference response, reflecting the way the analysand tended to deal with a parent, or a negative reaction by the analysand to a certain approach to therapy being adopted by the practitioner? How can anything that occurs in the therapy setting be considered inappropriate? If the analysand deliberately knocks over the analyst's lamp, isn't that telling? Isn't it, in fact, telling of what the therapist has not allowed the analysand to express in some other way or has not brought the analysand to express in some other way?

The analysand's behavior here could be understood as "acting out," in the psychoanalytic sense in which it is not construed as "the analysand's fault." As I indicated in Chapter 7, "acting out" has to do with things the patient finds it difficult or impossible to say, or with what the analyst is not enabling the analysand to say or come to grips with through speech (though often the term is reserved for actions that occur *outside* of the consulting room). Or the analysand's behavior here could be understood as resistance, which is ultimately the analyst's resistance to doing or saying something to keep the analysand talking and talking about what counts. I would be tempted to say that *there are no "inappropriate affects" in therapy—there are only inappropriate ways of practicing therapy* (and by "inappropriate" in the latter part of this formulation I mean ways that are not helpful to the analysand).

This is not to deny the existence of people who, regardless of the technique employed, are neither ready nor willing to engage in genuinely therapeutic work. But for those who are ready, willing, and indeed trying, there is no such thing as an inappropriate affect—*affects simply are*. Although a patient's seductive behavior may seem out of place in a "professional setting" like the consulting room, it obviously reflects something that is going on for the patient—whether that be that she construes all relationships as potentially sexual, that she deals with all men in positions of authority by acting seductively, or that she is sometimes led to focus on her feelings about the analyst as a person as a way of deflecting her attention away from the difficult work of remembering and elaborating. Such behavior may at first be difficult to handle in the analytic setting, but it often leads to very productive therapeutic work; indeed, what could be more apposite for the patient to express in the analytic setting than that?

Consider the way in which Freud (1909/1955) formulated what would undoubtedly be characterized by many contemporary therapists as "inappropriate affect": the Rat Man's intense self-reproaches for having allowed himself an hour of sleep while his father was dying, during which time his father in fact died (proving the doctor wrong who had told the Rat Man that his father would be out of danger within a day or two). Freud wrote:

> When there is a *mésalliance* [misalliance] . . . between an affect and its ideational content (in this instance, between the intensity of the self-reproach and the occasion for it), a layman will say that the affect is too great for the occasion—that it is exaggerated—and that consequently the inference following from the self-reproach (the inference that the patient is a criminal) is false. On the contrary, the [analyst] says: "No. The affect is justified. The sense of guilt is not in itself open to further criticism. But it belongs to some other content, which is unknown (*unconscious*), and which requires to be looked for. The known ideational content has only got into its actual position owing to a false connection. We are not used to feeling strong affects without their having any ideational content, and therefore, if the content is missing, we seize as a substitute upon some other content which is in some way or other suitable, much as our police, when they cannot catch the right murderer, arrest a wrong one instead. (pp. 175–176)

In Freud's view, the Rat Man's affect was not "inappropriate" but rather *displaced*: The affect (the self-reproaches, self-recriminations, and sense of being a criminal) was connected to the Rat Man's longstanding wish that his father would die (his affect could thus be characterized as "appropriate to" that wish, insofar as his moral sense condemned it), not to the fact that he missed his father's final moments. The latter was a "false connection." Indeed, *whenever the analyst is tempted to qualify someone's affect as "inappropriate," she should think displacement or projection instead.*[13]

---

[13] Freud (1894/1966) said much the same thing a number of years earlier:

> To the experienced physician, on the contrary, the affect [which the patient says she is astonished she has] seems justified and comprehensible; what *he* finds noticeable is only that an effect of that kind should be linked with an idea which does not merit it. The affect of the obsession appears to him, in other words, as being *dislodged* or *transposed*. (p. 54)

The use of terms like *appropriate* and *inappropriate* by practitioners to qualify behavior and affect[14]—and it is quite similar to their use of terms like *poor* or *inadequate affect regulation*, whose sinister overtones are hard to ignore—seems to signal one of two things:

- Either such practitioners fully endorse a developmental model that they believe allows them to legitimately assert that all mature people should show a specific affect (or range of affects) in a certain situation,
- Or else such practitioners have simply enlisted themselves in the service of conventional morality and norms, devoting themselves to molding patients' behavior so that it will be well adapted to modern-day working conditions and prevailing mores; for patients who display "appropriate affect" in therapy are thought to be likely to go on to display "appropriate behavior" at home, in the workplace, and in society at large.

To the extent that the latter is the case, psychology (and psychoanalysis too) reveals, in its ever greater use of such terms, that it is quite thoroughly engaged in the task of making individuals conform to widespread social, cultural, sexual, political, and economic norms, amounting to a disguised (and not always a well-disguised) method for exercising power. As Lacan (2006, p. 859) said in his usual no-holds-barred way, "Psychology has discovered a way to outlive itself by providing services to the technocracy." Like a number of the other "human sciences" (e.g., sociology and anthropology), psychology has enrolled in the service of goods, has become "a branch of the service of goods" (Lacan, 1992, p. 324), working in the service of a society in which the commodity is king.

In so doing, much of psychotherapeutic practice—not all, of course, for there are notable exceptions—has adopted lock, stock, and barrel the moral and cultural values of mainstream American society. Lacan was critical of the fact that the analysts who came to America before or during World War II often adapted psychoanalytic practice in such a way as to conform to ideals then prevalent in American culture (Lacan, 2006, pp. 402–403). Indeed, Lacan even criticized Anna Freud, who did not emigrate to America, for referring to such criteria as "the achievement of a higher income" to suggest that an analysis she had conducted had been successful (p. 604). Psychoanalysts themselves began to promise patients social and economic success, and they adapted their practice in such a way as to attempt to foster such goals in analysis.

---

[14] See, for example, McWilliams (2004, pp. 221, 230, 237).

In other words, practitioners seem to have adopted the goal of helping the patient perform better in the society of goods, in our present form of global capitalism. The patient, they feel, must be helped to overcome obstacles standing in the way of his improved concentration in the work arena, in the way of his getting along with his superiors, subordinates, and colleagues, and thus in the way of his getting a bigger piece of the pie for himself. Only in such a context could it possibly make sense to refer to a "patient" as a "client," for here the practitioner has made her patient's goals (and his explicitly formulated goals at the beginning of therapy often include returning to his former ability to "function" in society or "performing" better than he had before) her own, there being no hiatus between what he is aiming at and what she is aiming at for him (Renik, 2001, takes this position to the extreme).

Although Freud (1912b/1958, p. 119) said that psychoanalytic treatment strives to allow the analysand a "capacity for work and enjoyment,"[15] I do not think one could claim that his reference to work entailed helping the patient get ahead financially. Freud's technique seems to have been largely dedicated to the revelation of desire—the uncovering of the wishes the patient has been keeping out of sight and out of mind. The "work" he seems to have had in mind was often that of sublimation—creative, often artistic work—which is rarely well remunerated in Western culture (at least not until after the artist's death, in many cases).

To say that a patient shows "appropriate affect" is often tantamount, in the contemporary therapy world, to saying that the patient shows the same kind of affect that the analyst herself would show were she in a similar situation, as if she were the measure of all things,[16] or at least the kind and quantity of affect that she believes will help the patient get on in the world as she has come to understand it. To say that a patient shows "inappropriate affect" is ultimately tantamount to saying that the patient shows a kind and/or quantity of affect that the analyst cannot even imagine showing were she in a similar situation,

---

[15] The better known formulation, "love and work," was apparently attributed to Freud by Erik Erikson.
[16] Freud (1919/1955) cautioned analysts against seeing themselves in this way:

> We cannot avoid taking some patients for treatment who are so helpless and incapable of ordinary life that for them one has to combine analytic with educative influence; and even with the majority, occasions now and then arise in which the physician is bound to take up the position of teacher and mentor. But it must always be done with great caution, and the patient should be educated to liberate and fulfill his own nature, not to resemble ourselves. (p. 165)

Lacan (1988a, p. 18) ironized about the way in which analysts at his time seemed to believe that it was "the analyst's ego that serves as the yardstick of reality."

or that she thinks of as counterproductive for achieving the mainstream goals she endorses.

"High Functioning" and "Low Functioning"

Freud occasionally said that the unconscious is irrational, but that simply means that its rationality remains to be constructed; if the principle of contradiction . . . does not play the role in the unconscious that we think it does in classical logic, we must construct another logic, for classical logic has long been out of date.

— Lacan (1973–1974, November 20, 1973)

Appropriate and *inappropriate* are certainly not the only terms in contemporary psychotherapeutic jargon that signal normalizing tendencies. The ever-more-popular division of patients into the categories "high functioning" and "low functioning" (or "not-so-high functioning") clearly involves an assessment by the practitioner of the patient's ability to operate in the society around him as it is currently organized politically, economically, and socially—and to operate in a way that the practitioner deems suitable or "appropriate." This division also involves an implicit assumption that the patient should be able to operate well in society, whether that society endorses laissez-faire capitalism or is a dictatorship, whether it is a welfare state or a police state. What might it mean to function at a high level in a society that systematically persecutes a portion of the population? to be fortunate enough to be one of the persecutors, not one of the persecuted, and to follow persecutory orders when they are given? What might it mean to function at a high level in a society where the winners are those most adept at cutthroat competition? to stab others in the back and beat everyone at his own game? Although these might strike some readers as extreme cases, both could be said to characterize American society in certain ways, and I suspect that most clinicians, regardless of their political leanings, would agree that society abounds in injustices on larger and smaller scales. Perhaps it would be quite sensible to function poorly within an unjust society or a society whose injustices tend to target people like oneself! (As Pascal said in his *Pensées*, in certain situations "Men are so necessarily mad that it would be another twist of madness not to be mad.") All ethical and political perspective on the relation between the individual and society seems to drop out of the picture when clinicians use terms like *high functioning* and *low functioning*.

This division has, nevertheless, become so popular that, as I mentioned in the preface, one could argue that it is the primary diagnostic distinction made by many clinicians in the United States today, taking precedence over virtually all other forms of diagnosis, whether *DSM*-based or psychoanalytic. This strikes me as a very sorry state of affairs.

"Reality-testing"

Fantasy gives reality its frame.
— Lacan (*1969a, p. 96*)

In analytic practice, situating the subject in relation to reality, such as people assume it to constitute us, and not in relation to the signifier amounts to falling into the degrading trap of the psychological constitution of the subject.

— Lacan (*1978, p. 142*)

Another highly normalizing term in the contemporary clinician's arsenal is *reality-testing*. Whereas virtually all of the social sciences have moved in the direction of a notion of reality that is socially constructed—a notion of reality that is therefore shaped by a particular society's or group's language and worldview—psychology and psychoanalysis have often persisted in espousing a reality that is objective, not a product of our historically situated belief systems, and fully knowable. Many practitioners seem to think that they see reality more clearly than the vast majority of their patients do—not that they merely see reality differently because their own backgrounds (economic, cultural, religious, and so on) are different from those of their patients, nor that they simply see the world differently because of their own psychological makeup (e.g., their own desires, fantasies, neuroses, and so on). They consider themselves to be scientists of sorts who have somehow been able to extract themselves from their own historical circumstances—and the paradigms of thought peculiar to their time and place that both allow them to see and serve as blinders—and from the very vocabulary of their time (which, as I am trying to show in this chapter, includes an implicit paradigm), such that they have direct and unmediated access to reality, as if there could be such a thing!

Our access to reality is mediated by language (and all of the political, philosophical, and cultural assumptions it contains and conveys) and—just as we cannot step outside of the transference, as I indicated in Chapter 7—we cannot step outside of language to somehow experience reality directly. Even our specialized vocabularies and symbols (our "metalanguages") are made of the stuff of language and can only be explained with more language (the definition of one term or symbol always referring to other terms and symbols). There is no escape from language's mediation (except perhaps for the autist, whom language has failed, as we saw in Chapter 1).

Some clinicians might maintain that their use of the term *reality-testing* is far more limited than this, referring only to the patient's reported misreadings of the feelings and intentions of those around him—for example, when a patient repeatedly states that he believes that his wife is angry with him when she is not. But how does the clinician determine in such a case that the wife really is not angry with him? Can the clinician rely merely upon the wife's denial of anger, as reported by the patient? Couldn't it be that she is unaware of her own anger? or that she does not want to admit that she is angry? (Things are, of course, complicated still further by the possibility that the patient does not hear or remember what she actually says to him, or reports only a very small portion of it.)

Suppose an analysand were to talk at length about his boss's dislike of him and his fear of being fired. Can he be assumed to have "poor reality-testing" (or "poor reality-contact") if he is kept on—nay, promoted? It would be a risky assumption, to say the least. Perhaps he was on the verge of being fired, perhaps not; perhaps his promotion was his boss's way of getting him out of her hair (by, say, transferring him to a different department); or perhaps he was kept on or promoted due to a power struggle between his boss and others higher up in the chain of command (there being "wheels within wheels"). The analyst simply cannot know these things! She cannot know the reality he is up against, even if we were to assume that this reality is one single thing rather than a series of different constructions of a situation by the varied parties involved (a story always has more than one side).

At a time when a large number of those even in the "hard sciences" have come to the realization that they do not touch matter directly but only in a mediated way—only through the dominant scientific terminology and theories that inform their research and delimit their ways of thinking (see, for example, Kuhn, 1962)—it is curious that psychotherapists appeal to seemingly "paradigm-free" notions like "reality-testing" and good or bad "reality-contact."[17]

Ironically, many therapists think that Freud is the one who provided the theoretical foundations for the notion of reality-testing that they are employing. If they took the time, however, to read Freud's initial attempts to explain what he later came to term "reality-testing"—namely, how the psyche differentiates between images formed in the mind on the basis of wishes (in other words,

---

[17] Consider, for example, the following comment made by Bion (1959, p. 309) about one of his patients: "I knew that he had contact with reality because he came for analysis by himself."

hallucinatory reviving of things remembered or "wishful thinking," sometimes referred to today as "magical thinking") and images formed on the basis of perceptions of the outside world (in other words, "real perceptions")—they would realize just how shaky those foundations are, just how questionable Freud's whole discussion of the matter is. Consider the following passage:

> [There must be] an indication to distinguish between a perception and a memory (idea).
>
> It is probably the ω neurones [the neurons involved in perception] which furnish this indication: the *indication of reality*. In the case of every external perception a qualitative excitation occurs in ω, which in the first instance, however, has no significance for ψ [the memory apparatus]. It must be added that the ω excitation leads to ω discharge, and information of this, as of every discharge, reaches ψ. *The information of the discharge from ω is thus the indication of quality or of reality for ψ.*
>
> If the wished-for object is abundantly cathected, so that it is activated in a hallucinatory manner, the same indication of discharge or of reality follows too as in the case of external perception. In this instance the criterion fails. But if the wishful cathexis takes place subject to *inhibition*, as becomes possible when there is a cathected ego, a quantitative instance can be imagined in which the wishful cathexis, not being intense enough, produces no *indication of quality*, whereas the external perception would produce one. In this instance, therefore, the criterion would retain its value. For the difference is that the *indication of quality* follows, if it comes from outside, whatever the intensity of the cathexis, whereas, if it comes from ψ, it does so only when there are large intensities. It is accordingly inhibition by the ego which makes possible a criterion for distinguishing between perception and memory. (Freud, 1895/1966, pp. 325–326)

In this difficult passage from one of his earliest works, Freud hypothesized that signs or indications of reality (*Realitätszeichen*) are produced by the perceptual system (ω) when a perception comes from the outer world, but that the same kinds of signs can also be produced when a perceptual memory is revived from the inner world in cases in which "the wished-for object is abundantly cathected"—that is, when the wish is very strong (here the ego presumably allows primary-process wishful thinking to follow its bent because the ego is too weak to inhibit it, as, for example, when a hungry baby revives the image of its mother's breast).

There is thus no way to know in advance if one is dealing with a perception of something outside oneself (of something in the "real world") or with a hallucinatorily revived memory image. If the ego is strong, such hypothetical signs or indications of reality (for which, let us note, no neurological evidence has ever been found, to the best of my knowledge) will only be produced by "real perceptions," Freud argued, whereas if the ego is weak, such signs or indications of reality may be produced by both "real perceptions" and "remembered/fantasized perceptions." The individual thus seems capable of distinguishing between real perceptions and fantasy if he or she has a strong ego, and incapable of doing so if he or she has a weak ego. Real perceptions do not provide different signs or indications of reality than fantasies provide, signs that one can learn to read correctly; rather, according to Freud in this early text, it would seem that the more we inhibit our wishes (preventing them from becoming so invested with libidinal energy that they cross the threshold—that is, achieve "discharge," better known as satisfaction, through fantasy), the better we can distinguish genuine perceptions from fantasies.

Although much of this may concur with the way many contemporary clinicians think of reality-testing, I hope it is clear from this brief discussion that for Freud, reality-testing does not involve our ability to really and truly know the "outside world" in some sort of direct, unmediated way, but rather our ability to tell whether what we are experiencing is a perception or (the intrapsychic or endogenous recathecting of) a memory—that is, our ability to distinguish between perception and fantasy.[18] It has nothing to do with the *actual content* of the perception. And as we have known since the pre-Socratics, the information conveyed to us by sense perception (the content) is often misleading (a branch lying partway in a pool of water and partway out does not look straight even when it is, for example) and must be corroborated or corrected by other

---

[18] Note that the entire discussion hinges on what we understand by "signs or indications of reality," which is anything but clear. Freud's only gloss on their nature seems to be that they provide "information . . . of the discharge of the released reflex movement" to the cerebral cortex (Freud, 1895/1966, p. 318)—in other words, they inform the psyche that satisfaction has been achieved. Freud seems to suggest that they consist of "fresh sensory excitations (from the skin and muscles) which give rise to a *motor* [kinaesthetic] *image*" (p. 318). Lacan (1992, Chapters 2–5) argued that they are essentially sounds that we ourselves make that cue us into the fact that we have been satisfied. In either case, Freud's model suggests that we become aware of what has gone on inside of us by feeling a change in our bodies or hearing ourselves speak, react, cry out, and so on (on this point, see also Freud, 1940/1964, p. 162). We can retroactively deduce that a certain perception was not simply intrapsychic or endogenous (that is, the hallucinatory revival of a memory) because of a signal we receive from our skin or muscles (or through our ears from our own mouths, in Lacan's version) indicating that a genuine discharge has occurred. Again it should be noted that such a discharge can occur even in cases where we have simply fantasized the satisfaction; indeed, it can occur repeatedly, the stumbling block being that the hunger that may have been at its source keeps coming back, never being more than momentarily satisfied by imagining that one is being fed (even if in conjunction with thumb sucking). It is only a satisfaction based on a "real perception" of the breast and "real sucking sensations" that can lead to a more lasting discharge. Note that so-called wet dreams can, nevertheless, provide a discharge without involving "real perceptions."

perceptions. Freud (1900/1958, p. 613) was well aware that we have no direct access to reality, our access being mediated by our senses: The unconscious *"is as much unknown to us as [is] the reality of the external world, and it is as incompletely presented by the data of consciousness as is the external world by the communications of our sense organs."*

Freud's later work makes it abundantly clear that memory constantly informs and skews the content of perception, which is precisely why we so often "see" what we expect or want to see, and why we so often "perceive" other people to be behaving toward us the way we expect or want to have them behave toward us. *There is no such thing as a pure perception:*[19] What we think we are perceiving in the present is very much based on what we think we have perceived in the past; and when we are faced with unfamiliar or unexpected objects we often do not notice them at all or perceive very few of their actual characteristics (recall some of the examples given in Chapter 1). In other words, what we think we see when we have a perception is preinterpreted: It is interpreted as a function of all of our prior experiences and the way we have come to understand them (as a function of our worldview, in a word), and as a function of what we are expecting at a particular time and place. Except perhaps in the first few days of life, there can be no all-or-nothing distinction between the content of a perception and memory.

As has occurred with so many psychoanalytic terms, the meaning of *reality-testing* has drifted very far from Freud's originally intended meaning.[20]

Regarding the issue of "ego strength," note that, if we are to lend credence to Freud's later work, it is precisely those people with strong egos who are best able to repress things, which means that they are often the ones who have the most repressed material striving to find expression, that expression often being found in the form of projection—for example, "perceiving" that other people are angry with them when they themselves are angry with other people. If (and I think it is a big if) people with strong egos are better able to tell whether something they are experiencing is a perception or a memory than people with

---

[19] Except perhaps for the autist.

[20] Consider, in this connection, what Lacan (1978) said about "reality" as it is often understood by psychoanalysts:

> Let us not overlook what is, in the first place, highlighted by Freud as part and parcel of the dimension of the unconscious—namely, sexuality. Because psychoanalysis has ever more forgotten what is meant by the relation between the unconscious and the sexual, we will see that it has inherited a conception of reality that no longer has anything to do with reality such as Freud situated it at the level of the secondary process. (p. 146)

Two pages later he added, "The reality of the unconscious is—and this is an unbearable truth—sexual reality" (p. 150).

weak egos are, that hardly means that they are better able to tell whether the *content* of the perception most accurately describes themselves or other people. Indeed, we might hypothesize that in many cases *the stronger one's ego, the less able one is to know the repressed within oneself and therefore the less able one is to distinguish whether what one "sees" is coming from oneself or from other people*. Perhaps this observation can shed a new light on psychoanalysis' fascination with strengthening patients' egos.

To the best of my knowledge, Freud never claimed that the analyst, because she has gone through her own analysis, sees the "external world" more clearly or has better "reality contact" than the analysand. Certainly, she sees the world and thinks of reality differently than she did prior to her analysis. How can we describe the change that has occurred for her? Lacan hypothesized, as I mentioned in Chapter 6, that neurotics each have a fundamental fantasy that organizes their relations with others and with the world in general. While we each have many different conscious fantasies, the majority of them can be seen to follow a similar scenario in which we cast ourselves in a particular role, as a victim of others' punitive passions, as an object desired by or used by others, as a user of other people, or as a hero who saves victims, for example. Our individual fundamental fantasy colors the way we see the world and interact with it, leading us to create and recreate the same kind of scenario, the same kind of relationship with others again and again (for example, seeing ourselves as exploited by certain bosses, co-workers, family members, and potential spouses). As Lacan (1968a, p. 25) put it, "Fantasy constitutes for each of us our window onto reality." In the course of analysis that fundamental fantasy is shaken up and ultimately reconfigured (Lacan sometimes used the term *traversed*); this is not to say that it is eradicated, but rather that a somewhat different fundamental fantasy that we find more bearable forms. What this suggests is that we each continue to see the world—to see "reality"—through the lenses of our fundamental fantasy (through the lenses of what we want, what turns us on, and what we feel we cannot live without), even if it is no longer the same fundamental fantasy that we began with.

Our relationship to the world continues to be mediated by our own psychical reality, by our own fantasies,[21] and in the best of cases we will have learned something about how our own fantasies affect other people and our relations with them. By going through her own analysis, the analyst should acquire a

---

[21] Lacan (1975b, p. 193) playfully asserted that "we are all subject to the reality principle, that is, to fantasy." At one point he even went so far as to proffer, "As astonishing as it may seem, I will say that psychoanalysis . . . is reality" (Lacan, 2001, p. 351); further on he said that "fantasy serves as a frame for reality" (p. 366).

better sense of the desires and drives that inhabit her and of how they affect
the work she does with her analysands. She will be in "contact" with reality
no more and no less than she was before, if "reality" is understood in some
objective sense; she will, however, know far more about her own psychical
reality than she did at the outset. In the best of cases, she will realize by then
that she has no business attempting to impose her own notions of reality on
others.

"Disorder," "Dysfunction," "Stress," and Others

I have constructed a topology [real, symbolic, and imaginary] with which I dare to divide
up differently what Freud propped up with the term "psychical reality."
                                        — Lacan (1973–1974, December 18, 1973)

Many other terms in the practitioner's current lexicon reflect similar normalizing tendencies as those I have already mentioned. *Disorder*, which has become
ubiquitous, obviously presupposes an "order" that is considered standard or
ideal from which a "disorder" deviates. It implies that when someone's personality or psyche is "well ordered," all will be well in the world for that person
and for those around him or her: No one will think there is a problem. When,
on the contrary, someone's personality or psyche is "disordered," all will not
be well in the world for that person or for those around him or her: People
will think there is a problem. Although decked out in more scientific clothing,
the term *disorder* is simply a new version of the term *abnormal* (as are the related
terms *impairment* and *impaired*).

The same can obviously be said of the term *dysfunctional*, which assumes
that a person or social unit like the family is supposed to serve a specific
function—which presumably can be unambiguously defined, the resulting definition meeting with unanimous approval. Social histories of the family (see,
for example, Ariès, 1960/1962) suggest that different cultures and different
historical eras have assigned vastly different functions to the family—in other
words, there can be little or no universal agreement as to the family's ideal
functions. The attempt to assign a function or set of functions to an individual
encounters all the same pitfalls as the attempt (discussed earlier in this chapter)
to define human nature in general. *Regression* and *regressed* similarly appeal to an
ideal level of functioning from which someone has purportedly fallen away or
retreated; *adaptive* and *maladaptive* suggest that behavior should conform to an
ideal level of functioning—functioning in harmony with (that is, adapted to)
the world around us—but sometimes fails to do so.

Every era has its favorite catch-all explanations, and we should be wary of every term that takes the nation or profession by storm. Such is the case with the term *stress*, which was originally defined in physiology as "any stimulus, such as fear or pain, that disturbs or interferes with the normal physiological equilibrium of an organism." Over the last 30 years clinicians have latched onto the term—attracted no doubt to its seemingly scientific foundation—and have applied it to virtually all aspects of psychic life. Almost anything can now be considered to be a generator of stress: a so-called stressor.

Note first that implicit in clinicians' use of the term is the idea that one should not have stress, that one's life should be free of stress. Just as one can wonder if one should be "high functioning" in an unjust society, one can wonder whether one's life should actually be free of stress under a fascist dictatorship or could even theoretically be free of stressors in a society governed by "the law of the survival of the fittest" (that is, competitive capitalism). The presumption behind the current use of the term seems to be that one should have the absolute minimum of stress conceivable, regardless of one's profession or one's cultural, economic, or political context. But perhaps a certain amount of stress is beneficial, inspiring one to engage in cultural or political action.

Secondly, although clinicians were no doubt attracted to the seemingly objective state to which the term refers in physiology—disturbance of the normal physiological equilibrium of an organism—they seemed to willfully ignore the fact that, according to physiology's definition, such positive experiences as falling in love, winning the lottery, winning a gold medal, and so on should also be considered stressors, since they too generally disturb "the normal physiological equilibrium of an organism"! Moreover, real live human beings react very differently to the kinds of stressors usually invoked in clinical situations: One party to a divorce may be devastated while the other party is relieved; one child in a family may be thrown into a suicidal depression upon the death of a parent while another child may rejoice; one person who learns he has a life-threatening illness may fall into deep despair while another takes the opportunity to turn his life around. Stress in the psychological realm—and even to some degree in the physiological realm—is something that is experienced subjectively: It is not something that can be measured with a "stress test."[22]

I hope that this brief foray into the language of contemporary clinical terminology will serve to at least raise a question in practitioners' minds regarding

---

[22] I have discussed related matters at further length in Fink (1999).

the well-foundedness of the belief that we know what is good for our patients because we have at our disposal a widely accepted theory of what is good or best for human beings, which is based on a veritable science of human nature, and from which judgments of what is normal and abnormal, appropriate and inappropriate, functional and dysfunctional flow like water from the Trevi fountains in Rome (or, at the very least, from Old Faithful in Yellowstone). There is precious little agreement among philosophers, political theorists, and economists—much less psychoanalysts—regarding the right or best way for human beings to feel, act, develop, and live; and even if there were, the clinician would simply be making moralistic judgments on the basis of what some majority of theoreticians believes. Can such judgments be of any genuine use to our analysands? Can they even be of any use to us in our discussions with colleagues about our analysands? It would seem that, more than anything else, they simply incline us fall into the ruts of contemporary psychologistic thinking that takes the values of the world around us at face value.

10

Treating Psychosis

Psychoses ... are therefore not suitable for psychoanalysis, at least not for the method as it has been practised up to the present. I do not regard it as by any means impossible that by suitable changes in the method we may succeed in overcoming this contraindication—and so be able to initiate a psychotherapy of the psychoses.

— Freud (1904/1953, p. 264)

The role of the analyst ... must vary according to the diagnosis of the patient. ... The vast majority of people who may come to us for psycho-analysis are not psychotic and students must be first taught the analysis of non-psychotic cases. [1]

— Winnicott (1960/1965c, p. 162)

VIRTUALLY NONE OF the approaches to technique that I have articulated thus far in this book applies to the treatment of psychosis as it is understood in Lacanian psychoanalysis. The term *psychosis* does not cover the same ground in Lacan's usage as it does in more contemporary psychiatry and psychology (in the *DSM-IV*, for example), being in different ways both more specific and more extensive—more specific in that it is based on a particular mechanism of negation that Lacan terms "foreclosure" (which is quite different from

---

[1] Despite what he said here, Winnicott's regression-based approach to the treatment of psychosis does not, he said, require any change in approach compared to the treatment of neurotics. Moreover, he explicitly stated that he is "not asking [the analyst] to take on psychotic patients," especially not "in the first decade of his analytic career" (Winnicott, 1954/1958b, p. 293). He did, however, claim that in work with psychotics, "the setting becomes more important than the interpretation" (Winnicott, 1955–1956/1958c, p. 297).

Lacan (1977a, p. 12), on the other hand, maintained that "An analyst must not back away from psychosis," by which I think he meant that analysts must try to learn to work with psychotics, not that each individual analyst must take on psychotic analysands even when he knows nothing yet about how to work with them.

repression),[2] and more extensive in that it covers not only all those who have already had a psychotic break (even if it has long since subsided) but also all those who could potentially have one (the latter are sometimes referred to as "prepsychotics" and are said to be characterized by "psychotic structure"; for a detailed account of this, see Fink, 1997, Chapter 7). Just as there are several different forms of neurosis and different approaches to treatment that can be helpful for the different forms (see Fink, 1997, Chapter 8), there are different forms of psychosis—paranoia, schizophrenia, erotomania, melancholia, mania, and so on—and treatment should not be thought to proceed in exactly the same way for each form or even for all cases of the same form.[3] As creative as psychoanalytic work is with neurotic analysands, each case requiring the analyst to exercise a great deal of mental muscle to construct helpful interpretations and intervene in a manner that is felicitous for that particular person, psychoanalytic work must, as we shall see, be perhaps more creative still with psychotic analysands.

I will not try to lay out Lacan's entire theory of psychosis here, as it is beyond the scope of this book and as I have done so elsewhere (Fink, 1995, Chapters 4, 5, 1997, Chapters 6, 7). Confining myself to the theoretical contention that there is no repression, and thus strictly speaking no unconscious, in psychosis (a complex and no doubt controversial contention),[4] I will begin by offering

---

[2] His first mention of it can be found in Lacan (1993, pp. 150–151).

[3] See Freud's (1911a/1958, p. 77) comments on the distinction between paranoia and schizophrenia, which he often referred to as "dementia praecox." Vanneufville (2004) reported on a serious case of melancholia. Soler (2002) provided an excellent account of the different forms of psychosis from a highly sophisticated Lacanian perspective, providing separate chapters on erotomania, melancholia, autism, mania, paranoia, and schizophrenia. It may be of interest to certain readers to know that, whereas I have theorized that psychotics have not undergone what Lacan calls "alienation" (Fink, 1997, Chapters 7 and 9), Soler (2002, pp. 118–121) theorized that whereas autists and schizophrenics have not undergone alienation, paranoiacs have; what the latter have not undergone, in her view, is what Lacan calls "separation." She also postulated that in order to be inscribed within a discourse, one has to have undergone separation (p. 63). Note, too, that to her mind, the paternal metaphor is not all or nothing (p. 140).

[4] Early on in his work, Lacan (1993) put this rather differently than I have here:

> My starting point is as follows: The unconscious is there, it is present in psychosis. Psychoanalysts agree with this, rightly or wrongly, and I agree with them that this is in any case a *possible* starting point. The unconscious is there *but it does not function* [italics added]. Contrary to what people had thought, the fact that it is there does not automatically imply any sort of resolution; on the contrary, it implies a quite particular inertia. (p. 143–144; translation modified [note that a sentence is missing here in the published English translation; see French edition, p. 164])

Some 20 years later, Lacan (1990) spoke of a "rejection of the unconscious" in psychosis (it is mistranslated in the English text cited as a "reject of the unconscious," p. 22), using this expression as something of a synonym for the act or process of foreclosure. He also referred to James Joyce at one point (2005b,

some simple contrasts between the treatment of psychosis and the treatment of neurosis based on what has been said heretofore in this book; after that, I will try to indicate how psychosis (as defined by Lacan) can be detected through the kind of clinical work that proves to be possible with the analysand. This will lead to some more theoretical considerations about the nature of psychosis and to a discussion of a few possible avenues for treatment. It should be kept in mind throughout this chapter that the approach to treatment I lay out here is more applicable to paranoia than it is to the other forms of psychosis.[5]

---

p. 164) as, in a manner of speaking, "having cancelled his subscription to the unconscious" or as being "unsubscribed to the unconscious" (*désabonné à l'inconscient*). Freud (1917/1957, p. 235) said something somewhat similar when he indicated that in schizophrenia the unconscious is decathected. In a similar vein, Freud (1915b/1957, p. 203) said, "As regards schizophrenia . . . a doubt must occur to us whether the process here termed repression has anything at all in common with the repression which takes place in the transference neuroses."

By saying that there is, strictly speaking, no unconscious in psychosis, I do not mean to imply that the psychotic always knows why she does what she does; rather, I am suggesting that the knowledge found in the unconscious does not function in the same way as it does in neurosis—in particular, it is not projected onto the analyst as a subject supposed to know.

Freud (1925c/1959, p. 60) commented on the nonexistence or nonfunctionality of the unconscious in psychosis in a slightly different way when he said that "so many things that in the neuroses have to be laboriously fetched up from the depths are found in the psychoses on the surface, visible to every eye"; this is, no doubt, the origin of Lacan's well-known expression *à ciel ouvert*, meaning right out in the open, there for all the world to see (see, for example, Lacan, 2006, p. 825). The idea here is that in the very first session the psychotic may come right out and unembarrassedly say, "My wife took the place of my mother," whereas the neurotic may eventually say the same thing after a great deal of analytic work designed to get at the repressed.

My claim that there is no unconscious in psychosis flies in the face of many uses of the term *unconscious* by other analysts (for example, Klein, Bion, and Winnicott). Freud himself was not always consistent in his usage of the term, especially when he developed his second topography (1921), and subsequent analysts have emphasized one aspect or another of the unconscious as developed by Freud or have added their own two cents to the discussion. As De Masi (2001) showed, analysts mean very different things by the same word. Rather than dilute the specificity of the unconscious by embracing everything meant by it by all analysts, as De Masi did, in this book I adopt Lacan's notion of the unconscious as a chain of signifiers—largely equivalent, in his work, to what he calls the "symbolic order"—that does not function in the absence of repression. Rather than provide a long theoretical discussion of it here, I will refer the reader to Lacan (2006, pp. 11–61, 829–850) and to Fink (1995, Chapter 2, Appendix I).

[5] Lacan (2006, p. 392) provided a distinction between schizophrenia and paranoia when he said that, for the schizophrenic, "all of the symbolic is real."

Diagnosis is of considerable importance even to practitioners who do not think that it is. Should any of my readers eventually decide to practice or end up practicing in a totally nonpsychoanalytic way—employing psychodrama, gestalt techniques, and so on—they should nevertheless realize that they must not ask psychotics or prepsychotics to role play their fathers, for instance, as it is likely to drive them crazy or lead them to leave therapy altogether (for an example, see Garcia-Castellano's comments on a psychotic patient of his who had at first worked with a gestalt therapist; IRMA, 1997, p. 252).

What Not To Do with Psychotics

Paranoia means getting bogged down in the imaginary.
          — *Lacan* (*1974–1975, April 8, 1975*)

This dream we call reality . . .
          — *Lacan* (*1974–1975, February 11, 1975*)

Although the analyst must strive to listen to the psychotic analysand's speech
from a symbolic position—in which he does not take himself to be the measure
of all things, to be the target of all of the analysand's complaints, or jump
to conclusions about what the analysand means based on what he himself
would have meant had he said what the analysand said—he should generally
avoid making pointed "hmm" and "huh" sounds that can easily be construed as
suspicious or skeptical. Since there is, as I am proposing here, no repression
in psychosis, such sounds do not encourage the analysand to bring in parts of
the story that she had been leaving out, facets of the story that struck her as
shameful or reprehensible; indeed, they are more often taken as accusatory,
as charging her with lying or not acting in good faith. Psychotics who have
been through what I call the "psychiatric wringer" (innumerable encounters
with psychiatrists and other mental health workers who tell them that their
hallucinations or delusions are part of their illness and must be ignored or
forgotten, and who are quick to prescribe them drugs or hospitalize them
when they speak of them) may, of course, learn to omit certain parts of stories.
However, those who have not been through that wringer often make it clear
that they find it very difficult to lie, and that even when they intend not to
mention certain thoughts or feelings, they tend to let them slip out.

   Although it can be very helpful to the analyst to listen carefully for slips
and verbal stumblings at the beginning of his work with any patient, he will
generally find that psychotics make very few Freudian slips—that is, slips that
can be readily mobilized to open up the analysand to thinking about thoughts
and desires she had not planned to discuss and that may in fact run quite
counter to the ones she had anticipated conveying. Since, in psychosis, there
is no unconscious that is striving for expression against strong opposing forces,
slips are not produced by the interference of unconscious thoughts or wishes
with conscious ones. If the analyst emphasizes slips at the outset—and he
should, albeit gently, especially when he is not entirely sure of the diagnosis—
he will find that they are few and far between and that his efforts at putting

them to the work of the therapy bear no fruit.[6] If the analysand has some familiarity with psychoanalytic theory, she may laugh when he emphasizes a slip, and she may even agree with his proposed interpretation of its meaning, but she is not likely to propose meanings of her own. Sometimes a cigar *is* just a cigar: A slip made by a psychotic is not of the Freudian strain; it is simply a mistake. (Note too that the psychotic is generally quite uninterested in the analyst's own slips of the tongue and bungled actions, whereas the neurotic is often quite attentive to them and inclined to speculate about their meaning.)

Although it is generally quite important to ask the psychotic analysand myriad exploratory questions to get a better sense of her life and experience, there are times when this is contraindicated. For example, if a psychotic analysand's father played a very problematic role in her life (as is often the case), the analysand may become extremely anxious when specific events from her past involving her father are discussed. Were the analyst working with an analysand who was clearly neurotic, he might continue to probe despite the appearance of a certain quantum of anxiety in his analysand in the hope of overcoming her reluctance to reveal (or her shame at revealing) certain details, or in the hope of inducing her to remember them.[7] Were the anxiety somewhat stronger, he might simply make a mental note to himself to come back to this in the next session or in some future session, or he might convey to the analysand— especially if it is still early on in the treatment—that he would like her to speak about it further but that she need not elaborate on it any more right now if she is not comfortable doing so. However, if the analysand is psychotic, the analyst would do well to change the subject when memories related to missing fathers become anxiety-provoking; such memories may be elucidated in the years to come in the treatment, but there may be no need to ever elucidate them, especially as such thoughts may lead the analysand toward a gaping hole, the kind of hole in the symbolic that can trigger a psychotic break (on such holes in the symbolic, see Lacan, 2006, pp. 558, 582; see also the later section of this chapter entitled "Sinthome"). Even though such a break might potentially lead to the formation of a delusion that, as we shall see, must be understood as part of the curative process (and not part of the illness, as so

---

[6] According to J.-L. Belinchon and colleagues (1988, p. 294), Gérard Miller has gone so far as to say that slips are impossible in psychosis. By this he presumably means that "Freudian slips"—slips that have both an intended and an unintended meaning—are impossible, for mistakes of other kinds are obviously possible in psychosis.

[7] The psychoanalytic approach I present here to the treatment of neurosis runs quite counter to the contemporary American approach, introduced in many a training institute, wherein the analyst is taught not to do anything that might increase the analysand's anxiety.

many in the mental health professions are wont to think),[8] it is generally safer to carefully avoid provoking a break that might well make matters worse, at least at the outset. Once the proverbial genie is out of the bottle, it is unlikely to ever go back in and nothing is likely to ever be the same thereafter. *Primum non nocere*: Our first duty is to do no harm.

Since the purpose of most forms of punctuation (including scansion, which, as I said in Chapter 4, is merely a more emphatic form of punctuation) is to get at the repressed, loosely speaking, punctuation is not of much value in working with psychotics. If the analyst highlights certain words the psychotic analysand enunciates, they should preferably not be ambiguous or polyvalent words; the analyst's underscorings should be designed simply to get the analysand to clarify something he has not understood, explain specific words further, or go on with what she is saying. The same is true for the gentle "hmms" the analyst might utter: They should be provided only to indicate that he is listening and to encourage the analysand to go on speaking.

Abrupt scansions should be avoided, especially ones that would serve in neurosis to emphasize an ambiguous formulation the analysand has just proffered, a slip of the tongue, or a surprising reversal of perspective. The majority of the work with a psychotic analysand takes place during the session itself, not in between sessions as is often the case with neurotics. Whereas in neurosis the analyst strives to put the analysand's unconscious to work, in psychosis there is no unconscious to put to work; leaving the analysand unsure about why the session was stopped at a particular point does not achieve the same effect as it does in neurosis—in fact, it is likely to prompt perplexity, annoyance, and anxiety instead of associative work.

Insofar as interpretation is understood to target the repressed—to bring out, for example, the unconscious wish in a dream—it has no place in work with psychotics. Time and again, I have seen psychotic patients become highly agitated when a therapist has tried to point to something in a dream, fantasy, or slip that they themselves had not seen, or had not thought was there. Therapists who repeatedly interpret to psychotics what they believe to be unconscious in their discourse often become irremediably situated by their analysands as persecutors—as people who are trying to read their thoughts, influence them with their thoughts, or put foreign thoughts into their heads. If the analyst is to engage in interpretive work with the psychotic, it should be meaning-based—in other words, it should aim at conveying a very specific meaning (often a calming, nonpersecutory meaning, as discussed later), not at

---

[8] See Freud's (1911a/1958, pp. 71, 77) comments on this.

exploding the analysand's preexisting system of meanings or undermining the register of meaning itself.[9]

Whereas in his work with neurotics the analyst often does well to employ ambiguous phrasing so that the analysand can take up what he says in several different possible ways[10]—what the analysand hears often being of more interest than what the analyst intended—in his work with psychotics the analyst generally does well to say things as clearly as possible. Oracular speech, elusiveness, and equivocation should be avoided (of course, one is never able to remove all ambiguity from one's speech, try as one might, but in any case the psychotic will not necessarily hear "accidental" double meanings), and one should, as always, try to work within the analysand's vocabulary to the greatest extent possible. The goal is not at all to bring the psychotic analysand face to face with the lack of ultimate explanations, with the fact that the Other (as a putatively complete meaning system that covers everything) is lacking, or with castration as such—there is nothing curative for the psychotic in such an endeavor.

Diagnosing Psychosis

One can no longer consider psychosis to involve some sort of failure on the subject's part to correspond to reality but to involve instead a type of relation to language.
                                                        — Freda and colleagues (1988, p. 149)

Before I say more about what not to do in treating psychotics, let me first make a few points about diagnosis. In my experience, clinicians often find it difficult to distinguish between neurosis and psychosis and are consequently wont to make a mess of things with a considerable number of psychotic patients.

Without going into all the details of Lacan's theory of what leads to psychosis, and confining my attention here to the absence of repression that is characteristic of psychosis, I would like to mention several readily observable features of the analysand's speech and of the analysand's relation to the analyst that can help us make a differential diagnosis (that is, convincingly distinguish

---

[9] Paul Williams (2001, p. 1), in his introduction to a recent collection of papers on psychosis from non-Lacanian perspectives, argued that "the core of the [psychotic] patient's crisis [is] the destruction of meaning" and that "clinicians from different psychoanalytic orientations approach the task of restoring meaning."

[10] This is, of course, not true of matters directly related to the continuation of the analysis, such as scheduling and payment.

between neurosis and psychosis).[11] It should not be thought that the traditional signs of psychosis, such as voices, hallucinations, and delusions, are any
more conclusive than the criteria I will describe, for what exactly constitutes
a psychotic "voice" is a matter of much debate (after all, virtually all of us hear
voices of one kind or another at some point in time—these intrapsychic or en-
dopsychic voices are in many cases associated with the Freudian superego—
and it requires considerable subtlety to plausibly distinguish between your
run-of-the-mill superego voice and a "psychotic voice").[12] The same is true of
"hallucinations," a term that is often used quite loosely by neurotics to describe
any kind of unusual visual or auditory experience and that is often not used
by psychotics, who refer instead to visions or experiences (see Fink, 1997,
pp. 82–86). Reports (whether by the patient herself or by clinic or hospital
staff) of voices and hallucinations cannot be taken at face value by the analyst,
nor can what may initially seem to be delusional thinking. We must not be
quick to jump to the conclusion that the patient is imagining things, because,
in the majority of cases, it is quite difficult, if not altogether impossible, for
the average clinician to determine whether the FBI is spying on someone, for
example. It is rarely some particular thought that can serve us as convincing
proof that someone is delusional but, rather, the *certainty* with which she expresses that thought (in other words, when she does not *wonder* whether the FBI
is spying on her but instead is *absolutely convinced* of it and cannot even entertain
the thought that the FBI might be spying on her next-door neighbors rather
than on her).[13] It is not so much the content of her discourse as its form that
is crucial here.

---

[11] One should not assume that it is *always* possible to convincingly distinguish between neurosis and
psychosis; see IRMA (1997) for a detailed debate about the diagnosis of a number of unusual cases by
a prominent group of Lacanian analysts. I have opted not to discuss the treatment of perversion, the
third major diagnostic category, in this book. For a discussion of perversion, see Fink (1997, Chapter
9, 2003).

[12] Lacan (1974–1975, January 21,1975) suggested that "in psychosis, the subject not only believes
in the [existence of the] voices, he also believes them," whereas in neurosis the subject may well
believe that she hears voices, but she does not necessarily believe what they say: She is not certain
that they are right, as the psychotic tends to be. Certainty is a very important feature of psychosis.

[13] It is precisely because the psychotic has certainty that she is not looking for knowledge from the
analyst; the neurotic is uncertain or even full of doubts and seeks corroboration, validation, and assurance
from the analyst. This does not mean that the psychotic is *always* certain and never doubtful (see Soler,
1997, p. 215), but rather that the psychotic does not look for corroboration, validation, and assurance
from the analyst as the neurotic does.

Forms of Discourse

It is difficult not to see that the notion of the unconscious is in part founded on slips.
— *Lacan* (2005b, p. 97)

Behind every slip there is a signifying finality. If there is an unconscious, the error tends to want to express something.
— *Lacan* (2005b, p. 148)

The form of the analysand's discourse can tell us a great deal indeed. I mentioned earlier that psychotics make very few Freudian slips. The clinician who has effectively trained himself to hear slips and slight stumblings and slurs in a variety of contexts (in social situations, radio broadcasts, and analytic sessions) will hear one or more slips in virtually every session with his neurotic analysands—sometimes as many as one per minute. When such a "hearing-enabled" clinician finds himself working with someone who speaks at a fairly typical speed but only makes a slip every month or so, he should begin to suspect that there is no repressed material trying to interrupt that analysand's flow of speech.

Similarly, when the analyst pays careful attention to his analysands' speech, he will notice that statements are rarely if ever couched, by certain analysands, in the blatantly defensive way in which they are so often couched by neurotics. For example, the neurotic analysand regularly introduces statements with disclaimers like "here's a ridiculous thought for you," "the stupidest thing just came to mind," "I'm sure this has nothing to do with anything," or "this is totally irrelevant." She editorializes about her discourse, terming it "stupid," "irrelevant," "farfetched," "dumb," "trite," "absurd," "out of the blue," or "just a joke,"[14] and she denies things that no one has accused her of (in other words, she proffers unprovoked denials, as I called them in Chapter 3). All of these are signs of defense on the neurotic's part, and they indicate the direction in which the analyst can aim at the neurotic's repressed truth (for what the analysand terms "stupid" is often the smartest, and "irrelevant" the most relevant). When these signs of defense are totally absent from an analysand's discourse, the analyst should consider a diagnosis of psychosis.

Certain peculiarities of the psychotic's way of speaking are summarized in contemporary psychiatry by the rather vague term *concrete*. This term renders,

---

[14] We must always keep in mind that many a true word is spoken in jest. Such editorializing comments arise, no doubt, from what certain analysts term the "observing ego"; they might better be thought to arise from what Freud calls the "censor" or "censorship."

of course, an aspect of the psychotic's speech, but it seems to contrast it with the fluidity of the neurotic's speech, which is to put the emphasis in the wrong place. We must not confuse a slow, plodding cadence or conceptual stagnation with psychotic speech. "Concrete" also seems to emphasize an absence of imagery, which is not necessarily the case either. The more crucial difference between psychotic and neurotic speech is the inability (in psychosis) or ability (in neurosis) to see several different meanings in one and the same portion of speech. This brings us to the relation between speech and meaning—in linguistic terms, between the signifier and the signified—which is very different in neurosis and psychosis.

The signifier is what you hear when someone speaks—in other words, the signifier is essentially the sounds produced by a person in speaking—and the signified is what those sounds mean. A court stenographer records the *sounds* of words, and those sounds can at times be divided up differently, leaving the meaning of the text ambiguous (should, for example, the sound that can be written "disciplined answers," be understood instead as "discipline dancers," a syntagm pronounced in a session by one of my analysands?). The flow of sound, or "ribbon of sound" as Saussure (1916/1959) called it, can be broken down in a number of different ways in certain instances.

But to the psychotic analysand, meaning and sound, signified and signifier, are inseparable: The signifiers that she intended to pronounce are indissolubly attached, in her mind, to the meaning she intended to convey with them. There can be no slippage here, no other meaning in what she said than what she intended, no other way of reading the same words differently, or cutting up the ribbon of sound differently so that it means something else. The signifier and the signified are soldered or welded together here—there can be no gap between them. This means that although the psychotic generally speaks a language (if not more than one) and may indeed speak it extremely well by all accounts, she does not speak it or operate within it the way a neurotic does. The properly symbolic dimension of language, involving a potential gap between signifier and signified, is missing in psychosis.[15]

---

[15] In particular, the psychotic is apt to focus on the fact that a particular set of phonemes or sounds shows up in a number of different contexts (for example, steak or stake), without being able to appreciate the several different meanings that this set of phonemes can *simultaneously* convey. In one example, a French analysand could not get beyond the fact that the computer term *bit* is pronounced exactly like *bitte* in French (which is slang for penis), instead of being able to joke about its "metaphorical value" as his fellow students could (Nominé, 2005, p. 209). We do, of course, find examples of psychotics seeing or hearing multiple meanings in one and the same word or name; Georges (1997, p. 40) discussed a young Frenchman who, during a consultation, mentioned that in the name of a woman he had met, Edevine, he heard Edwige, divine, Eve, and *devine*, meaning "guess." Still, I do not believe that I have ever heard of a psychotic divining such multiple meanings in his own speech.

The neurotic analysand feels that she often fails to convey what she means in speech. She has an idea in mind, but she may very well feel that she has not adequately conveyed it in speaking to someone else. She has said more or less than she wanted to say; her words somehow did not live up to the idea she had in mind.

What we can say most generally is that *two fundamentally different levels* have come into existence for the neurotic—word and meaning (that is, signifier and signified)—and they have a tendency *not* to be as closely tied together as the neurotic would like:

- What she says ends up being ambiguous and she and her interlocutor both realize that what she says can be understood in different ways.
- What she means is not so easy to put into words and she is often frustrated at her own inability to put it well, to say it forcefully and elegantly, in a way that seems to do justice to the thought.[16]

There is no such gap for the psychotic between meaning and expression. *The psychotic cannot say one thing and mean another.* This is why there is no such thing as what I would call genuine irony in a psychotic's speech.[17] The neurotic is

---

Clearly, we do not find the same play of significations in psychosis as we do in neurosis, where one signifier refers to another signifier. Instead, we find in psychosis that there is a static, undialectizable relationship between signifier and signified. As Soler (2002, p. 63) put it, "The psychotic is not outside of language, but rather outside of discourse." In commenting on Lacan's remark that for the schizophrenic, "all of the symbolic is real," Soler added:

> That is to say that the schizophrenic, who nevertheless speaks and has his mother tongue at his disposal, does not have the symbolic at his disposal. We are very close here to Freud's formulation that the schizophrenic treats words like things. For the fact is that access to the symbolic assumes more than the learning of one's mother tongue, it assumes the emptying out of the living being as real which is produced by promoting a signifier. (p. 118)

In other words, it is only when the word becomes the death of the thing—when, for example, the child's words "fort" and "da" (gone and here) introduce a gap into the real presence or absence of the mother (see Freud, 1920, pp. 14–17), allowing the child to talk about her as present when absent and absent when present—and when language overwrites the body, turning it into a social body, a socialized body that enjoys in more or less socially acceptable ways correlated with the well-known erogenous zones, that the symbolic comes into being (see Fink, 1995, Chapter 3).

[16] Indeed, Lacan considered this to be one of the goals the neurotic analysand eventually sets for him- or herself: *le bien dire*, putting it well.

[17] Note, however, that Miller (1993, p. 8) proposed that the schizophrenic employs irony of a certain kind: the "comic form taken by the knowledge that the Other does not know—that is, that the Other, as Other of knowledge, is nothing." He later (IRMA, 1997) gave the example of a schizophrenic who played a kind of guessing game with his analyst, asking her questions to which he was quite sure she did not have the not-at-all-obvious answers, and then snickered because he had the answers that she did not have. According to Miller (IRMA, 1997, p. 202), "such guessing games incarnate the position of schizophrenic irony very well." It should be clear that I am using the term *irony* in a rather different sense. When analysts refer to a psychotic's use of irony, it is often very clear that *they* see something

very aware of her ability to deliberately use language to dupe the other by saying the exact opposite of what she means or by using irony to insinuate the opposite of what her words semantically mean. She has no problem telling the analyst, "I'm doing *so much better* since I started seeing you," all the while intending to convey that nothing has changed or that she is doing even worse than before.

This two-faced use of language is not available to the psychotic. *The psychotic does not employ irony*—not intentionally, at any rate. The duplicity language affords the neurotic—the social use of language to be very polite when annoyed at someone or to say the sweetest things when the angriest—is not available to the psychotic. Although the practitioner may see a great deal of irony in things the psychotic analysand says or believe that his analysand deliberately makes witty plays on words, he must be careful to distinguish between what he himself reads into things and what the analysand herself intends. Once again, we see here that the *form* of the analysand's speech can tell us a great deal indeed.[18]

---

ironic in that usage, whereas the patient does not. Sureau (IRMA, 1997, p. 204), for example, mentioned a patient who referred to her as her "guardian angel"; Sureau considered that to be very ironic because the patient was worried about being "guarded" (that is, forcibly detained) in a mental hospital. What is not at all clear is that the patient herself intended any irony in my sense of the term—in other words, it is not clear that the patient herself felt that she was needling or provoking Sureau with this sobriquet because she realized that it could be read at two very different levels. Here it seems evident that irony is in the eye of the beholder.

Similarly, one does not generally find much intentional humor in a psychotic's speech. Castanet & de Georges (2005, p. 41) noted the same thing regarding melancholia and those disposed toward it when they referred to the "attraction to seriousness and the relative incapacity for humor of the pre-melancholic subject, humor which would imply the possibility of a mediation, a distancing from pregiven values." Decool (1997, pp. 29–36), on the other hand, reported on a case in which a schizophrenic became a jokester: He told jokes that clearly relied upon plays on words and innuendo in order to make people laugh. The question that I would raise in this case is whether the patient invented the jokes himself or simply heard them from others and observed that they made people laugh, even though he himself did not understand them.

[18] One of the things that frequently arises in work with neurotics is that the analysand, early on, wants to bring in her spouse or lover so that the analyst can *really* see what the patient is up against, her words having, she feels, failed to convey this. She believes that the analyst must encounter this impossible partner in order to fully grasp and sympathize with her plight in life. Should the analyst refuse to meet with the partner, the analysand may resort to bringing in pictures, tape recordings, letters, and so on as evidence of her plight. Somehow, the analyst must be made to see things from precisely the same perspective that the patient sees them from in order for the analyst to fully appreciate the patient's predicament. (This is often accompanied by the statement that it is not really the patient who needs therapy but rather the partner.)

Virtually none of this occurs in psychosis. There is rarely if ever a concern on the psychotic's part that his or her description of the situation has been inadequate to convey to the analyst a proper appreciation of the patient's plight—indeed, the analyst is often far more worried about the patient's situation than the patient is. The neurotic would like to convince the analyst of a certain kind of personal drama that the analyst is perhaps perceived as taking too lightly, whereas the psychotic is far more likely to matter-of-factly recount situations that shock and trouble the analyst.

Transference

In psychosis, the analyst's position is determined by knowledge. But the knowledge in question is not knowledge regarding the unconscious as Other—that is, a knowledge that must be deciphered—but knowledge regarding the Other's jouissance.
— Kizer and colleagues (1988, p. 146)

The analyst can also learn to distinguish between neurosis and psychosis by considering the kind of transferential relationship the analysand forms with the analyst. Freud thought that psychoanalysis was impossible with psychotics because he believed they were incapable of forming a transference to the analyst. (Some writers have suggested that he may have revised his point of view on this matter in the 1930s.) What is clear is that the kind of relationship that the psychotic forms with the analyst is quite different from that formed by the neurotic. Let us begin with the difference in relationship with regard to knowledge.

The neurotic, who has repressed so many things about herself, believes that the knowledge she is missing about herself, the knowledge she does not have about herself, is located in the analyst as Other with a capital O. This may not be obvious from the outset, and young practitioners may find this aspect of the transference less pronounced than older clinicians, but it becomes clear sooner or later in every neurotic's analysis, albeit to a greater or lesser extent. The neurotic analysand spontaneously feels love for the person to whom she attributes the knowledge that she does not think she has but feels she needs, and she often repeatedly asks the analyst pointblank to tell her the meaning of her symptoms, fantasies, and dreams.

The psychotic analysand does no such thing. She may think that the analyst knows a few techniques about eating well, a few medications that can help her sleep, or a few tips about how to get by better in the world, but she does not assume that the analyst knows anything in particular about the meaning of her own difficulties in life. The psychotic does not spontaneously have the impression that the analyst must see something in what she says that she herself does not see, which is absolutely classic among neurotics. If the analyst insinuates that an expression the neurotic analysand used was ambiguous and could be interpreted in a number of different ways, she may dispute this initially and be loath to credit the legitimacy of the analyst hearing something in what she said that was not intended. She may be annoyed at the insinuation or jubilant that the analyst has found her out at some level, but she will rarely dispute the potentially ambiguous nature of what she said—especially after a certain amount of therapy. The neurotic is not likely to say, "No, what I said was very clear, and it does not grammatically allow for any misinterpretation, indeed, for any other interpretation at all." She is not likely to deny the possibility of any and all *equivocation* (whether homophonic or grammatical), and she is likely to occasionally lament the fact that she cannot control the meaning of everything she says. She implicitly acknowledges thereby that she is aware that while she may intend to convey one meaning, other people are at liberty to attribute other meanings to what she says, as disturbing as those other meanings may be to her.

When I pointed out to a neurotic analysand of mine that his phrase "my attraction to porn" could possibly also mean that he thinks of porn as attracted to him, he was initially nonplussed and did not know how to respond. At the beginning of the next session, however, he indicated that he had been mulling over my remark and wondered if I was referring to the possibility that he might be envisioning himself as an object for the women in the pornographic images he looked at, which would turn the tables on his assumption that he was the desiring subject looking at passive sexual objects. This led him to discuss his long-held belief that women neither wanted nor enjoyed sex, or at least *should* not want or enjoy sex, for there could only be one desirer in sex, which he referred to as a "zero-sum game" (if one person desired, the other person could not). This neurotic analysand clearly felt that what I heard in his speech might well have some legitimacy, and that if I had underscored this phrase it was no doubt because I knew something about him that he himself did not yet know. Even such a subtle grammatical ambiguity as this can be of use in work with neurotics, whereas it would fall completely flat with psychotics, who would not be interested in what the analyst heard in their speech that was not intended because they do not assume that he has any special knowledge of their innermost workings.

When the analyst finds that his knowledge is considered so useless by the analysand—and when I say useless I do not simply mean challenged, as it may well be by the hysteric, or trampled upon, as it may well be by the obsessive, both of whom generally reveal that the analyst's interpretations, although initially rejected, are nevertheless eventually assimilated or at least worked over at some level (sometimes even being repeated by the analysand almost verbatim several sessions after they were first uttered by the analyst, but without any seeming recognition on her part that they were ever uttered by the analyst)—that it is not even spontaneously solicited by the analysand, he should begin to suspect that he is dealing with someone with psychotic structure.

The analyst must not hastily jump to the conclusion that he is not being situated by the analysand as the Other with a capital O just because the analysand claims to have no faith in talk therapy. While it may occasionally be possible to conclude with some degree of confidence right from the first session that a patient is situating the analyst as a symbolic Other through the many direct references she makes to his supposed prior knowledge of everything she is about to say, or because she gives him a thumbnail sketch of her life story and then expects him to magically provide a solution or diagnosis and prognosis, on other occasions it may be possible to draw a similar conclusion when the analysand protests right from the outset (and perhaps for quite some time) that she does not believe in psychoanalysis, thinks all psychotherapists are lunatics, and has no respect whatsoever for headshrinkers, no matter what their persuasion. With Shakespeare, we may well suspect that "she doth protest too much," for her very contesting of the analyst's knowledge nevertheless points to *the existence of a place in her world for such knowledge*, even if she seems to want to deny the analyst access to that place. At least it is clear in this instance that such an ideal exists for the analysand, that the notion of the all-knowing Other has come into being, and that someone was perhaps at some point in time situated there, the patient's very disappointment being related to the fact that no one seems to occupy or live up to that position anymore.

The very fact that a patient contests the analyst's knowledge right from the outset means that, in spite of herself, she assumes the analyst has some and that she wants to deny it—by way of provocation, perhaps, or just to see how he will react (or possibly for other reasons as well). In other words, such statements act as typical Freudian denials. This is especially true when the analyst has not explicitly claimed to have any particular knowledge—the point being that his having knowledge came to the patient's mind. (Of course, the social or institutional context itself can suggest that the analyst has a certain power related to knowledge, even when the analyst himself does not profess to have any.) For his knowledge to be denied, it first had to come to her mind. In a word, the patient's fervent *denial* that he has some kind of knowledge that can help her may be as clear an indication of neurosis as her *assertion* that he has some kind of knowledge (often accompanied by a complaint that he is withholding it).

I have seen cases, for example, where someone from a non-Western culture has come to therapy saying that she has absolutely no faith in the ability of Western medicine or psychology to help her, whereas she believes that she was helped significantly at some point in her past by a faith healer or medicine man from her own culture. In other cases, a patient professes to have been helped by a coach, scout leader, or religious leader of some kind who gave the patient physical and spiritual challenges or deeds to accomplish, but the patient does not believe that just talking can do any good. The analyst need not be upset by these skeptical pronouncements, for they suggest that the patient has formed at least some idea of an Other who knows (Lacan, 2006, pp. 230–243, referred to this Other as "the subject supposed to know"), an Other who knows what is good for her, and he can at least hope that he will eventually be in some way associated by her with that Other, even if it takes quite some time.

The psychotic, on the other hand, does not subscribe to the illusion that "leads the [neurotic] subject to believe that her truth is already there in us, that we know it in advance" (Lacan, 2006, p. 308). The psychotic does *not* take the analyst as an Other who supposedly knows what ails her—who knows what the secret origin of that ailment is and how to fix it. The neurotic does, and this is often registered in the passing remark "But you've already heard all this before," or in her response to the analyst's question "What's going through your mind?" when she lapses into silence—"I was wondering what *you* thought of all this."

If the analyst pays close attention to such statements and does his best to elicit such thoughts even when they have not yet become statements (as, for example, when the analysand falls silent), he will be struck by the total absence of them in certain cases. In other words, he will become aware of the fact that certain patients are simply not concerned with what therapists know or think. Whereas one class of patients repeatedly mentions that they are worried the analyst thinks they are crazy or thinks badly of them, another class seems not to be preoccupied by such questions. Even though this latter class, the psychotics, may wonder about *their own sanity* or whether they are going crazy, the crucial point is that *they do not wonder whether the analyst thinks they are crazy.*[19]

They may think the analyst can help in some way—that he is helpful when he recommends a change of jobs, more sleep, a different diet, or whatever—but they do not attribute any sort of special insight or knowledge to him regarding their childhood, inner conflicts, or true feelings, for to their minds he is fundamentally no different from them: he is an other, not an Other, to them. He is not qualitatively different: There is only quantitative difference here.

This should not be taken to imply that anyone who believes in a qualitatively different, omniscient Other (for example, God) is automatically neurotic. The crucial question is whether or not the analysand's presumption that some knowledge regarding her exists beyond (or outside of) her can be transferred

---

[19] Those who wonder whether they are crazy are far more likely to be neurotic than those who never wonder about it at all. The wondering itself can serve as a useful diagnostic barometer.

onto the analyst—in other words, whether the analysand is able to view her analyst as an all-knowing Other. *If a patient is able to situate the analyst in the place of knowledge, the analyst can rule out psychosis.* (The neurotic's belief that the analyst knows something about what the analysand herself considers to be symptomatic must be sharply distinguished from the paranoiac's conviction that the analyst can read her mind, a conviction based at least in part on the belief that the analyst is putting thoughts and impulses into her head. The position of the omniscient persecutory other is one that the analyst wants to avoid being put into!)

Insofar as analysts tend to expect analysands to situate them in the place of knowledge as a regular part of the transference, they tend to sense that there is no transference at all in cases in which analysands do not attribute any special knowledge to them. Due no doubt to their extensive work with neurotics, they so closely associate transference with the analysand's projection onto them of the subject supposed to know that when there is no sign of this projection, there seems to them to be no sign of transference whatsoever. Rather than say that there is no transference, strictly speaking, in analytic work with psychotics, we might do better to say that *the transference takes place solely at the imaginary and real levels with psychotics, not at all three levels* (imaginary, symbolic, and real) *as it does with neurotics.* This is not to say that the analyst's work with psychotics bypasses speech: The majority of the work continues to involve speech, but speech in this case does not bring the symbolic into play, language and speech being imaginarized (that is, rendered imaginary) in psychosis.

The psychotic may well transfer something, in the strict sense of the term, onto the analyst—evil or persecutory intentions, for example, which were part of the psychotic's experience with prior figures in her life—but what she transfers, when indeed she does transfer, is imaginary in character insofar as it involves either a passionate love or a passionate hatred on the part of the other like herself. In other words, such a transference may be above all erotic in nature (erotomania being the delusional conviction that the analyst loves the analysand) or aggressive (persecutory paranoia being the delusional conviction that the analyst wants to cruelly enjoy, exploit, and/or destroy the analysand).[20] Transference in psychosis tends to involve passion, not knowledge (except insofar as it is related to passion), whereas in neurosis it tends to involve both.

---

[20] For a discussion of the different forms of paranoia, see Freud's (1911/1958, pp. 63–65) case history of Schreber.

What Kind of Other Is the Analyst for the Psychotic?

Being as far outside of transference as they are outside of discourse, these subjects may nevertheless come to confide in a few of their fellow beings. It is not transference, strictly speaking, for transference is a symbolic relationship that includes the subject supposed to know, and the schizophrenic does not enter there. But it leaves a possible place for an object relationship, which is both imaginary and real, that is easily confused with transference, a place from which one can sometimes obtain certain effects.

— *Soler* (2002, p. 123)

Since the symbolic dimension (another name for the unconscious) is missing in psychosis, there is no place in the psychotic's world for a symbolic Other, an all-knowing Other, a benevolent Other with whom a "symbolic pact" is possible (Lacan, 2006, p. 303; see also pp. 272, 308, 430, and 686). In the neurotic's world, the ground for such an Other is generally prepared (to put it in the simplest terms possible) by an at least sometimes kind caretaker who seems to know many things and who also enforces a law (moral, political, and/or religious) in the household—a law that is not strictly of his or her own making. Out of this ground grows the notion of a being who knows how to make things better when one is hurting, knows all of one's thoughts, knows when one has been good or bad, and who rewards or punishes, not arbitrarily, but rather on the basis of a rule that is discernible, even if only with great mental exertion on the child's part. The notion of such a being is often associated at first with a parent, then with a teacher or religious figure, and eventually with the Supreme Being, the neurotic's Other generally being characterized by omniscience and justice (individual parents, teachers, and religious figures are usually found by the child not to live up to the lofty ideals of omniscience and absolute justice she had initially associated with them).

Although the psychotic may well believe in God, the parental Other the psychotic has come to know is not an Other of knowledge but rather of cruel, exploitative jouissance.[21] The psychotic has generally not been exposed (or only for a very short period of time, or only later in life) to a kind, knowledgeable caretaker who enforces a law in the household that is not strictly of his or her own making; the ground has been prepared only for an Other who wishes to consume or annihilate the subject's very being, an Other who strives to penetrate and take possession of the subject's very body and soul, an Other who seeks to exploit and/or dispossess the subject of her very mind.

---

[21] As Miller (1993, p. 11) put it, the Other exists in paranoia not as symbolic but as real.

Should the analyst be so foolhardy as to attempt to occupy the position of an authority for the psychotic, the position of someone with authoritative knowledge of what really makes the psychotic tick, he is likely to quickly find himself associated with this cruel, persecutory Other who is experienced as taking advantage of the psychotic, sexually exploiting her, stealing her thoughts, and generally ruining her life (of course, not all of these elements need be present in any one particular case).

It is the attempt by the analyst to occupy a symbolic position (that of the Other with whom a symbolic pact is possible) for someone when there has been no precedent for such a position in that person's history—that is, no establishment of the symbolic order as such—that is most likely to trigger a psychotic break. (Outside of the therapeutic context, it is often when a psychotic's superior officer, boss, or landlord takes a firm or severe stand with the psychotic that she becomes destabilized or has a break; such figures unknowingly try to occupy a position in the psychotic's psychical space that is simply not there.[22]) It is therefore crucial that the analyst know his place and stay in it; when he is not sure of the diagnosis, he must tread very lightly, being sure to avoid abrupt punctuations and scansions and to steer clear of interventions or insinuations that might be taken as persecutory.

What is the place he must stay in, once he is quite sure that his analysand is psychotic? Since he cannot occupy a symbolic role, he is left with an imaginary role (to put it as simply as possible). Although the imaginary dimension can be characterized by rivalry and jealousy (see Fink, 2005b), the important aspect of the imaginary relationship here is that analyst and analysand are qualitatively the same: They are more like siblings than like parent and child. They are similar to each other in many respects—they are "semblables," as Lacan put it, people who resemble each other more than they differ.

The analyst must continue to avoid the pitfalls of the imaginary, as I described them in Chapter 1. He must not try to understand everything the analysand says in terms of his own experience and must not constantly concern himself with what it means about him (e.g., whether the analysand finds him dull-witted or intelligent, well dressed or sloppy). None of that is of any more value with the psychotic than it was with the neurotic. Nor is self-disclosure of any more value with the psychotic than it was with the neurotic: The less the analysand knows about the analyst the better, generally speaking. Although the psychotic may situate the analyst in an imaginary position from the outset,

---

[22] Imagine trying to have a chess piece land on a certain square on a chess board when that square has simply been cut out of the board.

that does not mean that the analyst must agree to occupy all facets of that position.[23]

Nevertheless, the analyst may occasionally do well to be less opaque and instead more transparent with his psychotic analysands regarding what has led him to reschedule sessions or regarding where he is going on vacation; the scenarios that neurotics are likely to imagine about the analyst's reasons for rescheduling or about the analyst's pastimes and leisure activities when he gives no details about them often provide good grist for the analytic mill, whereas certain psychotics are more likely to imagine persecutory scenarios in which the analyst is conspiring with certain authorities to have them involuntarily committed or is traveling somewhere to check up on their stories. For similar reasons, the analyst should generally avoid using the couch in work with psychotics: It is better for them to see what he is up to than to imagine he is up to no good behind their backs (there are other more complex reasons to avoid the couch with psychotics as well).

It is also of value to ally with the psychotic in a way that one would generally avoid with the neurotic (unless, for example, the neurotic analysand is a child). Whereas with a neurotic the analyst should keep his own ideas about what is good or bad for the analysand to himself as far as possible, intervening in the decisions the neurotic makes and the acts she engages in as rarely as possible (indeed, only when they threaten to put at risk the continuation of the analysis by endangering the neurotic's life and livelihood), it may be helpful at times—once one has gained the analysand's trust and has considerable knowledge of the analysand's life, interests, abilities, and current circumstances—to encourage the pursuits of the psychotic analysand that seem to foster stabilization and to discourage those that have often led to considerable conflict in her life, if not outright psychotic breaks. The analyst strives to act here in certain ways like the best friend one could ever possibly hope for—a friend who encourages one's pursuits not for his own purposes or profit but, to the highest degree possible, for what he assesses to be one's own best interest.[24] Such an assessment cannot be made quickly or definitively; it requires extensive knowledge of the analysand and must be open to continual revision.

---

[23] Note that, although the neurotic may situate the analyst in a symbolic position from the outset, the analyst does not agree to occupy that position with the neurotic, preferring to occupy the position of the cause of the analysand's desire (see, for example, Lacan, 2007, p. 41, and Fink, 1997, Chapter 4).

[24] My suspicion is that the majority of psychoanalysts today, at least in the English-speaking world, adopt this sort of "best friend" position with all of their analysands, regardless of diagnosis, working with them on the basis of their own-view of reality and of what is good for people, rather than adopting different positions with neurotics and psychotics.

Garcia-Castellano (IRMA, 1997) provided a good example of this approach in his discussion of his work with a psychotic woman who, in the second year of her analysis with him, made the "improbable discovery" that she had been raped by her father, her mother, and several brothers, even though she had absolutely no recollection of this having ever happened. Garcia-Castellano wrote:

> She was perplexed by the absence of any memory of the event, but found traces of what had happened to her in her body: her pains. It should be noted that her speculations regarding the subject remained confined, for the most part, to the analytic setting. She envisioned initiating an actual inquiry— a project laden with violence—but I discouraged her from doing so. She acquiesced, saying, "It's better that I speak and cry about the rape here rather than elsewhere." Years later, when she mentioned this intervention on my part, the patient indicated that she had "felt" at that time "a kind hand that was protecting me." (pp. 104–105)

Whereas with neurotics the analyst attempts to avoid imposing or in any way conveying his own notions of what is good and bad, striving to act in such a way as to further the analysand's Eros rather than her supposed Good (see Lacan, 1991, and Fink, 1999),[25] he does, in some sense, the opposite with psychotics: He must strive to further the psychotic analysand's good, as best as he can discern it, to help limit, localize, and give meaning to the jouissance she has that she finds unbearable and incomprehensible and that threatens to destabilize her when it comes over her (and give a pacifying meaning to the malicious will to jouissance she may sometimes believe she has detected in others).

The Helpful Other

What the psychotic requests is a witness and not a subject supposed to know.
— *Forbes and colleagues (1988, p. 321)*

The analyst's position with psychotics should be that of the "helpful other," as I propose to call it, not that of the knowledgeable Other.[26] Exactly who or

---

[25] In discussing work with neurotics, Lacan (2005a, p. 19) said "Psychoanalysts know very well that it is not by wanting what is good for people that they manage to bring it about and that, most of the time, it is even the contrary. . . . It would be helpful if more people realized that it is not because one wants so badly to do good things for one's fellow man that one actually does him good."

[26] Although these two different others may be easy to distinguish in theory, they are not always so easy to distinguish in practice, for the helpful other may be attributed a certain kind of

what is this helpful other, and is the psychotic looking for such an other when she seeks therapy?

At least one of the things that the neurotic is often seeking in coming to therapy is recognition, and although the analyst does not provide recognition of what it is that she would like him to recognize—her position as a victim or martyr, for example—the analyst lets her know that he *hears* what she is saying, but that *what he recognizes is the desire that lurks within her discourse of which she herself is unaware*. In other words, rather than recognize her alienation in some sense, the analyst seeks to emphasize, bring out, and recognize the desire within her for something else.

What does a psychotic want in coming to speak to a therapist? And does the analyst *refuse* to give the psychotic what she wants, as he does in work with neurotics? In therapy, psychotics seem to seek someone who will listen and who will not immediately tell them that what they are saying is part of their illness and should be forgotten about. They will continue to talk with someone who accepts to be a *witness* to what has happened to them and what is still happening to them without judging it, without criticizing it, and without necessarily believing or disbelieving it—someone who is able to accept it within a certain context, that context being the confines of the analytic situation. (While it may be helpful to the analyst to adopt the same position in some of the preliminary meetings with neurotics, they are likely to consider the analyst to be a simpleton or a dupe should he continue to adopt that position beyond a certain point.)

---

knowledge—a knowledge, for example, of how to get what one wants from the system (e.g., from social service agencies that provide housing, food stamps, healthcare, unemployment, disability, and so on) or a knowledge of psychiatric medications, herbal remedies, physical therapies, good hygiene, exercises, and so on that the patient finds helpful. Note that the kind of knowledge involved here has nothing to do with the patient's "inner life," nothing to do with the why and wherefore of her actions, and nothing to do with the cause of her distressing thoughts, hallucinations, and so on.

But even this is not entirely true, for the patient may very well come to think that the reason she was experiencing such thoughts and hallucinations was because she was having difficulty sleeping, a problem that could potentially be resolved by a coach's or doctor's recommendation that she do more exercise, not eat so close to bedtime, and stop reading or watching television in bed before turning the lights out. In other words, this helpful other could be attributed *a knowledge of the cause of her problems*, at a certain level.

The inner versus outer distinction becomes blurry here: "Exterior causes" could be seen to be the cause of painful "inner states." We can nevertheless note that patients for whom only the helpful other exists never seem to expect the analyst to know anything about early events in their lives that might have contributed to their current difficulties, to know anything about the kinds of family configurations that lead to the kinds of problems they complain of (except perhaps the usual banalities of "sexual abuse" and ADHD), and so on.

This does not mean that the analyst is required to accept all of the psychotic's actions outside of the analytic setting, but he must at least accept what she has to say within what we might call the "parenthesis" of the analytic setting. This allows the analysis to be situated in a different place than the rest of the patient's life—in a place that is isolated, separated off, or bracketed off from everyday life, in a place in which words can be taken very seriously, even though they need not imply any specific actions. A fabric of meaning can be spun, partially unwoven and rewoven, and elaborated in great detail without implying that anything in particular be done outside the consulting room (for an example of this, see Fink, 2001).

One might be tempted to think that just as the neurotic, in coming to therapy, spontaneously situates the analyst in the position of the knowledgeable Other and tries to work out her conflict with this abstract authority figure via the analyst, the psychotic spontaneously situates the analyst in the position of the persecutory Other and tries to work out her conflict with this obscene, lethal Other via the analyst. But the psychotic is not necessarily looking to transfer the imago or role of the persecutor in her everyday life onto the analyst to "work it out" in the therapy setting. This may happen more often than the analyst likes, but it is usually the result of his own missteps, owing to his mistaken agenda about how things should proceed, about the kind of things the patient should talk about and not talk about, and the kind of interventions he should make.

Whereas the analyst is most helpful in treating neurosis when he lends himself to any and every projection the neurotic makes onto him (assuming he proceeds to put those projections to the work of interpretation), the analyst is not a "helpful other" to the psychotic when he lends himself to any and every projection. While the analyst neither accepts nor rejects the neurotic's projections and tries to discern what is behind them, as it were, he must do his best to dispel any of the psychotic's projections that seem to situate him as this dangerous Other who enjoys at the psychotic's expense.

This may be more easily said than done, especially when the analyst knows little about the analysand. As I said in Chapter 7, once a transferential projection has been made, everything the analyst says thereafter is heard as coming from the person he is imputed to be by the analysand; he cannot find a place to stand outside of the transference (a metaposition or "transference of the transference") and may find himself digging himself in deeper instead of defusing the situation as he had hoped. An unswervingly supportive stance and direct statements like "I haven't the slightest interest in taking your ideas from you," "I would never exploit you in any such way," and "I have never tried to get you fired" are the best one can usually do and fortunately often suffice.

Therapeutic Goals

The notion that the psychotic is outside of discourse allows us to situate what creates a stumbling block for psychoanalysis. It does not mean that psychotic subjects cannot seek out analysts—experience proves that they do—but the use they make of them is not the analysis of the unconscious.

— Soler (2002, pp. 97–98)

As we have seen, the neurotic's ego is, in the vast majority of cases, too strong for its own good. It is so strong and rigid that repression occurs whenever one of the neurotic's own sexual or aggressive thoughts does not fit in with her view of herself, leading to the return of the repressed in symptoms. There would be no symptoms were the ego too weak to push such impulses outside of itself. Thus one of the goals of analysis with neurotics is to loosen up the rigidity of the ego, for it is that very rigidity that requires so many things to be put out of mind. To do so the analyst calls into question or looks for holes in the wholes the ego is constantly reconstituting in its attempt to rationalize the analysand's behavior and impulses. The analyst deconstructs the analysand's view of herself, which constantly recrystallizes in such a way that it excludes a part of herself.[27]

The psychotic's ego is, on the contrary, fragile in certain respects. The ego is never sealed off or totalized in psychosis because the symbolic dimension is never instated (see Fink, 1997, Chapter 7). It remains open or incomplete, in some sense: There is, we might say, a hole in the psychotic's ego and it is, figuratively speaking, when the analysand gets too close to the hole in her ego that things fall apart and she is more likely to have a psychotic break.[28] Rather than trying to deconstruct the analysand's view of herself, rather than seeking out or picking holes in an overly totalized self-view, the analyst needs to help her patch it up, cover over the hole that is already there. This is a simplistic way of talking about what Lacan (2006, p. 582) referred to as "supplementation."[29]

Whereas in neurosis we seek to decomplete the analysand's view of herself and her world—which has been totalized due to the solid division between self and other brought on by the instatement of the symbolic register or axis

---

[27] The ego can be seen here to be like an ideological system that attempts to explain everything that goes on in a palatable way, providing ad hoc or what are considered to be acceptable reasons for what would otherwise be considered unexplainable or unacceptable events.

[28] Here we might say that there are gaps in the patient's ideological framework and that it needs to be extended to cover everything.

[29] Lacan (2006, p. 582) explicitly referred in this context to "supplementing the . . . void constituted by the inaugural *Verwerfung* [foreclosure]."

(see Fink, 1997, Chapters 7, 8)—in psychosis we seek to help her complete her view of herself and her world by somehow supplementing it. How can the analysand's worldview be shored up or supplemented?

First we have to be clear about what exactly is missing.

Fostering the Construction of an Explanatory Principle

The schizophrenic, Lacan says, "faces his organs without the help of an established discourse."
But what good is an established discourse when it comes to organs? It helps to establish limits,
standard barriers to jouissance. This is why every discourse brings with it some castration.
— Soler (2002, p. 121)

For the neurotic, there is always a little story, vague and confusing as it may be, about why her parents wanted her or perhaps did not want her at first but grew to love her. This little story tells her something about the place she occupies in their desire, and that space in their desire, small as it may be, is her foothold in life. At the most minimal level it explains the why and wherefore of her existence in the world, explaining why she is here. In this sense, the story serves as an explanatory principle.

But that is not the whole of the matter: What is she wanted for? That is the question.[30] If she has the sense that she is wanted only as an extension of one parent, or is expected to devote herself to that parent's "sexual service" (Lacan, 2006, p. 852), trouble ensues. Far better is it for her to be wanted for something else, something perhaps extremely obscure: "We just want you to be happy, dear" or "We want you to be good at whatever it is you want to do." As anxiety-producing as such parental desires often are to the neurotic, they make it clear to the child that she is separate from her parents in certain ways and has a place of her own in the world. There is a reason why she is here, a reason that does not necessarily go so far as to provide a mission or overriding purpose to her entire life, but that at least grounds her in the world.

The psychotic has no such consistent explanatory principle and nothing that grounds her in the world. Again and again psychotics recount how they were never treated by one or both parents as if they were people who had a right to exist, as if their bodies were inviolate and belonged to them alone, as if there were real limits to the things people could do to them and legal recourse that could be taken if those limits were not respected. In one case of

---

[30] The answer to that question, according to Lacan, in neurosis is provided in the fundamental fantasy. According to J.-L. Belinchon and colleagues (1988, p. 294), there is no fundamental fantasy in psychosis; there is only jouissance.

mine, the analysand's father claimed that when his wife got pregnant early in their marriage he wanted to keep the child (his wife, he asserted, had wanted to abort the fetus); the analysand's mother, on the other hand, claimed that the analysand's father had wanted her to give the child up for adoption, but she had refused. The two sides of the story were irreconcilable and were not able to tell the analysand why he was here, why he was wanted, to what extent he was wanted, and so on; in a word, they were not able to serve him as an explanatory principle.

In the absence of such an explanatory principle, some psychotics founder, never finding their feet, so to speak; others are lucky enough to find a *project* that gives meaning to their lives; others still, however, form delusional systems that, if allowed to develop fully, provide a special place in the world for the subject. This special place may be that of an international spy, a religious figure like Christ, or the wife of God (like Freud's Schreber)—in short, a place not necessarily assented to easily and in fact often objected to strenuously at the outset by the psychotic herself as well as by those around her. But such a delusional system generally provides more than just a modicum of stability and it often gives the subject a purpose and mission in life that is at least not thoroughly incompatible with life in her time and place on earth. In the best of cases, that purpose and mission is quite compatible with the goals pursued by those around her: She may be an educator (see the case discussed by Morel & Wachsberger, 2005, p. 79), a nurse, or a missionary, or engage in any number of other activities.

The psychotic sets out—via the delusional process—to generate explanations for things that happen in her world and, in particular, to foment an explanatory principle of her own. *The delusion constructed by a psychotic serves to make up for the lack of an explanatory principle; it supplements this lack.* Delusional activity, when it is allowed to run its course rather than being silenced by a therapist's intervention and/or medications, eventually leads—and this process may take years—to the construction of what Lacan (2006, p. 577) called a "delusional metaphor," a new starting point on the basis of which the psychotic establishes the meaning of her life and world.[31] The psychotic's delusions—when allowed to pursue their own course—move in a direction of creating a

---

[31] Lacan referred to such a new worldview as a delusional metaphor because it stands in for the more usual "paternal metaphor" found in neurosis, in certain respects, allowing words and meanings to be bound together in a relatively stable, enduring way. Freud's Schreber, for example, spent years fomenting a new, highly idiosyncratic cosmology, but the end result was a stable world of meanings—meanings not shared by many, but meanings all the same—in which a space, a bearable role, was reserved for Schreber. Schreber at last managed to find a place for himself in a world of his own making. Lacan (2006, p. 571) referred to that as the "terminal" point of Schreber's "psychotic process." It was once he

world in which the psychotic is assigned an important place, a critical role. The psychotic's delusional cosmology serves to explain the why and wherefore of the psychotic's birth and the purpose of her life on earth.

If there is as yet no sign of any delusional activity on the patient's part (if, for example, she is a prepsychotic), the analyst should strive to help the patient construct meanings that can sustain her in life without recreating the entire universe à la Schreber. There is no cookbook method by which this can be done: The analyst must try to discern what it is that threatens to destabilize the analysand and construct meanings with her that can be both satisfying and load-bearing, so to speak—meanings that can bear the stress of circumstances the analysand is likely to encounter in the course of her life. There is nothing necessarily finite about this process, and *the analyst should be prepared to form a relationship with the analysand that may last indefinitely*. Although the intensity of the work may be much greater at the outset than after 10 or 15 years, the analysand may continue to find it helpful for many decades to speak with the analyst from time to time to make it through rough spots.

If, on the other hand, there are already signs of delusional activity on the patient's part, the analyst must not take it upon himself to rid the analysand of the delusions. As Freud (1911a/1958, pp. 71, 77) pointed out in his commentary on the case of Judge Schreber, delusions are part of the curative process. Hallucinations and delusions are often very dear to the patient—she loves them more than she loves herself, as Freud said—and the patient may feel quite bereft should they be taken away from her through the imposition of electroconvulsive therapy or medication. The fact that she sees, hears, or believes things that others do not may be part of what makes her special, part of what gives her an exceptional role and purpose in life. The difficulty for the analyst is to witness the formation of the delusional system and to attempt to work within it. Without calling into question the most important aspects of it, and while working within a conceptual universe that may be quite foreign to the analyst's own, the analyst must at times try to persuade the analysand to see certain things a little bit differently—especially when the analysand has arrived at an interpretation of something that might well lead her to harm herself, harm someone else, or get her thrown out of her home or fired from her job.

---

reached that "terminal point" that he was able to successfully argue that he should be released from the mental hospital (I believe that he nevertheless destabilized again some years later).

Note that the pervert, like the psychotic, engages in an attempt to *supplement the paternal function* that brings the symbolic Other into existence. The pervert does it by staging or enacting the enunciation of the law; the psychotic does it by fomenting a delusional metaphor. See, on this point, Fink (1997, Chapter 9).

The analyst must also attempt to dissipate projections on the analysand's part that attribute evil intentions to people in the analysand's entourage and to smooth over the hurtful implications of things they have said to her. Should, for example, the analysand begin to feel that her friends are persecuting her with their repeated telephone calls when she has dropped out of sight for a few days and start attributing maleficent intentions to people who, to the best of the analyst's knowledge, have hitherto been the mainstay of her existence, the analyst might (as did one of my supervisees) propose the idea that they are simply concerned about her because they have not heard from her for some time. In other words, he might attempt to dispel the paranoid meaning the analysand has attached to her friends' behavior and palliate things, deescalate the situation. Soler (1997, p. 214) referred to this technique as "countering the Other's jouissance," for here the analyst attempts to stop the analysand from placing someone (or several people) in the position of the maleficent Other who will enjoy devouring or destroying her.

Stevens (2005, p. 193) discussed a case in which an analyst "let the air out of a [potentially dangerous] scenario" that her analysand had begun to play out in his mind. When the analysand told her in a session, "I think that I am becoming the spiritual son of my boss!" the analyst replied that he had been employed by that boss simply to work, simply to do his job. The analyst may well have suspected that it was only one short step in the analysand's mind from the boss's position of spiritual father to that of malevolent, persecutory Other.

The analyst must walk a fine line between witnessing the development of a new conceptual system and steering it, when necessary, away from potentially catastrophic collisions. Again, there is no cookie-cutter way of doing this; the analyst must adapt his technique to each different case and the unique way in which it unfolds. (For a few examples of how such cases unfold, see École de la Cause Freudienne, 1993, and Fink, 2001).

In all such cases, however, we are obliged to work as far as possible within the framework of the belief system to which the patient already ascribes, whether that be a fundamentalist religious framework or that of black magic. As objectionable as the patient's belief system may be to us as individuals with our own worldviews, it is not by imposing our own views from the outside, as it were, that we are likely to bring about any sort of stability. We need to try to help the patient find a place within her own belief system that she can occupy—an important place with a mission attached to it that can give her a project and something to guide her actions.

Caveat Sanator

*The work with psychotics will always involve finding a way for the subject . . . to bring
about conversions that civilize jouissance until it is rendered bearable. . . . The solutions that
can be most easily located are those that involve a supplementary symbolic, which consist in
constructing a fiction other than the Oedipal fiction and bringing it to a point of stabilization.*
— Soler (2002, p. 189)

Given that there are many different forms of psychosis, it is impossible to
provide a prescription for all of them. I would like, nevertheless, to briefly
discuss what might be thought of as a kind of intermediary stage between so-
called prepsychosis and psychosis as characterized by delusions. In this stage,
which I have encountered on a number of occasions in my practice and in
supervising others, the gap in the psychotic's meaning system is plugged up
by a particular term that serves as an explanatory device (we will see later that
this "intermediary stage" can be understood in terms of what Lacan calls the
"sinthome"). In the cases with which I am familiar, the term was not so much
sought out by the subject as happened upon, being provided by mental health
professionals who diagnosed the subjects with attention deficit disorder. ADD
(or ADHD) soon came to serve these subjects as an explanatory device, as
something that explained everything in their universe: why they turned out
the way they turned out, why things happened the way they did, and why they
had a certain place in the world. In one case, the label even provided the subject
with an existential project or mission in life: that of helping other people with
the same diagnosis and lobbying for benefits and privileges for other people
like himself. Even though it was certainly not the clinicians' intention to help
these subjects plug up a certain hole in their worldview, the signifying material
provided by contemporary "scientific" discourse was woven into the fabric of
the meanings the subjects gave to their worlds and led to a certain stability, to
stable belief systems.

When practitioners encounter such subjects, they are likely to be frustrated.
They are often convinced that they are, in fact, dealing with neurotics who have
simply latched onto a label that explains everything and lets them off the hook,
releasing them from responsibility for what has gone on in their lives. While
this of course occasionally happens, they must be careful not to try to call this
particular element of the patient's worldview into question too quickly, as it
may be the element that is covering over an abyss, covering over a gaping hole
in the person's history. As long as it does not lead the person to subject himself
to harmful medications or other nefarious forms of treatment, this "stopgap"

explanatory principle may serve the psychotic subject well and should not be undermined by the clinician. Georges (1997, pp. 39–47) reported that he was consulted by a young man who was convinced he was suffering from a banal case of depression and simply wanted the analyst to confirm that this was so to his father. Although Georges was tempted to call the man's conviction into question, he soon thought better of it, given the otherwise psychotic clinical picture and the fact that the term *depression* seemed to be grounding the young man in the world, providing him with a recognizable place in the world.[32]

"Borderline"

I must admit that the unconscious that I have to concern myself with at the theoretical level is also the personified unconscious of analysts' resistances. In fact, every post-Freudian development (in the chronological sense of the term) in psychoanalysis is the consequence of a major rejection of the unconscious.

— *Lacan (1969b)*

Some of the people who would be considered prepsychotic according to Lacanian criteria might well be considered "borderline" (or "narcissistic") in contemporary psychoanalytic parlance.[33] If, however, one adopts the perspective that neurosis and psychosis are distinguished by the presence or absence, respectively, of repression (or, to put it in more strictly Lacanian terms, that neurosis is defined by repression whereas psychosis is defined by foreclosure), and one further accepts the notion that repression is an all-or-nothing phenomenon—either it has occurred or it has not—then there can be no genuine borderland between neurosis and psychosis. It may, as I mentioned earlier, be extremely difficult at times to reliably determine the correct diagnosis, but it is the clinician who is hesitating or vacillating between the two diagnoses, not the analysand.

Although in certain theoretical approaches it is common to speak of patients becoming psychotic and then going into "remission," presumably in the sense of no longer being psychotic, and in other traditions it is not uncommon to

---

[32] The moral here is that we have to be careful not to try to remove, willy-nilly, what we take to be someone's symptom: It may well be a sinthome (as we shall see later) holding the real, symbolic, and imaginary together for that person. Even if it is not, it may still be serving as a certain kind of provisional button tie (discussed later). This example suggests how foolish it is to make symptom removal our primary goal in therapy.

[33] People who would be considered neurotic (especially hysteric) according to Lacanian criteria are also often considered "borderline" in contemporary psychoanalytic parlance.

speak of "psychotic and non-psychotic parts of the personality" (Bion, 1957, p. 269), *in the Lacanian tradition there is no continuum between neurotic and psychotic, but rather a sharp discontinuity*—nor is there any moving back and forth across the line between neurotic and psychotic at different points in one's life.

Whereas much of contemporary psychological, psychoanalytic, and psychiatric thinking has moved in the direction of classifying patients according to whether they employ "primitive defenses" as opposed to more "mature defenses" (so much so that the authors of the *DSM-IV* are purportedly considering adding a fifth axis to their diagnostic schema for the *DSM-V*, which will cover defense mechanisms; Millon & Davis, 2000, p. 25), I would propose that it is sounder to subsume the defenses under the broader structural headings of neurosis and psychosis.[34] Repression should not be viewed as just one defense mechanism among others on a long laundry list of defenses used by neurotics, but rather as the very condition for the possibility of those defenses (such as denial, displacement, isolation of affect, compromise formation, omission, conversion, turning against the self, reaction formation, suppression of affect, and undoing).[35]

In one of his early papers, Freud (1894/1966) said that through repression an idea is detached from its accompanying affect and the latter is then displaced onto another idea (in the case of obsession) or is converted into a bodily symptom (in the case of hysteria). He went on to say that the idea is thereby substantially "weakened" (p. 52) and "separated from all association," meaning that it becomes part of a "second psychical group" (p. 55)—in other words, it becomes unconscious. None of these transformations of ideas and affects (which, roughly speaking, correspond to displacement, conversion, and dissociation, respectively) would be possible if the unconscious had not already come into being through the action of what Freud (1914b/1957, p.148) called "primal repression." Although they cannot be equated with repression, strictly

---

[34] Note that what I am saying here contradicts Freud's (1926/1959, p. 163) recommendation that repression be viewed as simply one defense among others, a relatively late reversal of his long-held perspective that repression was far more crucial than the various defense mechanisms. Anna Freud (1946, p. 54) took this single, isolated statement of her father's as an invitation to establish an entire "chronological classification" of the defenses, which is, unfortunately, still bearing fruit today. Note, however, that even in that context Freud (1926/1959, p. 164) did not establish a continuum of diagnoses and defenses, but rather hypothesized that "before its sharp cleavage into an ego and an id, and before the formation of a super-ego, the mental apparatus makes use of different methods of defence from those which it employs after it has reached these stages of organization." In other words, Freud postulated a possible set of defenses that are used prior to the formation of the ego through primal repression (and that may continue to be used in the absence of primal repression—that is, in psychosis), and a separate set of defenses that are premised upon primal repression.

[35] Recall that, as I indicated in Chapter 1, many of these have a corresponding term in rhetoric: Displacement corresponds to metonymy, omission to ellipsis, and so on.

speaking, they cannot occur in subjects for whom primal repression has not occurred. None of them are possible in psychosis, where primal repression has not occurred. Freud used the term *verwirft* in his text from 1894 (which Lacan translated first as "rejected" and then later as "foreclosed") to characterize an idea as being *obliterated*, as opposed to being displaced, converted into bodily symptoms, or isolated from all other ideas. When such obliteration occurs, the person "behaves as if the idea had never occurred to [him] at all" (p. 58). In such cases, there is no creation of the unconscious through primal repression, and therefore the kinds of defenses available to the neurotic do not function.[36] This theoretical perspective leads to an either/or—primal repression or foreclosure—with no gray area or borderland in between.[37]

Sinthome

In the psychoses, what almost always has to be done is to tie [the three dimensions] together where a knot has trouble getting tied, to avoid an untying when the subject runs the risk of that happening, or to help retie a knot where the former knot came untied, as in triggered adult psychoses.

— *Nominé (2005, p. 198)*

In his later work (from approximately 1973 to 1981), Lacan approached neurosis and psychosis in a rather different fashion: Rather than say that there is no genuinely symbolic dimension, and thus no functioning unconscious, in psychosis, he postulated that while all three dimensions—imaginary, symbolic, and real—are generally present in psychosis they are not tied together as they are in neurosis and do not operate together in the way that they do in neurosis.[38] Simplistically stated, these three dimensions become firmly tied together in neurosis by the formation of a kind of knot—a knot that Freud referred to as the Oedipus complex and that Lacan generalized as the "paternal metaphor." The way the knot is tied is not always felicitous, and this may lead to all kinds of problems for the neurotic, but the knot is secure and its infelicitous effects can, in the best of cases, be substantially mitigated through analysis.[39]

---

[36] This is not to say that every single defense falls neatly on one side or the other of the neurosis/psychosis divide; projection, for example, occurs in both groups.

[37] Note that in rejecting this either/or perspective, we might say, following a line of thought I proposed in an earlier footnote, psychoanalysis has eschewed a neurotic logic in favor of a perverse (if not a psychotic) logic.

[38] Lacan suggested, however, that in schizophrenia all of the symbolic is real; hence there are not really three dimensions that could even potentially be tied together in schizophrenia.

[39] Lacan's (1973–1974, December 11, 1973) early account of this is somewhat more nuanced than the account I have given here. He claimed that in normal people (this is one of his rare uses of the term

In psychosis, on the other hand, the imaginary, symbolic, and real are never tied together via the Oedipus complex (theoretically speaking, the latter does not occur in psychosis, at least not in any complete form). In cases in which the psychosis does not manifest itself clearly until a somewhat advanced age, the three dimensions are held together in some other way, through some "nonstandard" knot ("nonstandard" from the point of view of the Oedipus complex)—a knot that comes undone when the psychosis is triggered. As it turns out, the three different dimensions can be held together in a range of ways, as we see in the many widely varying cases of psychosis when we examine the events that led to destabilization or triggering: loss of a partner who allowed the psychotic to play a specific role in a family and whose body served as a limit for the psychotic's jouissance; loss of the ability to engage in an artistic or otherwise creative activity due to an accident of some kind; loss of a job that served to give the psychotic a purpose in life. In each of these cases, we can retroactively hypothesize that what allowed the subject to keep her body image, language, and jouissance working together was not the Oedipus complex (or paternal metaphor), but rather a life partner, an artistic endeavor, or a particular occupation or activity, respectively.

What does it look like when the three dimensions do not work together as they tend to in neurosis?[40] Lacan (2005b) suggested that we can catch a glimpse of their failure to work together in the manner determined by the Oedipus complex by looking at James Joyce's character Stephen Daedalus (who is based heavily on Joyce himself), in *A Portrait of the Artist as a Young Man* (1916/1964). Stephen is at one point ridiculed by his classmates for suggesting

---

normal), the imaginary, symbolic, and real dimensions are tied together in such a way that when one of them is cut or eliminated, the other two do not hang together; in neurotics, on the other hand, when one of them is cut or eliminated, the other two do hang together. As he put it, "In the best of cases, when one of the rings of string [corresponding to the three dimensions] is missing, you must go crazy. . . . If there is something normal, it is that when one of the dimensions gives way for whatever reason, you must truly go crazy." Nevertheless, his most often repeated comment about neurosis in the 1970s is that imaginary, symbolic, and real hang together (that is, stay connected to each other) because of the durable way in which they are tied together. That way is symptomatic, even at the end of one's analysis, which is why one never arrives at a point at which there is no symptom at all. This is not to say, however, that one does not arrive at a point at which there are no symptoms that one finds bothersome.

[40] Note that such a question could not even, it seems, arise for someone like Bowlby (1982), for whom the body, the central nervous system, and instincts provide the initial and in some sense automatic unity of human beings. Since, however, we encounter people whose bodies do not operate in a coordinated manner—whose legs may be walking, for example, without any assistance from their torso or arms, or who may be straining to defecate without any sign of that effort appearing on their faces (see Bettleheim, 1967)—it seems clear that we have to explain how an at least partially unified sense of self and partially unified bodily functioning come into being in some cases (Lacan's first attempt was through the "mirror stage"; Lacan, 2006, pp. 93–100) but not in others.

that Byron was the greatest poet ever and is beaten rather brutally by them when he refuses to take it back. Curiously enough, he very quickly "bore no malice . . . to those who had tormented him" and "felt that some power was divesting him of that suddenwoven anger as easily as a fruit is divested of its soft ripe peel" (p. 82). Rather than conjecture that Stephen is simply masochistic—that is, that he perhaps enjoyed being roughed up by his classmates—Lacan (2005b, pp. 148–150) suggested that Stephen manifests an unusual relationship to his body here, for the anger that one would generally feel as a somewhat long-lasting bodily sensation is instead stripped away like a banana peel. Rather than becoming agitated, on edge, full of adrenaline, or steaming with rage, Stephen shrugs off "that suddenwoven anger" like a snake's old skin—without any transcendent thoughts of forgiveness (for example, thinking "forgive them Father for they know not what they do") or a firm resolve to get even with them sooner or later (that is, forming a symbolic plan of action). Rather, it is as if the thrashing did not go to the core of his being in any way; it did not affect him in the way that it would most others. It seems that Stephen's body—which can be associated here with the imaginary dimension insofar as the imaginary first and foremost concerns images (visual, tactile, auditory, and so on) of the body and its boundaries—is not connected to him in any fundamental way: He does not seem to sense that if his body is under attack, he as a person is being threatened; there does not appear to be any sort of unrecognized, unconscious enjoyment of the pain; he does not seem to feel that he has been notably wronged or violated; nor does the incident lead to the formation of a grudge.

This lack of connection between the imaginary register and the symbolic and real registers is a recipe for psychosis, according to Lacan, leading in many cases to depersonalization, out-of-body experiences, and so on (these should not be taken in isolation to be "signatures" of psychosis, however, as they can occur in neurosis as well).[41] Simplistically stated, Lacan suggested that it is Joyce's writing and the name that he makes for himself through his writing that prevents the imaginary from becoming completely detached from the symbolic and real in his case. In this sense, his writing serves him as what

---

[41] Deffieux (1997, pp. 16–17) reported on the case of a patient who told him that at age eight he was waylaid in the woods by a stranger who severely beat him and took out a knife with the apparent intent to cut his penis off. The patient then remarked to Deffieux, "I have no idea whether it hurt." When Deffieux later asked him to tell him as many details of the scene as he could remember, he said that when the man began beating him he recalled having abandoned his body, distanced himself from it, disappeared: "'For an instant I saw the little boy, it was me, and it was then that I fled,'" mentally, not physically (pp. 17–18). The tendency to disconnect from or flee from one's own body in such circumstances is commonly associated with psychosis, as is the tendency in men to be completely flummoxed (far more so than usual) when faced with sexual excitation in the form of erections, since there is no meaning they can attach to them (see, for example, Castanet, 1997, p. 25).

Lacan called a "sinthome" (which is an old French spelling of "symptom")—a symptom or knot that takes the place of the Oedipus complex for him—which almost literally allows him to keep body and soul together.[42]

Joyce's sinthome seems to have been particularly robust and did not require psychoanalytic assistance. Others for whom the imaginary, symbolic, and real are not held together by what we commonly refer to as the Oedipus complex are not always so lucky. A sinthome may have been found or constructed by the individual at one point in time, but it gives way or begins to come undone under the pressure of certain life circumstances that threaten the stability of the individual's solution to the problem of keeping body and soul together, so to speak. The analyst's goal in such cases is to help the analysand find a way back to the former stability or find a new situation that will lead to stability of the same or of a slightly different kind.

In certain cases—when, for example, the analysand's former stability stemmed from a close relationship with a child or life partner who has died—no return will be possible and something related or altogether new will have to be found. In other cases, a return may be possible once certain obstacles have been cleared out of the way. And in yet other cases, "the analytic bond itself can constitute a sinthome for the subject if the analyst sticks to the attempt to guarantee the new order of the universe [constructed by the analysand]. This is precisely what the subject expects: that the analyst become the witness, that he guarantee this order" (Kizer et al., 1988, p. 146). As I indicated earlier, this argues in favor of a lifelong engagement on the analyst's part with certain psychotic analysands, there being a structural reason in these cases for an analysis that has no internally necessitated end.

Generalized *Capitonnage*

A quiet delusional metaphor orients the life, thoughts, actions, and bonds of a subject with others far more frequently than we tend to think, without it seeming to anyone to be pathological.
— *Deffieux (1997, p. 19)*

In this section, I provide a highly compressed account of some of the theory behind Lacan's formulation of psychosis from the 1950s to the 1970s, which should be viewed as nothing more than an appetizer. I can only hope that my

---

[42] What Joyce managed to do by becoming *the* artist was to become "the father of his own name. It is a button tie that is not a metaphor, but it is a button tie all the same that short-circuits the Oedipus complex and that nevertheless supplements it" (Soler, 2002, p. 209). This is how, according to Lacan, Joyce managed to consolidate his ego. And this is, according to Soler, the precise definition of stabilization, in the strongest sense of the term, as opposed to a simple amelioration of the psychotic's troubles.

discussion here will inspire readers to look further into Lacan's various texts on the subject.

In reformulating "psychopathology" as he did in the 1970s, Lacan essentially postulated that we are all—whether neurotic or psychotic—held together, "knotted together," or "stitched together" in a particular symptomatic way. Although the type of knot or stitch that holds the majority of us together is related to the Oedipus complex, there are other types of stitches as well (one might refer to this reformulation as akin to the shift from the special theory of relativity to the general theory, and as indicative of a move away from a "deficit model," whereby psychosis is considered to involve a lack of something that is present in neurosis). Interestingly enough, in the 1950s Lacan had already employed a metaphor from the realm of knotting and sewing (the "button tie") when he reformulated Freud's Oedipus complex as the paternal metaphor, wherein the father prohibits the child's desire for the mother and the mother's desire for the child, and names the mother's lack or desire as being related to the father (she wants something from the father that the child cannot give her). The paternal metaphor, according to Lacan, permanently ties a loss of bodily jouissance to a name—that is, it knots together the child's loss of close contact with the mother and the "Name-of-the-Father" (which is both the father as the name of what the mother wants that goes beyond the child and the name given by the father to what the mother is lacking).[43]

Lacan (2006) referred to this first and indissoluble connection between language and the experience of a loss of jouissance as a "button tie" (*point de capiton* in French; p. 805), which is a kind of stitch or knot employed by upholsterers to keep the stuffing in a piece of furniture from shifting in relation to the fabric that covers it. Upholsterers do this by attaching a button to a thread that runs through the stuffing and the fabric, thereby holding them together *in relation to each other*, although they are not necessarily attached to any more structural part of the furniture (for example, the frame).[44] Viewed from the point of view of the theory expounded by Lacan in the 1970s, we can see that the button tie is already a sinthome, in a sense, since it is a stitch

---

[43] I will not address the broader social/political implications of Lacan's use of terms like "Name-of-the-Father" and "paternal metaphor" in this book, as I have done so elsewhere (Fink, 1997, Chapter 7). What seems to me most crucial here is the structure of something beyond the parent, *in the name of which* the parent makes certain demands on the child and *in the name of which* both the child and the parent make certain sacrifices.

[44] This is clearly related for Lacan to the connection in Saussurian linguistics between the signifier and the signified, which does not include any referent; Richards & Ogden (1923/1945) criticized Saussure for this and introduced a tripartite approach to linguistics that included the referent. See Lacan (2006, pp. 271, 351, 498, 836).

or knot that ties together language (the symbolic), the body (the imaginary), and jouissance (the real). The button tie constituted by the paternal metaphor can then be thought of as just one possible stitch among many.[45]

The sinthome can thus also be understood as a continuation or extension of the notion of *capitonnage* (quilting, anchoring, stitching, buttoning, or tying together), which Lacan developed starting in Seminar V and wrote about in 1960 ("Subversion of the Subject," Lacan, 2006, pp. 804–819). The concept of *capitonnage* grew out of his fundamental insight into how meaning is made: Just as the beginning of a sentence does not necessarily make any sense until one has heard or read the end of the sentence (see Fink, 2004, pp. 88–91), an event that occurs at one point in one's life does not necessarily take on meaning or make sense until afterward. Indeed, a crucial part of psychoanalytic work with neurotics involves examining critical moments from one's past and attempting to figure out what it was that made them so critical—indeed, what made them into major turning points. This often involves returning to a specific event again and again at different moments in the course of the analysis in the attempt to hone in on the libidinal stakes that were involved.

The kinds of events that analysands return to repeatedly vary widely in tenor and age of occurrence. In one case of mine, it was a hysterical scene by a mother shortly after regaining custody over her young child in which the mother cried bitterly about her treatment by the world and especially by men; her child was never quite the same again, having made a number of obscure and complex choices during and in the aftermath of that scene which took

---

[45] One could formulate this by saying that virtually everyone has a sinthome, the Oedipus complex (or paternal metaphor) being but one sinthome among others, albeit a particularly robust form of sinthome. Or one could say, as Miller (IRMA, 1997, p.156) did, that there are two forms of button ties (or stitches): the Name-of-the-Father and the sinthome.

Alternatively, one could try to force the language of symptoms in such a way that what Lacan referred to as the "metaphorical structure" of the neurotic symptom (where, for example, the neurotic is conscious of being furious at her father but the unconscious meaning of the fury seems to be related to the mother, the father having replaced the mother in a sort of substitutional metaphor) is generalized to include the psychotic "symptom." This would require us to construe the psychotic "symptom" as a substitutional metaphor in which the delusion takes the place of the perceived desire of the subject's mother to engulf or destroy the child:

$$\frac{\text{Fury at father}}{\text{Fury at mother}} \quad \frac{\text{Delusion}}{\text{Mother's desire}}$$

The difficulty that arises in this case is that the psychotic "symptom" does not necessarily take the form of a metaphor (perhaps it does most often in paranoia, and less often in other forms of psychosis). Hence the continued value of distinguishing between the neurotic symptom and the psychotic sinthome, or of using sinthome as the more general category, substitutional metaphors (like the paternal metaphor) being just one possible form of sinthome.

Miller (1998, p. 16) also proposed that the sinthome be considered the more global term, suggesting that it includes, in the case of neurosis, both the symptom and the fundamental fantasy.

many years to unravel and reconstruct. In another case, it was the untimely death of a mother and her husband's almost instantaneous remarriage that led her adult child to call into question the entire foundation of the family up until that time: Had the father actually ever loved the mother? Had the children truly been wanted by the father? The sudden revival of the father's libido and the disturbance this caused in the child's libido constituted a major event that the analysand returned to time and again in an attempt to "get a handle on it."

In yet another case, the event was a near-suicide by alcohol poisoning that was initially thought of by the analysand as nothing more than an early attempt to see what it was like to be drunk. It soon became clear that it also involved a strong identification with a father-like figure from a comic book series and hence with the analysand's own alcoholic father. The analysand's struggles with his mother later led to the realization that he was no doubt trying to deprive her of something, even if it had to be at the cost of his own life, and still later meanings attributed to the event involved reproaches he might have been making to his father as well. The struggles occurring between the analysand and each of his family members came progressively into focus, and the initial event or situation (which I will refer to here as S_1) was given a whole series of meanings—meanings that did not necessarily cancel each other out or contradict each other, but that each presented a piece of the puzzle—based on what had thus far been elaborated in the analysis (in other words, on later events or situations, each of which I will refer to here as an S_2). A neurotic analysand attempts in this way to tie down or fix the meaning of an earlier event retroactively, years or even decades after the fact, each rereading serving to tie down (*capitonner*) the meaning momentarily, some rereadings tying down the meaning for longer periods than others. Note that this work has the structure of a substitutional metaphor in the sense that one interpretation (expressed in words or signifiers) is put in the place of another, a new one in the place of an old one.

Each of the new meanings achieved serves as a kind of anchor (even if it is only temporary or provisional), tying together the realms of meaning and experience for the analysand, and each is structured like the major anchor Lacan referred to as the "paternal metaphor" (which puts the Name-of-the-Father in the place of the mother's desire and/or the child's desire for the mother; see Lacan, 2006, p. 557). Once the first button tie constituted by the paternal metaphor has been put in place, other stable meanings (that is, other button ties) can be established—and reestablished, when necessary, through the work of analysis. Each of these meanings has an effect on the analysand's unconscious, which Lacan denoted with the symbol $\mathbf{S}$ (designating the subject,

S, as divided into conscious and unconscious, which Lacan often referred to as the "barred subject").

This highly abbreviated discussion has allowed me to assemble virtually all of the elements (known as "mathemes") of what Lacan considered to be the fundamental structure of signification itself, which is clearly operative in neurosis but not in psychosis:

$$\frac{S_1}{\cancel{S}} \rightarrow \frac{S_2}{a}$$

Without going into all of the details of this formulation,[46] let me simply note that both terms that appear on the bottom line, the barred subject and object a, have to do with a certain fixity or even fixation: a fixity of meaning in the case of the barred subject, and a fixation of the subject's desire in the case of object a. Object a is Lacan's term for what most primordially causes one's desire, what most fundamentally arouses one's desire (as opposed to the plethora of concrete objects in the world that one's desire might alight upon). The cause of the neurotic's desire is, generally speaking, quite specific, according to Lacan, even if it is extremely difficult to describe; examples of object a include a particular way of being looked at ("the gaze"), a particular tone or timbre of voice, the breast, and so on. The essential notion here is that the neurotic's desire is aroused by one particular object (even if, like the gaze, it is not terribly object-like in quality) and by little else.

The fundamental structure of signification, which is instated in neurosis, implies both fixity of meaning and fixation of desire. Fixity of meaning implies limitation of who and what one is—in other words, castration, in the psychoanalytic sense of the term—and fixation of desire implies limitation of jouissance, not unlimited, unbounded, uncontrollable jouissance.

In psychosis, we often fail to find such fixity or fixation. What psychoanalysts have pejoratively referred to as "narcissism" (as in "narcissistic personality disorder") and as "grandiosity" can be better understood as *a lack of limitation*. For in psychosis no initial button tie is ever established—the paternal metaphor is never instated, meaning that Oedipalization does not occur—which implies that no other specifically signifying connections between the realms of experience and meaning can be established either. We do not find in analytic work with psychotics that they return to the same event again and again, each time

---

[46] Lacan (2007) eventually came to refer to this formulation as the "Master's discourse." The reader can find discussions of it in Fink (1995, Chapter 9) and in Fink (2004, Chapter 5), where I discuss the parallelism between this discourse and Lacan's "graph of desire," which is based on the button tie.

giving it new meanings that flesh out other facets of the experience.[47] They are unable to produce an S_2 that would retroactively tie down the meaning of an earlier event (imagine an arrow running backward from S_2 to S_1 in the fundamental structure of signification just depicted), a new interpretation that would take the place of an old interpretation, thereby constituting a substitutional metaphor. What they are able to articulate simply constitutes a series of new events (a series of S_1s, so to speak), each of which seems to operate independently of the others, none of them retroactively affecting the prior ones in such a way as to "close signification"—that is, provisionally pin down their signification (Soler, 2002, pp. 95–96). In the case of the neurotic, on the other hand, the production in the course of the analysis of a new S_2 has an important impact on the subject as split between conscious and unconscious insofar as the new interpretation hits something that had previously been unconscious.

What we often find in psychosis, instead, is a difficulty stopping the flow or movement of ideas at any particular point—hence the difficulty of finding any suitable place (an S_2), any significant meaning that has been produced, on which to scand a session (as I mentioned in Chapter 4). Indeed, in mania we find what is often referred to as "derailment" or "flight of ideas," a movement of speech that seems unable to ever retroactively pin down or delimit any particular meaning with which the psychotic might be satisfied (*jouis-sens*). This inability is sometimes subsumed, in psychiatry, under the rubric of "thought disorders," a nebulous basket category, in my view, that needs to be articulated in terms of the very structure of meaning making.[48] Whereas it seems possible to drain certain painful events in the psychotic analysand's past of the morbid jouissance attached to them, the fixing of their meaning is far more difficult—as is the fixing or limiting of her jouissance, once the psychosis is triggered, for at that point her "body, rather than being the desert that it is for [neurotics], is laid siege to and traversed by an unspeakable and indecipherable jouissance" (Soler, 2002, p. 113).[49]

Object *a*, which also appears on the lower line of the fundamental structure of signification presented earlier, localizes jouissance for the neurotic in a durable and enduring manner—indeed, the neurotic often complains that she cannot find anyone, except in fantasy, who will speak to her in the tone of voice in which she wants to be spoken to, or look at her in the manner in which she wants to be looked at, there seeming to be no other way for her to experience

---

[47] One specific meaning can, of course, be provided by a delusional metaphor.

[48] The inability to provide an S_2 and thereby close signification may be related to what Bion (1959) called "attacks on linking."

[49] This is particularly true in schizophrenia, in which jouissance invades the body. In paranoia, the subject most often identifies jouissance in the Other (that is, thinks that someone else will delight in devouring or killing her).

jouissance. In psychosis, on the other hand, object *a* does not operate in the same manner, and the psychotic's jouissance may, when a break occurs, be difficult if not impossible to localize and limit.[50] This all too often leads the psychotic to try to localize and limit her own jouissance by mutilating or cutting out the "offending organs," the parts of her body that she experiences as becoming invaded by jouissance. As Miller (IRMA, 1997, p. 222) put it, "When castration is not symbolized, it seeks to be carried out in the real," which suggests that much of the cutting and self-mutilation we encounter in clinics today may well reflect attempts on the part of psychotics to carry out a kind of "real castration" (a physical castration) where no "symbolic castration" has been able to occur.

The analyst's goal is obviously to help the psychotic limit and delimit her jouissance without cutting herself to pieces, and to help her find a way to put a stop to the kind of sudden evacuation of all stable meanings that may occur during a psychotic episode. Since, however, the psychotic does not operate within the fundamental structure of signification depicted earlier, limits and meanings have to be found in other ways than they are found in work with neurotics. The work with psychotics is unpredictable and, as in all psychoanalytic work, the analyst must always be open to surprise and ready to use whatever presents itself. Stabilization with the help of an imaginary supplementation—that is, something in the imaginary dimension that can supplement or hold together the three registers that are not working together—is one fairly well-known and documented path; in the attempt to foster an imaginary supplementation, the analyst may encourage artistic pursuits to which the analysand is already inclined, whether photography, painting, sculpture, dance, music, or other arts (for an example, see Cambron, 1997, p. 100). Stabilization with the help of a symbolic supplementation is another well-known path, the analyst attempting to take advantage of a common propensity among psychotics to write (fiction, poetry, and so on), when he is not obliged, as he often is in cases of triggered psychosis, to simply witness and assist in the production of a delusional meaning system—a delusional metaphor that stands in for the paternal metaphor and, more generally speaking, constructs the symbolic dimension as a whole.

---

[50] In neurosis, object *a* includes what Lacan denoted as "minus phi," something related to castration (Lacan, 2006, pp. 823–826), whereas "in psychosis, the inclusion of minus phi in little *a* is problematic.... There is in psychosis an appeal to castration, in the guise of a subtraction, but since it cannot be accomplished in the symbolic register, it is incessantly reiterated in the real" (Miller, in IRMA, 1997, p. 227).

Lacan (2004, p. 388) commented that "In mania ... it is the nonfunctioning of object *a* that is at stake, not simply its misrecognition. The subject is not ballasted here by any *a*, meaning that he is delivered over to the pure, infinite, and ludic metonymy of the signifying chain, often without any possibility of being freed from it."

The treatment implications of Lacan's 1970s theory of psychosis broaden his earlier approach: The analyst need not simply try to either prevent a break from occurring or guide a delusional project in a nondangerous direction; other options now appear on the horizon as well, such as returning the analysand to an earlier stable state (restoring the knot to its earlier form, so to speak) or working toward a new stable state that need not necessarily be based on the delusional reconstruction of the entire universe. While few if any specific guidelines as to how to proceed are ever provided by Lacan, new therapeutic strategies are at least conceivable here.

Note that, unlike some analysts, Lacan did not believe that we can turn the adult psychotics who come to us into neurotics. In his view, if the paternal metaphor has not been instated prior to six to eight years of age, more or less, it will never be instated. Unlike Winnicott, Spotnitz, and certain other analysts, Lacan did not believe that patients can "regress" to all the earlier "stages of development" and go through them anew with the analyst. Someone who has reached adulthood and has become psychotic cannot theoretically become a subject split between unconscious and conscious at the end of her analysis. Although Lacan's views on the treatment of psychosis may not be as optimistic as those of other analysts, he nevertheless seems more hopeful about the prognosis for paranoiacs than for schizophrenics.

Concluding Remarks

When faced with someone who is insane and delusional, do not forget that you too are or were once an analysand and that you too spoke about what does not exist.
— Miller (1993, p. 13)

It should be clear that my discussion here of a Lacanian approach to the treatment of psychosis is very cursory, providing as it does only a thumbnail sketch of how the analyst should situate himself in the therapy and a few basic notions about what he should and should not do. Although my discussion earlier in this book of a Lacanian approach to the treatment of neurosis is far more elaborate, it covers the earlier stages of treatment far better than it does the later stages, and it certainly cannot be taken as a comprehensive guide: There will be cases to which it does not apply, cases in which it is not effective, and cases where basic rules must be bent at one point or another to allow the analysis to begin or continue. This is all the more true of my discussion of the treatment of psychosis here, a more complete guide to which I hope to provide on another occasion.

Afterword

Reading Freud in itself trains us.
— Lacan (1977b, p. 11)

IN MY ATTEMPT TO become conversant with other approaches to psychoanalytic theory and practice, I have noticed that analysts are often very poor readers of each other's work. A certain lackadaisicalness is built into the very reference format, which includes the name of the author and the date of publication but does not include any page number, adopted by many analysts and psychologists—the apparent implication being that what they are saying about that author's work is self-evident or widely agreed upon, and that there is no need to point to any particular passage or comment on it. Again and again in the course of preparing this book I found that what the authors were saying was anything but self-evident or widely agreed upon, and that even a cursory comparison of the commentator's interpretation and the original text revealed a considerable gap.

At a time in the development of psychoanalytic institutes and other kinds of training programs where students and faculty alike seem to concentrate on getting through the material faster and faster (whereas the field continues to grow rather than shrink) and are inclined to read nothing but secondary sources, I think it important to emphasize that there is no substitute for reading the original texts by important analysts. It is not, after all, Sandler, Mitchell and Black, or Segal—the authors of well-known commentaries on psychoanalytic thinkers—who are considered to be the expert clinicians and theorists (much less the writers of ever-more-prevalent textbooks, which are essentially commentaries based almost solely on other commentaries), but rather Freud, Klein, Winnicott, Bion, and so on. Analysts seem to take very little care in reading each other's work in such a way as to really get a serious feel for it.

273

This is true not only for writers of commentaries, but even for some of the best-known theoreticians: When, for example, Winnicott (1967/2005) referred to Lacan's (2006, pp. 93–100) article on the mirror stage, he retained little if anything of Lacan's original concept, and instead used the term "mirroring" to talk about something entirely different. Indeed, we might say that he borrowed nothing but the word *mirror* itself. Similarly, when Heimann, Racker, and Bion encountered the term *projective identification* in Klein's work, they clearly read a meaning into it that was their own, not Klein's. The most one could say, it seems, is that when a certain analyst was reading an article by another analyst, an idea struck him or her and he or she then attributed it to the author of the article (Lacan, too, occasionally seems to do this with Freud). This is quite a curious process, to say the least, for we might have expected analysts to try to claim originality for their own notions, whereas, in these cases at least, we perhaps see them seeking cover behind a "big-name" analyst, sneaking their own ideas in through the back door, as it were, using the same terms to mean something entirely different.

This greatly complicates the student's task: Analysts from virtually every school of psychoanalysis use the same words, but they mean vastly different things by them! Study of the history and evolution of psychoanalytic concepts seems indispensable to achieving a firm grasp of the field.

A study of introductory works on technique is no substitute for in-depth study of the major works on psychoanalytic theory and practice. I hope that my quotes from and discussion of Freud and Lacan will inspire the reader to consult the many works I have cited—and to consult them not just casually, for one often gets far more from reading such works again and again, and from reading them with a group of other people so that one is forced to articulate the main points aloud to others. Each clinician's technique must evolve over time through study and experience and as forms of pathology themselves evolve, and it is only on the basis of a profound knowledge of the foundations of psychoanalysis that practitioners can move technique in new directions that are not simply a rejection of psychoanalysis or a return to prepsychoanalytic views (those who cannot learn from the past are condemned to repeat it).

Technique Must Always Evolve

We need not, of course, make a habit of this, or indeed of any other policy in analysis, because as soon as the patient has grasped the new idea he immediately plays up to it and endeavours to fool us.
— Glover (1955, p. 177)

English-speaking analysts reputedly love to talk about technique whereas French-speaking analysts avoid it like the plague. The latter is especially true of Lacanians, but I think that they would do well to spend more time illustrating the implications of their ample psychoanalytic theorizing at the level of practice. Their aversion to discussing technique has led a number of English-speaking clinicians who have no formal training in Lacanian psychoanalysis to believe that they practice in a Lacanian manner whereas, in my view at least, they do nothing of the sort. When pressed on the issue, they are likely to claim one of following: (1) They are doing the same thing Lacanians are doing but simply calling it something else; (2) no one really knows what Lacanian technique is anyway, because no one ever describes it; and (3) since we are all, after all, faced with the same problems, mustn't we all be doing the same things with our patients? The French might perhaps deign to attempt to translate their theory into practice (or to "reduce it to practice," as U.S. patent law puts it) if they knew what people who were calling themselves Lacanians were doing or if they knew that their own terms—including that of the Other with a capital O (Bollas, 1983, pp. 3 and 11) and of dialectics and subjectivity (Ogden, 1992, pp. 517ff)—were being co-opted for utterly foreign purposes essentially designed to reduce the heterogeneity of the symbolic dimension to the homogeneity of the imaginary dimension. This seems to be occurring above all in the relational, interpersonal, and intersubjective schools. Ogden's (1994) so-called analytic third, for example, in no wise transcends the imaginary; indeed, it might well be equated with the imaginary axis itself (Ogden himself admits that it is not "third" in Lacan's sense of the symbolic that interrupts the dyadic relation; p 464).

It is crucial to indicate what kind of practice logically flows from one's theory—otherwise, clinicians may end up thinking that they are basing their practice on a particular theory when their practice would in fact be contraindicated by the theory. We are therefore required to provide a "theory of practice," just as we are required to discuss the practice of theory (building). One and the same practice may plausibly follow from several different theories, but I suspect that this is more often the exception than the rule (it seems to me to make far more sense to expect different practices to stem from different theories). At the present time in the English-speaking world, certain clinicians who are interested in Lacan's work are beginning to claim that their form of practice follows from Lacanian theory, whereas I suspect that no coherent conceptual link could be established between the two.

The translation of theory into practice is all the more urgent with regard to the treatment of psychosis; analysts, most of whom are not, in the best of cases, psychotic, can fairly easily deduce many elements of technique from the analyses they themselves go through, but they cannot extrapolate from their own neurotic experience in analysis to that of the psychotic. In other words, in the course of the adventure that is one's own psychoanalysis, the analyst-in-training tends to learn a good deal about the treatment of neurosis and precious little about the treatment of psychosis.

Perhaps every specific technique, every specific technical device, must at some point exhaust itself: Once the patient population becomes so familiar with particular psychoanalytic ideas and approaches, they can no longer have the impact that they had before. Such was the case with the kinds of interpretations sometimes made in the early decades of psychoanalytic practice, which targeted very specific Oedipal meanings. By the 1920s, Freud found that such interpretations no longer had any of the shock value that they had had prior to that time. Technique must thus continually evolve, but that does not mean that—in the search by certain analysts for "the next big thing"—the baby must be thrown out with the bath water: The general goal in work with neurotics of getting at what has been repressed must be maintained. In the analyst's lifelong learning about psychoanalysis (and loving it, hopefully) from study and from the adventure that is each new analysis he or she conducts, the guiding principle must remain: to have an impact upon the unconscious.

Where Is Objectivity To Be Found?

No matter how you articulate psychoanalysis, your articulation always tends to wear thin, but that does not stop analysis from being something else, all the same.
                                                                    — Lacan (1998b, p. 434)

A great deal of the analytic tradition has sought a basis for objectivity in clinical work in some utterly knowable relationship to reality—a reality thought to be independent of both analyst and analysand, and thus serving as a limit to the actions and speculations of both. This supposedly knowable reality is viewed as better known to the analyst than to the analysand at the outset of an analysis, but it serves as a sort of Other or objective referent for both of them, ensuring, in the view of many practitioners, that analysis does not become a *délire à deux*—an ungrounded, unmoored, unhinged dialogue about unicorns and leprechauns.

In the parts of the analytic tradition into which deconstruction and postmodernism have seeped, "reality" is no longer so sure a reference point and the psychoanalytic "frame" itself has been latched onto as the analysand's only remaining safeguard against the omnipotence of analysts left to their own devices—left to their own countertransference. (In Winnicott's view, the frame lets analysts express their hatred for their patients so they presumably will not have to express it in other ways.) Without the frame, analysts worry they will be working without a guardrail, without a net.

Lacanian psychoanalysis proposes that we look instead for secure landmarks in the symbolic dimension—that is, what the analysand actually says and all the meanings it can take on in the Other—and for reliable signposts in the real that resists symbolization (object *a*). These provide us with far more trustworthy and useful guidelines than do the trumped-up notion of an objective, knowable, external reality; the belief that respecting the frame can ensure anything other than that analyst and analysand find themselves in the same room regularly for a set amount of time; and the idea that the only fixed reference point for psychoanalytic practice is the patient's profession that he feels better and is "experiencing desired life changes" (Renik, 2001, p. 237). The first of these notions predominated in psychoanalysis during the first half of the 20th century, the second during the second half, and the third has been proposed for the 21st century. For Renik, this third approach gives the analyst "an outcome criterion that is relatively independent of his or her own theory and presumed expertise" (p. 238), but it would seem to suggest that a particular analysis I conducted would have been successful if and only if I enabled one of my analysands, who desired to achieve power over everyone and to humiliate everyone in relation to whom he had always felt inferior, to actually do so and to feel good doing so. This is tantamount, in the end, to adopting the capitalist adage that "the customer is always right."

As I indicated earlier, the only form of objectivity we can aspire to in psychoanalysis is work based on the symbolic material: the analysand's speech and the symbolic coordinates it provides us with. That is, after all, what allows us to discuss our cases with other analysts and allows them to form their own opinions of those cases— opinions that may well differ from our own. Their potential validity depends on the degree to which they explain the symbolic material of the case.

A Convergence in the Offing?

Theories are themselves marked by repression.
— *Miller (2002, p. 21)*

Kernberg (2001, pp. 534–538) provided an intriguing account of "the two major currents of the English language psychoanalytic mainstream," which he referred to as the "contemporary psychoanalytic mainstream" and the "intersubjectivist-interpersonal-self psychology" current. The Lacanian approach that I have presented in this book runs counter to virtually every technique Kernberg attributed to the contemporary psychoanalytic mainstream (early and systematic interpretation of the transference, a central focus on countertransference analysis, systematic character analysis, affective dominance, technical neutrality, and so on) and to many of the techniques he attributed to the intersubjectivist-interpersonal-self psychology schools (stress on countertransference and its occasional communication to the patient, emphasis on empathy, employment of a deficit model of early development, and so on). Kernberg went on to provide a brief account of what he calls the "French psychoanalytic approach," mentioning but never actually quoting or citing Lacan himself, and arrived at the following conclusion: "If the trend toward mutual modification of previously hotly defended differences continues, one might expect a degree of convergence in the French and English schools in the years to come" (p. 543). I hope it is clear from my account in this book that the Lacanian approach to psychoanalytic technique is not likely to converge any time soon with any of the English schools of which I am aware or that Kernberg mentions. The disagreements between them seem far too structural, based as they are on irremediable differences in theoretical perspective.

Bibliography

Ablon, J. S., & Jones, E. E. (1998). How expert clinicians, prototypes of an ideal treatment correlate with outcome in psychodynamic and cognitive-behavioral therapy. *Psychotherapy Research, 8*, 71–83.

Alexander, F., & French, T. (1946). *Psychoanalytic therapy: Principles and application.* New York: Ronald.

Aparicio, S. (1996). Le médium de l'interprétation [The medium of interpretation]. *La cause freudienne, 32*, 52–55.

Ariès, P. (1962). *Centuries of childhood: A social history of family life.* New York: Vintage. (Original published 1960)

Arnst, C. (2006, May 29). Health as a birthright. *BusinessWeek, 3986*, 30–32.

Basescu, S. (1990). Show and tell: Reflection on the analyst's self-disclosure. In G. Stricker & M. Fisher (Eds.), *Self-disclosure in the therapeutic relationship* (pp. 47–59). New York: Plenum.

Bauer, G. P., & Mills, J. A. (1994). Patient and therapist resistance to use of the transference in the here and now. In G. P. Bauer (Ed.), *Essential papers on transference analysis* (pp. 195–213). Northvale, NJ: Jason Aronson. (Original published 1989)

Belinchon, J.-L., Cabrera, A., Cortell, H., Duarto, M.-J., Garcia, M.-J., & Porras, J. (1988). Entrées en analyse du psychotique? [How psychotics enter analysis]. In *Clinique différentielle des psychoses* (pp. 291–296). Paris: Navarin.

Bettelheim, B. (1967). *The empty fortress: Infantile autism and the birth of the self.* New York: Free Press.

Bibring, E. (1937). Therapeutic results of psycho-analysis. *International Journal of Psycho-Analysis, 18*, 170–189.

Bibring-Lehner, G. (1990). A contribution to the subject of transference-resistance. In A. H. Esman (Ed.), *Essential papers on transference* (pp. 115–123). New York & London: New York University Press. (Original published 1936)

Bion, W. R. (1955). Language and the schizophrenic. In M. Klein, P. Heimann, & R. E. Money-Kyrle (Eds.), *New directions in psycho-analysis* (pp. 220–239). London: Tavistock.

Bion, W. R. (1957). Differentiation of the psychotic from the non-psychotic personalities. *International Journal of Psycho-Analysis, 38*, 266–275.

Bion, W. R. (1959). Attacks on linking. *International Journal of Psycho-Analysis, 40*, 308–315.

Bion, W. R. (1962). *Learning from experience.* New York: Basic.

Bleger, J. (1967). Psychoanalysis of the psychoanalytic frame. *International Journal of Psycho-Analysis, 48*, 511–519.

Bollas, C. (1983). Expressive uses of the countertransference. *Contemporary Psychoanalysis*, *19*, 1–34.

Bollas, C. (1987). *The shadow of the object*. New York: Columbia University Press.

Bowlby, J. (1982). *Attachment and loss* (Vol. 1). New York: Basic.

Brenner, C. (1990). Working alliance, therapeutic alliance, and transference. In A. H. Esman (Ed.), *Essential papers on transference* (pp. 172–187). New York & London: New York University Press. (Original published 1979)

Bruno, P. (1995). L'avant-dernier mot [The second to last word]. *La lettre mensuelle*, *140*, 5–6.

Cambron, C. (1997). D'une tache à l'autre [From one stain to another]. In *La conversation d'Arcachon: Cas rares, les inclassables de la clinique* (pp. 93–100). Paris: Agalma-Seuil.

Cardinal, M. (1983). *The words to say it*. Cambridge, MA: VanVactor & Goodheart.

Carey, J. (2006, May 29). Medical guesswork. *BusinessWeek*, *3986*, 73–79.

Carrade, J.-B. (2000). L'art de la coupure [The art of the cut]. *La cause freudienne*, *46*, 83–86.

Casement, P. J. (1991). *Learning from the patient*. New York & London: Guilford.

Castanet, H. (1997). Un sujet dans le brouillard [A subject in the fog]. In *La conversation d'Arcachon: Cas rares, les inclassables de la clinique* (pp. 21–26). Paris: Agalma-Seuil.

Castanet, H., & Georges, P. de (2005). Branchements, débranchements, rebranchements [Connections, disconnections, and reconnections]. In *La psychose ordinaire: La convention d'Antibes* (pp. 13–44). Paris: Agalma-Seuil.

Castonguay, L. G., Goldfried, M. R., Wiser, S., Raue, P. J., & Hayes, A. M. (1996). Predicting the effect of cognitive therapy for depression: A study of unique and common factors. *Journal of Consulting and Clinical Psychology*, *64*, 497–504.

Cottet, S. (1994). Le principe de l'interprétation [The crux of interpretation]. *La lettre mensuelle*, *134*, 1–2.

Decool, C. (1997). Une suppléance rare [An unusual supplementation]. In *La conversation d'Arcachon: Cas rares, les inclassables de la clinique* (pp. 27–36). Paris: Agalma-Seuil.

Deffieux, J.-P. (1997). Un cas pas si rare [A not so unusual case]. In *La conversation d'Arcachon: Cas rares, les inclassables de la clinique* (pp. 11–19). Paris: Agalma-Seuil.

De Masi, F. (2001). The unconscious and psychosis: Some considerations of the psychoanalytic theory of psychosis. In Williams, P. (Ed.), *A language for psychosis: Psychoanalysis of psychotic states* (pp. 69–97). New York & Hove, U.K.: Brunner-Routledge.

Eco, U. (1984). Horns, hooves, insteps: Some hypotheses on three types of abduction. In U. Eco & T. A. Sebeok (Eds.), *The sign of three: Dupin, Holmes, Pierce* (pp. 198–220). Bloomington, IN: Indiana University Press.

École de la Cause Freudienne. (1993). L'énigme & la psychose. [Enigmas and psychosis] *La cause freudienne*, *23*.

École de la Cause Freudienne. (1996). Vous ne dites rien [You aren't saying anything]. *La cause freudienne*, *32*.

École de la Cause Freudienne. (2000). La séance analytique [The analytic session]. *La cause freudienne*, *46*.

École de la Cause Freudienne. (2004). La séance courte [The short session]. *La cause freudienne*, *56*.

Ferenczi, S. (1990). Introjection and transference. In A. H. Esman (Ed.), *Essential papers on transference* (pp. 15–27). New York & London: New York University Press. (Original published 1909).

Fink, B. (1995). *The Lacanian subject: Between language and jouissance*. Princeton, NJ: Princeton University Press.

Fink, B. (1997). *A clinical introduction to Lacanian psychoanalysis: Theory and technique.* Cambridge, MA: Harvard University Press.

Fink, B. (1999). The ethics of psychoanalysis: A Lacanian perspective. *The Psychoanalytic Review 86, 4,* 529–545.

Fink, B. (2001). Psychoanalytic approaches to severe pathology: A Lacanian perspective. *Newsletter of the International Federation for Psychoanalytic Education.* www.ifpe.org/news_1001_p14.html

Fink, B. (2003). The use of Lacanian psychoanalysis in a case of fetishism. *Clinical Case Studies, 2, 1,* 50–69.

Fink, B. (2004). *Lacan to the letter: Reading* Écrits *closely.* Minneapolis, MN: University of Minnesota Press.

Fink, B. (2005a). Lacan in "translation." *Journal of Lacanian Studies, 2, 2,* 264–281.

Fink, B. (2005b). Lacanian clinical practice. *The Psychoanalytic Review, 92, 4,* 553–579.

Fliess, R. (1942). The metapsychology of the analyst. *Psychoanalytic Quarterly, 11,* 211–227.

Florence, J. (1984). *L'identification dans la théorie freudienne* [Identification in Freud's theory]. Brussels: Facultés Universitaires Saint-Louis.

Forbes, J., Galletti Ferretti, M. C., Gauto Fernandez, C. G., Nogueira, L. C., & Sampaio Bicalho, H. M. (1988). Entretiens préliminaires et fonction diagnostique dans les névroses et les psychoses [Preliminary meetings and diagnostics in the neuroses and the psychoses]. In *Clinique différentielle des psychoses* (pp. 315–324). Paris: Navarin.

Freda, F. H., Yemal, D., Alisse, M.-L., Aparicio, S., Barrère, L., Berthouse, E., et al. (1988). Forclusion, monnayage et suppléance du Nom-du-Père [Foreclosure, exchange, and supplementation of the Name-of-the-Father]. In *Clinique différentielle des psychoses* (pp. 148–160). Paris: Navarin.

Freud, A. (1946). *The ego and the mechanisms of defence.* New York: International Universities Press.

Freud, S. (1966). The neuro-psychoses of defence. In J. Strachey (Ed. & Trans.), *The standard edition of the complete psychological works of Sigmund Freud* (Vol. 3, pp. 45–61). London: Hogarth. (Original published 1894)

Freud, S. (1966). Project for a scientific psychology. In J. Strachey (Ed. & Trans.), *The standard edition of the complete psychological works of Sigmund Freud* (Vol. 1, pp. 295–397). London: Hogarth. (Original published 1895)

Freud, S. (1958). The interpretation of dreams. In J. Strachey (Ed. & Trans.), *The standard edition of the complete psychological works of Sigmund Freud* (Vols. 4–5). London: Hogarth. (Original published 1900)

Freud, S. (1953). On psychotherapy. In J. Strachey (Ed. & Trans.), *The standard edition of the complete psychological works of Sigmund Freud* (Vol. 7, pp. 257–268). London: Hogarth. (Original published 1904)

Freud, S. (1953). Three essays on the theory of sexuality. In J. Strachey (Ed. & Trans.), *The standard edition of the complete psychological works of Sigmund Freud* (Vol. 7, pp. 130–243). London: Hogarth. (Original published 1905a)

Freud, S. (1960). Jokes and their relation to the unconscious. In J. Strachey (Ed. & Trans.), *The standard edition of the complete psychological works of Sigmund Freud* (Vol. 8, pp. 9–238). London: Hogarth. (Original published 1905b)

Freud, S. (1959). Creative writers and day-dreaming. In J. Strachey (Ed. & Trans.), *The standard edition of the complete psychological works of Sigmund Freud* (Vol. 9, pp. 143–153). London: Hogarth. (Original published 1908)

Freud, S. (1955). Notes upon a case of obsessional neurosis. In J. Strachey (Ed. & Trans.), *The standard edition of the complete psychological works of Sigmund Freud* (Vol. 10, pp. 155–318). London: Hogarth. (Original published 1909)

Freud, S. (1957). The future prospects of psycho-analytic therapy. In J. Strachey (Ed. & Trans.), *The standard edition of the complete psychological works of Sigmund Freud* (Vol. 11, pp. 141–151). London: Hogarth. (Original published 1910)

Freud, S. (1958). Psychoanalytic notes on an autobiographical account of a case of paranoia [Schreber]. In J. Strachey (Ed. & Trans.), *The standard edition of the complete psychological works of Sigmund Freud* (Vol. 12, pp. 9–82). London: Hogarth. (Original published 1911a)

Freud, S. (1958). The handling of dream-interpretation in psycho-analysis. In J. Strachey (Ed. & Trans.), *The standard edition of the complete psychological works of Sigmund Freud* (Vol. 12, pp. 91–96). London: Hogarth. (Original published 1911b)

Freud, S. (1958). The dynamics of transference. In J. Strachey (Ed. & Trans.), *The standard edition of the complete psychological works of Sigmund Freud* (Vol. 12, pp. 99–108). London: Hogarth. (Original published 1912a)

Freud, S. (1958). Recommendations to physicians practising psycho-analysis. In J. Strachey (Ed. & Trans.), *The standard edition of the complete psychological works of Sigmund Freud* (Vol. 12, pp. 111–120). London: Hogarth. (Original published 1912b)

Freud, S. (1958). On beginning the treatment. In J. Strachey (Ed. & Trans.), *The standard edition of the complete psychological works of Sigmund Freud* (Vol. 12, pp. 123–144). London: Hogarth. (Original published 1913) [In German, see *Gesammelte Werke* (Vol. 8, pp. 454–478). Frankfurt: S. Fischer Verlag, 1945.]

Freud, S. (1958). Remembering, repeating and working-through. In J. Strachey (Ed. & Trans.), *The standard edition of the complete psychological works of Sigmund Freud* (Vol. 12, pp. 147–156). London: Hogarth. (Original published 1914a)

Freud, S. (1957). Repression. In J. Strachey (Ed. & Trans.), *The standard edition of the complete psychological works of Sigmund Freud* (Vol. 14, pp. 146–158). London: Hogarth. (Original published 1914b)

Freud, S. (1958). Observations on transference-love. In J. Strachey (Ed. & Trans.), *The standard edition of the complete psychological works of Sigmund Freud* (Vol. 12, pp. 159–171). London: Hogarth. (Original published 1915a)

Freud, S. (1957). The unconscious. In J. Strachey (Ed. & Trans.), *The standard edition of the complete psychological works of Sigmund Freud* (Vol. 14, pp. 166–215). London: Hogarth. (Original published 1915b)

Freud, S. (1963). Introductory lectures on psycho-analysis. In J. Strachey (Ed. & Trans.), *The standard edition of the complete psychological works of Sigmund Freud* (Vols. 15–16). London: Hogarth. (Original published 1916–1917)

Freud, S. (1957). A metapsychological supplement to the theory of dreams. In J. Strachey (Ed. & Trans.), *The standard edition of the complete psychological works of Sigmund Freud* (Vol. 14, pp. 221–235). London: Hogarth. (Original published 1917)

Freud, S. (1955). Lines of advance in psycho-analytic therapy. In J. Strachey (Ed. & Trans.), *The standard edition of the complete psychological works of Sigmund Freud* (Vol. 17, pp. 159–168). London: Hogarth. (Original published 1919)

Freud, S. (1955). Beyond the pleasure principle. In J. Strachey (Ed. & Trans.), *The standard edition of the complete psychological works of Sigmund Freud* (Vol. 18, pp. 7–64). London: Hogarth. (Original published 1920)

Freud, S. (1955). Group psychology and the analysis of the ego. In J. Strachey (Ed. & Trans.), *The standard edition of the complete psychological works of Sigmund Freud* (Vol. 18, pp. 67–143). London: Hogarth. (Original published 1921)

Freud, S. (1961). Remarks on the theory and practice of dream-interpretation. In J. Strachey (Ed. & Trans.), *The standard edition of the complete psychological works of Sigmund Freud* (Vol. 19, pp. 109–121). London: Hogarth. (Original published 1923a)

Freud, S. (1961). The ego and the id. In J. Strachey (Ed. & Trans.), *The standard edition of the complete psychological works of Sigmund Freud* (Vol. 19, pp. 12–66). London: Hogarth. (Original published 1923b)

Freud, S. (1961). The economic problem of masochism. In J. Strachey (Ed. & Trans.), *The standard edition of the complete psychological works of Sigmund Freud* (Vol. 19, pp. 159–170). London: Hogarth. (Original published 1924)

Freud, S. (1961). Some additional notes on dream-interpretation as a whole. In J. Strachey (Ed. & Trans.), *The standard edition of the complete psychological works of Sigmund Freud* (Vol. 19, pp. 127–138). London: Hogarth. (Original published 1925a)

Freud, S. (1961). Negation. In J. Strachey (Ed. & Trans.), *The standard edition of the complete psychological works of Sigmund Freud* (Vol. 19, pp. 235–239). London: Hogarth. (Original published 1925b)

Freud, S. (1959). An autobiographical study. In J. Strachey (Ed. & Trans.), *The standard edition of the complete psychological works of Sigmund Freud* (Vol. 20, pp. 7–74). London: Hogarth. (Original published 1925c)

Freud, S. (1959). Inhibitions, symptoms and anxiety. In J. Strachey (Ed. & Trans.), *The standard edition of the complete psychological works of Sigmund Freud* (Vol. 20, pp. 87–175). London: Hogarth. (Original published 1926)

Freud, S. (1964). New introductory lectures on psycho-analysis. In J. Strachey (Ed. & Trans.), *The standard edition of the complete psychological works of Sigmund Freud* (Vol. 22, pp. 5–182). London: Hogarth. (Original published 1933)

Freud, S. (1964). The subtleties of a faulty action. In J. Strachey (Ed. & Trans.), *The standard edition of the complete psychological works of Sigmund Freud* (Vol. 22, pp. 233–235). London: Hogarth. (Original published 1935)

Freud, S. (1964). Analysis terminable and interminable. In J. Strachey (Ed. & Trans.), *The standard edition of the complete psychological works of Sigmund Freud* (Vol. 23, pp. 216–253). London: Hogarth. (Original published 1937)

Freud, S. (1964). Splitting of the ego in the process of defence. In J. Strachey (Ed. & Trans.), *The Standard edition of the complete psychological works of Sigmund Freud* (Vol. 23, pp. 275–278). London: Hogarth. (Original published 1938)

Freud, S. (1964). An outline of psycho-analysis. In J. Strachey (Ed. & Trans.), *The standard edition of the complete psychological works of Sigmund Freud* (Vol. 23, pp. 144–207). London: Hogarth. (Original published 1940)

Freud, A. (1946). *The ego and the mechanisms of defence.* New York: International Universities Press.

Freud, S. (1985). *The complete letters of Sigmund Freud to Wilhelm Fliess 1887–1904.* Cambridge, MA & London: Harvard University Press.

Freud, S., & Breuer, J. (1955). Studies on hysteria. In J. Strachey (Ed. & Trans.), *The standard edition of the complete psychological works of Sigmund Freud* (Vol. 2, pp.1–307). London: Hogarth. (Original published 1893–1895)

Frieswyck, S. H., Allen, J. G., Colson, D. B., Coyne, L., Gabbard, G. O., Horwitz, L., & Newsom, G. (1986). Therapeutic alliance: Its place as a process and outcome variable in dynamic psychotherapy research. *Journal of Consulting and Clinical Psychology, 54,* 32–38.

Gaston, L. (1990). The concept of the alliance and its role in psychotherapy: Theoretical and empirical considerations. *Psychotherapy, 27,* 143–153.

Georges, P. de (1997). Paradigme de déclenchement: Un mot de trop [Triggering paradigm: One word too many]. In *Le conciliabule d'Angers* (pp. 39–47). Paris: Agalma-Seuil.

Gilet-Le Bon, S. (1995). L'interprétation: 'Apophantic' et 'oraculaire' [Interpretation: Apophantic and oracular]. *La lettre mensuelle*, *138*, 5–8.

Gill, M. M. (1982). *Analysis of transference. Vol. I: Theory and technique*. New York: International Universities Press.

Gill, M. M., & Hoffman, I. Z. (1982). *Analysis of transference. Vol. II: Studies of nine audio-recorded psychoanalytic sessions*. New York: International Universities Press.

Glover, E. (1931). The therapeutic effect of inexact interpretation: A contribution to the theory of suggestion. *International Journal of Psycho-Analysis*, *12* (4), 397–411.

Glover, E. (1955). *The technique of psycho-analysis*. New York: International Universities Press.

Goldfried, M. R. (1991). Research issues in psychotherapy integration. *Journal of Psychotherapy Integration*, *1*, 5–25.

Grandin, T. (1995). *Thinking in pictures*. New York: Doubleday.

Grandin, T., & Johnson, C. (2005). *Animals in translation*. New York: Scribner.

Green, M. F. (2001). *Schizophrenia revealed: From neurons to social interactions*. New York: Norton.

Greenson, R. (1990). The working alliance and the transference neurosis. In A. H. Esman (Ed.), *Essential papers on transference* (pp. 150–171). New York & London: NewYork University Press. (Original published 1965)

Greenson, R. (1967). *The technique and practice of psychoanalysis*. New York: International Universities Press.

Grosskurth, P. (1987). *Melanie Klein: Her world and her work*. Cambridge, MA: Harvard University Press.

Guntrip, H. (1971). *Psychoanalytic theory, therapy and the self*. New York: Basic.

Heidegger, M. (1982). *The basic problems of phenomenology*. Translated by A. Hofstadter. Bloomington, IN: Indiana University Press (Original published 1975)

Heimann, P. (1950). On counter-transference. *International Journal of Psycho-Analysis*, *31*, 81–84.

Heinlein, R. (1968). *Stranger in a strange land*. New York: Berkeley Publishing Co. (Original published 1961)

IRMA. (1997). *La conversation d'Arcachon: Cas rares, les inclassables de la clinique* [The Arcachon conversation: Unusual cases, clinically unclassifiable]. Paris: Agalma-Seuil.

Joseph, E. D. (1982). Presidential address: Normal in psychoanalysis. *International Journal of Psycho-analysis*, *63*, 3–13.

Joyce, J. (1964). *A portrait of the artist as a young man*. New York: Viking. (Original published 1916)

Joyce, J. (1975). *Finnegans wake*. London and Boston: Faber and Faber. (Original published 1939)

Kernberg, O. (2001). Recent developments in the technical approaches of English-language psychoanalytic schools. *Psychoanalytic Quarterly*, *70*, 519–547.

King, C. D. (1945). The meaning of normal. *Yale Journal of Biological Medicine*, *17*, 493–501.

Kirsner, D. (2000). *Unfree associations: Inside psychoanalytic institutes*. London: Process Press.

Kizer, M., Vivas, E. L., Luongo, L., Portillo, R., Ravard, J., & Réquiz, G. (1988). L'Autre dans les psychoses [The Other in the psychoses]. In *Clinique différentielle des psychoses* (pp. 135–147). Paris: Navarin.

Klein, M. (1950). *Contributions to psycho-analysis*. London: Hogarth.

Klein, M. (1952). Notes on some schizoid mechanisms. In J. Riviere (Ed.), *Developments in psycho-analysis* (pp. 292–320). London: Hogarth. (Original published 1946)

Klein, M. (1955). On identification. In M. Klein, P. Heimann, & R. E. Money-Kyrle (Eds.), *New directions in psycho-analysis* (pp. 309–345). London: Tavistock.

Klein, M. (1957). *Envy and gratitude, a study of unconscious sources.* New York: Basic.

Kohut, H. (1984). *How does analysis cure?* Chicago: University of Chicago Press.

Kuhn, T. S. (1962). *The structure of scientific revolutions.* Chicago: University of Chicago Press.

Lacan, J. (1965–1966). *Séminaire XIII, L'objet de la psychanalyse* [Seminar XIII, The object of psychoanalysis] (unpublished).

Lacan, J. (1966). Réponses à des étudiants en philosophie sur l'objet de la psychanalyse [Responses to philosophy students about the object of psychoanalysis]. *Cahiers pour l'analyse,* 3, 5–13.

Lacan, J. (1966–1967). *Séminaire XIV, La logique du fantasme* [Seminar XIV, The logic of fantasy] (unpublished).

Lacan, J. (1967–1968). *Séminaire XV, L'acte psychanalytique* [Seminar XV, The psychoanalytic act] (unpublished).

Lacan, J. (1968a). Proposition du 9 octobre 1967 sur le psychanalyste de L'Ecole [The October 9, 1967 proposition regarding the Psychoanalyst of the School]. *Scilicet,* 1, 14–30.

Lacan, J. (1968b). La méprise du sujet supposé savoir [The misunderstanding of the subject supposed to know]. *Scilicet,* 1, 31–41.

Lacan, J. (1969a). Intervention sur l'exposé de M. Ritter: 'Du désir d'être psychanalyste' [Remarks on Ritter's talk: "On the desire to be a psychoanalyst"]. *Lettres de L'Ecole Freudienne,* 6, 87–96.

Lacan, J. (1969b). Interview by Paolo Caruso. In P. Caruso (Ed.), *Conversaciones con Lévi-Strauss, Foucault y Lacan.* Barcelona, Spain: Anagrama.

Lacan, J. (1970–1971). *Séminaire XVIII, D'un discours qui ne serait pas du semblant* [Seminar XVIII, On a discourse that would not want to be mere semblance] (unpublished).

Lacan, J. (1971–1972). *Séminaire XIX, . . . ou pire* [Seminar XIX, . . . or worse] (unpublished).

Lacan, J. (1973). *L'Étourdit. Scilicet,* 4, 5–52.

Lacan, J. (1973–1974). *Séminaire XXI, Les non-dupes errent* [Seminar XXI, Nondupes go astray] (unpublished).

Lacan, J. (1974–1975). *Séminaire XXII, R.S.I.* (unpublished).

Lacan, J. (1975a). Introduction à l'édition allemande d'un premier volume des *Écrits* [Introduction to the German edition of a first volume of *Écrits*]. *Scilicet,* 5, 11–17.

Lacan, J. (1975b). La Troisième [The third]. *Lettres de l'École Freudienne,* 16, 177–203.

Lacan, J. (1976). Conférences et entretiens dans des universités nord-américaines [Lectures and interviews at North American universities]. *Scilicet,* 6/7, 5–63.

Lacan, J. (1976–1977). *Séminaire XXIV, L'insu que sait de l'une-bévue s'aile à mourre* (unpublished).

Lacan, J. (1977a). Ouverture de la section clinique [Inauguration of the clinical program]. *Ornicar?,* 9, 7–14.

Lacan, J. (1984). Préface à l'ouvrage de Robert Georgin [Preface to Robert Georgin's book]. In R. Georgin. *Lacan* (2nd ed., pp. 9–17). Paris: L'Age d'homme. (Original published 1977b).

Lacan, J. (1977–1978). *Séminaire XXV, Le moment de conclure* [The moment for concluding] (unpublished).

Lacan, J. (1978). *The four fundamental concepts of psychoanalysis (1964)* (J.-A. Miller, Ed., & A. Sheridan, Trans.). New York & London: Norton.

Lacan, J. (1988a). *The seminar of Jacques Lacan, Book I: Freud's papers on technique (1953–1954)* (J.-A. Miller, Ed., & J. Forrester, Trans.). New York & London: Norton.

Lacan, J. (1988b). *The seminar of Jacques Lacan, Book II: The ego in Freud's theory and in the technique of psychoanalysis (1954–1955)* (J.-A. Miller, Ed., & S. Tomaselli, Trans.). New York & London: Norton.

Lacan, J. (1990). *Television: A challenge to the psychoanalytic establishment* (D. Hollier, R. Krauss, & A. Michelson, Trans.). New York & London: Norton.

Lacan, J. (1991). *Le séminaire de Jacques Lacan, Livre VIII: Le transfert (1960–1961)* [The seminar of Jacques Lacan, Book VIII: Transference (1960–1961)]. (J.-A. Miller, Ed.). Paris: Seuil.

Lacan, J. (1992). *The seminar of Jacques Lacan, Book VII: The ethics of psychoanalysis (1959–1960)* (J.-A. Miller, Ed.,. & D. Porter, Trans.). New York & London: Norton.

Lacan, J. (1993). *The seminar of Jacques Lacan, Book III: The Psychoses (1955–1956)* (J.-A. Miller, Ed., & R. Grigg, Trans.). New York & London: Norton.

Lacan, J. (1994). *Le séminaire de Jacques Lacan, Livre IV: La relation d'objet (1956–1957)* [The seminar of Jacques Lacan, Book IV: The relation to the object (1956–1957)] (J.-A. Miller, Ed.,). Paris: Seuil.

Lacan, J. (1998a). *The seminar of Jacques Lacan, Book XX, Encore: On feminine sexuality, the limits of love and knowledge (1972–1973)* (J.-A. Miller, Ed., & B. Fink, Trans.). New York & London: Norton.

Lacan, J. (1998b). *Le séminaire de Jacques Lacan, Livre V: Les formations de l'inconscient (1957–1958)* [The seminar of Jacques Lacan, Book V: Unconscious formations (1957–1958)] (J.-A. Miller, Ed.). Paris: Seuil.

Lacan, J. (2001). *Autres écrits* [Other writings]. Paris: Seuil.

Lacan, J. (2004). *Le séminaire de Jacques Lacan, Livre X: L'angoisse (1962–1963)* [The seminar of Jacques Lacan, Book X: Anguish (1962–1963)] (J.-A. Miller, (Ed.). Paris: Seuil.

Lacan, J. (2005a). *Mon enseignement* [My teaching]. Paris: Seuil.

Lacan, J. (2005b). *Le séminaire de Jacques Lacan, Livre XXIII: Le sinthome (1975–1976)* [The seminar of Jacques Lacan, Book XXIII: The sinthome] (J.-A. Miller, Ed.). Paris: Seuil.

Lacan, J. (2006). *Écrits: The first complete edition in English* (B. Fink, Trans.). New York & London: Norton. (Pages cited refer to the page numbers in the margins that correspond to the pagination of the 1966 French edition.)

Lacan, J. (2007). *The seminar of Jacques Lacan, Book XVII: The other side of psychoanalysis (1969–1970)* (J.-A. Miller, Ed., & R. Grigg, Trans.). New York & London: Norton. (Pages cited refer to the page numbers in the margins that correspond to the French edition.)

Laing, J. R. (2006, June 26). Is your CEO lying? *Barron's*, 21–23.

Levenson, H. (1995). *Time-limited dynamic psychotherapy: A guide to clinical practice.* New York: Basic.

Lichtenberg, J., & Slap, J. (1977). Comments on the general functioning of the analyst in the psychoanalytic situation. *The Annual of Psychoanalysis, 5*, 295–314. New York: International Universities Press.

Little, M. (1951). Counter-transference and the patient's response to it. *International Journal of Psycho-Analysis, 32*, 32–40.

Little, M. (1990). *Psychotic anxieties and containment: A personal record of an analysis with Winnicott.* Northvale, NJ & London: Jason Aronson.

Macalpine, I. (1990). The development of the transference. In A. H. Esman (Ed.), *Essential papers on transference* (pp. 188–220). New York & London: New York University Press. (Original published 1950)

Mack, A., & Rock, I. (1998). *Inattentional blindness.* Cambridge, MA: MIT Press.

Mahler, M. S. (1972). On the first three subphases of the separation-individuation process. *International Journal of Psycho-Analysis, 53,* 333–338.

Malan, D. H. (2001). *Individual psychotherapy and the science of psychodynamics.* London: Arnold. (Original published 1995)

McWilliams, N. (2004). *Psychoanalytic psychotherapy: A practitioner's guide.* New York & London: Guilford.

Miller, J.-A. (1993). Clinique ironique [Ironic clinic]. *La cause freudienne, 23,* 7–13.

Miller, J.-A. (1996). L'interprétation à l'envers [The flip side of interpretation]. *La cause freudienne, 32,* 9–13.

Miller, J.-A. (1998). Le sinthome, un mixte de symptôme et fantasme [The sinthome: a mixture of symptom and fantasy]. *La cause freudienne, 39,* 7–17.

Miller, J.-A. (1999, July 3). Vers le corps portable [Toward the portable body]. *Libération.*

Miller, J.-A. (2002). Le dernier enseignement de Lacan [Lacan's final teaching]. *La cause freudienne, 51,* 7–32.

Miller, J.-A. (2003). Contre-transfert et intersubjectivité [Countertransference and intersubjectivity]. *La cause freudienne, 53,* 7–39.

Miller, J.-A. (2005). *Le transfert négatif* [Negative transference]. Paris: Navarin.

Millon, T., & Davis, R. (2000). *Personality disorders in modern life.* New York: John Wiley & Sons.

Milner, M. (1952). Aspects of symbolism in comprehension of the not-self. *International Journal of Psycho-Analysis, 33,* 181–195.

Mitchell, S. A., & Black, M. J. (1995). *Freud and Beyond.* New York: Basic Books.

Money-Kryle, R. (1956). Normal counter-transference and some of its deviations. *International Journal of Psycho-Analysis, 37,* 360–366.

Morel, G., & Wachsberger, H. (2005). Recherches sur le début de la psychose [Studies on the beginning of psychosis]. In *La psychose ordinaire: La convention d'Antibes* (pp. 69–88). Paris: Agalma-Seuil.

Nacht, S. (1956). La thérapeutique psychanalytique [Psychoanalytic therapeutics]. In *La Psychanalyse d'aujourd'hui* (pp. 123–168). Paris: Presses Universitaires de France.

Nobus, D. (2000). *Jacques Lacan and the Freudian practice of psychoanalysis.* London & Philadelphia: Routledge.

Nominé, B. (2005). Le psychanalyst comme aide contre [The analyst as a help against]. In *La psychose ordinaire: La convention d'Antibes* (pp. 195–218). Paris: Agalma-Seuil.

Ogden, T. H. (1979). On projective identification. *International Journal of Psycho-Analysis, 60,* 357–373.

Ogden, T. H. (1982). *Projective identification and psychotherapeutic technique.* Northvale, NJ: Jason Aronson.

Ogden, T. H. (1992). The dialectically constituted/decentred subject of psychoanalysis. I. The Freudian subject. *International Journal of Psycho-Analysis, 73,* 517–526.

Ogden, T. H. (1999). The analytic third: Working with intersubjective clinical facts. In S. A. Mitchell & L. Aron (Eds.), *Relational psychoanalysis: The emergence of a tradition* (pp. 461–492). Hillsdale, NJ: Analytic Press. (Original published 1994)

Ormont, L. R. (1969). Acting in and the therapeutic contract in group psychoanalysis. *International Journal of Group Psychotherapy, 19,* 4, 420–432.

Poe, E. A. (1938). The purloined letter. In *The complete tales and poems of Edgar Allan Poe* (pp. 208–222). New York: Modern Library. (Original published 1845)

Queneau, R. (1971). *On est toujours trop bon avec les femmes* [One is always too good to women]. Paris: Gallimard. (Original published 1947)

Racker, H. (1968). *Transference and countertransference*. New York: International Universities Press.

Reik, T. (1937). *Surprise and the psychoanalyst*. New York: E. P. Dutton.

Renik, O. (1999). Playing one's cards face up in analysis: An approach to the problem of self-disclosure. *Psychoanalytic Quarterly, 68,* 521–539.

Renik, O. (2001). The patient's experience of therapeutic benefit. *Psychoanalytic Quarterly, 70,* 231–241.

Richards, A., & Goldberg, F. (2000). A survey of Division 39 members regarding telephone therapy. Paper presented at the American Psychological Association Conference in a panel entitled Telephone Therapy—Advantages and Disadvantages. August 2000, Washington D.C. (unpublished).

Richards, I. A., & Ogden, C. K. (1945). *The meaning of meaning*. New York: Harcourt, Brace. (Original published 1923)

Rogers, C. (1951). *Client-centered therapy*. Boston: Houghton Mifflin.

Sandler, J. (1987). *Projection, identification, projective identification*. Madison, CT: International Universities Press.

Saussure, F. de (1959). *Course in general linguistics* (W. Baskin, Trans.). New York: McGraw-Hill. (Original published 1916)

Segal, H. (1964). *Introduction to the work of Melanie Klein*. New York: Basic.

Silberer, H. (1921). *Der Zufall und die Koboldstreiche des Unbewussten* [Chance and the impish pranks of the unconscious]. Bern: Bircher.

Sleek, S. (1997, August). Providing therapy from a distance. *American Psychological Association Monitor, 1 & 38.*

Soler, C. (1996). Silences [Silences]. *La cause freudienne, 32,* 26–30.

Soler, C. (1997). Contributions to the discussion in *Le conciliabule d'Angers*. Paris: Agalma-Seuil.

Soler, C. (2002). *L'inconscient à ciel ouvert de la psychose* [Psychosis: The unconscious right out in the open]. Toulouse, France: Presses Universitaires du Mirail.

Spotnitz, H. (1999). *Modern psychoanalysis of the schizophrenic patient*. Northvale, NJ: Jason Aronson.

Spoto, D. (1993). *Marilyn Monroe: The biography*. New York: HarperCollins.

Sterba, R. (1934). The fate of the ego in analytic therapy. *International Journal of Psycho-Analysis, 15*(2-3), 117–26.

Sterba, R. (1990). The dynamics of the dissolution of the transference resistance. In A. H. Esman (Ed.), *Essential papers on transference* (pp. 80–93). New York & London: New York University Press. (Original published 1940)

Stevens, A. (2005). Le transfert et psychose aux limites [Transference and psychosis at the borders]. In *La psychose ordinaire: La convention d'Antibes* (pp. 179–194). Paris: Agalma-Seuil.

Strachey, J. (1990). The nature of the therapeutic action of psycho-analysis. In A. H. Esman (Ed.), *Essential Papers on Transference* (pp. 49–79). New York & London: New York University Press. (Original published 1934)

Szasz, T. (1963). The concept of transference. *International Journal of Psycho-Analysis, 44,* 432–443.

Twain, M. (1996). *Tom Sawyer abroad*. Oxford, England: Oxford University Press. (Original published 1896)

Vanneufville, M. (2004). Un cas de mélancolie grave [A serious case of melancholia]. *Savoirs et clinique: Revue de psychanalyse, 5,* 91–96.

Williams, P. (Ed.). (2001). *A language for psychosis: Psychoanalysis of psychotic states*. New York & Hove, U.K.: Brunner-Routledge.

Winnicott, D. W. (1949). Hate in the counter-transference. *International Journal of Psycho-Analysis, 30*(2), 69–74.

Winnicott, D. W. (1958a). Mind and its relation to the psyche-soma. In *Collected papers: Through pediatrics to psycho-analysis* (pp. 243–254). London: Tavistock. (Original published 1949)

Winnicott, D. W. (1958b). Metapsychological and clinical aspects of regression within the psycho-analytical set-up. In *Collected papers: Through pediatrics to psycho-analysis* (pp. 278–294). London: Tavistock. (Original published 1954)

Winnicott, D. W. (1958c). Clinical varieties of transference. In *Collected papers: Through pediatrics to psycho-analysis* (pp. 295–299). London: Tavistock. (Original published 1955–1956)

Winnicott, D. W. (1965a). Ego distortion in terms of true and false self. In *The maturational processes and the facilitating environment* (pp. 140–152). London: Hogarth. (Original published 1960)

Winnicott, D. W. (1965b). The theory of the parent-infant relationship. In *The maturational processes and the facilitating environment* (pp. 37–55). London: Hogarth. (Original published 1960)

Winnicott, D. W. (1965c). Counter-transference. In *The maturational processes and the facilitating environment* (pp. 158–165). London: Hogarth. (Original published 1960)

Winnicott, D. W. (1977). *The piggle*. New York: International Universities Press.

Winnicott, D. W. (2005). Mirror-role of mother and family in child development. In *Playing and reality* (pp. 111–118). London and New York: Routledge. (Original published 1967)

Wodehouse, P. G. (1981). Heavy weather. In *Life at Blandings* (pp. 533–828) London: Penguin. (Original published 1933)

Zalusky, S. (1998). Telephone analysis: Out of sight, but not out of mind. *Journal of the American Psychoanalytic Association, 46*, 1221–1242.

Zalusky, S., Argentieri, S., Mehler, J. A., Rodriguez de la Sierra, L., Brainsky, S., Habib, L. E. Y., et al. (2003). Telephone analysis [special issue]. *International Psychoanalysis: News Magazine of the International Psychoanalytic Association, 12*, 1.

Zetzel, E. R. (1990). Current concepts of transference. In A. H. Esman (Ed.), *Essential papers on transference* (pp. 136–149). New York & London: New York University Press. (Original published 1956)

Index